Food Matters

A BEDFORD SPOTLIGHT READER

Food Matters

THIRD EDITION

A BEDFORD SPOTLIGHT READER

Holly Bauer

University of California, San Diego

bedford/st.martin's
Macmillan Learning
Boston | New York

Vice President: Leasa Burton
Program Director, English: Stacey Purviance
Senior Program Manager: John E. Sullivan III
Director, Content Development: Jane Knetzger
Executive Development Manager: Susan McLaughlin
Development Editor: Cari Goldfine
Executive Media Editor: Adam Whitehurst
Advanced Media Project Manager: Rand Thomas
Executive Marketing Manager: Joy Fisher Williams
Director, Content Management Enhancement: Tracey Kuehn
Senior Managing Editor: Michael Granger
Senior Manager of Publishing Services: Andrea Cava
Senior Content Project Manager: Louis C. Bruno Jr.
Senior Workflow Project Manager: Jennifer Wetzel
Production Coordinator: Brianna Lester
Director of Design, Content Management: Diana Blume
Interior Design: Castle Design; Janis Owens, Books By Design, Inc.; Claire
    Seng-Niemoeller
Cover Design: William Boardman
Director, Rights and Permissions: Hilary Newman
Text Permissions Researcher: Elaine Kosta, Lumina Datamatics, Inc.
Photo Permissions Editor: Angie Boehler
Photo Researcher: Lisa Passmore, Lumina Datamatics, Inc.
Senior Director, Digital Production: Keri deManigold
Project Management: Lumina Datamatics, Inc.
Project Manager: Ronald Dsouza, Lumina Datamatics, Inc.
Editorial Services: Lumina Datamatics, Inc.
Copyeditor: Jon Preimesberger
Composition: Lumina Datamatics, Inc.
Cover Image: Claudia Totir/Moment/Getty Images
Printing and Binding: LSC Communications

Library of Congress Control Number: 2020936455
ISBN: 978-1-319-24459-0

Printed in the United States of America.
1 2 3 4 5 6   25 24 23 22 21 20

Acknowledgments
Text acknowledgments and copyrights appear at the back of the book on pages 350–51, which constitute an extension of the copyright page. Art acknowledgments and copyrights appear on the same page as the art selections they cover.

For information, write: Bedford/St. Martin's, 75 Arlington Street, Boston, MA 02116

About The Bedford Spotlight Reader Series

The Bedford Spotlight Reader Series is a line of single-theme readers, each featuring Bedford's trademark care and quality. The readers in the series collect thoughtfully chosen readings sufficient for an entire writing course—about thirty-five selections—to allow instructors to provide carefully developed, high-quality instruction at an affordable price. Bedford Spotlight Readers are designed to help students make inquiries from multiple perspectives, opening up topics such as food, sustainability, gender, happiness, borders, monsters, American subcultures, science and technology, and intelligence to critical analysis. An editorial board of a dozen compositionists whose programs focus on specific themes has assisted in the development of the series.

Bedford Spotlight Readers offer plenty of material for a composition course while keeping the price low. Each volume in the series includes multiple perspectives on the topic and its effects on individuals and society. Chapters are built around central questions such as "What Does It Mean to Eat Ethically?" and "Has Technology Made Us the Gods of the Natural World?" and so offer numerous entry points for inquiry and discussion. High-interest readings, chosen for their suitability in the classroom, represent a mix of genres and disciplines as well as a choice of accessible and challenging selections to allow instructors to tailor their approach. Each chapter thus brings to light related—even surprising—questions and ideas.

A rich editorial apparatus provides a sound pedagogical foundation. A general introduction, chapter introductions, and headnotes supply context. Following each selection, writing prompts provide avenues of inquiry tuned to different levels of engagement, from reading comprehension ("Understanding the Text"), to critical analysis ("Reflection and Response"), to the kind of integrative analysis appropriate to the research paper ("Making Connections"). The instructor resources tab of the catalog page for *Food Matters* offers support for teaching, with sample syllabi, web links to additional readings and videos, and more; visit **macmillanlearning .com/spotlight**.

Food matters to everyone. What we eat, where it comes from, and how we share it are important and increasingly visible issues in our public life. The ongoing debates about food that surround us present a real opportunity for writers; the complexities, nuances, and difficulties around the issues make food a compelling writing subject. This is surely a large part of the reason why so many professional writers focus on food—and why a writing course should center on food issues. Food offers real and engaging opportunities for students to weigh in on the issues and to learn about academic writing while doing so.

The idea for this book came from my own food-focused writing course. And many of the ideas for this third edition came from teaching *Food Matters* and from ideas shared with me by reviewers and instructors who use the book in their courses. My food-themed writing courses have been popular with students because they could see many ways to connect their own experiences and lives to the larger academic questions posed by the reading selections. A course that centers on a theme like food provides a real writing opportunity: Everyone has a lot of experiences with food and something at stake in the present and future food supply. There are many ways to join the conversation. Students can examine food from a variety of angles and write about it from a variety of perspectives—personal, academic, journalistic, historical, cultural, and scientific. Students can analyze, explain, argue, and advocate. While it goes without saying that everyone eats food, many people do not think much about the broader implications of their food choices or the political and socioeconomic structures that help determine what they eat. Because there are no easy answers or obviously right ways to think about food, the topic offers legitimate—and interesting—contested terrain for students to explore. Thinking and writing about food helps students learn to care about ideas; ideally, they will link their own experiences with food to larger academic questions that they can explore in writing.

After all, the course in which you will use this reader is not primarily about food; food is simply the occasion for engaging in the many practices that will help make your students successful college students: careful reading, critical thinking, textual analysis, argumentation, working with sources, synthesis, and academic writing. *Food Matters* offers meaningful ways to practice inquiry and engage with ideas through different genres: academic essays, journalistic accounts, personal narratives, interviews, blogs, memoirs, and arguments of various sorts. The book also includes photographs and diagrams that support and clarify arguments about food as well as images of the federal nutrition guidelines. A range of disciplinary viewpoints are represented—science, history, social sciences, philosophy. The texts come from a variety of sources—newspapers, magazines, academic journals, government recommendations, online forums and blogs, and chapters from books.

In selecting texts, I have taken care to represent a range of viewpoints, many of which are in conversation with each other. I hope that this variety of tenable and legitimate perspectives, grouped carefully to respond to the questions that frame each chapter, will help your students to weigh the evidence, consider their values and beliefs, and think through what really matters to them when they write their narratives, analyze the various authors' positions, and construct their own arguments. The inquiry-based nature of the questions that introduce each chapter, along with the headnotes that introduce the readings and the questions that follow them, will spark productive discussion, critical engagement, and engaging assignments.

Food is a pertinent contemporary topic. We all eat to stay alive, and the way food is and will be produced matters to us all—whether we care to think about it or not. This reader provides real opportunities for students to engage with and write about the multidimensional controversies and debates surrounding food. My writing courses on food have been successful in engaging students in meaningful writing activities. I hope you and your students find this material as engaging as I do.

New to the Third Edition

Current and Diverse Reading Selections

Of this edition's thirty-seven reading selections, sixteen are new, providing more perspectives, topics, and disciplines to choose from and giving instructors more flexibility for using the topic of food in their writing courses. Notable new readings include **Taffy Brodesser-Akner's** "Why I've Never Learned How to Cook"; **Amanda Little's** "Stop the Rot"; **Georgina Gustin's** "Can a Climate Conscious Diet Include Meat or Dairy?"; **Abaki Beck's** "How One Tribe Is Fighting for Their Food Culture in the Face of Climate Change"; **Joon Yun, David Kessler, and Dan Glickman's** "We Need Better Answers on Nutrition"; and more.

New Chapter, "How Does Our Food System Contribute to the Climate Crisis?"

Based on feedback from instructors, the third edition features a new chapter delving into food and the climate crisis. This timely chapter interrogates how our food choices and food production both contribute to and will be affected by the climate crisis, identifying both problems and potential solutions. In addition to a tried-and-true favorite by Jonathan Foley, we've added seven brand-new readings, investigating the food system and the climate crisis from numerous angles. Key readings include authors such as **Paul Greenberg, Rowan Jacobsen, Nicole Walker,** and **Bren Smith.**

New Appendix, "Sentence Guides for Academic Writers"

Following the last chapter of the book, this new section helps with an essential skill: working with and responding to others' ideas in writing. This practical module helps students develop an academic writing voice by giving them sentence guides, or templates, to follow in a variety of composing situations.

Contents by Rhetorical Purpose

In addition to the existing tables of contents grouped by theme and by discipline, we've added a table of contents grouped by rhetorical purpose. These three alternative tables of contents are designed to give you flexibility as you teach your course and may help you as you create your syllabus or reading list.

Acknowledgments

Many people helped and supported me in the creation of this book. First, I'd like to acknowledge the students in the courses I have taught that have focused on food; these students have offered insights and ideas that have helped me understand why our food choices matter in new ways. These students have also helped me think through how best to select materials and teach a writing course that focuses on food. I also would like to thank the writing instructors in the Analytical Writing Program and in the Warren College Writing Program at the University of California, San Diego, with whom I have taught courses on food. Teaching with so many talented instructors and observing how they use this material and how they teach writing in general have helped me develop and improve it.

I also would like to thank these friends with whom I chat (and learn) about food: Sam Przywitowski, Melissa Leasure, Andrea Lamberti, Brian Keyser, Eugene Ahn, and Matthew Rich. In their own ways, each has nourished me with thoughts, suggestions, images, recipes, ideas, and arguments that have helped me to better understand the subject of food and to select texts for this book.

I am also grateful to all the reviewers who provided thoughtful and detailed feedback during the development process for this edition: Scott Ash, Nassau Community College; Karen Davies, Fresno City College; Elaine Folayan, Cypress College; Jeff Gagnon, University of California, San Diego; Claudia McIsaac, Santa Clara University; Rebecca Monks, Bakersfield College; Lori Owens, Owens Community College; Linda Rogers, University of Louisville; Jeffrey Schneider, St. Louis Community College, Meramec; Emily Shearer Stewart, Del Mar College; Jan Thompson, University of Nebraska, Kearney; and Lynn Wytenbroek, Vancouver Island University, Nanaimo.

I also must acknowledge all of the wonderful people I have met at Bedford/St. Martin's. Amy Shefferd, sales representative, has provided immeasurable support. I also would like to thank Leasa Burton, vice president of editorial humanities at Macmillan Learning; and John Sullivan, senior program manager, for encouraging me to take on this project (even when I hesitated) and for seeing me through the process. This project would not have been possible without Stacey Purviance, program director for English; Elaine Kosta and Lisa Passmore, permissions researchers; Louis Bruno, content project manager, and Ronald Dsouza, project manager. My biggest shout-outs go to Sophia Snyder, editor of the first edition; Leah Rang, editor of the second edition; and Cari Goldfine, editor of this third edition. I talked food and shared articles and links about food for more than a year with each of them. I appreciate their careful attention to the text and the many valuable suggestions they made. I am a better writer for having worked with each of them.

Last, my family deserves special recognition — especially my mother, Gayle Bauer, who taught me to value cooking, shopping for produce, and healthy eating; my late father, Walter Bauer, who used to squeeze orange juice for us every single morning and who made certain dishes (beef Wellington!) over and over again until he perfected them; and my children, Kai and Stella, who might not always be ready to help me grow and harvest the kale but who always drink it down in a breakfast smoothie. I am thankful for our rich food life and our ability to reflect on that life in conversation and in writing. I also thank them for the patience they offered when I spent large chunks of time on this project instead of with them.

Holly Bauer

Bedford/St. Martin's Puts You First

From day one, our goal has been simple: to provide inspiring resources that are grounded in best practices for teaching reading and writing. For more than thirty-five years, Bedford/St. Martin's has partnered with the field, listening to teachers, scholars, and students about the support writers need. We are committed to helping every writing instructor make the most of our resources.

How Can We Help *You*?

- Our editors can align our resources to your outcomes through correlation and transition guides for your syllabus. Just ask us.
- Our sales representatives specialize in helping you find the right materials to support your course goals.
- Our learning solutions and product specialists help you make the most of the digital resources you choose for your course.
- Our *Bits* blog on the Bedford/St. Martin's English Community (**community.macmillan.com**) publishes fresh teaching ideas weekly. You'll also find easily downloadable professional resources and links to author webinars on our community site.

Contact your Bedford/St. Martin's sales representative or visit **macmillanlearning.com** to learn more.

Print and Digital Options for *Food Matters*

Choose the format that works best for your course, and ask about our packaging options that offer savings for students.

Print

- *Paperback.* To order the paperback edition, use ISBN 978-1-319-24459-0. To order *Food Matters* (print) packaged with Achieve, use ISBN 978-1-319-37901-8.

Digital

- *Achieve for Readers and Writers.* Achieve puts student writing at the center of your course and keeps revision at the core, with a dedicated composition space that guides students through drafting, peer review, plagiarism prevention, reflection, and revision. Developed to support best practices in commenting on student drafts, Achieve is a flexible, integrated suite of tools for designing and facilitating writing assignments, paired with actionable insights that make students' progress toward outcomes clear and measurable. Achieve offers instructors a quick and flexible solution for targeting instruction based on students' unique needs. For details, visit **macmillanlearning.com/college/us/englishdigital**.

- *Popular e-book formats.* For details about our e-book partners, visit **macmillanlearning.com/ebooks**.
- *Inclusive Access.* Enable every student to receive their course materials through your LMS on the first day of class. Macmillan Learning's Inclusive Access program is the easiest, most affordable way to ensure all students have access to quality educational resources. Find out more at **macmillanlearning.com/inclusiveaccess**.

Your Course, Your Way

No two writing programs or classrooms are exactly alike. Our Curriculum Solutions team works with you to design custom options that provide the resources your students need. (Options below require enrollment minimums.)

- *ForeWords for English.* Customize any print resource to fit the focus of your course or program by choosing from a range of prepared topics, such as Sentence Guides for Academic Writers.
- *Macmillan Author Program (MAP).* Add excerpts or package acclaimed works from Macmillan's trade imprints to connect students with prominent authors and public conversations. A list of popular examples or academic themes is available upon request.
- *Mix and Match.* With our simplest solution, you can add up to fifty pages of curated content to your Bedford/St. Martin's text. Contact your sales representative for additional details.
- *Bedford Select.* Build your own print anthology from a database of more than 800 selections, or build a handbook, and add your own materials to create your ideal text. Package with any Bedford/ St. Martin's text for additional savings. Visit **macmillanlearning .com/bedfordselect**.

Instructor Resources

You have a lot to do in your course. We want to make it easy for you to find the support you need—and to get it quickly. Instructor resources, including sample syllabi and a list of related resources, are available from **macmillanlearning.com**.

Contents

Introduction for Students   1

Chapter 1   What Is the Purpose of Food?   7

kids. I didn't cook after my mother, on a visit after I had a baby, kept the Food Network on nonstop for six weeks, hoping it would take. I didn't cook."

Chapter 3   What Does It Mean to Eat Ethically?   135

Chapter 5　What Is the Future of Food?　285

Contents by Discipline

Agricultural Studies and Farming

Creative Nonfiction

Cultural Studies

Economics

History

Journalism

Nutrition Science

Philosophy and Ethics

Public Policy

Contents by Theme

Animal Rights

Autobiography

Cooking

Environment

Food Justice

Food Movements

Globalization

Government and Food Policy

Junk Food

Nutrition

Organic Farming and Industrial Agriculture

Race and Food

Contents by Rhetorical Purpose

Argument

Autobiography

Introduction for Students

When we sit down to write, we need something to write about, something that will stimulate our thinking and will interest others, too. All writers need a topic — journalists, historians, professional writers, poets, humorists, textbook authors like myself, and students like you. This book, *Food Matters*, aims to provide you with a topic: the subject of food. It offers reading and writing assignments that ask you to consider a range of questions about what you eat, how you make food choices, what those choices say about you and your culture, and why they matter. The book invites you to explore what others have written about food, and it provides a variety of writing opportunities for students with varied interests and backgrounds.

While the subject is food, the real purpose of this book is to provide you with a set of texts that provoke critical inquiry and lead to productive writing opportunities. To write well at the college level, you need to practice critical reading and critical thinking; you need to learn to analyze and evaluate the ideas you are asked to write about. Food is a great topic for engaging in a range of interesting, complex, thought-provoking issues — and thus for practicing critical reading, thinking, and writing. This book asks you to consider a range of issues, debates, problems, and questions about food. These are matters about which I hope you will care deeply — and thus about which you will have something to say, and, more important, *something to write*.

Why Food?

Do you eat breakfast? Is it from a box, your garden, or the corner coffee shop? Do you sit down with your family to eat? Or do you eat in your car, on the bus, or walking to work or school? Have you ever thought about where your food comes from? When you buy food, do you select what is cheapest, healthiest, or most ethically produced? Do you care if it is organic or conventionally grown? Does it matter if it was produced near where you live or on the other side of the globe? Do you think about whether it was picked or packaged or processed by workers who were compensated fairly? What is food anyway? Is it a product of nature? Is it a product of food science? Does it matter? What does it mean to *eat food*? Do you eat for health, for sustenance, for pleasure, or for something else? Where does your food come from? Do you know? Do you care? Is eating supposed to be pleasurable? social? for survival? How should we decide what to eat? On what should our decisions be based — on our sense of what is healthy, what is fast and easy, the organic food movement, the slow food movement, federal health guidelines, or on concern for the environment, animal rights, labor rights, or other ethical considerations?

These questions probably would not have been posed this way until recently. But an increasing number of authors and movements have propelled the topic of food to the forefront. News headlines, blogs, TV shows, documentaries, books, and advertisements bombard us with talk about food. What we eat, where it comes from, and why our food choices are important are issues that are increasingly visible in U.S. political, social, and cultural life. We are surrounded by writing about food, and the more we read about food and think through the lists of considerations, the more complex and confusing it gets.

You might start to wonder, as some prominent writers have, if much of what we eat can even be called food anymore. Or you might think that certain critics are too particular and their critiques are overblown. These complexities and difficulties are what make *food* such a viable writing subject. The confusion and controversy I describe — and the ongoing debates about food that accompany it — are a real opportunity for writers. I imagine that this is why so many professional writers focus on food, and I am certain that this is why writing about food is such a great opportunity for students like you to practice critical reading, thinking, and writing. In fact, it is because there are no easy answers and obviously right ways to think about food that the topic offers legitimate — and interesting — contested terrain for you to explore. There are many ways for you to join the conversation, and providing ways for you to consider, analyze, and write about real issues and controversies is the purpose of this book.

Reading, Thinking, Writing

Although this book focuses on food and asks you to contemplate difficult questions, it does not advocate a particular ethical stance or political point of view. Instead, the book offers a range of tenable and legitimate positions and invites you to weigh the evidence, consider your values and beliefs, and think through what really matters to you as you construct narratives and arguments about food. After all, the course in which you will use this reader is not primarily a course about food. This is a writing course; food is simply the occasion for writing.

When you sit down to write, how do you decide what to do? The authors in this book demonstrate the importance of considering the purpose and audience for which they are writing, the idea or emotion or position that they are trying to put forward or communicate, and the argument they want to make. How they write about their ideas — the form and structure their writings take — is at least partially determined by what they want to say. I encourage you to compare the genres included here and how the writers use rhetorical strategies that help them say what they want to say. I have chosen pieces that take a range of forms — essays, blogs, humor, magazine articles, academic arguments, book excerpts, and images. Not only do the pieces offer a variety of viewpoints on food, they also offer a range of models for writing and taking a stand on a particular issue or problem.

One unique quality of this reader is that by focusing on a theme, it allows you to delve into the topic of food on various levels — personal, political, social, moral, academic, environmental, and scientific. As you develop a base of knowledge about the topic, a sense of the key issues, and an understanding of the values and beliefs that motivate and inform various perspectives, you will become a kind of expert; this will allow you an opportunity to write about the issues in meaningful and legitimate ways. I hope your engagement with these texts will lead you to feel that it is worth your while to figure out where you stand in relation to the narratives, arguments, and materials offered here. This book invites you to join the scholarly conversation and to position yourself in relation to real issues, ongoing problems, and contested positions.

Organization of the Book

Food Matters provides a sense of the contemporary conversations and debates about the purpose of food, the social and political forces that affect food choices, the ethics of eating, the relationship between food and the climate crisis, and the future of food. Each chapter poses a question and includes a set of carefully chosen selections that speak to the question by defining key terms, providing context, or taking a position. Although each chapter includes selections you can use to explore the chapter's guiding question, you might find that these are artificial divisions, as many of the selections could be responses to the lead questions of other chapters, too. I encourage you to make connections between and among them as you go.

Each chapter begins with an introduction that summarizes the themes and issues that are central to that chapter and poses some questions to think about as you read. Headnotes for each piece introduce the author and contextualize the selection. Following the readings, three sets of questions ask you to demonstrate your understanding of the text, to reflect on and respond to it, and to make connections between the readings and to conduct research. Effective responses to these questions will also take into account how your own values, beliefs, and experiences contribute to your understanding of the issues and the positions you take on them.

The book is organized around five questions for you to explore. These questions are intended as starting points for inquiry, though they are certainly not exhaustive in scope or topic. The first chapter, "What Is the Purpose of Food?," explores how we define food, the reasons we eat, and the varied purposes food serves in our lives — purposes that extend beyond nutrition to culture, politics, environment, and pleasure. The selections explore the complex ways food nourishes us, and in so doing they tie the definition and purpose of food to historical, cultural, spiritual, and political matters.

The second chapter, "What Forces Affect Our Food Choices?," examines the complex mix of laws, social realities, health guidelines, cultural pressures, and socioeconomic factors that help determine what we eat. While in one sense *we* determine what we eat, the selections in this chapter ask us to look at the many larger forces at work that direct what food choices are available, where, and for whom.

The third chapter, "What Does It Mean to Eat Ethically?," turns to an exploration of the role of ethics in determining what we eat and why our food choices matter. While acknowledging the larger political, social, cultural, and economic forces that affect food choices, the selections in this chapter ask us to consider what it means to declare that eating is necessarily a moral act.

The fourth chapter, "How Does Our Food System Contribute to the Climate Crisis?," focuses on the ways food production both contributes to and will be affected by climate change. While the authors help explain the complex connections between our food system and climate change, they also identify problems we must confront and suggest potential solutions to the problems. This chapter challenges us to consider if and how we might change our eating habits to sustain the planet.

The fifth and last chapter, "What Is the Future of Food?," identifies problems and possibilities that will influence the future of food. The readings indicate that this future will be no less complex than the present and that food production and consumption will continue to evolve as other aspects of society, culture, science, business, politics, and environment change. The chapter returns to themes of previous chapters and asks us to think critically about the scope and variety of influences that will affect our food choices in the future.

While each chapter focuses on a specific aspect of food, the chapters also include a range of genres and approaches to the topic. Academic essays, journalistic accounts, personal narratives, blogs, memoirs, images, and arguments are included. A range of disciplinary viewpoints are represented — science, history, social sciences, philosophy. The texts come from a variety of sources — newspapers, magazines, academic journals, government recommendations, online forums, blogs, and chapters of books. The selections represent a range of viewpoints, which are in conversation with one another. Although the questions are meant to be starting points for thinking, discussing, and writing, they are certainly not exhaustive. Thus, you might choose to pursue other fruitful questions, connections, and potential occasions for writing that this collection suggests.

Writing That Matters

A course that centers on a theme provides real writing opportunities for you. You can examine a topic from a variety of angles and write about it from a variety of perspectives — personal, cultural, political, academic, journalistic, and ethical. Working with this book, you will read and write personal narratives, political pieces, and academic arguments. One benefit of spending a significant amount of time studying one topic is that doing so yields more substantial writing opportunities. Writing about food is a great way to stimulate your thinking about how your own experiences, values, and positions are related to larger scientific, cultural, academic, and ethical questions. While it goes without saying that everyone eats food, many people do not think much about the broader implications of their food choices. We wake up and eat breakfast, or we order a sandwich in a deli. But we do not always think or know much about where our food comes from, how it was produced, how it contributes to the climate crisis, or who harvested our vegetables or raised the livestock. Food matters to all of us, and we make food choices that affect the world around us whether we are aware of this or not.

We all need to eat to stay alive (or live to eat), and we all have a stake in the present and future food supply. This book gives you opportunities to examine, analyze, and write about the major arguments in the myriad controversies and debates surrounding food. This is good practice for the other kinds of writing you will be doing in college, work, and life. I hope you will find this to be an engaging and productive way to practice and develop your writing skills.

1

What Is the Purpose of Food?

S trictly speaking, food is defined as edible and nutritious substances that we consume in order to live and grow. But food can be much more than this. The many ways we define food — and the varied purposes it serves in our lives — say something important about our health, values, culture, identities, and even our psychology. Is food a product of nature? Is it a product of science? We eat and drink many things that we categorize as food even though they are produced in labs and no longer resemble their plant and animal sources. Why do we eat them? What purposes do they serve for us — sustenance, cultural reinforcement, comfort, status, enlightenment? Where does our food come from? Do we know, and do we care? What makes food "real"? What makes food "good"? And are those the same things?

The readings in this chapter ask us to consider these questions and more. Taken together, these readings complicate the definition of what food "really" is and suggest various purposes of food. Michael Pollan provides a set of rules on how to define food, which he differentiates from "foodish products." Eric Schlosser looks at the flavoring industry and how it affects the "authenticity" of our dining experiences. The very manufactured flavors and artificially produced "foodish products" that Pollan and Schlosser criticize are what Jill McCorkle loves most about food. Her vivid memories of her life as a junk-food junkie indicate that there might be more to authentic eating than the freshness, quality, and origin of what we eat.

Most people would agree that one purpose of food, at least, is nutrition. But how do we know what foods will keep us healthy? Marion Nestle focuses on the effects that food has on our bodies and reminds us that nutrition science can sometimes lead us astray. Although Wendell Berry shares with Nestle a belief in healthy eating, he emphasizes that one important purpose of food is pleasure and that truly grasping the pleasure of eating requires an understanding of one's role in its production. Lily Wong reminds us that the pleasure of eating is linked to cultural identity in her exploration of her food choices. Finally, Thich Nhat Hanh and Lilian Cheung encourage us to be mindful of what we eat as a way to rethink our relationship to our food, nature, other people, and the world.

To explore the purpose of food, then, it seems that an understanding of its nutritional components is not enough. Taken together, the readings in this chapter suggest that we need a broader set of considerations to understand the purpose of food in our lives. What roles does food play? Do we eat for nutrition? pleasure? cultural connection? spiritual health? status? What purposes might food be said to serve beyond being something we consume? Is the purpose of food largely cultural, linked to our historical, political, ethnic, and socioeconomic origins? Does the purpose of food complicate what counts as "food"? How does food nourish us — through certain chemical properties, or through something larger and more difficult to define? What are the different "pleasures" of food? This chapter encourages you to reflect on these questions.

Eat Food: Food Defined

Michael Pollan

Best known for his engaging writing about food and his ability to tell complex stories that weave together politics, culture, nutrition, ethics, and history, Michael Pollan is an award-winning author, *New York Times Magazine* writer, and professor of journalism at the University of California, Berkeley. He has written numerous articles and books, including five *New York Times* best sellers: *Cooked: A Natural History of Transformation* (2013); *Food Rules: An Eater's Manual* (2010); *In Defense of Food: An Eater's Manifesto* (2008); *The Omnivore's Dilemma: A Natural History of Four Meals* (2006); and *The Botany of Desire: A Plant's-Eye View of the World* (2001). This selection comes from *In Defense of Food: An Eater's Manifesto*, a book in which Pollan works to define just what should count as food. He argues that "food" must be differentiated from "foodish products" and makes a case for how to define the difference.

The first time I heard the advice to "just eat food" it was in a speech by Joan Gussow, and it completely baffled me. Of course you should eat food—what else is there to eat? But Gussow, who grows much of her own food on a flood-prone finger of land jutting into the Hudson River, refuses to dignify most of the products for sale in the supermarket with that title. "In the thirty-four years I've been in the field of nutrition," she said in the same speech, "I have watched real food disappear from large areas of the supermarket and from much of the rest of the eating world." Taking food's place on the shelves has been an unending stream of foodlike substitutes, some seventeen thousand new ones every year—"products constructed largely around commerce and hope, supported by frighteningly little actual knowledge." Ordinary food is still out there, however, still being grown and even occasionally sold in the supermarket, and this ordinary food is what we should eat.

But given our current state of confusion and given the thousands of products calling themselves food, this is more easily said than done. So consider these related rules of thumb. Each proposes a different sort of map to the contemporary food landscape, but all should take you to more or less the same place.

• **DON'T EAT ANYTHING YOUR GREAT GRANDMOTHER WOULDN'T RECOGNIZE AS FOOD.** Why your great grandmother? Because at this point your mother and possibly even your grandmother is as confused as the rest of us; to be safe we need to go back at least a couple generations, to a time before the advent of most modern foods. So depending on your age (and your grandmother), you may need to go back to your great- or even great-great grandmother. Some nutritionists recommend going back even further. John Yudkin, a British nutritionist whose early alarms about the dangers of refined carbohydrates were overlooked in the 1960s and 1970s, once advised, "Just don't eat anything your Neolithic° ancestors wouldn't have recognized and you'll be ok."

What would shopping this way mean in the supermarket? Well, imagine your great grandmother at your side as you roll down the aisles. You're standing together in front of the dairy case. She picks up a package of Go-Gurt Portable Yogurt tubes—and has no idea what this could possibly be. Is it a food or a toothpaste? And how, exactly, do you introduce it into your body? You could tell her it's just yogurt in a squirtable form, yet if she read the ingredients label she would have every reason to doubt that that was in fact the case. Sure, there's some yogurt in there, but there are also a dozen other things that aren't remotely yogurtlike, ingredients she would probably fail to recognize as foods of any kind, including high-fructose corn syrup, modified corn starch, kosher gelatin, carrageenan, tri-calcium phosphate, natural and artificial flavors, vitamins, and so forth. (And there's a whole other list of ingredients for the "berry bubblegum bash" flavoring, containing everything but berries or bubblegum.) How did yogurt, which in your great grandmother's day consisted simply of milk inoculated with a bacterial culture, ever get to be so complicated? Is a product like Go-Gurt Portable Yogurt still a whole food? A food of any kind? Or is it just a food product?

There are in fact hundreds of foodish products in the supermarket that 5 your ancestors simply wouldn't recognize as food: breakfast cereal bars transected by bright white veins representing, but in reality having nothing to do with, milk; "protein waters" and "nondairy creamer"; cheeselike foodstuffs equally innocent of any bovine° contribution; cakelike cylinders (with creamlike fillings) called Twinkies that never grow stale. Don't eat anything incapable of rotting is another personal policy you might consider adopting.

There are many reasons to avoid eating such complicated food products beyond the various chemical additives and corn and soy derivatives they contain. One of the problems with the products of food science is that, as Joan Gussow has pointed out, they lie to your body; their artificial colors and flavors and synthetic sweeteners and novel fats confound the senses we rely on to assess new foods and prepare our bodies to deal

---

Neolithic: of or relating to the period of human history about 10,000 years ago, when humans began to develop agriculture and polished stone tools.
bovine: relating to cows.

with them. Foods that lie leave us with little choice but to eat by the numbers, consulting labels rather than our senses.

It's true that foods have long been processed in order to preserve them, as when we pickle or ferment or smoke, but industrial processing aims to do much more than extend shelf life. Today foods are processed in ways specifically designed to sell us more food by pushing our evolutionary buttons—our inborn preferences for sweetness and fat and salt. These qualities are difficult to find in nature but cheap and easy for the food scientist to deploy, with the result that processing induces us to consume much more of these ecological rarities than is good for us. "Tastes great, less filling!" could be the motto for most processed foods, which are far more energy dense than most whole foods: They contain much less water, fiber, and micronutrients, and generally much more sugar and fat, making them at the same time, to coin a marketing slogan, "More fattening, less nutritious!"

The great grandma rule will help keep many of these products out of your cart. But not all of them. Because thanks to the FDA's° willingness, post-1973, to let food makers freely alter the identity of "traditional foods that everyone knows" without having to call them imitations, your great grandmother could easily be fooled into thinking that that loaf of bread or wedge of cheese is in fact a loaf of bread or a wedge of cheese. This is why we need a slightly more detailed personal policy to capture these imitation foods; to wit:

• **AVOID FOOD PRODUCTS CONTAINING INGREDIENTS THAT ARE A) UNFAMILIAR, B) UNPRONOUNCEABLE, C) MORE THAN FIVE IN NUMBER, OR THAT INCLUDE D) HIGH-FRUCTOSE CORN SYRUP.** None of these characteristics, not even the last one, is necessarily harmful in and of itself, but all of them are reliable markers for foods that have been highly processed to the point where they may no longer be what they purport to be. They have crossed over from foods to food products.

Consider a loaf of bread, one of the "traditional foods that everyone 10 knows" specifically singled out for protection in the 1938 imitation rule. As your grandmother could tell you, bread is traditionally made using a remarkably small number of familiar ingredients: flour, yeast, water, and a pinch of salt will do it. But industrial bread—even industrial whole-grain bread—has become a far more complicated product of modern food science (not to mention commerce and hope). Here's the complete ingredients list for Sara Lee's Soft & Smooth Whole Grain White Bread.

FDA: United States Food and Drug Administration, the federal agency that is responsible for regulating and supervising food safety.

(Wait a minute—isn't "Whole Grain White Bread" a contradiction in terms? Evidently not anymore.)

Enriched bleached flour [wheat flour, malted barley flour, niacin, iron, thiamin mononitrate (vitamin B₁), riboflavin (vitamin B₂), folic acid], water, whole grains [whole wheat flour, brown rice flour (rice flour, rice bran)], high fructose corn syrup [hello!], whey, wheat gluten, yeast, cellulose. Contains 2% or less of each of the following: honey, calcium sulfate, vegetable oil (soybean and/or cottonseed oils), salt, butter (cream, salt), dough conditioners (may contain one or more of the following: mono- and diglycerides, ethoxylated mono- and diglycerides, ascorbic acid, enzymes, azodicarbonamide), guar gum, calcium propionate (preservative), distilled vinegar, yeast nutrients (monocalcium phosphate, calcium sulfate, ammonium sulfate), corn starch, natural flavor, beta-carotene (color), vitamin D₃, soy lecithin, soy flour.

There are many things you could say about this intricate loaf of "bread," but note first that even if it managed to slip by your great grandmother (because it is a loaf of bread, or at least is called one and strongly resembles one), the product fails every test proposed under rule number two: It's got unfamiliar ingredients (monoglycerides I've heard of before, but ethoxylated monoglycerides?); unpronounceable ingredients (try "azodicarbonamide"); it exceeds the maximum of five ingredients (by roughly thirty-six); and it contains high-fructose corn syrup. Sorry, Sara Lee, but your Soft & Smooth Whole Grain White Bread is not food and if not for the indulgence of the FDA could not even be labeled "bread."

Sara Lee's Soft & Smooth Whole Grain White Bread could serve as a monument to the age of nutritionism. It embodies the latest nutritional wisdom from science and government (which in its most recent food pyramid recommends that at least half our consumption of grain come from whole grains) but leavens that wisdom with the commercial recognition that American eaters (and American children in particular) have come to prefer their wheat highly refined—which is to say, cottony soft, snowy white, and exceptionally sweet on the tongue. In its marketing materials, Sara Lee treats this clash of interests as some sort of Gordian knot°—it speaks in terms of an ambitious quest to build a "no compromise" loaf—which only the most sophisticated food science could possibly cut.

And so it has, with the invention of whole-grain white bread. Because the small percentage of whole grains in the bread would render it that

---

Gordian knot: in legend, a knot impossible to untangle. Alexander the Great "untied" the knot by cutting it with his sword.

much less sweet than, say, all-white Wonder Bread—which scarcely waits to be chewed before transforming itself into glucose—the food scientists have added high-fructose corn syrup and honey to make up the difference; to overcome the problematic heft and toothsomeness of a real whole-grain bread, they've deployed "dough conditioners," including guar gum and the aforementioned azodicarbonamide, to simulate the texture of supermarket white bread. By incorporating certain varieties of albino wheat, they've managed to maintain that deathly but apparently appealing Wonder Bread pallor.

Who would have thought Wonder Bread would ever become an ideal of aesthetic and gustatory perfection to which bakers would actually aspire—Sara Lee's Mona Lisa?

Very often food science's efforts to make traditional foods more nutritious make them much more complicated, but not necessarily any better for you. To make dairy products low fat, it's not enough to remove the fat. You then have to go to great lengths to preserve the body or creamy texture by working in all kinds of food additives. In the case of low-fat or skim milk, that usually means adding powdered milk. But powdered milk contains oxidized cholesterol, which scientists believe is much worse for your arteries than ordinary cholesterol, so food makers sometimes compensate by adding antioxidants, further complicating what had been a simple one-ingredient whole food. Also, removing the fat makes it that much harder for your body to absorb the fat-soluble vitamins that are one of the reasons to drink milk in the first place.

All this heroic and occasionally counterproductive food science has been undertaken in the name of our health—so that Sara Lee can add to its plastic wrapper the magic words "good source of whole grain" or a food company can ballyhoo the even more magic words "low fat." Which brings us to a related food policy that may at first sound counterintuitive to a health-conscious eater:

• **AVOID FOOD PRODUCTS THAT MAKE HEALTH CLAIMS.** For a food product to make health claims on its package it must first *have* a package, so right off the bat it's more likely to be a processed than a whole food. Generally speaking, it is only the big food companies that have the wherewithal to secure FDA-approved health claims for their products and then trumpet them to the world. Recently, however, some of the tonier fruits and nuts have begun boasting about their health-enhancing properties, and there will surely be more as each crop council scrounges together the money to commission its own scientific study. Because all plants contain antioxidants, all these studies are guaranteed to find *some*thing on which to base a health oriented marketing campaign.

But for the most part it is the products of food science that make the boldest health claims, and these are often founded on incomplete and often erroneous science—the dubious fruits of nutritionism. Don't forget that trans-fat-rich margarine, one of the first industrial foods to claim it was healthier than the traditional food it replaced, turned out to give people heart attacks. Since that debacle, the FDA, under tremendous pressure from industry, has made it only easier for food companies to make increasingly doubtful health claims, such as the one Frito-Lay now puts on some of its chips—that eating them is somehow good for your heart. If you bother to read the health claims closely (as food marketers make sure consumers seldom do), you will find that there is often considerably less to them than meets the eye.

Consider a recent "qualified" health claim approved by the FDA for (don't laugh) corn oil. ("Qualified" is a whole new category of health claim, introduced in 2002 at the behest of industry.) Corn oil, you may recall, is particularly high in the omega-6 fatty acids we're already consuming far too many of.

Very limited and preliminary scientific evidence suggests that eating about one tablespoon (16 grams) of corn oil daily may reduce the risk of heart disease due to the unsaturated fat content in corn oil.

The tablespoon is a particularly rich touch, conjuring images of moms administering medicine, or perhaps cod-liver oil, to their children. But what the FDA gives with one hand, it takes away with the other. Here's the small-print "qualification" of this already notably diffident health claim:

[The] FDA concludes that there is little scientific evidence supporting this claim.

And then to make matters still more perplexing:

To achieve this possible benefit, corn oil is to replace a similar amount of saturated fat and not increase the total number of calories you eat in a day.

This little masterpiece of pseudoscientific bureaucratese was extracted from the FDA by the manufacturer of Mazola corn oil. It would appear that "qualified" is an official FDA euphemism for "all but meaningless." Though someone might have let the consumer in on this game: The FDA's own research indicates that consumers have no idea what to make of qualified health claims (how would they?), and its rules allow companies to promote the claims pretty much any way they want—they can use really big type for the claim, for example, and then print the disclaimers in teeny-tiny type. No doubt we can look forward to a qualified health claim for high-fructose corn syrup, a tablespoon of which probably does contribute to your health—as long as it replaces a comparable amount of, say, poison in your diet and doesn't increase the total number of calories you eat in a day.

When corn oil and chips and sugary breakfast cereals can all boast being good for your heart, health claims have become hopelessly corrupt. The American Heart Association currently bestows (for a fee) its heart-healthy seal of approval on Lucky Charms, Cocoa Puffs, and Trix cereals, Yoo-hoo lite chocolate drink, and Healthy Choice's Premium Caramel Swirl Ice Cream Sandwich—this at a time when scientists are coming to recognize that dietary sugar probably plays a more important role in heart disease than dietary fat. Meanwhile, the genuinely heart-healthy whole foods in the produce section, lacking the financial and political clout of the packaged goods a few aisles over, are mute. But don't take the silence of the yams as a sign that they have nothing valuable to say about health.

Bogus health claims and food science have made supermarkets particularly treacherous places to shop for real food, which suggests two further rules:

- **SHOP THE PERIPHERIES OF THE SUPERMARKET AND STAY OUT OF THE MIDDLE.** Most 25 supermarkets are laid out the same way: Processed food products dominate the center aisles of the store while the cases of ostensibly fresh food—dairy, produce, meat, and fish—line the walls. If you keep to the edges of the store you'll be that much more likely to wind up with real food in your shopping cart. The strategy is not foolproof, however, because things like high-fructose corn syrup have slipped into the dairy case under cover of Go-Gurt and such. So consider a more radical strategy:

- **GET OUT OF THE SUPERMARKET WHENEVER POSSIBLE.** You won't find *any* high-fructose corn syrup at the farmers' market. You also won't find any elaborately processed food products, any packages with long lists of unpronounceable ingredients or dubious health claims, nothing microwavable, and, perhaps best of all, no old food from far away. What you *will* find are fresh whole foods picked at the peak of their taste and nutritional quality—precisely the kind your great grandmother, or even your Neolithic ancestors, would easily have recognized as food.

Indeed, the surest way to escape the Western diet is simply to depart the realms it rules: the supermarket, the convenience store, and the fast-food outlet. It is hard to eat badly from the farmers' market, from a CSA box (community-supported agriculture, an increasingly popular scheme in which you subscribe to a farm and receive a weekly box of produce), or from your garden. The number of farmers' markets has more than doubled in the last ten years, to more than four thousand, making it one of the fastest-growing segments of the food marketplace. It is true that most farmers' markets operate only seasonally, and you won't find everything you need there. But buying as much as you can from the farmers' market, or directly from the farm when that's an option, is a simple act with a host of profound consequences for your health as well as for the health of the food chain you've now joined.

When you eat from the farmers' market, you automatically eat food that is in season, which is usually when it is most nutritious. Eating in season also tends to diversify your diet — because you can't buy strawberries or broccoli or potatoes twelve months of the year, you'll find yourself experimenting with other foods when they come into the market. The CSA box does an even better job of forcing you out of your dietary rut because you'll find things in your weekly allotment that you would never buy on your own. Whether it's a rutabaga or an unfamiliar winter squash, the CSA box's contents invariably send you to your cookbooks to figure out what in the world to do with them. Cooking is one of the most important health consequences of buying food from local farmers; for one thing, when you cook at home you seldom find yourself reaching for the ethoxylated diglycerides or high-fructose corn syrup. . . .

To shop at a farmers' market or sign up with a CSA is to join a short food chain, and that has several implications for your health. Local produce is typically picked ripe and is fresher than supermarket produce, and for those reasons it should be tastier and more nutritious. As for supermarket organic produce, it too is likely to have come from far away — from the industrial organic farms of California or, increasingly, China.[1] And while it's true that the organic label guarantees that no synthetic pesticides or fertilizers have been used to produce the food, many, if not most, of the small farms that supply farmers' markets are organic in everything but name. To survive in the farmers' market or CSA economy, a farm will need to be highly diversified, and a diversified farm usually has little need for pesticides; it's the big monocultures that can't survive without them.[2]

---

[1] One recent study found that the average item of organic produce in the supermarket had actually traveled farther from the farm than the average item of conventional produce. [Pollan's note.]

[2] Wendell Berry put the problem of monoculture with admirable brevity and clarity in his essay "The Pleasures of Eating": "But as scale increases, diversity declines; as diversity declines, so does health; as health declines, the dependence on drugs and chemicals necessarily increases." [Pollan's note.]

If you're concerned about chemicals in your produce, you can simply   30
ask the farmer at the market how he or she deals with pests and fertility
and begin the sort of conversation between producers and consumers
that, in the end, is the best guarantee of quality in your food. So many
of the problems of the industrial food chain stem from its length and
complexity. A wall of ignorance intervenes between consumers and producers, and that wall fosters a certain carelessness on both sides. Farmers
can lose sight of the fact that they're growing food for actual eaters rather
than for middlemen, and consumers can easily forget that growing good
food takes care and hard work. In a long food chain, the story and identity of the food (Who grew it? Where and how was it grown?) disappear
into the undifferentiated stream of commodities, so that the only information communicated between consumers and producers is a price. In a
short food chain, eaters can make their needs and desires known to the
farmer, and farmers can impress on eaters the distinctions between ordinary and exceptional food, and the many reasons why exceptional food
is worth what it costs. Food reclaims its story, and some of its nobility,
when the person who grew it hands it to you. So here's a subclause to the
get-out-of-the-supermarket rule: *Shake the hand that feeds you.*

As soon as you do, accountability becomes once again a matter of relationships instead of regulation or labeling or legal liability. Food safety
didn't become a national or global
problem until the industrialization of
the food chain attenuated° the relationships between food producers and eaters. That was the story Upton Sinclair
told about the Beef Trust in 1906, and
it's the story unfolding in China today,
where the rapid industrialization of
the food system is leading to alarming
breakdowns in food safety and integrity.
Regulation is an imperfect substitute
for the accountability, and trust, built
into a market in which food producers meet the gaze of eaters and vice
versa. Only when we participate in a short food chain are we reminded
every week that we are indeed part of a food chain and dependent for our
health on its peoples and soils and integrity—on its health.

"Only when we participate
in a short food chain are
we reminded every week
that we are indeed part of a
food chain and dependent
for our health on its peoples
and soils and integrity — on
its health."

"Eating is an agricultural act," Wendell Berry famously wrote, by which
he meant that we are not just passive consumers of food but cocreators
of the systems that feed us. Depending on how we spend them, our food

attenuated: made smaller, thinner, or weaker.

dollars can either go to support a food industry devoted to quantity and convenience and "value" or they can nourish a food chain organized around *values*—values like quality and health. Yes, shopping this way takes more money and effort, but as soon as you begin to treat that expenditure not just as shopping but also as a kind of vote—a vote for health in the largest sense—food no longer seems like the smartest place to economize.

Understanding the Text

1. What is the "industrial food chain"?

2. What are "foodish products"? What reasons does Pollan offer for avoiding "foodish products"?

3. What are the differences between processed and whole foods? Why does this distinction matter to Pollan?

Reflection and Response

4. What does the advice to "just eat food" mean to you?

5. Does Pollan think we can trust food labels? Explain.

6. Select a packaged or processed food product that you like to eat, and examine the ingredients. Would Pollan classify your item as "food"? Why or why not? Do you classify it as "food"? Explain.

7. How would following Pollan's advice change your eating patterns? How might you benefit? What would you give up?

Making Connections

8. How might Pollan evaluate the Food Pyramid and Food Plate developed by the U.S. Department of Agriculture (p. 68)? Locate textual evidence to support your case.

9. Pollan quotes Wendell Berry, author of "The Pleasures of Eating" (p. 46), in the last paragraph of this selection. What ideals do Pollan and Berry share? What selections in this book complicate these ideals? How?

10. In his exploration of plant-based meat substitutes and their potential role in responding to the climate crisis, Rowan Jacobsen ("The Biography of a Plant-Based Burger," p. 232) references a *New York Times* essay written by Michael Pollan. How does Jacobsen complicate Pollan's prescription to eat only what your great grandmother would recognize as food?

Why the Fries Taste Good

Eric Schlosser

Eric Schlosser is an award-winning journalist best known for his exhaustive research on the fast-food industry and his best-selling book *Fast Food Nation* (2001), which began as a two-part article in *Rolling Stone*. Schlosser began his writing career as a fiction writer, then turned to nonfiction and became a correspondent for *The Atlantic Monthly*. His other books include *The New York Times* bestsellers *Command and Control* (2013) and *Reefer Madness* (2003). He appeared in the documentary *Food, Inc.* (2008), which draws on his searing critiques of the food industry to demonstrate their potential for damaging our health and environment. In this essay, excerpted from *Fast Food Nation*, Schlosser discusses how McDonald's flavors its fries as an example of larger industry flavoring practices. He offers an in-depth look at the flavor industry and how it differentiates "natural" and "artificial" flavorings.

The taste of McDonald's french fries has long been praised by customers, competitors, and even food critics. James Beard loved McDonald's fries. Their distinctive taste does not stem from the type of potatoes that McDonald's buys, the technology that processes them, or the restaurant equipment that fries them. Other chains buy their french fries from the same large processing companies, use Russet Burbanks, and have similar fryers in their restaurant kitchens. The taste of a fast food fry is largely determined by the cooking oil. For decades, McDonald's cooked its french fries in a mixture of about 7 percent cottonseed oil and 93 percent beef tallow. The mix gave the fries their unique flavor—and more saturated beef fat per ounce than a McDonald's hamburger.

Amid a barrage of criticism over the amount of cholesterol in their fries, McDonald's switched to pure vegetable oil in 1990. The switch presented the company with an enormous challenge: how to make fries that subtly taste like beef without cooking them in tallow. A look at the ingredients now used in the preparation of McDonald's french fries suggests how the problem was solved. At the end of the list is a seemingly innocuous, yet oddly mysterious phrase: "natural flavor." That ingredient helps to explain not only why the fries taste so good, but also why most fast food—indeed, most of the food Americans eat today—tastes the way it does.

Open your refrigerator, your freezer, your kitchen cupboards, and look at the labels on your food. You'll find "natural flavor" or "artificial flavor" in just about every list of ingredients. The similarities between these two broad categories of flavor are far more significant than their differences.

Both are man-made additives that give most processed food its taste. The initial purchase of a food item may be driven by its packaging or appearance, but subsequent purchases are determined mainly by its taste. About 90 percent of the money that Americans spend on food is used to buy processed food. But the canning, freezing, and dehydrating techniques used to process food destroy most of its flavor. Since the end of World War II, a vast industry has arisen in the United States to make processed food palatable. Without this flavor industry, today's fast food industry could not exist. The names of the leading American fast food chains and their best-selling menu items have become famous worldwide, embedded in our popular culture. Few people, however, can name the companies that manufacture fast food's taste.

The flavor industry is highly secretive. Its leading companies will not divulge the precise formulas of flavor compounds or the identities of clients. The secrecy is deemed essential for protecting the reputation of beloved brands. The fast food chains, understandably, would like the public to believe that the flavors of their food somehow originate in their restaurant kitchens, not in distant factories run by other firms.

The New Jersey Turnpike runs through the heart of the flavor industry,   5 an industrial corridor dotted with refineries and chemical plants. International Flavors & Fragrances (IFF), the world's largest flavor company, has a manufacturing facility off Exit 8A in Dayton, New Jersey; Givaudan, the world's second-largest flavor company, has a plant in East Hanover. Haarmann & Reimer, the largest German flavor company, has a plant in Teterboro, as does Takasago, the largest Japanese flavor company. Flavor Dynamics has a plant in South Plainfield; Frutarom is in North Bergen; Elan Chemical is in Newark. Dozens of companies manufacture flavors in New Jersey industrial parks between Teaneck and South Brunswick. Indeed, the area produces about two-thirds of the flavor additives sold in the United States.

The IFF plant in Dayton is a huge pale blue building with a modern office complex attached to the front. It sits in an industrial park, not far from a BASF plastics factory, a Jolly French Toast factory, and a plant that manufactures Liz Claiborne cosmetics. Dozens of tractor-trailers were parked at the IFF loading dock the afternoon I visited, and a thin cloud of steam floated from the chimney. Before entering the plant, I signed a nondisclosure form, promising not to reveal the brand names of products that contain IFF flavors. The place reminded me of Willy Wonka's chocolate factory. Wonderful smells drifted through the hallways, men and women in neat white lab coats cheerfully went about their work, and hundreds of little glass bottles sat on laboratory tables and shelves. The bottles contained powerful but fragile flavor chemicals, shielded from light by the brown glass and the round plastic caps shut tight. The long chemical names on the little white labels were as mystifying to me as medieval Latin. They were the odd-sounding names of things that would be mixed and poured and turned into new substances, like magic potions.

I was not invited to see the manufacturing areas of the IFF plant, where it was thought I might discover trade secrets. Instead, I toured various laboratories and pilot kitchens, where the flavors of well-established brands are tested or adjusted, and where whole new flavors are created. IFF's snack and savory lab is responsible for the flavor of potato chips, corn chips, breads, crackers, breakfast cereals, and pet food. The confectionery lab devises the flavor for ice cream, cookies, candies, toothpastes, mouthwashes, and antacids. Everywhere I looked, I saw famous, widely advertised products sitting on laboratory desks and tables. The beverage lab is full of brightly colored liquids in clear bottles. It comes up with the flavor for popular soft drinks, sport drinks, bottled teas, and wine coolers, for all-natural juice drinks, organic soy drinks, beers, and malt liquors. In one pilot kitchen I saw a dapper chemist, a middle-aged man with an elegant tie beneath his lab coat, carefully preparing a batch of cookies with white frosting and pink-and-white sprinkles. In another pilot kitchen I saw a pizza oven, a grill, a milk-shake machine, and a french fryer identical to those I'd seen behind the counter at countless fast food restaurants.

In addition to being the world's largest flavor company, IFF manufactures the smell of six of the ten best-selling fine perfumes in the United States. It makes the smell of Estée Lauder's Beautiful, Clinique's Happy, Ralph Lauren's Polo, and Calvin Klein's Eternity. It also makes the smell of household products such as deodorant, dishwashing detergent, bath soap, shampoo, furniture polish, and floor wax. All of these aromas are made through the same basic process: the manipulation of volatile chemicals to create a particular smell. The basic science behind the scent of your shaving cream is the same as that governing the flavor of your TV dinner.

The aroma of a food can be responsible for as much as 90 percent of its flavor. Scientists now believe that human beings acquired the sense of taste as a way to avoid being poisoned. Edible plants generally taste sweet; deadly ones, bitter. Taste is supposed to help us differentiate food that's good for us from food that's not. The taste buds on our tongues can detect the presence of half a dozen or so basic tastes, including: sweet, sour, bitter, salty, astringent, and umami (a taste discovered by Japanese researchers, a rich and full sense of deliciousness triggered by amino acids in foods such as shellfish, mushrooms, potatoes, and seaweed). Taste buds offer a relatively limited means of detection, however, compared to the human olfactory system, which can perceive thousands of different chemical aromas. Indeed "flavor" is primarily the smell of gases being released by the chemicals you've just put in your mouth.

The act of drinking, sucking, or chewing a substance releases its 10 volatile gases. They flow out of the mouth and up the nostrils, or up the passageway in the back of the mouth, to a thin layer of nerve cells called the olfactory epithelium, located at the base of the nose, right between the eyes. The brain combines the complex smell signals from the epithelium with the simple taste signals from the tongue, assigns a flavor to what's in your mouth, and decides if it's something you want to eat.

Babies like sweet tastes and reject bitter ones; we know this because scientists have rubbed various flavors inside the mouths of infants and then recorded their facial reactions. A person's food preferences, like his or her personality, are formed during the first few years of life, through a process of socialization. Toddlers can learn to enjoy hot and spicy food, bland health food, or fast food, depending upon what the people around them eat. The human sense of smell is still not fully understood and can be greatly affected by psychological factors and expectations. The color of a food can determine the perception of its taste. The mind filters out the overwhelming majority of chemical aromas that surround us, focusing intently on some, ignoring others. People can grow accustomed to bad smells or good smells; they stop noticing what once seemed overpowering. Aroma and memory are somehow inextricably linked. A smell can suddenly evoke a long-forgotten moment. The flavors of childhood foods seem to leave an indelible mark, and adults often return to them, without always knowing why. These "comfort foods" become a source of pleasure and reassurance, a fact that fast food chains work hard to promote. Childhood memories of Happy Meals can translate into frequent adult visits to McDonald's, like those of the chain's "heavy users," the customers who eat there four or five times a week.

The human craving for flavor has been a largely unacknowledged and unexamined force in history. Royal empires have been built, unexplored lands have been traversed, great religions and philosophies have been forever changed by the spice trade. In 1492 Christopher Columbus set sail to find seasoning. Today the influence of flavor in the world marketplace is no less decisive. The rise and fall of corporate empires—of soft drink companies, snack food companies, and fast food chains—is frequently determined by how their products taste.

The flavor industry emerged in the mid-nineteenth century, as processed foods began to be manufactured on a large scale. Recognizing the need for flavor additives, the early food processors turned to perfume companies that had years of experience working with essential oils and volatile aromas. The great perfume houses of England, France, and the Netherlands produced many of the first flavor compounds. In the early part of the twentieth century, Germany's powerful chemical industry assumed the technological lead in flavor production. Legend has it that a German scientist discovered methyl anthranilate, one of the first artificial flavors, by accident while mixing chemicals in his laboratory. Suddenly the lab was filled with the sweet smell of grapes. Methyl anthranilate later became the chief flavoring compound of grape Kool-Aid. After World War II, much of the perfume industry shifted from Europe to the United States, settling in New York City near the garment district and the fashion houses. The flavor industry came with it, subsequently moving to New Jersey to gain more plant capacity. Man-made flavor additives were used mainly in baked goods, candies, and sodas until the 1950s, when sales of processed food began to soar. The invention of gas chromatographs and mass spectrometers—machines capable of detecting volatile gases at low levels—vastly increased the number of flavors that could be synthesized. By the mid-1960s the American flavor industry was churning out compounds to supply the taste of Pop Tarts, Bac-Os, Tab, Tang, Filet-O-Fish sandwiches, and literally thousands of other new foods.

The American flavor industry now has annual revenues of about $1.4 billion. Approximately ten thousand new processed food products are introduced every year in the United States. Almost all of them require flavor additives. And about nine out of every ten of these new food products fail. The latest flavor innovations and corporate realignments are heralded in publications such as *Food Chemical News, Food Engineering, Chemical Market Reporter,* and *Food Product Design.* The growth of IFF has mirrored that of the flavor industry as a whole. IFF was formed in 1958, through the merger of two small companies. Its annual revenues have grown almost fifteenfold since the early 1970s, and it now has manufacturing facilities in twenty countries.

The quality that people seek most of all in a food, its flavor, is usu- 15 ally present in a quantity too infinitesimal to be measured by any traditional culinary terms such as ounces or teaspoons. Today's sophisticated spectrometers, gas chromatographs, and headspace vapor analyzers provide a detailed map of a food's flavor components, detecting chemical aromas in amounts as low as one part per billion. The human nose, however, is still more sensitive than any machine yet invented. A nose can detect aromas present in quantities of a few parts per trillion—an amount equivalent to 0.000000000003 percent. Complex aromas, like those of coffee or roasted meat, may be composed of volatile gases from nearly a thousand different chemicals. The smell of a strawberry arises from the interaction of at least 350 different chemicals that are present in minute amounts. The chemical that provides the dominant flavor of bell pepper can be tasted in amounts as low as .02 parts per billion; one drop is sufficient to add flavor to five average size swimming pools. The flavor additive usually comes last, or second to last, in a processed food's list of ingredients (chemicals that add color are frequently used in even smaller amounts). As a result, the flavor of a processed food often costs less than its packaging. Soft drinks contain a larger proportion of flavor additives than most products. The flavor in a twelve-ounce can of Coke costs about half a cent.

The Food and Drug Administration does not require flavor companies to disclose the ingredients of their additives, so long as all the chemicals are considered by the agency to be GRAS (Generally Regarded As Safe). This lack of public disclosure enables the companies to maintain the secrecy of their formulas. It also hides the fact that flavor compounds sometimes contain more ingredients than the foods being given their taste. The ubiquitous phrase "artificial strawberry flavor" gives little hint of the chemical wizardry and manufacturing skill that can make a highly processed food taste like a strawberry.

A typical artificial strawberry flavor, like the kind found in a Burger King strawberry milk shake, contains the following ingredients: amyl acetate, amyl butyrate, amyl valerate, anethol, anisyl formate, benzyl acetate, benzyl isobutyrate, butyric acid, cinnamyl isobutyrate, cinnamyl valerate, cognac essential oil, diacetyl, dipropyl ketone, ethyl acetate, ethyl amylketone, ethyl butyrate, ethyl cinnamate, ethyl heptanoate, ethyl heptylate, ethyl lactate, ethyl methylphenylglycidate, ethyl nitrate,

Nutrition Facts	
Serving Size 2.6 oz (75g)	
Servings Per Container 1	

Amount Per Serving

Calories 230	Calories from Fat 100
	% Daily Values*
Total Fat 11g	**17%**
Saturated Fat 1.5g	**8%**
Trans Fat 0g	
Sodium 130mg	**5%**
Total Carbohydrate 30g	**10%**
Dietary Fiber 2g	**8%**
Sugars 0g	
Protein 2g	**4%**

*Percent Daily Values are based on a 2,000 calorie diet.

INGREDIENTS: Potatoes, Vegetable Oil (Canola Oil, Soybean Oil, Hydrogenated Soybean Oil, Natural Beef Flavor [Wheat and Milk Derivatives]*, Citric Acid [Preservative]), Dextrose, Sodium Acid Pyrophosphate (Maintain Color), Salt. Prepared in Vegetable Oil (Canola Oil, Corn Oil, Soybean Oil, Hydrogenated Soybean Oil) with TBHQ and Citric Acid to preserve freshness of the oil and Dimethylpolysiloxane to reduce oil splatter when cooking.
CONTAINS: WHEAT AND MILK.
*Natural beef flavor contains hydrolyzed wheat and hydrolyzed milk as starting ingredients.

A nutrition label with ingredients for one small order of McDonald's french fries.

ethyl propionate, ethyl valerate, heliotropin, hydroxyphrenyl 2-butanone (10 percent solution in alcohol), α-ionone, isobutyl anthranilate, isobutyl butyrate, lemon essential oil, maltol, 4-methylacetophenone, methyl anthranilate, methyl benzoate, methyl cinnamate, methyl heptine carbonate, methyl naphthyl ketone, methyl salicylate, mint essential oil, neroli essential oil, nerolin, neryl isobutyrate, orris butter, phenethyl alcohol, rose, rum ether, γ-undecalactone, vanillin, and solvent.

Although flavors usually arise from a mixture of many different volatile chemicals, a single compound often supplies the dominant aroma. Smelled alone, that chemical provides an unmistakable sense of the food. Ethyl-2-methyl butyrate, for example, smells just like an apple. Today's highly processed foods offer a blank palette: whatever chemicals you add to them will give them specific tastes. Adding methyl-2-peridylketone makes something taste like popcorn. Adding ethyl-3-hydroxybutanoate makes it taste like marshmallow. The possibilities are now almost limitless. Without affecting the appearance or nutritional value, processed foods could even be made with aroma chemicals such as hexanal (the smell of freshly cut grass) or 3-methyl butanoic acid (the smell of body odor).

> "The distinction between artificial and natural flavors can be somewhat arbitrary and absurd, based more on how the flavor has been made than on what it actually contains."

The 1960s were the heyday of artificial flavors. The synthetic versions of flavor compounds were not subtle, but they did not need to be, given the nature of most processed food. For the past twenty years food processors have tried hard to use only "natural flavors" in their products. According to the FDA, these must be derived entirely from natural sources—from herbs, spices, fruits, vegetables, beef, chicken, yeast, bark, roots, etc. Consumers prefer to see natural flavors on a label, out of a belief that they are healthier. The distinction between artificial and natural flavors can be somewhat arbitrary and absurd, based more on how the flavor has been made than on what it actually contains. "A natural flavor," says Terry Acree, a professor of food science technology at Cornell University, "is a flavor that's been derived with an out-of-date technology." Natural flavors and artificial flavors sometimes contain exactly the same chemicals, produced through different methods. Amyl acetate, for example, provides the dominant note of banana flavor. When you distill it from bananas with a solvent, amyl acetate is a natural flavor. When you produce it by mixing vinegar with amyl alcohol, adding sulfuric acid as a catalyst, amyl acetate is an artificial flavor. Either way it smells and tastes the same. The phrase "natural flavor" is now listed among the ingredients of everything from Stonyfield Farm Organic Strawberry Yogurt to Taco Bell Hot Taco Sauce.

A natural flavor is not necessarily healthier or purer than an artificial 20 one. When almond flavor (benzaldehyde) is derived from natural sources, such as peach and apricot pits, it contains traces of hydrogen cyanide, a deadly poison. Benzaldehyde derived through a different process—by mixing oil of clove and the banana flavor, amyl acetate—does not contain any cyanide. Nevertheless, it is legally considered an artificial flavor and sells at a much lower price. Natural and artificial flavors are now manufactured at the same chemical plants, places that few people would associate with Mother Nature. Calling any of these flavors "natural" requires a flexible attitude toward the English language and a fair amount of irony.

The small and elite group of scientists who create most of the flavor in most of the food now consumed in the United States are called "flavorists." They draw upon a number of disciplines in their work: biology, psychology, physiology, and organic chemistry. A flavorist is a chemist with a trained nose and a poetic sensibility. Flavors are created by blending scores of different chemicals in tiny amounts, a process governed by scientific principles but demanding a fair amount of art. In an age when delicate aromas, subtle flavors, and microwave ovens do not easily coexist, the job of the flavorist is to conjure illusions about processed food and, in the words of one flavor company's literature, to ensure "consumer likeability." The flavorists with whom I spoke were charming, cosmopolitan, and ironic. They were also discreet, in keeping with the dictates of their trade. They were the sort of scientist who not only enjoyed fine wine, but could also tell you the chemicals that gave each vintage its unique aroma. One flavorist compared his work to composing music. A well-made flavor compound will have a "top note," followed by a "dry-down," and a "leveling-off," with different chemicals responsible for each stage. The taste of a food can be radically altered by minute changes in the flavoring mix. "A little odor goes a long way," one flavorist said.

In order to give a processed food the proper taste, a flavorist must always consider the food's "mouthfeel"—the unique combination of textures and chemical interactions that affects how the flavor is perceived. The mouthfeel can be adjusted through the use of various fats, gums, starches, emulsifiers, and stabilizers. The aroma chemicals of a food can be precisely analyzed, but mouthfeel is much harder to measure. How does one quantify a french fry's crispness? Food technologists are now conducting basic research in rheology, a branch of physics that examines the flow and deformation of materials. A number of companies sell sophisticated devices that attempt to measure mouthfeel. The Universal TA-XT2 Texture Analyzer, produced by the Texture Technologies Corporation, performs calculations based on data derived from twenty-five separate probes. It is essentially a mechanical mouth. It gauges the most important rheological properties of a food—the bounce, creep, breaking point, density, crunchiness, chewiness, gumminess, lumpiness, rubberiness, springiness, slipperiness, smoothness, softness, wetness, juiciness, spreadability, spring-back, and tackiness.

Some of the most important advances in flavor manufacturing are now occurring in the field of biotechnology. Complex flavors are being made through fermentation, enzyme reactions, fungal cultures, and tissue cultures. All of the flavors being created through these methods—including the ones being synthesized by funguses—are considered natural flavors by the FDA. The new enzyme-based processes are responsible for extremely lifelike dairy flavors. One company now offers not just butter flavor, but also fresh creamy butter, cheesy butter, milky butter, savory melted butter, and super-concentrated butter flavor, in liquid or powder form. The development of new fermentation techniques, as well as new techniques for heating mixtures of sugar and amino acids, have led to the creation of much more realistic meat flavors. The McDonald's Corporation will not reveal the exact origin of the natural flavor added to its french fries. In response to inquiries from *Vegetarian Journal*, however, McDonald's did acknowledge that its fries derive some of their characteristic flavor from "animal products."

Other popular fast foods derive their flavor from unexpected sources. Wendy's Grilled Chicken Sandwich, for example, contains beef extracts. Burger King's BK Broiler Chicken Breast Patty contains "natural smoke flavor." A firm called Red Arrow Products Company specializes in smoke flavor, which is added to barbecue sauces and processed meats. Red Arrow manufactures natural smoke flavor by charring sawdust and capturing the aroma chemicals released into the air. The smoke is captured in water and then bottled, so that other companies can sell food which seems to have been cooked over a fire.

In a meeting room at IFF, Brian Grainger let me sample some of the   25 company's flavors. It was an unusual taste test; there wasn't any food to taste. Grainger is a senior flavorist at IFF, a soft-spoken chemist with graying hair, an English accent, and a fondness for understatement. He could easily be mistaken for a British diplomat or the owner of a West End brasserie with two Michelin stars. Like many in the flavor industry, he has an Old World, old-fashioned sensibility which seems out of step with our brand-conscious, egocentric age. When I suggested that IFF should put its own logo on the products that contain its flavors—instead of allowing other brands to enjoy the consumer loyalty and affection inspired by those flavors—Grainger politely disagreed, assuring me such a thing would never be done. In the absence of public credit or acclaim, the small and secretive fraternity of flavor chemists praises one another's work. Grainger can often tell, by analyzing the flavor formula of a product, which of his counterparts at a rival firm devised it. And he enjoys walking down supermarket aisles, looking at the many products that contain his flavors, even if no one else knows it.

Grainger had brought a dozen small glass bottles from the lab. After he opened each bottle, I dipped a fragrance testing filter into it. The filters were long white strips of paper designed to absorb aroma chemicals without producing off-notes. Before placing the strips of paper before my nose, I closed my eyes. Then I inhaled deeply, and one food after another was conjured from the glass bottles. I smelled fresh cherries, black olives, sautéed onions, and shrimp. Grainger's most remarkable creation took me by surprise. After closing my eyes, I suddenly smelled a grilled hamburger. The aroma was uncanny, almost miraculous. It smelled like someone in the room was flipping burgers on a hot grill. But when I opened my eyes, there was just a narrow strip of white paper and a smiling flavorist.

Understanding the Text

1. How are "artificial" and "natural" flavors similar? How are they different?
2. How does Schlosser describe the process through which food flavors are made?
3. According to Schlosser, what role does "taste" play in our health?

Reflection and Response

4. Why does Schlosser conclude that the distinction between artificial and natural flavors is often "arbitrary and absurd"? Do you agree or disagree? Explain.
5. Why is the production of flavors so secretive? What are the potential benefits of the secrecy to consumers? What are the potential drawbacks?
6. Does Schlosser's article make you think about french fries, fast food, or processed food flavors differently? Will his at-times searing critique change how you eat? Explain.

Making Connections

7. Why is the flavor industry so important? What role does the flavor industry play in what Michael Pollan calls the "industrial food chain" ("Eat Food: Food Defined," p. 10)? Using your campus library resources, locate two external sources to help support your response.
8. Compare Schlosser's description of the flavor industry to Donald L. Barlett and James B. Steele's description of Monsanto and the patented seed industry ("Monsanto's Harvest of Fear," p. 165). What commonalities exist? What differences do you see? How do these industries affect consumers?

Her Chee-to Heart

Jill McCorkle

Jill McCorkle is an award-winning novelist, essayist, and short story writer who has published many collections and novels, most recently *Life After Life* (2013). Several of her stories have been chosen for inclusion in *Best American Short Stories* collections. She teaches creative writing in the MFA Program at North Carolina State University and is a faculty member of the Bennington College Writing Seminars. In this essay, published in the collection *We Are What We Ate* (1998), McCorkle offers vivid memories of life as a "junk-food junkie."

If I could have a perfect day of eating, this would be it: I'd begin with pancakes and sausage patties drenched in Log Cabin syrup. Then I'd visit my grandmother's kitchen, where my sister and I used to watch ravenously as Gramma made her famous pound cake (a real pound cake — a pound of butter, a pound of sugar, egg after egg after egg swirled in Swans Down cake flour). We'd each slurp batter off the mixer whisks and then split what was left in the red-and-white Pyrex bowl. My grandmother also made chicken and pastry (her pastry was more like dumplings) and homemade biscuits (the secret ingredient is lard), which might be dipped in redeye gravy or covered in butter and Karo syrup (doughboys) and eaten as dessert. She made homemade apple pies (the fruit part of our diet) fried in Crisco and filled with sugar.

If I couldn't have homemade food, then I would settle for what could be bought. A foot-long hot dog at the B&R Drive-In, for example; french fries limp with grease and salt from the bowling alley; a barbecue sandwich (Carolina style — chopped fine and spiced up with hot sauce); a triple-chocolate milk shake from Tastee-Freez. Banana splits and hot-fudge sundaes. Maybe a frozen Zero candy bar or a Milky Way, a Little Debbie snack cake and a moon pie, too.

I am a junk-food junkie and always have been. My college roommate and my husband both blame me for their slides into high-fat, preservative-filled meals, like the frozen Mexican TV dinners that my roommate and I ate all the way through college, or the microwavable burritos I now stash at the back of my freezer for desperate moments (desperate meaning a craving for Tex-Mex or a need to drive a nail and not being able to find a hammer). Forget meals, anyway; the truly good treats for a junk-food junkie get served up in between: colorful Ben & Jerry's pints, natural in an ethical way (the money goes to good places, at least) that makes me feel healthy; names — Chubby Hubby, Chunky Monkey, Wavy

Gravy—that make me laugh. Good Humor is what it's all about and has been since childhood: kids trained to respond to the ringing of a bell, to chase alongside trucks in neighborhood streets like so many pups for a Nutty Buddy. Ice cream is near the top of any junk-food junkie's list to be sure, but I haven't even begun to mention the Chee-tos, the Pecan Sandies.

There's something about unnatural food colors that has always attracted me. What tastes or looks better than the frosting on grocery-store-bakery birthday cakes? Hot pink or blue roses that melt in your mouth. The fluorescent brilliance of a crunchy Chee-to. Not too long ago my children (ages four and seven) were eating at a friend's. They were served a lovely meal of homemade macaroni and cheese, white, the way something without any additives and preservatives should be. I was on the other side of the room, helpless to defend myself when I heard my daughter say, "But my mom's macaroni and cheese is bright orange." Well? What can I say? I also love that fuchsia-colored sweet-and-sour sauce that you often find on Chinese food buffets.

At the last big dinner party we had, my husband bought Yodels to throw out on the dessert table along with a fresh-fruit concoction, which had taken me forever to cut up, and little cheesecakes. At the end of the night, there was not a Yodel in sight, but very few people had openly indulged. These scrumptious lunch-box treats (creme-filled chocolate rolls, 140 calories and 8 grams of fat each, which means, of course, that they are good) had instead been slyly tucked away into pockets and purses for the ride home. Yodels, Twinkies, Hostess Snoballs. They make people nostalgic for elementary school, those wonderful years when we were advised to eat beef and pork. Children thriving on sloppy joes and Saturday T-bones. Pork chops with applesauce. Sausage gravy over home-made biscuits. A good green vegetable in the South, where I grew up, was a green-bean casserole in which the beans were camouflaged in Campbell's cream of mushroom soup and canned fried onion rings. All the recipes in my favorite cookbooks begin with Campbell's cream-of-some-thing soup.

I was enamored of a boy named Michael in the first grade who licked Kool-Aid powder from his palm whenever the teacher wasn't looking. He moved away before the end of the year, and yet thirty-one years later, I still remember him with a fond mixture of repulsion at the sticky red saliva that graced his notebook paper and admiration for the open ease with which he indulged his habit. I loved Pixy Stix straws, which, let's face it, were nothing more than dry Kool-Aid mix poured right into your mouth. Sweetarts. Jawbreakers. Firecrackers. Mary Janes. Any item that I was told was *very* bad for my teeth.

Maybe it's an oral-gratification thing. I'm sure that's why I smoked for fifteen years. When I quit nine years ago, I rediscovered my taste buds. I found flavors I had forgotten all about: Sugar Babies and Raisinets, that thick mashed-potato gravy that is the *real* secret ingredient at Kentucky Fried Chicken. I found flavors I had never had before, such as cheese blintzes and latkes smothered in sour cream. I found that wonderful, all-natural, fortified cereal Quaker 100% Natural Oats Honey and Raisins. I need oral participation, oral gratification.

> "There's something about unnatural food colors that has always attracted me. What tastes or looks better than the frosting on grocery-store-bakery birthday cakes?"

Despite what they will tell you on television, a little stick of Juicy Fruit is not going to get you there if you've been lighting up for years. But M&M's? Junior Mints? Those diablo-style peanuts thoroughly doused with cayenne pepper? Now, that's chewing satisfaction. A Coke (or diet Coke for the figure-minded; Jolt cola for the desperate-to-start-the-day-minded) chaser.

I could do a taste test. I can recognize all the sodas. The soda wanna-bes. I drink a good two to three cups of coffee when I get up, and by the time I drive the kids to school, I've switched over to diet Coke. People say, "Doesn't it keep you awake?" I wish! During one of my pregnancies I lost all taste for Coke. I couldn't believe it. I'd been drinking Coke for as long as I could remember. It was so sad; filling myself up on Hawaiian Punch (which is very good in its own right), Pop-Tarts, and ice cream, ice cream, ice cream. But I missed the Coke cans rolling around under the seat of my car. I missed the whoosh and zap of buying a Coke from a vending machine. And one day, like magic, it returned, this desire, like an old love resurfacing.

There are ways a junk-food junkie can feel less guilty about all this food, if indeed you ever do feel guilty. Did I mention caffeine? It's like air—essential for full enjoyment. And it burns calories. If that doesn't work, there are always things like the NordicTrack where I hang my clothes at the end of the day and the Suzanne Somers Thighmaster I keep in my closet for decoration.

Besides, I consider myself a purist; I don't like substitute things—like these new clear sodas. Who cares? I went into the all-natural health-food grocery store not long ago only to discover that there are a lot of things in this world that are foreign to me. The produce section had products you might find growing in a neglected basement. There were name brands I'd never heard of; certainly they don't buy airtime on television. 10

There were cereals without colored marshmallows or prizes in the box. They boasted of having no sugar (as if this were good). It did not take me long to get back to the familiar aisles of the Super Stop & Shop, the red-and-white Campbell's soup labels, the chip-and-cookie aisle (nothing there sweetened with fruit juice or carob imitating chocolate), and the candy bars at the checkout.

One of my fondest junk-food memories is of a rare snow day in Lumberton, North Carolina, when I was in the sixth grade, a wonderful age at which, though I liked boys, they were not nearly as exciting as the ice cream store nearby that served up an oversize cone called a Kitchen Sink. But that day, I sat with a couple of friends in the back of the Kwik-Pik (the South's version of the convenience store) and ate raw chocolate-chip-cookie dough while drinking Eagle Brand sweetened condensed milk straight from the can. My friends and I waddled home feeling sick but warmly nourished, our stomachs coated and glowing with sugar. I mean, really, there is no cake or cookie on earth that tastes as good as dough or batter.

My favorite food in the eighth grade was Slim Jim sausages. For the uninformed, these are the miniature pepperoni sticks usually found near the register of convenience stores, where you might also find the beef jerky and pickled eggs. When I was growing up, there was usually a big jar of pickled pig's feet too, but this was not a treat that ever caught my eye. No, I lived on Slim Jims, spicy and chewy. I kept them with me at all times, getting a good chew while at cheerleading practices. They reminded me of being an even younger kid and getting a little bit of raw, salty country ham from my grandmother and chewing it all day like a piece of gum. (Sorry, Juicy Fruit; failed again.)

My husband, a doctor whose specialty is infectious diseases, is certain that I have been host to many parasites. Maybe, but what I'm certain that I have been host to are the junk-food parasites who refuse to admit that they indulge, but they do. Just put out a bowl of pistachios and check out the red fingertips leaving; chips, M&M's. Ah, M&M's. It was a sad day long ago when they retired the red ones. I had spent years being entertained by a pack; segregate and then integrate, close your eyes and guess which color. I was thrilled when the red ones returned, and now blue! Lovely blue M&M's. I love the pastel ones at Easter, along with those Cadbury eggs, and my own personal favorite: malted Easter eggs. These are actually Whoppers (malted-milk balls) covered in a speckled candy shell. Sometimes they are called robin eggs and sometimes simply malteds, but a Whopper is a Whopper is a Whopper. I like to bite one in half and then suck in. When the air is pulled out of a Whopper, what's left is more like a Milk Dud.

Of course there is also the Whopper from Burger King. Once, after a Friday night high-school football game, I sat down at a table with a bag of food that looked similar to those of all the guys on the team. I had a Whopper with everything, large fries, an apple pie, and a chocolate shake. Our cheerleading adviser told me that I wouldn't always be able to do that.

Thank God I didn't know she was right. It would have ruined the next four years as I continued to down cream-filled Krispy Kreme doughnuts and my own special high-protein omelette that was filled with mayonnaise and cheese. I loved Funyuns, too, except that nobody wanted to sit next to me on the bus when I ate them. 15

After all these years, I've made some adjustments. I now buy Hebrew National for things like hot dogs and bologna. I figure the kosher laws probably serve me well in this particular purchase, and try as I might to dissuade them, my children love bologna with an absolute passion. They can smell the reject turkey substitute from fifty paces. They don't like *real* mac and cheese. They like the microwave kind. My niece (at age four) once invited me into her playhouse for lunch. She said, "Would you like a diet Coke while I cook lunch in the microwave?" So maybe it's a family thing. Maybe it's the potassium benzoate.

I would love a diet Coke and a cream horn right about now. Some salt-and-vinegar chips. Onion dip and Ruffles. S'mores. I like to get in bed to read with a stash of something close by. I have found that I am especially drawn to things with a high polyglycerol-ester-of-fatty-acids content. It makes me feel *happy*. I think maybe this is the key to a true junk-food junkie's heart: happiness. Just as Proust bit into his little madeleine and had a flood of memories, I bite into my Devil Dog, my Ring-Ding, Twinkie, Ho-Ho, Yodel. I bite into my Hostess Snoball and retreat to a world where the only worry is what to ask your mother to put in your lunch box the next day or which pieces of candy you will select at the Kwik-Pik on your way home from school. Ahead of you are the wasteland years: a pack of cigarettes, some Clearasil pads, a tube of Blistex, and breath spray. But for now, reach back to those purer, those sugar-filled, melt-in-your-mouth, forever-a-kid years. Who cares if there is a little polysorbate 60 and some diglycerides, some carrageenan, some Red 40 and Blue 1, some agar-agar? I have a dream that somewhere out there in the grown-up, low-fat world there is a boy named Michael licking his lips and getting all the fumaric acid that he can.

Understanding the Text

1. What is a "junk-food junkie"?
2. What role does food play in McCorkle's life? Consider how food affects both her self-perception and her relationships with others.

Reflection and Response

3. Does McCorkle's diet fascinate or horrify you? Explain your reaction.
4. Do you think her eating habits are normal in our society? Why or why not?
5. Why do you think she wrote this essay? What do you think she hopes her readers will learn from her stories about food?

Making Connections

6. What attitudes or values do Michael Pollan ("Eat Food: Food Defined," p. 10) and McCorkle share? What would Pollan praise about McCorkle's relationship with food? What would he question?
7. Consider Eric Schlosser's description of the flavor industry ("Why the Fries Taste Good," p. 20). What role does the flavor industry play in McCorkle's diet?
8. Think about what Dhruv Khullar ("Why Shame Won't Stop Obesity," p. 71) and Thich Nhat Hanh and Lilian Cheung ("Are You Really Appreciating the Apple?," p. 59) have to say about the role eating plays in our lives. How would they each analyze McCorkle's attitudes about food?
9. Make a list of what you have eaten in the last two days. In light of the views of Michael Pollan, Eric Schlosser, and Jill McCorkle, evaluate your diet.

Eating Made Simple

Marion Nestle

Marion Nestle is a professor emerita in the Department of Nutrition, Food Studies, and Public Health at New York University. She has spent much of her career in public service, consulting on government policies around food and health. She is the author of several books, including *What to Eat* (2007), *Food Politics: How the Food Industry Influences Nutrition and Health* (2007), *Safe Food: The Politics of Food Safety* (2010), *Why Calories Count: From Science to Politics* (2012), *Eat Drink Vote: An Illustrated Guide to Food Politics* (2013), and *Unsavory Truth: How Food Companies Skew the Science of What We Eat* (2018). Nestle's research focuses on food and nutrition policy and analysis and the social, political, and environmental influences on food choice. She regularly writes about her work in the *San Francisco Chronicle*, *The Atlantic*, and her blog *Food Politics*. In this essay, which originally appeared in *Scientific American*, Nestle provides advice on how to sort out the often confusing and sometimes contradictory messages about nutrition and dietary advice.

As a nutrition professor, I am constantly asked why nutrition advice seems to change so much and why experts so often disagree. Whose information, people ask, can we trust? I'm tempted to say, "Mine, of course," but I understand the problem. Yes, nutrition advice seems endlessly mired in scientific argument, the self-interest of food companies, and compromises by government regulators. Nevertheless, basic dietary principles are not in dispute: eat less; move more; eat fruits, vegetables, and whole grains; and avoid too much junk food.

"Eat less" means consume fewer calories, which translates into eating smaller portions and steering clear of frequent between-meal snacks. "Move more" refers to the need to balance calorie intake with physical activity. Eating fruits, vegetables, and whole grains provides nutrients unavailable from other foods. Avoiding junk food means to shun "foods of minimal nutritional value" — highly processed sweets and snacks laden with salt, sugars, and artificial additives. Soft drinks are the prototypical° junk food; they contain sweeteners but few or no nutrients.

If you follow these precepts, other aspects of the diet matter much less. Ironically, this advice has not changed in years. The noted cardiologist Ancel Keys (who died in 2004 at the age of 100) and his wife, Margaret,

prototypical: serving as an example of a type.

suggested similar principles for preventing coronary heart disease nearly 50 years ago.

But I can see why dietary advice seems like a moving target. Nutrition research is so difficult to conduct that it seldom produces unambiguous results. Ambiguity requires interpretation. And interpretation is influenced by the individual's point of view, which can become thoroughly entangled with the science.

Nutrition Science Challenges

This scientific uncertainty is not overly surprising given that humans eat so many different foods. For any individual, the health effects of diets are modulated° by genetics but also by education and income levels, job satisfaction, physical fitness, and the use of cigarettes or alcohol. To simplify this situation, researchers typically examine the effects of single dietary components one by one.

Studies focusing on one nutrient in isolation have worked splendidly to explain symptoms caused by deficiencies of vitamins or minerals. But this approach is less useful for chronic conditions such as coronary heart disease and diabetes that are caused by the interaction of dietary, genetic, behavioral, and social factors. If nutrition science seems puzzling, it is because researchers typically examine single nutrients detached from food itself, foods separate from diets, and risk factors apart from other behaviors. This kind of research is "reductive" in that it attributes health effects to the consumption of one nutrient or food when it is the overall dietary pattern that really counts most.

> "If nutrition science seems puzzling, it is because researchers typically examine single nutrients detached from food itself, foods separate from diets, and risk factors apart from other behaviors."

For chronic diseases, single nutrients usually alter risk by amounts too small to measure except through large, costly population studies. As seen recently in the Women's Health Initiative, a clinical trial that examined the effects of low-fat diets on heart disease and cancer, participants were unable to stick with the restrictive dietary protocols. Because humans cannot be caged and fed measured formulas, the diets of experimental and control study groups tend to converge, making differences indistinguishable over the long run—even with fancy statistics.

modulate: modify or control.

It's the Calories

Food companies prefer studies of single nutrients because they can use the results to sell products. Add vitamins to candies, and you can market them as health foods. Health claims on the labels of junk foods distract consumers from their caloric content. This practice matters because when it comes to obesity—which dominates nutrition problems even in some of the poorest countries of the world—it is the calories that count. Obesity arises when people consume significantly more calories than they expend in physical activity.

America's obesity rates began to rise sharply in the early 1980s. Sociologists often attribute the "calories in" side of this trend to the demands of an overworked population for convenience foods—prepared, packaged products and restaurant meals that usually contain more calories than home-cooked meals.

But other social forces also promoted the calorie imbalance. The 10 arrival of the Reagan administration in 1980 increased the pace of industry deregulation, removing controls on agricultural production and encouraging farmers to grow more food. Calories available per capita in the national food supply (that produced by American farmers, plus imports, less exports) rose from 3,200 a day in 1980 to 3,900 a day two decades later.

The early 1980s also marked the advent of the "shareholder value movement" on Wall Street. Stockholder demands for higher short-term returns on investments forced food companies to expand sales in a marketplace that already contained excessive calories. Food companies responded by seeking new sales and marketing opportunities. They encouraged formerly shunned practices that eventually changed social norms, such as frequent between-meal snacking, eating in book and clothing stores, and serving larger portions. The industry continued to sponsor organizations and journals that focus on nutrition-related subjects and intensified its efforts to lobby government for favorable dietary advice. Then and now food lobbies have promoted positive interpretations of scientific studies, sponsored research that can be used as a basis for health claims, and attacked critics, myself among them, as proponents of "junk science." If anything, such activities only add to public confusion.

Supermarkets as "Ground Zero"

No matter whom I speak to, I hear pleas for help in dealing with supermarkets, considered by shoppers as "ground zero" for distinguishing health claims from scientific advice. So I spent a year visiting supermarkets to help people think more clearly about food choices. The result was my book *What to Eat*.

Supermarkets provide a vital public service but are not social services agencies. Their job is to sell as much food as possible. Every aspect of store design — from shelf position to background music — is based on marketing research. Because this research shows that the more products customers see, the more they buy, a store's objective is to expose shoppers to the maximum number of products they will tolerate viewing.

If consumers are confused about which foods to buy, it is surely because the choices require knowledge of issues that are not easily resolved by science and are strongly swayed by social and economic considerations. Such decisions play out every day in every store aisle.

Are Organics Healthier?

Organic foods are the fastest-growing segment of the industry, in part 15 because people are willing to pay more for foods that they believe are healthier and more nutritious. The U.S. Department of Agriculture forbids producers of "Certified Organic" fruits and vegetables from using synthetic pesticides, herbicides, fertilizers, genetically modified seeds, irradiation, or fertilizer derived from sewage sludge. It licenses inspectors to ensure that producers follow those rules. Although the USDA is responsible for organics, its principal mandate is to promote conventional agriculture, which explains why the department asserts that it "makes no claims that organically produced food is safer or more nutritious than conventionally produced food. Organic food differs from conventionally grown food in the way it is grown, handled and processed."

This statement implies that such differences are unimportant. Critics of organic foods would agree; they question the reliability of organic certification and the productivity, safety, and health benefits of organic production methods. Meanwhile the organic food industry longs for research to address such criticisms, but studies are expensive and difficult to conduct. Nevertheless, existing research in this area has established that organic farms are nearly as productive as conventional farms, use less energy, and leave soils in better condition. People who eat foods grown without synthetic pesticides ought to have fewer such chemicals in their bodies, and they do. Because the organic rules require pretreatment of manure and other steps to reduce the amount of pathogens in soil treatments, organic foods should be just as safe — or safer — than conventional foods.

Similarly, organic foods ought to be at least as nutritious as conventional foods. And proving organics to be more nutritious could help justify their higher prices. For minerals, this task is not difficult. The mineral content of plants depends on the amounts present in the soil in which they are grown. Organic foods are cultivated in richer soils, so their mineral content is higher.

But differences are harder to demonstrate for vitamins or antioxidants (plant substances that reduce tissue damage induced by free radicals); higher levels of these nutrients relate more to a food plant's genetic strain or protection from unfavorable conditions after harvesting than to production methods. Still, preliminary studies show benefits: organic peaches and pears contain greater quantities of vitamins C and E, and organic berries and corn contain more antioxidants.

Further research will likely confirm that organic foods contain higher nutrient levels, but it is unclear whether these nutrients would make a measurable improvement in health. All fruits and vegetables contain useful nutrients, albeit in different combinations and concentrations. Eating a variety of food plants is surely more important to health than small differences in the nutrient content of any one food. Organics may be somewhat healthier to eat, but they are far less likely to damage the environment, and that is reason enough to choose them at the supermarket.

Dairy and Calcium

Scientists cannot easily resolve questions about the health effects of dairy 20 foods. Milk has many components, and the health of people who consume milk or dairy foods is influenced by everything else they eat and do. But this area of research is especially controversial because it affects an industry that vigorously promotes dairy products as beneficial and opposes suggestions to the contrary.

Dairy foods contribute about 70 percent of the calcium in American diets. This necessary mineral is a principal constituent of bones, which constantly lose and regain calcium during normal metabolism. Diets must contain enough calcium to replace losses, or else bones become prone to fracture. Experts advise consumption of at least one gram of calcium a day to replace everyday losses. Only dairy foods provide this much calcium without supplementation.

But bones are not just made of calcium; they require the full complement of essential nutrients to maintain strength. Bones are stronger in people who are physically active and who do not smoke cigarettes or drink much alcohol. Studies examining the effects of single nutrients in dairy foods show that some nutritional factors—magnesium, potassium, vitamin D, and lactose, for example—promote calcium retention in bones. Others, such as protein, phosphorus, and sodium, foster calcium excretion. So bone strength depends more on overall patterns of diet and behavior than simply on calcium intake.

Populations that do not typically consume dairy products appear to exhibit lower rates of bone fracture despite consuming far less calcium than recommended. Why this is so is unclear. Perhaps their diets contain less protein from meat and dairy foods, less sodium from processed foods, and less phosphorus from soft drinks, so they retain calcium more effectively. The fact that calcium balance depends on multiple factors could explain why rates of osteoporosis (bone density loss) are highest in countries where people eat the most dairy foods. Further research may clarify such counterintuitive observations.

In the meantime, dairy foods are fine to eat if you like them, but they are not a nutritional requirement. Think of cows: they do not drink milk after weaning, but their bones support bodies weighing 800 pounds or more. Cows feed on grass, and grass contains calcium in small amounts—but those amounts add up. If you eat plenty of fruits, vegetables and whole grains, you can have healthy bones without having to consume dairy foods.

A Meaty Debate

Critics point to meat as the culprit responsible for elevating blood choles- 25 terol, along with raising risks for heart disease, cancer, and other conditions. Supporters cite the lack of compelling science to justify such allegations; they emphasize the nutritional benefits of meat protein, vitamins, and minerals. Indeed, studies in developing countries demonstrate health improvements when growing children are fed even small amounts of meat.

But because bacteria in a cow's rumen attach hydrogen atoms to unsaturated fatty acids, beef fat is highly saturated—the kind of fat that increases the risk of coronary heart disease. All fats and oils contain some saturated fatty acids, but animal fats, especially those from beef, have more saturated fatty acids than vegetable fats. Nutritionists recommend eating no more than a heaping tablespoon (20 grams) of saturated fatty acids a day. Beef eaters easily meet or exceed this limit. The smallest McDonald's cheeseburger contains 6 grams of saturated fatty acids, but a Hardee's Monster Thickburger has 45 grams.

Why meat might boost cancer risks, however, is a matter of speculation. Scientists began to link meat to cancer in the 1970s, but even after decades of subsequent research they remain unsure if the relevant factor might be fat, saturated fat, protein, carcinogens°, or something

carcinogen: any substance that directly causes cancer.

else related to meat. By the late 1990s experts could conclude only that eating beef probably increases the risk of colon and rectal cancers and possibly enhances the odds of acquiring breast, prostate and perhaps other cancers. Faced with this uncertainty, the American Cancer Society suggests selecting leaner cuts, smaller portions, and alternatives such as chicken, fish, or beans—steps consistent with today's basic advice about what to eat.

Fish and Heart Disease

Fatty fish are the most important sources of long-chain omega-3 fatty acids. In the early 1970s Danish investigators observed surprisingly low frequencies of heart disease among indigenous populations in Greenland that typically ate fatty fish, seals, and whales. The researchers attributed the protective effect to the foods' content of omega-3 fatty acids. Some subsequent studies—but by no means all—confirm this idea.

Because large, fatty fish are likely to have accumulated methylmercury and other toxins through predation, however, eating them raises questions about the balance between benefits and risks. Understandably, the fish industry is eager to prove that the health benefits of omega-3s outweigh any risks from eating fish.

Even independent studies on omega-3 fats can be interpreted differently. In 2004 the National Oceanic and Atmospheric Administration—for fish, the agency equivalent to the USDA—asked the Institute of Medicine (IOM) to review studies of the benefits and risks of consuming seafood. The ensuing review of the research on heart disease risk illustrates the challenge such work poses for interpretation.

The IOM's October 2006 report concluded that eating seafood reduces the risk of heart disease but judged the studies too inconsistent to decide if omega-3 fats were responsible. In contrast, investigators from the Harvard School of Public Health published a much more positive report in the *Journal of the American Medical Association* that same month. Even modest consumption of fish omega-3s, they stated, would cut coronary deaths by 36 percent and total mortality by 17 percent, meaning that not eating fish would constitute a health risk.

Differences in interpretation explain how distinguished scientists could arrive at such different conclusions after considering the same studies. The two groups, for example, had conflicting views of earlier work published in March 2006 in the *British Medical Journal*. That study found no overall effect of omega-3s on heart disease risk or mortality, although a subset of the original studies displayed a 14 percent reduction in total mortality that did not reach statistical significance. The IOM team interpreted the "nonsignificant" result as evidence for the need for caution, whereas the Harvard group saw the data as consistent with studies reporting the benefits of omega-3s. When studies present inconsistent results, both interpretations are plausible. I favor caution in such situations, but not everyone agrees.

Because findings are inconsistent, so is dietary advice about eating fish. The American Heart Association recommends that adults eat fatty fish at least twice a week, but U.S. dietary guidelines say: "Limited evidence suggests an association between consumption of fatty acids in fish and reduced risks of mortality from cardiovascular disease for the general population . . . however, more research is needed." Whether or not fish uniquely protects against heart disease, seafood is a delicious source of many nutrients, and two small servings per week of the less predatory classes of fish are unlikely to cause harm.

Sodas and Obesity

Sugars and corn sweeteners account for a large fraction of the calories in many supermarket foods, and virtually all the calories in drinks—soft, sports, and juice—come from added sugars.

In a trend that correlates closely with rising rates of obesity, daily 35 per capita consumption of sweetened beverages has grown by about 200 calories since the early 1980s. Although common sense suggests that this increase might have something to do with weight gain, beverage makers argue that studies cannot prove that sugary drinks alone—independent of calories or other foods in the diet—boost the risk of obesity. The evidence, they say correctly, is circumstantial. But pediatricians often see obese children in their practices who consume more than 1,000 calories a day from sweetened drinks alone, and several studies indicate that children who habitually consume sugary beverages take in more calories and weigh more than those who do not.

Nevertheless, the effects of sweetened drinks on obesity continue to be subject to interpretation. In 2006, for example, a systematic review funded by independent sources found sweetened drinks to promote obesity in both children and adults. But a review that same year sponsored in part by a beverage trade association concluded that soft drinks have no special role in obesity. The industry-funded researchers criticized existing studies as being short-term and inconclusive, and pointed to studies finding that people lose weight when they substitute sweetened drinks for their usual meals.

These differences imply the need to scrutinize food industry sponsorship of research itself. Although many researchers are offended by suggestions that funding support might affect the way they design or interpret studies, systematic analyses say otherwise. In 2007 investigators classified studies of the effects of sweetened and other beverages on health according to who had sponsored them. Industry-supported studies were more likely to yield results favorable to the sponsor than those funded by independent sources. Even though scientists may not be able to prove that sweetened drinks cause obesity, it makes sense for anyone interested in losing weight to consume less of them.

The examples I have discussed illustrate why nutrition science seems so controversial. Without improved methods to ensure compliance with dietary regimens, research debates are likely to rage unabated. Opposing points of view and the focus of studies and food advertising on single nutrients rather than on dietary patterns continue to fuel these disputes. While we wait for investigators to find better ways to study nutrition and health, my approach—eat less, move more, eat a largely plant-based diet, and avoid eating too much junk food—makes sense and leaves you plenty of opportunity to enjoy your dinner.

Understanding the Text

1. What is nutrition science? Why is nutrition science "reductive"?
2. What nutritional principles do experts agree on, according to Nestle?
3. If the basic principles are not in dispute, why is there so much conflicting nutritional advice? How does Nestle suggest reconciling it?

Reflection and Response

4. Nestle explains that nutrition science is controversial. Why is it so difficult to conduct nutrition research, and what makes the results so controversial? Select three of her examples to illustrate your position.
5. Think about what you eat. What have you learned about your own overall nutrition from reading Nestle's essay? Are there changes you think you should make? Why or why not?

Making Connections

6. What possible connections exist between the flavor industry described by Eric Schlosser ("Why the Fries Taste Good," p. 20) and the nutrition research described by Nestle? How might Thich Nhat Hanh and Lilian Cheung ("Are You Really Appreciating the Apple?," p. 59) analyze these connections?
7. Nestle served as a policy maker for the federal government nutrition guidelines. How do you think Nestle would interpret and evaluate the USDA's Food Pyramid in relation to the Food Plate guidelines (p. 68)? Which one do you think she would prefer and why?

8. Think about the story of nutrition in America that Nestle tells in relation to the argument David Freedman makes ("How Junk Food Can End Obesity," p. 75). How does Nestle's essay complicate the debate between Pollan and Freedman? How might they each use evidence presented by Nestle to support their views?

9. Messages regarding nutrition and dietary advice surround us, from stories in the media about cutting-edge studies to advertising and packaging labels (such as the FDA's new nutrition label, p. 69). Find several pieces of nutrition advice that employ nutrition science as evidence for why consumers should adopt the advice or buy the product. How do they use nutrition science? What would Nestle, Dhruv Khullar ("Why Shame Won't Stop Obesity," p. 71), and Wendell Berry ("The Pleasures of Eating," p. 46) say about the advice? What do you think of the advice? Would you follow it?

The Pleasures of Eating

Wendell Berry

Wendell Berry has spent his life as a poet and a farmer, drawing on his knowledge of and concern for the land, flora, and fauna in his more than thirty books of essays, poetry, and fiction. A prolific writer and man of letters, he uses his writing as a platform for speaking out about degradation of the land, environmental awareness, and conservation. He is well known for his essays on sustainable agriculture and food, many of which are collected in *Bringing It to the Table: On Farming and Food*, published in 2009. His many awards and lectures demonstrate his ability to connect with his audiences in meaningful ways. In this essay, Berry argues that we should think of eating as an "agricultural act" instead of thinking of food as an "agricultural product." He hopes that this will lead to a greater awareness of the complex relationships we have with our food and our responsibilities in its production.

Many times, after I have finished a lecture on the decline of American farming and rural life, someone in the audience has asked, "What can city people do?"

"Eat responsibly," I have usually answered. Of course, I have tried to explain what I mean by that, but afterwards I have invariably felt there was more to be said than I had been able to say. Now I would like to attempt a better explanation.

I begin with the proposition that eating is an agricultural act. Eating ends the annual drama of the food economy that begins with planting and birth. Most eaters, however, are no longer aware that this is true. They think of food as an agricultural product, perhaps, but they do not think of themselves as participants in agriculture. They think of themselves as "consumers." If they think beyond that, they recognize that they are passive consumers. They buy what they want — or what they have been persuaded to want — within the limits of what they can get. They pay, mostly without protest, what they are charged. And they mostly ignore certain critical questions about the quality and the cost of what they are sold: How fresh is it? How pure or clean is it, how free of dangerous chemicals? How far was it transported, and what did transportation add to the cost? How much did manufacturing or packaging or advertising add to the cost? When the food product has been manufactured or "processed" or "precooked," how has that affected its quality or price or nutritional value?

Most urban shoppers would tell you that food is produced on farms. But most of them do not know what farms, or what kinds of farms, or where the farms are, or what knowledge or skills are involved in farming.

They apparently have little doubt that farms will continue to produce, but they do not know how or over what obstacles. For them, then, food is pretty much an abstract idea—something they do not know or imagine—until it appears on the grocery shelf or on the table.

The specialization of production induces specialization of consumption. Patrons of the entertainment industry, for example, entertain themselves less and less and have become more and more passively dependent on commercial suppliers. This is certainly true also of patrons of the food industry, who have tended more and more to be mere consumers—passive, uncritical, and dependent. Indeed, this sort of consumption may be said to be one of the chief goals of industrial production. The food industrialists have by now persuaded millions of consumers to prefer food that is already prepared. They will grow, deliver, and cook your food for you and (just like your mother) beg you to eat it. That they do not yet offer to insert it, prechewed, into our mouth is only because they have found no profitable way to do so. We may rest assured that they would be glad to find such a way. The ideal industrial food consumer would be strapped to a table with a tube running from the food factory directly into his or her stomach.

Perhaps I exaggerate, but not by much. The industrial eater is, in fact, one who does not know that eating is an agricultural act, who no longer knows or imagines the connections between eating and the land, and who is therefore necessarily passive and uncritical—in short, a victim. When food, in the minds of eaters, is no longer associated with farming and with the land, then the eaters are suffering a kind of cultural amnesia that is misleading and dangerous. The current version of the "dream home" of the future involves "effortless" shopping from a list of available goods on a television monitor and heating precooked food by remote control. Of course, this implies and depends on a perfect ignorance of the history of the food that is consumed. It requires that the citizenry should give up their hereditary and sensible aversion to buying a pig in a poke. It wishes to make the selling of pigs in pokes an honorable and glamorous activity. The dreams in this dream home will perforce know nothing about the kind or quality of this food, or where it came from, or how it was produced and prepared, or what ingredients, additives, and residues it contains—unless, that is, the dreamer undertakes a close and constant study of the food industry, in which case he or she might as well wake up and play an active and responsible part in the economy of food.

There is, then, a politics of food that, like any politics, involves our freedom. We still (sometimes) remember that we cannot be free if our minds and voices are controlled by someone else. But we have neglected to understand that we cannot be free if our food and its sources are controlled by someone else. The condition of the passive consumer of food is not a democratic condition. One reason to eat responsibly is to live free.

But if there is a food politics, there are also a food esthetics and a food ethics, neither of which is dissociated from politics. Like industrial sex, industrial eating has become a degraded, poor, and paltry thing. Our kitchens and other eating places more and more resemble filling stations, as our homes more and more resemble motels. "Life is not very interesting," we seem to have decided. "Let its satisfactions be minimal, perfunctory, and fast." We hurry through our meals to go to work and hurry through our work in order to "recreate" ourselves in the evenings and on weekends and vacations. And then we hurry, with the greatest possible speed and noise and violence, through our recreation—for what? To eat the billionth hamburger at some fast-food joint hellbent on increasing the "quality" of our life? And all this is carried out in a remarkable obliviousness to the causes and effects, the possibilities and the purposes, of the life of the body in this world.

One will find this obliviousness represented in virgin purity in the advertisements of the food industry, in which food wears as much makeup as the actors. If one gained one's whole knowledge of food from these advertisements (as some presumably do), one would not know that the various edibles were ever living creatures, or that they all come from the soil, or that they were produced by work. The passive American consumer, sitting down to a meal of pre-prepared or fast food, confronts a platter covered with inert, anonymous substances that have been processed, dyed, breaded, sauced, gravied, ground, pulped, strained, blended, prettified, and sanitized beyond resemblance to any part of any creature that ever lived. The products of nature and agriculture have been made, to all appearances, the products of industry. Both eater and eaten are thus in exile from biological reality. And the result is a kind of solitude, unprecedented in human experience, in which the eater may think of eating as, first, a purely commercial transaction between him and a supplier and then as a purely appetitive transaction between him and his food.

And this peculiar specialization of the act of eating is, again, of obvi-   10
ous benefit to the food industry, which has good reasons to obscure the connection between food and farming. It would not do for the consumer to know that the hamburger she is eating came from a steer who spent much of his life standing deep in his own excrement in a feedlot, helping to pollute the local streams, or that the calf that yielded the veal cutlet on her plate spent its life in a box in which it did not have room to turn around. And, though her sympathy for the slaw might be less tender,

she should not be encouraged to meditate on the hygienic and biological implications of mile-square fields of cabbage, for vegetables grown in
huge monocultures are dependent on toxic chemicals—just as animals
in close confinements are dependent on antibiotics and other drugs.

The consumer, that is to say, must be
kept from discovering that, in the food
industry—as in any other industry—the
overriding concerns are not quality
and health, but volume and price. For
decades now the entire industrial food
economy, from the large farms and feedlots to the chains of supermarkets and
fast-food restaurants, has been obsessed
with volume. It has relentlessly increased
scale in order to increase volume in order
(probably) to reduce costs. But as scale

> "Eaters . . . must understand
> that eating takes place ines-
> capably in the world, that it
> is inescapably an agricultural
> act, and how we eat deter-
> mines, to a considerable
> extent, how the world is
> used."

increases, diversity declines; as diversity declines, so does health; as health
declines, the dependence on drugs and chemicals necessarily increases.
As capital replaces labor, it does so by substituting machines, drugs, and
chemicals for human workers and for the natural health and fertility of
the soil. The food is produced by any means or any shortcuts that will
increase profits. And the business of the cosmeticians° of advertising is to
persuade the consumer that food so produced is good, tasty, healthful, and
a guarantee of marital fidelity and long life.

It is possible, then, to be liberated from the husbandry and wifery of
the old household food economy. But one can be thus liberated only by
entering a trap (unless one sees ignorance and helplessness as the signs of
privilege, as many people apparently do). The trap is the ideal of indus-
trialism: a walled city surrounded by valves that let merchandise in but
no consciousness out. How does one escape this trap? Only voluntarily,
the same way that one went in: by restoring one's consciousness of what
is involved in eating; by reclaiming responsibility for one's own part in
the food economy. One might begin with the illuminating principle of
Sir Albert Howard's, that we should understand "the whole problem of
health in soil, plant, animal, and man as one great subject." Eaters, that
is, must understand that eating takes place inescapably in the world, that
it is inescapably an agricultural act, and how we eat determines, to a considerable extent, how the world is used. This is a simple way of describing a relationship that is inexpressibly complex. To eat responsibly is to

cosmetician: someone who sells or applies makeup.

understand and enact, so far as we can, this complex relationship. What can one do? Here is a list, probably not definitive:

1. Participate in food production to the extent that you can. If you have a yard or even just a porch box or a pot in a sunny window, grow something to eat in it. Make a little compost of your kitchen scraps and use it for fertilizer. Only by growing some food for yourself can you become acquainted with the beautiful energy cycle that revolves from soil to seed to flower to fruit to food to offal° to decay, and around again. You will be fully responsible for any food that you grow for yourself, and you will know all about it. You will appreciate it fully, having known it all its life.

2. Prepare your own food. This means reviving in your own mind and life the arts of kitchen and household. This should enable you to eat more cheaply, and it will give you a measure of "quality control": you will have some reliable knowledge of what has been added to the food you eat.

3. Learn the origins of the food you buy, and buy the food that is produced closest to your home. The idea that every locality should be, as much as possible, the source of its own food makes several kinds of sense. The locally produced food supply is the most secure, freshest, and the easiest for local consumers to know about and to influence.

4. Whenever possible, deal directly with a local farmer, gardener, or orchardist. All the reasons listed for the previous suggestion apply here. In addition, by such dealing you eliminate the whole pack of merchants, transporters, processors, packagers, and advertisers who thrive at the expense of both producers and consumers.

5. Learn, in self-defense, as much as you can of the economy and technology of industrial food production. What is added to the food that is not food, and what do you pay for those additions?

6. Learn what is involved in the best farming and gardening.

7. Learn as much as you can, by direct observation and experience if possible, of the life histories of the food species.

The last suggestion seems particularly important to me. Many people are now as much estranged from the lives of domestic plants and animals (except for flowers and dogs and cats) as they are from the lives of the

---

offal: scrap waste.

wild ones. This is regrettable, for these domestic creatures are in diverse ways attractive; there is such pleasure in knowing them, too.

It follows that there is great displeasure in knowing about a food economy that degrades and abuses those arts and those plants and animals and the soil from which they come. For anyone who does know something of the modern history of food, eating away from home can be a chore. My own inclination is to eat seafood instead of red meat or poultry when I am traveling. Though I am by no means a vegetarian, I dislike the thought that some animal has been made miserable in order to feed me. If I am going to eat meat, I want it to be from an animal that has lived a pleasant, uncrowded life outdoors, on bountiful pasture, with good water nearby and trees for shade. And I am getting almost as fussy about food plants. I like to eat vegetables and fruits that I know have lived happily and healthily in good soil, not the products of the huge, bechemicaled factory-fields that I have seen, for example, in the Central Valley of California. The industrial farm is said to have been patterned on the factory production line. In practice, it looks more like a concentration camp.

The pleasure of eating should be an extensive pleasure, not that of 15 the mere gourmet. People who know the garden in which their vegetables have grown and know that the garden is healthy and remember the beauty of the growing plants, perhaps in the dewy first light of morning when gardens are at their best. Such a memory involves itself with the food and is one of the pleasures of eating. The knowledge of the good health of the garden relieves and frees and comforts the eater. The same goes for eating meat. The thought of the good pasture and of the calf contentedly grazing flavors the steak. Some, I know, will think of it as bloodthirsty or worse to eat a fellow creature you have known all its life. On the contrary, I think it means that you eat with understanding and with gratitude. A significant part of the pleasure of eating is in one's accurate consciousness of the lives and the world from which food comes. The pleasure of eating, then, may be the best available standard of our health. And this pleasure, I think, is pretty fully available to the urban consumer who will make the necessary effort.

I mentioned earlier the politics, esthetics, and ethics of food. But to speak of the pleasure of eating is to go beyond those categories. Eating with the fullest pleasure — pleasure, that is, that does not depend on ignorance — is perhaps the profoundest enactment of our connection with the world. In this pleasure we experience and celebrate our dependence and our gratitude, for we are living from mystery, from creatures we did not make and powers we cannot comprehend. When I think of the meaning of food, I always remember these lines by the poet William Carlos Williams, which seem to me merely honest:

> There is nothing to eat,
> seek it where you will,
> but the body of the Lord.
> The blessed plants
> and the sea, yield it
> to the imagination intact.

Understanding the Text

1. What is an "industrial eater"?
2. Why does Berry think it is important to understand the connection between eating and the land?
3. According to Berry, how does the separation of food from farming and agriculture benefit the food industry?

Reflection and Response

4. Berry wrote this essay in 1989. Do you notice substantial changes from what he describes? Do you think he would be pleased with how farming and agricultural practices have changed since then? Why or why not?
5. Berry suggests that freedom depends on eating responsibly and understanding our place in the agricultural economy. Why does he think eating responsibly is a necessary condition of democracy? Explain your answer. Do you agree? Why or why not?
6. Why do you think Berry includes the poem by William Carlos Williams at the end of his essay? What does it add? How does it connect to the larger purpose of Berry's essay?

Making Connections

7. What is the "pleasure of eating," according to Berry? Compare the way Berry describes the purpose of food to the ways Jill McCorkle ("Her Chee-to Heart," p. 30) and Thich Nhat Hanh and Lilian Cheung ("Are You Really Appreciating the Apple?," p. 59) describe it.
8. Berry argues that eating is necessarily an "agricultural act" and makes seven suggestions for responsible eating. Compare them with Michael Pollan's rules for choosing foods to eat ("Eat Food: Food Defined," p. 10). What values do they share? Are they rules or suggestions you have tried or would consider trying? Which ones? What might you gain (or lose)? What might you learn about your food (and yourself)? How does Georgina Gustin's

("Can a Climate Conscious Diet Include Meat or Dairy?," p. 227) analysis of climate conscious eating complicate Berry and Pollan's rules?

9. Berry argues that there is a "food politics" that is impossible to separate from a "food esthetics" and a "food ethics." What is a "food politics"? Think about the community in which you live. What kinds of local food movements, organizations, programs, or activities exist that could be identified as political in nature (overtly or subtly)? Research at least one of them, and use the views of Berry, Barbara Kingsolver ("You Can't Run Away on Harvest Day," p. 150), and Bill McKibben ("The Only Way to Have a Cow," p. 161) to analyze its potential for contributing to awareness of the public's relationships with and responsibilities to food production.

Eating the Hyphen

Lily Wong

Lily Wong wrote this essay in a class she took on food and society when she was an undergraduate student at Williams College. After earning a bachelor's degree in history and Asian studies there, she has dabbled in food writing, taught English in Hong Kong, and worked in a museum conducting research and planning exhibits. This essay first appeared in *Gastronomica: The Journal of Food and Culture*, an academic journal that uses food as a source of knowledge about culture; it was selected for inclusion in *Best Food Writing 2013*. Wong loves food and cooking, and thinking and writing about food continue to intrigue her. Here she describes her love of dumplings eaten with a fork, a knife, a pair of chopsticks, and ketchup to illustrate the important relationship between food and identity.

Fork? Check. Knife? Check. Chopsticks? Check. It may seem odd to have all three of these eating utensils side by side for the consumption of a single meal, but for me, there's just no other way. Oh, and ketchup, that's key. Definitely need to have the ketchup, pre-shaken to avoid an awkward first squirt of pale red water. There's no place for that on my plate, not when I'm eating dumplings. Yes, that is what I said: I need a fork, a knife, a pair of chopsticks, and ketchup before I eat my dumplings.

Now I've just looked up "dumpling" on the online *Oxford English Dictionary* and discovered that it is "a kind of pudding consisting of a mass of paste or dough, more or less globular in form, either plain and boiled, or enclosing fruit and boiled or baked." I am definitely not talking about whatever unappetizing-sounding food that dumpling is supposed to be. I'm talking about Chinese dumplings, pot stickers, Peking ravioli, *jiaozi*, whatever you want to call them. Do you know what I mean yet? Maybe you've gotten a vague idea, but let me explain, because I am *very* picky about my dumplings.

To begin with, the skin has to be thick. I mean really thick. Thick and chewy and starchy and the bottom should be a bit burnt and dark golden brown from the pan-frying. Have you ever had *gyoza*, the Japanese dumplings? Yes, those thin, almost translucent skins just won't do it for me. Hands-down, no question, until my dying day, I will vouch that the skin is the make-or-break feature of a dumpling. Bad skin equals bad dumpling. Those boiled dumplings that are also a type of Chinese dumplings? The skin is too thin, too soggy, and frankly, rather flavorless. If I had to call it names, I'd say it was limp and weak and characterless. The thick-skinned dumplings that I know and love absorb more of the meaty-flavored goodness inside the dumplings. Also, because they are pan-fried (a key aspect of delicious dumplings), the bottom gets its own texture—a slightly charred crispiness to add that perfect smidgen of crunch. So, if you were to eat just the skin of the dumpling, it would be simultaneously chewy and crispy, with a bit of savory meat flavor mixed in with a burnt taste off the bottom—a wonderfulness that the words of the English language are hard-pressed to capture.

But what about the filling? To me, it's a bit peripheral. The dumplings I'm talking about have a standard pork filling with "Chinese vegetables." I've never been entirely sure what these elusively named Chinese vegetables actually are, but I imagine that they are some combination of leeks and Chinese cabbage. They're not too salty and they don't have cilantro. These dumplings also have enough savory broth secretly sequestered inside the skin so that when you cut them open, you get some oil spatterings, pretty much all over your clothes, plate, and table. That's the sign of a good, moist, and juicy meat section.

I should mention before you envision me slaving away in a kitchen 5 to create the perfect dumpling that the ones I like come out of the freezer. In plastic bags of fifty each. Imported to my house from Boston's Chinatown. It's strange, considering that most days I like the home-grown version of foods more than the store-bought version, but these are the exception. Even though I know they're handmade by a small company, so you get that same small-batch feel as if you made them at home, they're still store-bought and frozen rather than fresh.

But enough about finding the right dumplings; you're probably still confused as to why it's so imperative that I have a fork, knife, chopsticks, and ketchup. Here is your step-by-step guide to an entirely new dumpling eating experience.

1. On a large white plate, place six or seven dumplings (or more if you're particularly ravenous) and add some broccoli or beans for color and nutrition.

2. Squirt a glop of ketchup in one of the empty white spaces on your plate (as in not touching the broccoli or the dumplings). This is where it's key that the ketchup has been shaken a bit, otherwise that red ketchup juice runs all over your plate ruining everything.

3. Take that fork and knife on the side and cut each dumpling in half width-wise. Make sure to cut completely through the skin and meat.

4. Take the backside of your fork and push down on the top of each dumpling half until the meat abruptly pops out in a pool of brothy juice.

5. Once you've finished systematically cutting and squishing, you'll have lots of skins and meat pieces separated and you can put that knife and fork away. Grab the chopsticks.

6. Pick up a piece of the meat (just the meat now, no trying to get some skin in on this too) and dip it into the ketchup. Eat and repeat. If at any point you want to indulge in that steamed broccoli, it's a good idea. You wouldn't want to leave it all to the end. But don't dip it in ketchup. That's weird.

7. Now this is the best part. Use your chopsticks to one-by-one eat every last half dumpling's worth of skin. Savor every part because this is what it's all really been about. No ketchup or meat to obscure the flavor and chewiness, just pure starchy goodness.

And that's how it goes. Every single time. Confused? So was I the first time I really sat down to think about how I eat dumplings. It sounds a little like a grand mutilation of how a dumpling should be eaten for it to be "authentic" (using only chopsticks and with the dumpling left whole and dipped in black vinegar, no ketchup in sight). And I have unabashedly criticized and ridiculed Americanized Chinese food for being fake and something of a disgrace to "authentic" Chinese food. Yet here I am, still eating my dumplings with ketchup and a fork, unceremoniously and quite literally butchering my dumplings before I eat them. My grandmother meanwhile takes small bites out of whole dumplings, careful not to lose any of that broth from inside (with a face only three-quarters filled with disgust as I rush from the table to grab my ketchup from the fridge).

Bottled up in this entirely strange ritual is my status as a Chinese American. It is unclear to me where I ever came up with the idea that dumplings should be cut in half, or that the meat would taste better with ketchup (particularly since this is literally the only time that I use ketchup). Perhaps this combination has something to do with the fact that since both my parents grew up in the States, we've embraced many American traditions while abandoning or significantly modifying many Chinese ones. But even so, I have always embraced my Chinese culture and heritage. It gives me something larger to cling to when I'm feeling ostracized by American culture for looking "different." The suburb I grew up in is mostly white, but it's not as if I didn't have Chinese people around me; after all, there was always Chinatown. But Chinatown was full of people who spoke the language—whether Cantonese or Mandarin—who somehow just seemed so much more Chinese than I ever could be. And perhaps that's true. Maybe that's why I feel so gosh-darned American when I eat my dumplings with ketchup while holding my chopsticks "incorrectly." The notion that this somehow takes away from my ability to identify with Chinese culture is, I rationally understand, flawed. But in my pursuit to try and discover who I am, it's taken an oddly large place.

I'm not sure why I often think that to be a Chinese American means that you relish authentic Chinese food—and by authentic I mostly mean strictly what your grandmother cooks for you—but I do. I've told friends that they don't know what real Chinese food is because all they know is Panda Express. I pride myself on my Cantonese background, which leads me to look favorably on pig's ears and fungus of all shapes and sizes. My innate territorialism regard-ing my particular definition of what Chinese food is makes the choice to continue eating my dumplings in such a strange fashion slightly fraught. I'm not even sure that anyone besides my family knows that this is how I eat dumplings. In part, I think my reticence derives precisely from a fear that it would make me "less" Chinese.

> "I'm not sure why I often think that to be a Chinese American means that you relish authentic Chinese food — and by authentic I mostly mean strictly what your grandmother cooks for you — but I do."

Somehow, I've come to strange terms with these contradictions. 10 Somewhere along the way, dumplings, cut in half with ketchup on the meat and the skin separated as a special entity of its own, have become my comfort food. So whether or not it perverts some thousand-year-old tradition of the "proper" way to eat dumplings, this is what makes me happy. Although I sometimes catch myself overcompensating with extra delight in Chinese delicacies involving jellyfish and sea cucumber that cause most Americans to squirm, eating dumplings in my own style has become the hyphen between Chinese and American in my identity.

Understanding the Text

1. How does Wong define "food"? How does she define "Chinese food"?
2. How does Wong feel that her food preferences define her? Do you agree?
3. What constitutes an "authentic" food experience for Wong?

Reflection and Response

4. Why do you think Wong includes the dictionary definition of "dumpling"? What effect does it have on the rest of the piece?
5. How do you explain the significance of the title? What does it emphasize about Wong's story?

Making Connections

6. Compare Wong's description of her love of dumplings to the meditation on eating an apple offered by Thich Nhat Hanh and Lilian Cheung ("Are You Really Appreciating the Apple?," p. 59). What do they suggest about the relationships between food, awareness, and pleasure? Use specific textual references and quotations to support your comparisons.

7. Reflect on the relationship between your food preferences and your identity. Do your food choices express something about your identity or aspects of it? Why or why not?

8. Wong and Michael Pollan ("Eat Food: Food Defined," p.10) define food in relation to what grandmothers would consider authentic. Why do you think this is? Do you connect certain foods to your grandmother or to other family members? Explain.

Are You Really Appreciating the Apple?

Thich Nhat Hanh and Lilian Cheung

Revered across the globe for his teachings on mindfulness and his peace activism, Thich Nhat Hanh has written more than 100 books. He was born in Vietnam and ordained as a Buddhist monk at age sixteen. After years of travel and teaching internationally, including at several American universities, he returned to Vietnam to commit himself to peace work, for which he was later exiled. He now lives in France and continues to work for peace and to teach and encourage what he calls "engaged Buddhism," a form of mindfulness that helps us respond directly to daily needs. Hanh teamed up with nutrition expert Lilian Cheung to write *Savor: Mindful Eating, Mindful Life*, a book that encourages mindful eating as a way to cultivate healthier habits and a mindful life. Cheung teaches at the Harvard School of Public Health's Department of Nutrition and serves as the editorial director of The Nutrition Source, a website on nutrition research. Much of her work focuses on making scientific health research accessible to the public and to promote healthy eating and healthy lifestyles. In this excerpt from *Savor: Mindful Eating, Mindful Life*, Hanh and Cheung encourage us to rethink how we eat an apple as a way to encourage more mindful eating habits.

> The apple in your hand is the body of the Cosmos.
>
> —THICH NHAT HANH

Let's have a taste of mindfulness. Take an apple out of your refrigerator. Any apple will do. Wash it. Dry it. Before taking a bite, pause for a moment. Look at the apple in your palm and ask yourself: When I eat an apple, am I really enjoying eating it? Or am I so preoccupied with other thoughts that I miss the delights that the apple offers me?

If you are like most of us, you answer yes to the second question much more often than the first. For most of our lives, we have eaten apple after apple without giving it a second thought. Yet in this mindless way of eating, we have denied ourselves the many delights present in the simple act of eating an apple. Why do that, especially when it is so easy to truly enjoy the apple?

The first thing is to give your undivided attention to eating the apple. When you eat the apple, just concentrate on eating the apple. Don't think of anything else. And most important, be still. Don't eat the apple while you are driving. Don't eat it while you are walking. Don't eat it while you are reading. Just be still. Being focused and slowing down will allow you to truly savor all the qualities the apple offers: its sweetness, aroma, freshness, juiciness, and crispness.

Next, pick up the apple from the palm of your hand and take a moment to look at it again. Breathe in and out a few times consciously to help yourself focus and become more in touch with how you feel about the apple. Most of the time, we barely look at the apple we are eating. We grab it, take a bite, chew it quickly, and then swallow. This time, take note: What kind of apple is it? What color is it? How does it feel in your hand? What does it smell like? Going through these thoughts, you will begin to realize that the apple is not simply a quick snack to quiet a grumbling stomach. It is something more complex, something part of a greater whole.

Then, give the apple a smile and, slowly, take a bite, and chew it. Be aware 5 of your in-breath and out-breath a few times to help yourself concentrate solely on eating the apple: what it feels like in your mouth; what it tastes like; what it's like to chew and swallow it. There is nothing else filling your mind as you chew—no projects, no deadlines, no worries, no "to do" list, no fears, no sorrow, no anger, no past, and no future. There is just the apple.

When you chew, know what you are chewing. Chew slowly and completely, twenty to thirty times for each bite. Chew consciously, savoring

When was the last time you ate an apple? How much did you appreciate the experience?

Liam Daly/EyeEm/Getty Images

the taste of the apple and its nourishment, immersing yourself in the experience 100 percent. This way, you really appreciate the apple as it is. And as you become fully aware of eating the apple, you also become fully aware of the present moment. You become fully engaged in the here and now. Living in the moment, you can really receive what the apple offers you, and you become more alive.

> "If we are not conscious of the food we eat, if we are not actively thinking about that apple, how can we taste it and get the pleasure of eating it?"

By eating the apple this way, truly savoring it, you have a taste of *mindfulness*, the state of awareness that comes from being fully immersed in the present moment. Letting go for those few short minutes and living in the here and now, you can begin to sense the pleasure and freedom from anxiety that a life lived in mindfulness can offer.

In today's world, mindless eating and mindless living are all too common. We are propelled by the fast pace of high-tech living — high-speed Internet, e-mails, instant messages, and cell phones—and the expectation that we are always on call, always ready to respond instantly to any message we get. Thirty years ago, hardly anyone would have expected to receive a reply to a phone call or letter within the same day. Yet today, the pace of our lives is utterly harried and spinning out of control. We constantly have to respond to external stimuli and demands. We have less and less time to stop, stay focused, and reflect on whatever is in front of us. We have much less time to be in touch with our inner selves — our thoughts, feelings, consciousness, and how and why we have become the way we are, for better or worse. And our lives suffer because of it.

Some of us find that it is too inconvenient and difficult to eat a whole apple. So major food outlets now sell "value-added" apples—presliced apples, packed in bags and coated with an all-natural flavorless sealant so that they won't turn brown or lose their crispness for up to three weeks. These apples epitomize the new food-marketing concept of "snackability": There are no crumbs and no fuss, nothing to interrupt the repetitive movement of hand to bag and food to mouth. Aside from the inherent lack of freshness in these "snackable" precut apples, they also promote mindless eating—in the car, in front of the TV, at the computer, whenever and wherever. And while there are certainly much less healthy snack foods than precut apple slices, the pattern of eating is one we all experience and that food marketers promote with a vengeance.

Most of the time, we are eating on autopilot, eating on the run, 10
eating our worries or anxieties from the day's demands, anticipations,
irritations, and "to do" lists. If we are not conscious of the food we eat, if
we are not actively thinking about that apple, how can we taste it and get
the pleasure of eating it?

Eating an apple mindfully is not only a pleasant experience; it is good
for our health as well. The adage "An apple a day keeps the doctor away"
is actually backed by solid science. Research shows that eating apples can
help prevent heart disease because the fiber and antioxidants they contain can prevent cholesterol buildup in the blood vessels of the heart.
The fiber in apples can also help move waste through the intestines,
which can help lower the risk of problems such as irritable bowel syndrome. Eating the apple with the skin—especially when it is organic—is
better than eating it without the skin, as half of the vitamin C is under
the apple's skin; the skin itself is rich in phytochemicals, special plant
compounds that may fight chronic disease. Apples are also packed with
potassium, which can help keep blood pressure under control.

Beyond the health benefits and pleasure an apple can provide, when
we view the apple on an even grander scale we can see it as a representative of our cosmos. Look deeply at the apple in your hand and you see
the farmer who tended the apple tree; the blossom that became the fruit;
the fertile earth, the organic material from decayed remains of prehistoric marine animals and algae, and the hydrocarbons themselves; the
sunshine, the clouds, and the rain. Without the combination of these
far-reaching elements and without the help of many people, the apple
would simply not exist.

At its most essential, the apple you hold is a manifestation of the wonderful presence of life. It is interconnected with all that is. It contains the
whole universe; it is an ambassador of the cosmos coming to nourish our
existence. It feeds our body, and if we eat it mindfully, it also feeds our
soul and recharges our spirit.

Eating an apple consciously is to have a new awareness of the apple,
of our world, and of our own life. It celebrates nature, honoring what
Mother Earth and the cosmos have offered us. Eating an apple with
mindfulness is a meditation and can be deeply spiritual. With this awareness and insight, you begin to have a greater feeling of gratitude for and
appreciation of the food you eat, and your connection to nature and all
others in our world. As the apple becomes more real and vibrant, your
life becomes more real and vibrant. Savoring the apple is mindfulness
at work.

And it is mindfulness that will help you reconnect with yourself and 15
become healthier in mind, body, and spirit now and in the future.

Understanding the Text

1. According to Thich Nhat Hanh and Lilian Cheung, what is the difference between mindful and mindless ways of eating an apple?

2. Why do Thich Nhat Hanh and Lilian Cheung encourage us to live in the moment?

3. What is the problem with "snackability"?

Reflection and Response

4. Set aside time to complete an "apple meditation" as described by Thich Nhat Hanh and Lilian Cheung. Focus on moving through the various steps as they are described in the text. Then, write a reflection about your experience of eating an apple following mindfulness principles. What did you notice? What were you mindful of? Will the experience change how you eat? Why or why not? What about your life would have to change for you to becoming a more mindful eater?

5. Reflect on what Thich Nhat Hanh and Lilian Cheung mean when they say that the apple "contains the whole universe" (par. 13)? How is this similar or different to how you thought about an apple before reading this text?

6. Lilian Cheung is a nutrition expert and Thich Nhat Hanh is a Buddhist monk revered for his teachings on the art of mindful living. Why do you think they decided to pursue a book on mindful eating together? Does their collaboration change how you view the purpose and effect of the essay?

Making Connections

8. How would Thich Nhat Hanh and Lilian Cheung view McCorkle's "meditation" on junk food ("Her Chee-to Heart," p. 30)? Are there values that they share? Locate textual evidence to support your assertions. Offer specific textual references to support your conclusions.

9. Lilian Cheung and Marion Nestle ("Eating Made Simple," p. 36) are both nutrition experts. Compare Nestle's discussion of healthy eating with the values being promoted by Cheung and Thich Nhat Hanh. Why do you think Cheung and Hanh point out that the "adage 'An apple a day keeps the doctor away' is actually backed by solid science" (par. 11)? How might Nestle view this strategy?

10. Thich Nhat Hanh and Lilian Cheung write that an apple "is a manifestation of the wonderful presence of life" and that it "contains the whole universe" (par. 13). Research Thich Nhat Hanh's work on mindfulness and the art of mindful living. Write an open letter to students at your college or university on how it might change their daily lives to eat with mindfulness.

Claudia Totir/Moment/Getty Images

2

What Forces Affect Our Food Choices?

W e wake up in the morning and decide what to eat for breakfast. We go to the cafeteria or the fridge or a restaurant, and we make choices about what to select from the display or order from the menu. We might select an apple or some raspberries, or we might opt for a doughnut or a granola bar. In one sense, then, *we* determine what we eat. But our food choices aren't made in a vacuum; many larger political, social, economic, environmental, and cultural factors help direct what choices are available (and where) and if they are affordable (and for whom).

A variety of factors, then, affect what we eat — whether we realize it or not. Various laws, policies, patents, and trade agreements play a role in determining what food choices are available to us. Federal guidelines make recommendations about health. Restaurant options and portion sizes help dictate what we choose, and various food movements work to influence our habits and choices. Government agencies regulate buying and selling options. And so do cultural norms, including ones that are shaped by race, class, and gender.

We are thus surrounded by institutions, agencies, corporations, businesses, and attitudes that affect our food choices, as the readings in this chapter demonstrate. The federal government develops nutritional graphics and guidelines for us to use to decide what and how much to eat. Dhruv Khullar demonstrates that these guidelines are not always easy to follow in his discussion of the prevalence of readily available junk food and how this reality helps determine what we eat. David H. Freedman wonders if "junk food" is really so harmful as he critiques the wholesome-food movement and considers its relationship to the obesity epidemic. Joe Pinsker explores why children from families with higher socioeconomic status are more likely to enjoy the taste of healthy food, while Barry Yeoman explores the complex relationships among race, class, and food access. Taffy Brodesser-Akner questions gender assumptions about cooking, as Stephen Satterfield demonstrates why we must consider

photo: Claudia Totir/Moment/Getty Images

race when we think about food — both its production and consumption. While these authors point to the ways that gender, race, and socioeconomic factors affect food choices, Mary Roach looks to linguistics, history, and science to help us see just how complicated — and, at times, funny — our relationships with the foods we eat are.

The complex mix of laws, social realities, cultural norms, and health guidelines discussed in these selections are not usually on our minds when we ask "What's for dinner?" But federal health recommendations, corporate interests, farming practices, local trends, and even stereotypes influence the answer in important ways. The readings in this chapter ask us to attend to this broad range of forces that affect our food choices.

Nutritional Guidelines

United States Government

The U.S. Department of Agriculture established the Center for Nutrition Policy and Promotion in 1994 to promote the nutrition and well-being of Americans. One of the core ways the center supports this objective is through the advancement of dietary guidelines and the promotion of guidance systems like MyPyramid and MyPlate. The Food Pyramid was introduced in 1992, updated in 2005, and replaced in 2010 by MyPlate. These visual diagrams are widely used as educational tools for translating nutritional guidelines into simple images of how much to eat and what kinds of food to eat on a daily basis. More recently, in 2016, the U.S. Food and Drug Administration updated the Nutrition Facts labels on food packages sold in the United States. The update reflects new scientific research and public health concerns and represents another method by which the federal government works to promote health and nutrition.

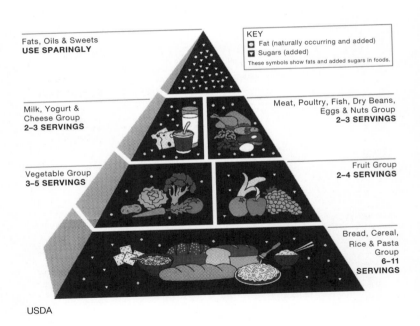

Fats, Oils & Sweets
USE SPARINGLY

KEY
☐ Fat (naturally occurring and added)
☑ Sugars (added)
These symbols show fats and added sugars in foods.

Milk, Yogurt & Cheese Group
2–3 SERVINGS

Meat, Poultry, Fish, Dry Beans, Eggs & Nuts Group
2–3 SERVINGS

Vegetable Group
3–5 SERVINGS

Fruit Group
2–4 SERVINGS

Bread, Cereal, Rice & Pasta Group
6–11 SERVINGS

USDA

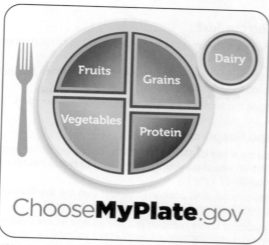

ChooseMyPlate.gov

USDA Center for Nutrition Policy and Promotion

Previous Label

Nutrition Facts
Serving Size 2/3 cup (55g)
Servings Per Container About 8

Amount Per Serving

Calories 230 Calories from Fat 72

	% Daily Values*
Total Fat 8g	**12%**
Saturated Fat 1g	**5%**
Trans Fat 0g	
Cholesterol 0mg	**0%**
Sodium 160mg	**7%**
Total Carbohydrate 37g	**12%**
Dietary Fiber 4g	**16%**
Sugars 1g	
Protein 3g	
Vitamin A	10%
Vitamin C	8%
Calcium	20%
Iron	45%

*Percent Daily Values are based on a 2,000 calorie diet. Your daily value may be higher or lower depending on your calorie needs

	Calories:	2,000	2,500
Total Fat	Less than	65g	80g
Sat Fat	Less than	20g	25g
Cholesterol	Less than	300mg	300mg
Sodium	Less than	2,400mg	2,400mg
Total Carbohydrate		300g	375g
Dietary Fiber		25g	30g

New Label

Nutrition Facts
8 servings per container
Serving size   **2/3 cup (55g)**

Amount per serving
Calories   230

	% Daily Value*
Total Fat 8g	**10%**
Saturated Fat 1g	**5%**
Trans Fat 0g	
Cholesterol 0mg	**0%**
Sodium 160mg	**7%**
Total Carbohydrate 37g	**13%**
Dietary Fiber 4g	**14%**
Total Sugars 12g	
Includes 10g Added Sugars	**20%**
Protein 3g	
Vitamin D 2mcg	10%
Calcium 260mg	20%
Iron 8mg	45%
Potassium 235mg	6%

* The % Daily Value (DV) tells you how much a nutrient in a serving of food contributes to a daily diet. 2,000 calories a day is used for general nutrition advice.

Understanding the Text

1. What did the Food Pyramid prioritize? What kinds of recommendations did it give?
2. How is the MyPlate different in scope and purpose than the Food Pyramid? What goals do they share?
3. What changes are most prominent in the new Nutrition Facts label?

Reflection and Response

4. Why do you think the USDA continues to rely on visual images to promote nutrition? Which visual do you think will lead to better health education? To healthier eating? Why?
5. What social, cultural, and economic tendencies are the federal nutritional guidelines and Nutrition Facts labels working against?
6. Were you aware of these nutrition guidelines and labels before reading them here? Where did you encounter them? Have you studied them in school? Have you tried to live by them?

Making Connections

7. Review Michael Pollan's "rules" ("Eat Food: Food Defined," p. 10). How do they compare with the advice of the USDA and the FDA? What would he applaud in this advice? What might he question? Would he see this as a good way to decide what to eat? Why or why not?
8. Do you think the federal government should play a role in nutrition education? Why or why not? Use Joon Yun, David Kessler, and Dan Glickman's "We Need Better Answers on Nutrition" (p. 301) and one or two other selections in this collection, as well as two or three sources you find through library research to help you construct your argument. Select at least one source that presents a challenge to your position. Refute that challenge as part of your support for your position.

Why Shame Won't Stop Obesity

Dhruv Khullar

Dhruv Khullar, a physician and assistant professor for the Weill Cornell Department of Healthcare Policy and Research, wrote this piece in 2012 for the *Bioethics Forum*, the blog published by the *Hastings Center Report*, while studying medicine at Yale University and public policy at the John F. Kennedy School of Government at Harvard University as a Zuckerman Fellow. Khullar's interest in public health and social justice has led him to do research that bridges the gap between medicine and public policy. He considers obesity a public health as well as a social justice issue, one that disproportionately affects minority groups and the poor. He is particularly interested in publishing his research for the general public in the hope that sound research can play a larger role in public discussion of health policies and contributes to *The New York Times* on health policy, medicine, and economics. In this essay, Khullar offers specific suggestions for reversing the trend of junk food and fast food as being more readily available and cheaper than healthy food choices.

I am still in medical school, but today I sigh the frustrated, disapproving sigh of a fully trained doctor. "You know," I scold the middle-aged man in front of me, "you really should start eating better."

Like many patients I saw in clinic that morning, this man is obese. His diabetes is poorly controlled. His blood pressure is through the roof. And he hasn't lost a single pound in months.

Oh well, it's lunchtime and I'm hungry. I slip off to the hospital cafeteria and begin to ponder why these patients can't seem to lead a healthier lifestyle. As I wait in line, I consider a more pressing problem: should I get the fried chicken or the four-cheese pizza? I settle on popcorn shrimp and some curly fries. Only then do I ask myself what exactly I would have recommended my patients eat — besides maybe a side of cheesy broccoli and some bruised bananas — had they joined me for lunch.

This, sadly, is the case in the cafeteria of a major hospital, an institution devoted to preserving and promoting health. It is a stark and telling microcosm of a much broader issue — one in large part responsible for the skyrocketing rates of obesity and associated disease in this country.

Americans today are exposed to an unprecedented amount of readily 5 available high-fat, high-calorie, and low-nutrient foods. We are saturated with junk food advertising. We are eating more and more meals outside the home, and portion sizes are bigger than ever. Healthy options are more frequently the exception than the rule.

It is hardly surprising, then, that we find ourselves in the midst of an obesity epidemic. Nearly three-quarters of Americans are overweight or obese, and a report by United Healthcare predicts that half of all American adults will develop diabetes or prediabetes by the end of the decade. The report further estimates that diabetes — which increases one's risk of stroke, cardiovascular disease, kidney failure, blindness, and amputations — will cost our society $500 billion a year by 2020.

In an effort to combat this disturbing trend, Georgia — the state with the nation's second highest obesity rates — recently launched a provocative and controversial ad campaign. It emphasizes the role of parents in failing to recognize and address childhood obesity. In the commercials, obese children sullenly ask questions like, "Mom, why am I fat?" and drive home poignant messages like, "It's hard to be a little girl, when you're not," or "Being fat takes the fun out of being a kid."

One might argue that Georgia's campaign is a bold and necessary step in the right direction, and to the extent that it raises awareness and sparks constructive conversation, it may be. However, these commercials miss the point. Shaming children and parents into losing weight is unlikely to be an effective strategy. It increases stigma on those already struggling with the psychosocial° consequences of being overweight, and shifts the focus of obesity control efforts to personal responsibility at a time when, for many individuals, options for improving eating habits may be limited.

> "While taking responsibility for one's health is certainly part of the solution, we must also recognize that we have created a food environment so ripe for obesity that to expect anything else would be irrational."

While taking responsibility for one's health is certainly part of the solution, we must also recognize that we have created a food environment so ripe for obesity that to expect anything else would be irrational. Even for the most knowledgeable and resourceful among us, consistently eating well is a challenge. It is difficult to distinguish healthy options from unhealthy ones, and purchasing the right foods once they are identified is no cakewalk. Furthermore, people living in low-income areas have limited access to healthy food options for a variety of reasons, a barrier that contributes to their particularly high risk for being obese.

There is much we can and should do to reverse the current trend. 10
An important step would be to provide monetary incentives to promote

psychosocial: relating to the interconnection of individual thoughts and behavior and external social factors.

the production of and access to fresh, healthy food. By subsidizing fresh fruits and vegetables and supporting restaurants and vendors that offer healthy alternatives, we might create an economic environment more conducive to healthy eating. Making healthy options more accessible and affordable, especially for those living in low-income areas of the country, is a vital component of reducing the burden of obesity. When you can buy 2,000 calories for under $10 at your neighborhood McDonald's, but have trouble getting your hands on an apple, it's difficult to justify trying to shame anyone into skinniness.

Another important measure would be to minimize junk food advertising, especially to children. Each year, the food industry spends nearly $2 billion marketing its products to children, and evidence suggests that children exposed to junk food advertising express greater preference for these types of foods. Asking the industry to refrain from advertising foods that contain unhealthful amounts of sugar, salts, and fats to youth could also encourage the production of healthier options. I think that initially the guidelines should be voluntary, but significant public and political pressure should be placed on the food industry to adopt them. If it becomes clear over time that they are unwilling to do so, then federal regulations may be needed.

A third initiative might center on education and empowering youth to make informed decisions. Instituting nutrition and health curriculums into public schools would help children learn how to read nutrition labels and identify healthy foods, as well as understand the negative long-term consequences of obesity. Today's youth may be the first generation of Americans to live shorter, more disease-riddled lives than their parents—a staggering prediction based largely on the rapid rise in childhood obesity. Let this not be our legacy.

Understanding the Text

1. What realization does Khullar have when he makes his trip to the cafeteria?
2. What dilemma does Khullar describe? What solutions does he propose?

Reflection and Response

3. Why does Khullar claim that shame will not help reduce the obesity epidemic? Does he make a good case? Why or why not? Do you agree with him? Why or why not?

4. Khullar indicates that personal responsibility for food choices is not the only factor that affects what people eat. On what does he base this conclusion? What evidence does he give?

Making Connections

5. David H. Freedman ("How Junk Food Can End Obesity," p. 75) quotes Robert Kushner, obesity scientist and clinical director at Northwestern University, who says, "The difference between losing weight and not losing weight is a few hundred calories a day" (par. 44). How do the essays by Khullar and Marion Nestle ("Eating Made Simple," p. 36) support this statement? How do they complicate it? What does each author suggest about the relationship between weight, calories, and eating practices? Are there other authors in this collection who would argue for a different view?

6. Do your eating habits and food choices reflect your values regarding food, or are they determined by other factors? Explain your answer using Khullar's argument, at least one other source from this book, and at least two other sources located in your campus library.

How Junk Food Can End Obesity

David H. Freedman

David H. Freedman studied physics at Oberlin College. As a Boston-based journalist, he writes about science, technology, medicine, and business for *The New York Times, Inc. Magazine, The Atlantic, Wired, Scientific American,* and many other publications. He is known for offering skeptical critiques of some popular scientific findings and how they are portrayed in the popular media. He also consults with university medical centers, working with them to improve health systems. Freedman has published several books, including *Wrong: Why Experts* Keep Failing Us — and How to Know When Not to Trust Them* (2010). In this essay, Freedman launches a strong critique of proponents of the whole-some-food movement and suggests that technology might have an important role to play in solving the obesity crisis.

Late last year, in a small health-food eatery called Cafe Sprouts in Oberlin, Ohio, I had what may well have been the most whole-some beverage of my life. The friendly server patiently guided me to an apple-blueberry-kale-carrot smoothie-juice combination, which she spent the next several minutes preparing, mostly by shepherding farm-fresh produce into machinery. The result was tasty, but at 300 calories (by my rough calculation) in a 16-ounce cup, it was more than my diet could regularly absorb without consequences, nor was I about to make a habit of $9 shakes, healthy or not.

Inspired by the experience nonetheless, I tried again two months later at L.A.'s Real Food Daily, a popular vegan restaurant near Hollywood. I was initially wary of a low-calorie juice made almost entirely from green vegetables, but the server assured me it was a popular treat. I like to brag that I can eat anything, and I scarf down all sorts of raw vegetables like candy, but I could stomach only about a third of this oddly foamy, bitter concoction. It smelled like lawn clippings and tasted like liquid celery. It goes for $7.95, and I waited 10 minutes for it.

I finally hit the sweet spot just a few weeks later, in Chicago, with a delicious blueberry-pomegranate smoothie that rang in at a relatively modest 220 calories. It cost $3 and took only seconds to make. Best of all, I'll be able to get this concoction just about anywhere. Thanks, McDonald's!

If only the McDonald's smoothie weren't, unlike the first two, so fattening and unhealthy. Or at least that's what the most-prominent voices in our food culture today would have you believe.

An enormous amount of media space has been dedicated to 5 promoting the notion that all processed food, and only processed food, is making us sickly and overweight. In this narrative, the food-industrial complex — particularly the fast-food industry — has turned all the powers of food-processing science loose on engineering its offerings to addict us to fat, sugar, and salt, causing or at least heavily contributing to the obesity crisis. The wares of these pimps and pushers, we are told, are to be universally shunned.

Consider *The New York Times*. Earlier this year, *The Times Magazine* gave its cover to a long piece based on Michael Moss's about-to-be-best-selling book, *Salt Sugar Fat: How the Food Giants Hooked Us*. Hitting bookshelves at about the same time was the former *Times* reporter Melanie Warner's *Pandora's Lunchbox: How Processed Food Took Over the American Meal*, which addresses more or less the same theme. Two years ago *The Times Magazine* featured the journalist Gary Taubes's "Is Sugar Toxic?," a cover story on the evils of refined sugar and high-fructose corn syrup. And most significant of all has been the considerable space the magazine has devoted over the years to Michael Pollan, a journalism professor at the University of California at Berkeley, and his broad indictment of food processing as a source of society's health problems.

"The food they're cooking is making people sick," Pollan has said of big food companies. "It is one of the reasons that we have the obesity and diabetes epidemics that we do . . . If you're going to let industries decide how much salt, sugar and fat is in your food, they're going to put [in] as much as they possibly can. . . . They will push those buttons until we scream or die." The solution, in his view, is to replace Big Food's engineered, edible evil — through public education and regulation — with fresh, unprocessed, local, seasonal, *real* food.

Pollan's worldview saturates the public conversation on healthy eating. You hear much the same from many scientists, physicians, food activists, nutritionists, celebrity chefs, and pundits. *Foodlike substances*, the derisive term Pollan uses to describe processed foods, is now a solid part of the elite vernacular. Thousands of restaurants and grocery stores, most notably the Whole Foods chain, have thrived by answering the call to reject industrialized foods in favor of a return to natural, simple, nonindustrialized — let's call them "wholesome" — foods. The two newest restaurants in my smallish Massachusetts town both prominently tout wholesome ingredients; one of them is called the Farmhouse, and it's usually packed.

A new generation of business, social, and policy entrepreneurs is rising to further cater to these tastes, and to challenge Big Food. Silicon Valley, where tomorrow's entrepreneurial and social trends are forged, has spawned a small ecosystem of wholesome-friendly venture-capital firms (Physic Ventures, for example), business accelerators (Local Food Lab), and Web sites (Edible Startups) to fund, nurture, and keep tabs on young companies such as blissmo (a wholesome-food-of-the-month club), Mile High Organics (online wholesome-food shopping), and Wholeshare (group wholesome-food purchasing), all designed to help reacquaint Americans with the simpler eating habits of yesteryear.

In virtually every realm of human existence, we turn to technology to 10 help us solve our problems. But even in Silicon Valley, when it comes to food and obesity, technology—or at least food-processing technology—is widely treated as if it *is* the problem. The solution, from this viewpoint, necessarily involves turning our back on it.

If the most-influential voices in our food culture today get their way, we will achieve a genuine food revolution. Too bad it would be one tailored to the dubious health fantasies of a small, elite minority. And too bad it would largely exclude the obese masses, who would continue to sicken and die early. Despite the best efforts of a small army of wholesome-food heroes, there is no reasonable scenario under which these foods could become cheap and plentiful enough to serve as the core diet for most of the obese population—even in the unlikely case that your typical junk-food eater would be willing and able to break life-long habits to embrace kale and yellow beets. And many of the dishes glorified by the wholesome-food movement are, in any case, as caloric and obesogenic° as anything served in a Burger King.

Through its growing sway over health-conscious consumers and policy makers, the wholesome-food movement is impeding the progress of the one segment of the food world that is actually positioned to take effective, near-term steps to reverse the obesity trend: the processed-food industry. Popular food producers, fast-food chains among them, are already applying various tricks and technologies to create less caloric and more satiating versions of their junky fare that nonetheless retain much of the appeal of the originals, and could be induced to go much further. In fact, these roundly demonized companies could do far more for the public's health in five years than the wholesome-food movement is likely to accomplish in the next 50. But will the wholesome-food advocates let them?

---

obesogenic: tending to cause excessive weight gain.

Michael Pollan Has No Clothes

Let's go shopping. We can start at Whole Foods Market, a critical link in the wholesome-eating food chain. There are three Whole Foods stores within 15 minutes of my house—we're big on real food in the suburbs west of Boston. Here at the largest of the three, I can choose from more than 21 types of tofu, 62 bins of organic grains and legumes, and 42 different salad greens.

Much of the food isn't all that different from what I can get in any other supermarket, but sprinkled throughout are items that scream "wholesome." One that catches my eye today, sitting prominently on an impulse-buy rack near the checkout counter, is Vegan Cheesy Salad Booster, from Living Intentions, whose package emphasizes the fact that the food is enhanced with spirulina°, chlorella°, and sea vegetables. The label also proudly lets me know that the contents are raw—no processing!—and that they don't contain any genetically modified ingredients. What the stuff does contain, though, is more than three times the fat content per ounce as the beef patty in a Big Mac (more than two-thirds of the calories come from fat), and four times the sodium.

What kind of food do you buy? Like this man, do you purchase all organic produce?
RubberBall/Alamy

spirulina: blue-green algae, used as a health food because it is loaded with good nutrients.
chlorella: green algae, recognized as a super food because of its high protein and Vitamin B content.

After my excursion to Whole Foods, I drive a few minutes to a 15 Trader Joe's, also known for an emphasis on wholesome foods. Here at the register I'm confronted with a large display of a snack food called "Inner Peas," consisting of peas that are breaded in cornmeal and rice flour, fried in sunflower oil, and then sprinkled with salt. By weight, the snack has six times as much fat as it does protein, along with loads of carbohydrates. I can't recall ever seeing anything at any fast-food restaurant that represents as big an obesogenic crime against the vegetable kingdom. (A spokesperson for Trader Joe's said the company does not consider itself a " 'wholesome food' grocery retailer." Living Intentions did not respond to a request for comment.)

This phenomenon is by no means limited to packaged food at upscale supermarkets. Back in February, when I was at Real Food Daily in Los Angeles, I ordered the "Sea Cake" along with my green-vegetable smoothie. It was intensely delicious in a way that set off alarm bells. RFD wouldn't provide precise information about the ingredients, but I found a recipe online for "Tofu 'Fish' Cakes," which seem very close to what I ate. Essentially, they consist of some tofu mixed with a lot of refined carbs (the RFD version contains at least some unrefined carbs) along with oil and soy milk, all fried in oil and served with a soy-and-oil-based tartar sauce. (Tofu and other forms of soy are high in protein, but per 100 calories, tofu is as fatty as many cuts of beef.) L.A. being to the wholesome-food movement what Hawaii is to Spam, I ate at two other mega-popular wholesome-food restaurants while I was in the area. At Café Gratitude I enjoyed the kale chips and herb-cornmeal-crusted eggplant parmesan, and at Akasha I indulged in a spiced-lamb-sausage flatbread pizza. Both are pricey orgies of fat and carbs.

I'm not picking out rare, less healthy examples from these establishments. Check out their menus online: fat, sugar, and other refined carbs abound. (Café Gratitude says it uses only "healthy" fats and natural sweeteners; Akasha says its focus is not on "health food" but on "farm to fork" fare.) In fact, because the products and dishes offered by these types of establishments tend to emphasize the healthy-sounding foods they contain, I find it much harder to navigate through them to foods that go easy on the oil, butter, refined grains, rice, potatoes, and sugar than I do at far less wholesome restaurants. (These dishes also tend to contain plenty of sea salt, which Pollanites hold up as the wholesome alternative to the addictive salt engineered by the food industry, though your body can't tell the difference.)

One occasional source of obesogenic travesties is *The New York Times Magazine*'s lead food writer, Mark Bittman, who now rivals Pollan as a shepherd to the anti-processed-food flock. (*Salon*, in an article titled

"How to Live What Michael Pollan Preaches," called Bittman's 2009 book, *Food Matters*, "both a cookbook and a manifesto that shows us how to eat better—and save the planet.") I happened to catch Bittman on the *Today* show last year demonstrating for millions of viewers four ways to prepare corn in summertime, including a lovely dish of corn sautéed in bacon fat and topped with bacon. Anyone who thinks that such a thing is much healthier than a Whopper just hasn't been paying attention to obesity science for the past few decades.

That science is, in fact, fairly straightforward. Fat carries more than twice as many calories as carbohydrates and proteins do per gram, which means just a little fat can turn a serving of food into a calorie bomb. Sugar and other refined carbohydrates, like white flour and rice, and high-starch foods, like corn and potatoes, aren't as calorie-dense. But all of these "problem carbs" charge into the bloodstream as glucose in minutes, providing an energy rush, commonly followed by an energy crash that can lead to a surge in appetite.

Because they are energy-intense foods, fat and sugar and other problem carbs trip the pleasure and reward meters placed in our brains by evolution over the millions of years during which starvation was an ever-present threat. We're born enjoying the stimulating sensations these ingredients provide, and exposure strengthens the associations, ensuring that we come to crave them and, all too often, eat more of them than we should. Processed food is not an essential part of this story: recent examinations of ancient human remains in Egypt, Peru, and elsewhere have repeatedly revealed hardened arteries, suggesting that pre-industrial diets, at least of the affluent, may not have been the epitome of healthy eating that the Pollanites make them out to be. People who want to lose weight and keep it off are almost always advised by those who run successful long-term weight-loss programs to transition to a diet high in lean protein, complex carbs such as whole grains and legumes, and the sort of fiber vegetables are loaded with. Because these ingredients provide us with the calories we need without the big, fast bursts of energy, they can be satiating without pushing the primitive reward buttons that nudge us to eat too much.

(A few words on salt: Yes, it's unhealthy in large amounts, raising blood pressure in many people; and yes, it makes food more appealing. But salt is not obesogenic—it has no calories, and doesn't specifically increase the desire to consume high-calorie foods. It can just as easily be enlisted to add to the appeal of vegetables. Lumping it in with fat and sugar as an addictive junk-food ingredient is a confused proposition. But let's agree we want to cut down on it.)

To be sure, many of Big Food's most popular products are loaded with appalling amounts of fat and sugar and other problem carbs (as well as salt), and the plentitude of these ingredients, exacerbated by large portion sizes, has clearly helped foment the obesity crisis. It's hard to find anyone anywhere who disagrees. Junk food is bad for you because it's full of fat and problem carbs. But will switching to wholesome foods free us from this scourge? It could in theory, but in practice, it's hard to see how. Even putting aside for a moment the serious questions about whether wholesome foods could be made accessible to the obese public, and whether the obese would be willing to eat them, we have a more immediate stumbling block: many of the foods served up and even glorified by the wholesome-food movement are themselves chock full of fat and problem carbs.

> "Many of the foods served up and even glorified by the wholesome-food movement are themselves chock full of fat and problem carbs."

Some wholesome foodies openly celebrate fat and problem carbs, insisting that the lack of processing magically renders them healthy. In singing the praises of clotted cream and lard-loaded cookies, for instance, a recent *Wall Street Journal* article by Ron Rosenbaum explained that "eating basic, earthy, fatty foods isn't just a supreme experience of the senses—it can actually be good for you," and that it's "too easy to conflate eating fatty food with eating industrial, oil-fried junk food." That's right, we wouldn't want to make the same mistake that all the cells in our bodies make. Pollan himself makes it clear in his writing that he has little problem with fat—as long as it's not in food "your great-grandmother wouldn't recognize."

Television food shows routinely feature revered chefs tossing around references to healthy eating, "wellness," and farm-fresh ingredients, all the while spooning lard, cream, and sugar over everything in sight. (A study published last year in the *British Medical Journal* found that the recipes in the books of top TV chefs call for "significantly more" fat per portion than what's contained in ready-to-eat supermarket meals.) Corporate wellness programs, one of the most promising avenues for getting the population to adopt healthy behaviors, are falling prey to this way of thinking as well. Last November, I attended a stress-management seminar for employees of a giant consulting company, and listened to a high-powered professional wellness coach tell the crowded room that it's okay to eat anything as long as its plant or animal origins aren't obscured by processing. Thus, she explained, potato chips are perfectly healthy, because they plainly come from potatoes, but Cheetos will make you sick and fat, because what plant or animal is a Cheeto? (For the record, typical potato chips and Cheetos have about equally nightmarish amounts of fat calories per ounce; Cheetos have fewer carbs, though more salt.)

The Pollanites seem confused about exactly what benefits their way of eating provides. All the railing about the fat, sugar, and salt engineered into industrial junk food might lead one to infer that wholesome food, having not been engineered, contains substantially less of them. But clearly you can take in obscene quantities of fat and problem carbs while eating wholesomely, and to judge by what's sold at wholesome stores and restaurants, many people do. Indeed, the more converts and customers the wholesome-food movement's purveyors seek, the stronger their incentive to emphasize foods that light up precisely the same pleasure centers as a 3 Musketeers bar. That just makes wholesome food stealthily obesogenic.

Hold on, you may be thinking. Leaving fat, sugar, and salt aside, what about all the nasty things that wholesome foods do not, by definition, contain and processed foods do? A central claim of the wholesome-food movement is that wholesome is healthier because it doesn't have the artificial flavors, preservatives, other additives, or genetically modified ingredients found in industrialized food; because it isn't subjected to the physical transformations that processed foods go through; and because it doesn't sit around for days, weeks, or months, as industrialized food sometimes does. (This is the complaint against the McDonald's smoothie, which contains artificial flavors and texture additives, and which is pre-mixed.)

The health concerns raised about processing itself—rather than the amount of fat and problem carbs in any given dish—are not, by and large, related to weight gain or obesity. That's important to keep in mind, because obesity is, by an enormous margin, the largest health problem created by what we eat. But even putting that aside, concerns about processed food have been magnified out of all proportion.

Some studies have shown that people who eat wholesomely tend to be healthier than people who live on fast food and other processed food (particularly meat), but the problem with such studies is obvious: substantial nondietary differences exist between these groups, such as propensity to exercise, smoking rates, air quality, access to health care, and much more. (Some researchers say they've tried to control for these factors, but that's a claim most scientists don't put much faith in.) What's more, the people in these groups are sometimes eating entirely different foods, not the same sorts of foods subjected to different levels of processing. It's comparing apples to Whoppers, instead of Whoppers to hand-ground, grass-fed-beef burgers with heirloom tomatoes, garlic aioli, and artisanal cheese. For all these reasons, such findings linking food type and health are considered highly unreliable, and constantly contradict one another, as is true of most epidemiological studies that try to tackle broad nutritional questions.

The fact is, there is simply no clear, credible evidence that any aspect of food processing or storage makes a food uniquely unhealthy. The U.S. population does not suffer from a critical lack of any nutrient because we eat so much processed food. (Sure, health experts urge Americans to get more calcium, potassium, magnesium, fiber, and vitamins A, E, and C, and eating more produce and dairy is a great way to get them, but these ingredients are also available in processed foods, not to mention supplements.) Pollan's "foodlike substances" are regulated by the U.S. Food and Drug Administration (with some exceptions, which are regulated by other agencies), and their effects on health are further raked over by countless scientists who would get a nice career boost from turning up the hidden dangers in some common food-industry ingredient or technique, in part because any number of advocacy groups and journalists are ready to pounce on the slightest hint of risk.

The results of all the scrutiny of processed food are hardly scary, 30 although some groups and writers try to make them appear that way. The Pew Charitable Trusts' Food Additives Project, for example, has bemoaned the fact that the FDA directly reviews only about 70 percent of the ingredients found in food, permitting the rest to pass as "generally recognized as safe" by panels of experts convened by manufacturers. But the only actual risk the project calls out on its Web site or in its publications is a quote from a *Times* article noting that bromine°, which has been in U.S. foods for eight decades, is regarded as suspicious by many because flame retardants containing bromine have been linked to health risks. There is no conclusive evidence that bromine itself is a threat.

In *Pandora's Lunchbox*, Melanie Warner assiduously catalogs every concern that could possibly be raised about the health threats of food processing, leveling accusations so vague, weakly supported, tired, or insignificant that only someone already convinced of the guilt of processed food could find them troubling. While ripping the covers off the breakfast-cereal conspiracy, for example, Warner reveals that much of the nutritional value claimed by these products comes not from natural ingredients but from added vitamins that are chemically synthesized, which must be bad for us because, well, they're *chemically synthesized*. It's the tautology° at the heart of the movement: processed foods are unhealthy because they aren't natural, full stop.

bromine: chemical element with an extremely offensive odor and recently the subject of much controversy over its safety.
tautology: redundant expression or needless repetition of an idea.

In many respects, the wholesome-food movement veers awfully close to religion. To repeat: there is no hard evidence to back any health-risk claims about processed food — evidence, say, of the caliber of several studies by the Centers for Disease Control and Prevention that have traced food poisoning to raw milk, a product championed by some circles of the wholesome-food movement. "Until I hear evidence to the contrary, I think it's reasonable to include processed food in your diet," says Robert Kushner, a physician and nutritionist and a professor at Northwestern University's medical school, where he is the clinical director of the Comprehensive Center on Obesity.

There may be other reasons to prefer wholesome food to the industrialized version. Often stirred into the vague stew of benefits attributed to wholesome food is the "sustainability" of its production — that is, its long term impact on the planet. Small farms that don't rely much on chemicals and heavy industrial equipment may be better for the environment than giant industrial farms — although that argument quickly becomes complicated by a variety of factors. For the purposes of this article, let's simply stipulate that wholesome foods are environmentally superior. But let's also agree that when it comes to prioritizing among food-related public-policy goals, we are likely to save and improve many more lives by focusing on cutting obesity — through any available means — than by trying to convert all of industrial agriculture into a vast constellation of small organic farms.

The impact of obesity on the chances of our living long, productive, and enjoyable lives has been so well documented at this point that I hate to drag anyone through the grim statistics again. But let me just toss out one recent dispatch from the world of obesity-havoc science: a study published in February in the journal *Obesity* found that obese young adults and middle-agers in the U.S. are likely to lose almost a decade of life on average, as compared with their non-obese counterparts. Given our obesity rates, that means Americans who are alive today can collectively expect to sacrifice 1 billion years to obesity. The study adds to a river of evidence suggesting that for the first time in modern history — and in spite of many health-related improvements in our environment, our health care, and our nondietary habits — our health prospects are worsening, mostly because of excess weight.

By all means, let's protect the environment. But let's not rule out the possibility of technologically enabled improvements to our diet — indeed, let's not rule out *any* food — merely because we are pleased by images of pastoral family farms. Let's first pick the foods that can most plausibly make us healthier, all things considered, and then figure out how to make them environmentally friendly.

The Food Revolution We Need

The one fast-food restaurant near [a] busy East L.A. intersection otherwise filled with bodegas was a Carl's Jr. I went in and saw that the biggest and most prominent posters in the store were pushing a new grilled-cod sandwich. It actually looked pretty good, but it wasn't quite lunchtime, and I just wanted a cup of coffee. I went to the counter to order it, but before I could say anything, the cashier greeted me and asked, "Would you like to try our new Charbroiled Atlantic Cod Fish Sandwich today?" Oh, well, sure, why not? (I asked her to hold the tartar sauce, which is mostly fat, but found out later that the sandwich is normally served with about half as much tartar sauce as the notoriously fatty Filet-O-Fish sandwich at McDonald's, where the fish is battered and fried.) The sandwich was delicious. It was less than half the cost of the Sea Cake appetizer at Real Food Daily. It took less than a minute to prepare. In some ways, it was the best meal I had in L.A., and it was probably the healthiest.

We know perfectly well who within our society has developed an extraordinary facility for nudging the masses to eat certain foods, and for making those foods widely available in cheap and convenient forms. The Pollanites have led us to conflate the industrial processing of food with the adding of fat and sugar in order to hook customers, even while pushing many faux-healthy foods of their own. But why couldn't Big Food's processing and marketing genius be put to use on genuinely healthier foods, like grilled fish? Putting aside the standard objection that the industry has no interest in doing so—we'll see later that in fact the industry has plenty of motivation for taking on this challenge—wouldn't that present a more plausible answer to America's junk-food problem than ordering up 50,000 new farmers' markets featuring locally grown organic squash blossoms?

According to Lenard Lesser, of the Palo Alto Medical Foundation, the food industry has mastered the art of using in-store and near-store promotions to shape what people eat. As Lesser and I drove down storied Telegraph Avenue in Berkeley and into far less affluent Oakland, leaving behind the Whole Foods Markets and sushi restaurants for gas-station markets and barbecued-rib stands, he pointed out the changes in the billboards. Whereas the last one we saw in Berkeley was for fruit juice, many in Oakland tout fast-food joints and their wares, including several featuring the Hot Mess Burger at Jack in the Box. Though Lesser noted that this forest of advertising may simply reflect Oakland residents' pre-existing preference for this type of food, he told me lab studies have indicated that the more signs you show people for a particular food product or dish, the more likely they are to choose it over others, all else being equal.

We went into a KFC and found ourselves traversing a maze of signage that put us face-to-face with garish images of various fried foods that presumably had some chicken somewhere deep inside them. "The more they want you to buy something, the bigger they make the image on the menu board," Lesser explained. Here, what loomed largest was the $19.98 fried-chicken-and-corn family meal, which included biscuits and cake. A few days later, I noticed that McDonald's places large placards showcasing desserts on the trash bins, apparently calculating that the best time to entice diners with sweets is when they think they've finished their meals.

Trying to get burger lovers to jump to grilled fish may already be a   40 bit of a stretch — I didn't see any of a dozen other customers buy the cod sandwich when I was at Carl's Jr., though the cashier said it was selling reasonably well. Still, given the food industry's power to tinker with and market food, we should not dismiss its ability to get unhealthy eaters — slowly, incrementally — to buy better food.

That brings us to the crucial question: Just how much healthier could fast-food joints and processed-food companies make their best-selling products without turning off customers? I put that question to a team of McDonald's executives, scientists, and chefs who are involved in shaping the company's future menus, during a February visit to McDonald's surprisingly bucolic° campus west of Chicago. By way of a partial answer, the team served me up a preview tasting of two major new menu items that had been under development in their test kitchens and high-tech sensory-testing labs for the past year, and which were rolled out to the public in April. The first was the Egg White Delight McMuffin ($2.65), a lower-calorie, less fatty version of the Egg McMuffin, with some of the refined flour in the original recipe replaced by whole-grain flour. The other was one of three new Premium McWraps ($3.99), crammed with grilled chicken and spring mix, and given a light coating of ranch dressing amped up with rice vinegar. Both items tasted pretty good (as do the versions in stores, I've since confirmed, though some outlets go too heavy on the dressing). And they were both lower in fat, sugar, and calories than not only many McDonald's staples, but also much of the food served in wholesome restaurants or touted in wholesome cookbooks.

In fact, McDonald's has quietly been making healthy changes for years, shrinking portion sizes, reducing some fats, trimming average salt content by more than 10 percent in the past couple of years alone, and adding fruits, vegetables, low-fat dairy, and oatmeal to its menu. In May, the chain dropped its Angus third-pounders and announced a new line

---

bucolic: pastoral, relating to an idyllic rural or country life.

of quarter-pound burgers, to be served on buns containing whole grains. Outside the core fast-food customer base, Americans are becoming more health-conscious. Public backlash against fast food could lead to regulatory efforts, and in any case, the fast-food industry has every incentive to maintain broad appeal. "We think a lot about how we can bring nutritionally balanced meals that include enough protein, along with the tastes and satisfaction that have an appetite-tiding effect," said Barbara Booth, the company's director of sensory science.

Such steps are enormously promising, says Jamy Ard, an epidemiology° and preventive-medicine researcher at Wake Forest Baptist Medical Center in Winston-Salem, North Carolina, and a co-director of the Weight Management Center there. "Processed food is a key part of our environment, and it needs to be part of the equation," he explains. "If you can reduce fat and calories by only a small amount in a Big Mac, it still won't be a health food, but it wouldn't be as bad, and that could have a huge impact on us." Ard, who has been working for more than a decade with the obese poor, has little patience with the wholesome-food movement's call to eliminate fast food in favor of farm-fresh goods. "It's really naive," he says. "Fast food became popular because it's tasty and convenient and cheap. It makes a lot more sense to look for small, beneficial changes in that food than it does to hold out for big changes in what people eat that have no realistic chance of happening."

According to a recent study, Americans get 11 percent of their calories, on average, from fast food—a number that's almost certainly much higher among the less affluent overweight. As a result, the fast-food industry may be uniquely positioned to improve our diets. Research suggests that calorie counts in a meal can be trimmed by as much as 30 percent without eaters noticing—by, for example, reducing portion sizes and swapping in ingredients that contain more fiber and water. Over time, that could be much more than enough to literally tip the scales for many obese people. "The difference between losing weight and not losing weight," says Robert Kushner, the obesity scientist and clinical director at Northwestern, "is a few hundred calories a day."

Which raises a question: If McDonald's is taking these sorts of steps, 45 albeit in a slow and limited way, why isn't it more loudly saying so to deflect criticism? While the company has heavily plugged the debut of its new egg-white sandwich and chicken wraps, the ads have left out even a mention of health, the reduced calories and fat, or the inclusion of whole grains. McDonald's has practically kept secret the fact that it

epidemiology: the study of causes, effects, and patterns of health and disease across defined populations.

has also begun substituting wholegrain flour for some of the less healthy refined flour in its best-selling Egg McMuffin.

The explanation can be summed up in two words that surely strike fear into the hearts of all fast-food executives who hope to make their companies' fare healthier: McLean Deluxe.

Among those who gleefully rank such things, the McLean Deluxe reigns as McDonald's worst product failure of all time, eclipsing McPasta, the McHotdog, and the McAfrika (don't ask). When I brought up the McLean Deluxe to the innovation team at McDonald's, I faced the first and only uncomfortable silence of the day. Finally, Greg Watson, a senior vice president, cleared his throat and told me that neither he nor anyone else in the room was at the company at the time, and he didn't know that much about it. "It sounds to me like it was ahead of its time," he added. "If we had something like that in the future, we would never launch it like that again."

Introduced in 1991, the McLean Deluxe was perhaps the boldest single effort the food industry has ever undertaken to shift the masses to healthier eating. It was supposed to be a healthier version of the Quarter Pounder, made with extra-lean beef infused with seaweed extract. It reportedly did reasonably well in early taste tests—for what it's worth, my wife and I were big fans—and McDonald's pumped the reduced-fat angle to the public for all it was worth. The general reaction varied from lack of interest to mockery to revulsion. The company gamely flogged the sandwich for five years before quietly removing it from the menu.

The McLean Deluxe was a sharp lesson to the industry, even if in some ways it merely confirmed what generations of parents have well known: if you want to turn off otherwise eager eaters to a dish, tell them it's good for them. Recent studies suggest that calorie counts placed on menus have a negligible effect on food choices, and that the less-health-conscious might even use the information to steer clear of low-calorie fare—perhaps assuming that it tastes worse and is less satisfying, and that it's worse value for their money. The result is a sense in the food industry that if it is going to sell healthier versions of its foods to the general public—and not just to that minority already sold on healthier eating—it is going to have to do it in a relatively sneaky way, emphasizing the taste appeal and not the health benefits. "People expect something to taste worse if they believe it's healthy," says Charles Spence, an Oxford University neuroscientist who specializes in how the brain perceives food. "And that expectation affects how it tastes to them, so it actually *does* taste worse."

Thus McDonald's silence on the nutritional profiles of its new menu 50 items. "We're not making any health claims," Watson said. "We're just saying it's new, it tastes great, come on in and enjoy it. Maybe once the product is well seated with customers, we'll change that message." If customers learn that they can eat healthier foods at McDonald's without even realizing it, he added, they'll be more likely to try healthier foods there than at other restaurants. The same reasoning presumably explains why the promotions and ads for the Carl's Jr. grilled-cod sandwich offer not a word related to healthfulness, and why there wasn't a whiff of health cheerleading surrounding the turkey burger brought out earlier this year by Burger King (which is not yet calling the sandwich a permanent addition).

If the food industry is to quietly sell healthier products to its mainstream, mostly non-health-conscious customers, it must find ways to deliver the eating experience that fat and problem carbs provide in foods that have fewer of those ingredients. There is no way to do that with farm-fresh produce and wholesome meat, other than reducing portion size. But processing technology gives the food industry a potent tool for trimming unwanted ingredients while preserving the sensations they deliver.

I visited Fona International, a flavor-engineering company also outside Chicago, and learned that there are a battery of tricks for fooling and appeasing taste buds, which are prone to notice a lack of fat or sugar, or the presence of any of the various bitter, metallic, or otherwise unpleasant flavors that vegetables, fiber, complex carbs, and fat or sugar substitutes can impart to a food intended to appeal to junk-food eaters. Some 5,000 FDA-approved chemical compounds—which represent the base components of all known flavors—line the shelves that run alongside Fona's huge labs. Armed with these ingredients and an array of state-of-the-art chemical-analysis and testing tools, Fona's scientists and engineers can precisely control flavor perception. "When you reduce the sugar, fat, and salt in foods, you change the personality of the product," said Robert Sobel, a chemist, who heads up research at the company. "We can restore it."

For example, fat "cushions" the release of various flavors on the tongue, unveiling them gradually and allowing them to linger. When fat is removed, flavors tend to immediately inundate the tongue and then quickly flee, which we register as a much less satisfying experience. Fona's experts can reproduce the "temporal profile" of the flavors in fattier foods by adding edible compounds derived from plants that slow the release of flavor molecules; by replacing the flavors with similarly flavored compounds that come on and leave more slowly; or by enlisting "phantom aromas" that create the sensation of certain tastes even when those tastes are not present on the tongue. (For example, the smell of vanilla can essentially mask reductions in sugar of up to 25 percent.) One triumph of this sort of engineering is the modern protein drink, a staple of many successful weight-loss programs and a favorite of those trying to build muscle. "Seven years ago they were unpalatable," Sobel said. "Today we can mask the astringent flavors and eggy aromas by adding natural ingredients."

I also visited Tic Gums in White Marsh, Maryland, a company that engineers textures into food products. Texture hasn't received the attention that flavor has, noted Greg Andon, Tic's boyish and ebullient° president, whose family has run the company for three generations. The result, he said, is that even people in the food industry don't have an adequate vocabulary for it. "They know what flavor you're referring to when you say 'forest floor,' but all they can say about texture is 'Can you make it more creamy?'" So Tic is inventing a vocabulary, breaking textures down according to properties such as "mouth coating" and "mouth clearing." Wielding an arsenal of some 20 different "gums"—edible ingredients mostly found in tree sap, seeds, and other plant matter—Tic's researchers can make low-fat foods taste, well, creamier; give the same full body that sugared drinks offer to sugar-free beverages; counter chalkiness and gloopiness; and help orchestrate the timing of flavor bursts. (Such approaches have nothing in common with the ill-fated Olestra, a fat-like compound engineered to pass undigested through the body, and billed in the late 1990s as a fat substitute in snack foods. It was made notorious by widespread anecdotal complaints of cramps and loose bowels, though studies seemed to contradict those claims.)

Fona and Tic, like most companies in their industry, won't identify 55 customers or product names on the record. But both firms showed me an array of foods and beverages that were under construction, so to speak, in the name of reducing calories, fat, and sugar while maintaining mass appeal. I've long hated the taste of low-fat dressing—I gave up on it a few years ago and just use vinegar—but Tic served me an in-development version of a low-fat salad dressing that was better than any I've ever had. Dozens of companies are doing similar work, as are the big food-ingredient manufacturers, such as ConAgra, whose products are in 97 percent of American homes, and whose whole-wheat flour is what McDonald's is relying on for its breakfast sandwiches. Domino Foods, the sugar manufacturer, now sells a low-calorie combination of sugar and the nonsugar sweetener stevia that has been engineered by a flavor company to mask the sort of nonsugary tastes driving many consumers away from diet beverages and the like. "Stevia has a licorice note we were

ebullient: enthusiastic.

able to have taken out," explains Domino Foods CEO Brian O'Malley. High-tech anti-obesity food engineering is just warming up. Oxford's Charles Spence notes that in addition to flavors and textures, companies are investigating ways to exploit a stream of insights that have been coming out of scholarly research about the neuroscience of eating. He notes, for example, that candy companies may be able to slip healthier ingredients into candy bars without anyone noticing, simply by loading these ingredients into the middle of the bar and leaving most of the fat and sugar at the ends of the bar. "We tend to make up our minds about how something tastes from the first and last bites, and don't care as much what happens in between," he explains. Some other potentially useful gimmicks he points out: adding weight to food packaging such as yogurt containers, which convinces eaters that the contents are rich with calories, even when they're not; using chewy textures that force consumers to spend more time between bites, giving the brain a chance to register satiety; and using colors, smells, sounds, and packaging information to create the belief that foods are fatty and sweet even when they are not. Spence found, for example, that wine is perceived as 50 percent sweeter when consumed under a red light.

Researchers are also tinkering with food ingredients to boost satiety. Cargill has developed a starch derived from tapioca that gives dishes a refined-carb taste and mouthfeel, but acts more like fiber in the body—a feature that could keep the appetite from spiking later. "People usually think that processing leads to foods that digest too quickly, but we've been able to use processing to slow the digestion rate," says Bruce McGoogan, who heads R&D for Cargill's North American food-ingredient business. The company has also developed ways to reduce fat in beef patties, and to make baked goods using half the usual sugar and oil, all without heavily compromising taste and texture.

> "Candy companies may be able to slip healthier ingredients into candy bars without anyone noticing. . . . 'We tend to make up our minds about how something tastes from the first and last bites, and don't care as much what happens in between.'"

Other companies and research labs are trying to turn out healthier, more appealing foods by enlisting ultra-high pressure, nanotechnology°, vacuums, and edible coatings. At the University of Massachusetts at Amherst's Center for Foods for Health and Wellness, Fergus Clydesdale,

---

nanotechnology: the science of manipulating matter on a very small (atomic or molecular) scale.

the director of the school's Food Science Policy Alliance — as well as a spry 70-something who's happy to tick off all the processed food in his diet — showed me labs where researchers are looking into possibilities that would not only attack obesity but also improve health in other significant ways, for example by isolating ingredients that might lower the risk of cancer and concentrating them in foods. "When you understand foods at the molecular level," he says, "there's a lot you can do with food and health that we're not doing now."

The Implacable Enemies of Healthier Processed Food

What's not to like about these developments? Plenty, if you've bought into the notion that processing itself is the source of the unhealthfulness of our foods. The wholesome-food movement is not only talking up dietary strategies that are unlikely to help most obese Americans; it is, in various ways, getting in the way of strategies that could work better.

The Pollanites didn't invent resistance to healthier popular foods, as the fates of the McLean Deluxe and Olestra demonstrate, but they've greatly intensified it. Fast food and junk food have their core customer base, and the wholesome-food gurus have theirs. In between sit many millions of Americans — the more the idea that processed food should be shunned no matter what takes hold in this group, the less incentive fast-food joints will have to continue edging away from the fat-and-problem-carb-laden fare beloved by their most loyal customers to try to broaden their appeal.

Pollan has popularized contempt for "nutritionism," the idea behind packing healthier ingredients into processed foods. In his view, the quest to add healthier ingredients to food isn't a potential solution, it's part of the problem. Food is healthy not when it contains healthy ingredients, he argues, but when it can be traced simply and directly to (preferably local) farms. As he resonantly put it in *The Times* in 2007: "If you're concerned about your health, you should probably avoid food products that make health claims. Why? Because a health claim on a food product is a good indication that it's not really food, and food is what you want to eat."

In this way, wholesome-food advocates have managed to pre-damn the very steps we need the food industry to take, placing the industry in a no-win situation: If it maintains the status quo, then we need to stay away because its food is loaded with fat and sugar. But if it tries to moderate these ingredients, then it is deceiving us with nutritionism. Pollan explicitly counsels avoiding foods containing more than five ingredients, or any hard-to-pronounce or unfamiliar ingredients. This rule eliminates

60

almost anything the industry could do to produce healthier foods that retain mass appeal — most of us wouldn't get past xanthan gum — and that's perfectly in keeping with his intention.

By placing wholesome eating directly at odds with healthier processed foods, the Pollanites threaten to derail the reformation of fast food just as it's starting to gain traction. At McDonald's, "Chef Dan" — that is, Dan Coudreaut, the executive chef and director of culinary innovation — told me of the dilemma the movement has caused him as he has tried to make the menu healthier. "Some want us to have healthier food, but others want us to have minimally processed ingredients, which can mean more fat," he explained. "It's becoming a balancing act for us." That the chef with arguably the most influence in the world over the diet of the obese would even consider adding fat to his menu to placate wholesome foodies is a pretty good sign that something has gone terribly wrong with our approach to the obesity crisis.

Many people insist that the steps the food industry has already taken to offer less-obesogenic fare are no more than cynical ploys to fool customers into eating the same old crap under a healthy guise. In his 3,500-word *New York Times Magazine* article on the prospects for healthier fast food, Mark Bittman lauded a new niche of vegan chain restaurants while devoting just one line to the major "quick serve" restaurants' contribution to better health: "I'm not talking about token gestures, like the McDonald's fruit-and-yogurt parfait, whose calories are more than 50 percent sugar." Never mind that 80 percent of a farm-fresh apple's calories come from sugar; that almost any obesity expert would heartily approve of the yogurt parfait as a step in the right direction for most fast-food-dessert eaters; and that many of the desserts Bittman glorifies in his own writing make the parfait look like arugula, nutrition-wise. (His recipe for corn-and-blueberry crisp, for example, calls for adding two-thirds of a cup of brown sugar to a lot of other problem carbs, along with five tablespoons of butter.)

Bittman is hardly alone in his reflexive dismissals. No sooner had McDonald's and Burger King rolled out their egg-white sandwich and turkey burger, respectively, than a spate of articles popped up hooting that the new dishes weren't healthier because they trimmed a mere 50 and 100 calories from their standard counterparts, the Egg McMuffin and the Whopper. Apparently these writers didn't understand, or chose to ignore, the fact that a reduction of 50 or 100 calories in a single dish places an eater exactly on track to eliminate a few hundred calories a day from his or her diet — the critical threshold needed for long-term weight loss. Any bigger reduction would risk leaving someone too hungry to stick to a diet program. It's just the sort of small step in the right direction we should be aiming for, because the obese are much more likely to take it than they are to make a big leap to wholesome or very-low-calorie foods.

Many wholesome foodies insist that the food industry won't make 65 serious progress toward healthier fare unless forced to by regulation. I, for one, believe regulation aimed at speeding the replacement of obesogenic foods with appealing healthier foods would be a great idea. But what a lot of foodies really want is to ban the food industry from selling junk food altogether. And that is just a fantasy. The government never managed to keep the tobacco companies from selling cigarettes, and banning booze (the third-most-deadly consumable killer after cigarettes and food) didn't turn out so well. The two most health-enlightened, regulation-friendly major cities in America, New York and San Francisco, tried to halt sales of two of the most horrific fast-food assaults on health—giant servings of sugared beverages and kids' fast-food meals accompanied by toys, respectively—and neither had much luck. Michelle Obama is excoriated by conservatives for asking schools to throw more fruits and vegetables into the lunches they serve. Realistically, the most we can hope for is a tax on some obesogenic foods. The research of Lisa Powell, the University of Illinois professor, suggests that a 20 percent tax on sugary beverages would reduce consumption by about 25 percent. (As for fatty foods, no serious tax proposal has yet been made in the U.S., and if one comes along, the wholesome foodies might well join the food industry and most consumers in opposing it. Denmark did manage to enact a fatty-food tax, but it was deemed a failure when consumers went next door into Germany and Sweden to stock up on their beloved treats.)

Continuing to call out Big Food on its unhealthy offerings, and loudly, is one of the best levers we have for pushing it toward healthier products—but let's call it out intelligently, not reflexively. Executives of giant food companies may be many things, but they are not stupid. Absent action, they risk a growing public-relations disaster, the loss of their more affluent and increasingly health-conscious customers, and the threat of regulation, which will be costly to fight, even if the new rules don't stick. Those fears are surely what's driving much of the push toward moderately healthier fare within the industry today. But if the Pollanites convince policy makers and the health-conscious public that these foods are dangerous by virtue of not being farm-fresh, that will push Big Food in a different direction (in part by limiting the profit potential it sees in lower-fat, lower-problem-carb foods), and cause it to spend its resources in other ways.

Significant regulation of junk food may not go far, but we have other tools at our disposal to prod Big Food to intensify and speed up its efforts to cut fat and problem carbs in its offerings, particularly if we're smart about it. Lenard Lesser points out that government and advocacy groups could start singling out particular restaurants and food products for praise or shaming—a more official version of "eat this, not that"—rather than sticking to a steady drumbeat of "processed food must go away." Academia could do a much better job of producing and highlighting solid research into less obesogenic, high-mass-appeal foods, and could curtail its evidence-light anti-food-processing bias, so that the next generation of social and policy entrepreneurs might work to narrow the gap between the poor obese and the well-resourced healthy instead of inadvertently widening it. We can keep pushing our health-care system to provide more incentives and support to the obese for losing weight by making small, painless, but helpful changes in their behavior, such as switching from Whoppers to turkey burgers, from Egg McMuffins to Egg White Delights, or from blueberry crisp to fruit-and-yogurt parfaits.

And we can ask the wholesome-food advocates, and those who give them voice, to make it clearer that the advice they sling is relevant mostly to the privileged healthy—and to start getting behind realistic solutions to the obesity crisis.

Understanding the Text

1. What is the wholesome food movement, and what does Freedman think is wrong with it?

2. How does Freedman think that the fast-food and processed-food industries could improve public health?

3. What happened with the McLean Deluxe? Why does it matter to Freedman's argument?

Reflection and Response

4. Freedman argues that telling people to eat more fruits and vegetables and less fat and calories hasn't and won't work. How does he support this assertion? Do you agree with his line of reasoning? Why or why not?

5. Freedman rejects the claim that "processed foods are unhealthy because they aren't natural" (par. 31) in favor of the idea that we could engineer healthier processed foods that are popular and tasty and actually have the potential to help the poor and the obese lose weight. How does he support his rejection of the "processed foods are unhealthy" view? Based on your analysis of this essay, as well as your own experience, which position do you think is more valid? Why?

6. How does Freedman depict the media's role in building brand reputations? How does the media affect how you see brands? Does your experience support or complicate Freedman's depiction?

Making Connections

7. Compare Freedman's description of the texture industry to Eric Schlosser's description of the flavor industry ("Why the Fries Taste Good," p. 20), and then go online and research both industries. Write a descriptive essay about their influences on food choices.

8. Imagine that Freedman and Jill McCorkle ("Her Chee-to Heart," p. 30) are discussing the pleasures of food. How might their perspectives on eating complicate each other?

9. Freedman offers a harsh critique of Michael Pollan and the wholesome-food movement. He not only objects to Pollan's position, he criticizes it as impractical and goes so far as to accuse him of hypocrisy. Does Freedman offer a fair critique of Pollan? Does Freedman's critique hold up to scrutiny? Might some of his ideas be called impractical and hypocritical, too? How do we make sense of the debate they are having? Join their conversation, supporting your ideas with concrete evidence and strong analysis that helps your reader understand how you are interpreting the evidence and why you think it is support for your position. You may want to visit Pollan's website, read "Eat Food: Food Defined" on p. 10, or look at other essays that he has written to develop your response.

10. Frances Moore Lappé ("Biotechnology Isn't the Key to Feeding the World," p. 317) argues that democracy, not technology, is the answer to solving global hunger issues. Freedman argues for the benefits of using technology to solve the obesity crisis. Research the relationship between food production and new technologies. Select a few recent innovations, and explore if and how they might help us improve our health or make our food supply more sustainable, stable, or healthy. Evaluate the positives and negatives of the innovations you select.

Why So Many Rich Kids Come to Enjoy the Taste of Healthier Foods

Joe Pinsker

Joe Pinsker is a staff writer for *The Atlantic*, a monthly magazine that provides cultural and political commentary on various aspects of American life. Based in Washington, DC, Pinsker covers issues relating to families, parenting, and education. In this essay, published in *The Atlantic* in 2016, Pinsker uses various academic studies to explore the complex reasons that children from families with higher socioeconomic status are more likely to eat health foods.

Broccoli is nutritious, and it knows it.

Since humans and other plant-eating animals have reason to consume a lot of broccoli, it has come to produce goitrin, a compound that tastes very bitter to people with a certain gene — which serves as a (meager) defense against getting eaten. Other vegetables that come from the very same plant, including kale, brussels sprouts, and collard greens, all employ a similar protective strategy. But, as the podcast *Surprisingly Awesome* recently noted, broccoli's flavor armor can be actually quite effective, as evidenced by many kids' disgusted reaction to tasting it for the first time.

But those kids can learn to like it, eventually: One 1990 study found that kids need to be presented with unknown foods somewhere between eight and 15 times before they come to accept them. This, of course, doesn't come cheap. Once rejected, a good number of those eight to 15 servings of broccoli (or carrots or whole grains or fish) are going to end up on the floor and then in the garbage. And on top of that, parents need to buy a dependable backup food to have on hand.

Who can afford that sort of waste? Not parents with tight food budgets. A recently published study looking into the eating and shopping habits of both low-income and high-income parents suggests that the steep up-front cost of introducing foods to children is enough to deter a number of parents from trying. This cost-cutting decision may explain some of the differences between how rich and poor Americans eat.

This basic idea about how humans come to like novel° foods, sur- 5 prisingly, doesn't come up very much in discussions about the price of

---

novel: new, of a kind not seen before.

healthy eating—a topic that economists, public-health researchers, and journalists all disagree about. On one side there are a number of economists who say that on a per-calorie basis, it's more affordable (not to mention less time-consuming) to buy fast food than it is to cook a meal using fresh produce. On the other side are those who maintain that thinking by the calorie doesn't make sense, because Americans eat too many calories anyway. This latter group, which includes other economists as well as the food writer Mark Bittman, insists that it's not all that difficult to cook a filling, nutritious meal for less money than it takes to go to McDonald's, as long as one isn't hung up on buying organic or local food.

Both arguments have their virtues and their shortcomings, but both overlook the basic fact that food purchased is not necessarily the same as food consumed. When many economists estimate the price of eating fresh foods, the cost when a child eats half of a 50-cent carrot is recorded as 25 cents, even if the other half goes to waste.

Could this unaccounted-for cost be part of the explanation for why high-income and low-income Americans tend to have different diets? Caitlin Daniel, a doctoral student in sociology at Harvard, recently published a study in the journal *Social Science & Medicine* suggesting that this cost might actually be large enough to change the shopping decisions of some low-income families, but small enough for wealthier parents to shrug off. In other words, richer parents might have plenty of room in their budgets to force brussels sprouts on their children 10 times and throw out what remains, while poorer parents tend to stick to dependable but less-nutritious foods that their kids are known to like.

Daniel arrived at this finding after interviewing 75 Boston-area parents from a range of economic backgrounds about their food-shopping habits. She spent an average of two hours with each interviewee, and followed a number of them on their trips to the grocery store. (And apparently, having a sociologist looking over their shoulder with a notepad didn't deter the research subjects from their usual shopping behavior: Daniel reports that three interviewees stole from the grocery store even though they knew she was watching.)

The data that came out of Daniel's study is qualitative, but it provides some insight into how parents of different economic backgrounds think about the costs of feeding their children. "I try not to buy things that I don't know if he'll like because it's just, it's a waste," one lower-income mother told Daniel. Parents talked about wanting to serve "real" food, but out of necessity resorting to more dependable, easier-to-love foods such as frozen burritos or Hot Pockets. Whether the rejected food was eaten by another family member, stashed in the fridge, or thrown out entirely, parents mentally counted it as a loss.

Daniel found that parents with higher incomes framed the conver- 10
sation about food waste in very different terms. Similar to less wealthy
parents, they didn't like the idea of throwing food out, but they tended
to be bothered only by the principle of it, not focusing on the loss of
money. One well-off mother who kept packing grapes in her son's
lunchbox only to find them uneaten day after day, told Daniel, "I do
feel bad about the waste, but I feel worse about my son not eating well."
Of the parents that Daniel interviewed, those with higher incomes were
more likely to say they can afford to waste food, and that rejected food
wouldn't go uneaten.

While it's not clear just how big of a role these discrepancies play in
shaping different families' eating habits—Daniel stresses that this is just
one sample of parents in one American city—it does seem to be the case
that poorer parents feel they don't have enough wiggle room in their
budgets to present acquired tastes to their children, whereas wealthier
parents aren't as constrained in teaching their children what to like. And,
as Daniel notes in her paper, the tastes that children come to enjoy are
likely to stick around into adolescence and beyond.

About 3,500 miles away and likely around the same time when Daniel
was interviewing Bostonians about their shopping habits, two Danish
researchers were independently working on another important, and
related, question: Why do well-educated adults have healthier diets than
those with less education?

The standard answer is that well-educated people are more aware of
the health benefits of eating well, so they purchase and eat foods that are
more nutritious. The theory is a little more complicated than that (because
wealth, leisure time, and other variables come into play), but it fits with a
central, popular assumption about healthy eating: that the most indulgent
foods are the ones that should be avoided. Healthy eaters, the thinking
goes, are armed with enough informa-
tion to resist the temptations of cupcakes
and Doritos.

What Sinne Smed and Lars Gårn
Hansen, the two researchers at the University of Copenhagen's Institute of
Food and Resource Economics, wanted
to do was test this idea. They knew that
there was a body of research showing
that people with less education tend to
eat more saturated fats and sugars, and
they wanted to figure out why.

> "Any sound model of
> healthy eating should
> account for the strong possi-
> bility that the tastes children
> acquire in early childhood go
> on to shape their shopping
> habits later in life — and that
> acquiring those tastes in
> the first place can be more
> costly than it seems."

So they turned to a dataset, provided to them by the market-research 15
firm GfK, that described the eating habits of roughly 2,500 Danes in great
detail. The data tracked everything from a consumer's education level to
whether the milk she was buying was whole, low-fat, skim, or chocolate.
Smed and Hansen's first finding was that the Danes matched with previous patterns encompassing education level and diet: While everyone
could stand to eat less sugar and saturated fat, it was the least-educated
who were exceeding recommendations the most.

Because the dataset they were working with was so fine-grained°, Smed
and Hansen essentially got to look at the grocery-store receipts of all those
Danish shoppers. They realized that this could let them do something
that was potentially very revealing of why eating habits vary by education
levels. Their method is a bit complicated, but the idea is that a shopper's
overall monthly spending hints at how much she was willing to spend for
all of the, say, saturated fat she consumed in a month (which says something about how healthy or unhealthy she perceives saturated fat to be).
Meanwhile, the money she spent on milk during a month hints at how
much money she's willing to spend on saturated fat in milk (which says
something about her preference for milk specifically, as opposed to other

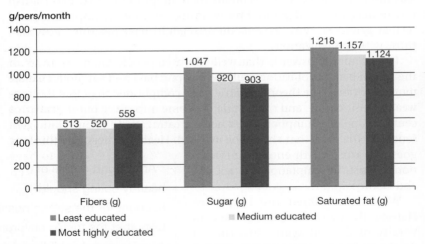

g/pers/month

Monthly Consumption of Fiber, Sugar, and Saturated Fat, by Education Level

Note: "Highly educated" more or less refers to a bachelor's degree, "medium" to an associate's
degree, and "least" to no higher education. (Smed and Hansen)

Smed, S., & Hansen, L. G. (2016). Consumer valuation of health attributes in food. Frederiksberg:
Department of Food and Resource Economics, University of Copenhagen. IFRO Working Paper,
No. 2016/01

fine-grained: richly detailed.

	Healthiest Diet	Healthiest Health Preferences	Healthiest "Taste" Preferences
Sugar	Most highly Educated	Least Educated	Most highly Educated
Fibre	Most highly Educated	No difference	Most highly Educated
Saturated fat	Most highly Educated	No difference	Most highly Educated

How Education Level Correlates with Perceptions of How Healthy a Nutrient Is, and If It Tastes Good

Note: "Highly educated" more or less refers to a bachelor's degree, "medium" to an associate's degree, and "least" to no higher education. (Smed and Hansen)

Smed, S., & Hansen, L. G. (2016). Consumer valuation of health attributes in food. Frederiksberg: Department of Food and Resource Economics, University of Copenhagen. IFRO Working Paper, No. 2016/01

foods). In other words, Smed and Hansen's analysis let them use shoppers' spending records to draw conclusions about how they perceived both the nutritional value and the taste of different nutrients.

What they found was striking: Those with the most education and those with the least education had extremely similar understandings of how healthy (or unhealthy) sugar, fiber, and saturated fat were. But the big difference between these two groups was that more-educated people liked the taste of more-nutritious foods—foods lower in sugar, lower in saturated fat, and higher in fiber—than less-educated people.

This pattern is hard to accept at first, because it goes against the way a lot of people think about nutrition: The reason that more-educated people have healthier diets may not be because they have more of an appreciation for the importance of a good diet, but because to an extent they're following their palates. This explanation undoes a basic assumption about healthy eating—that for everyone, a better diet is a matter of overcoming the temptation of salty, sweet, and fatty foods.

Instead, better-educated people might be being somewhat indulgent and pleasure-seeking when they buy food. They just happen to have a preference for different sorts of foods—foods they might have been exposed to when they were growing up.

When taken together, Daniel's research and Smed and Hansen's 20 research suggests that any sound model of healthy eating should account for the strong possibility that the tastes children acquire in early childhood go on to shape their shopping habits later in life—and that acquiring those tastes in the first place can be more costly than it seems.

Public-health messaging often emphasizes the health benefits of eating certain foods. But if eating well is a matter of taste (and, of course, access), then those billboards and commercials may be missing the point.

It's not clear exactly how public policy could change to accommodate all this, but Daniel has some ideas. She heard from some of her interviewees that when children were given fruits they'd never heard of at school, such as pomegranates and Asian pears, the parents started buying them at home. Perhaps schools could absorb the upfront losses that low-income parents worry about when feeding their children novel, but healthy, foods. (Smed and Hansen also mention this possibility in their paper.) And if policy solutions don't materialize, Daniel notes that buying frozen produce can reduce waste, since it can be stored for long periods of time and doled out in small servings.

In the end, though, it seems like the most important thing a parent can do is to keep repeating a timeless three-word phrase, even after a string of rejections: "Eat your vegetables." Research, and thousands of years of human experience, suggests that eventually, they will.

Understanding the Text

1. Why do many kids dislike the taste of broccoli?
2. Why do wealthier children tend to enjoy healthier foods?
3. How and why do we learn to like foods we initially disliked?

Reflection and Response

4. What does Pinsker identify as potential hidden costs of healthy eating, and why does Pinsker think it is important to understand them?
5. Identify all of the studies and research projects that Pinsker references. Notice the fields and disciplines represented. How would you characterize this evidence? Why do you think he decided to support his position this way?
6. Examine the chart and graph that accompany Pinsker's essay. What do they add to the argument? Do they help convince you of the validity of his position? Why or why not?

Making Connections

7. Not only do Pinsker and Dhruv Khullar ("Why Shame Won't Stop Obesity," p. 71) both critique conventional thinking on how to improve eating habits, they both make arguments that suggest a need to see improving eating habits as a social justice matter. Imagine that they were to sit down together to work on an ad campaign to promote healthy eating. What values would they share? What messages would they emphasize? Create an ad campaign that draws on both arguments and works to overcome the problems they identify.
8. Pinsker ends his essay with a simple, timeless, oft-repeated rule: "Eat your vegetables." Yet he also examines all the ways this guideline is more

complex than it sounds. Why is this so complicated? How do authors like Michael Pollan ("Eat Food: Food Defined," p. 10), Marion Nestle ("Eating Made Simple," p. 36), and Mary Roach ("Liver and Opinions," p. 114) help us understand the complexities? If you follow this rule, why do you do so? If you do not, do any of the authors in this collection inspire you to do so? How and why?

9. If we accept Pinsker's assertion that "eating well is a matter of taste (and, of course, access)," (par. 21) how might we change public health messaging to be more effective? Draw on the work of Michael Pollan ("Eat Food: Food Defined," p. 10), Marion Nestle ("Eating Made Simple," p. 36), and Thich Nhat Hanh and Lilian Cheung ("Are You Really Appreciating the Apple?," p. 59) to support your response.

The Hidden Resilience of "Food Desert" Neighborhoods

Barry Yeoman

Barry Yeoman majored in journalism at New York University before becoming an investigative journalist for *The Independent*, a weekly magazine published in Durham, North Carolina. Yeoman worked there for more than a decade. For the past twenty years, Yeoman has worked full time as a freelance journalist for a range of publications; he is known for writing in-depth nonfiction narrative pieces that bring a human element to complex political, environmental, racial, and social issues. He is the recipient of many prestigious awards for his writing and also teaches journalism and writing courses at Duke University and Wake Forest University. In this essay, originally published in SAPIENS and reprinted by *Civil Eats*, Yeoman offers a unique look into the ways academic experts are connected to the communities that they research as he explores the power and limitations of resilience in African American neighborhoods with limited access to healthy, nutritious foods.

Even before Ashanté Reese and I reach the front gate, retired schoolteacher Alice Chandler is standing in the doorway of her brick home in Washington, D.C. She welcomes Reese, an anthropologist whom she has known for six years, with a hug and apologizes for having nothing to feed us during this spontaneous visit.

Chandler, 69 years old, is a rara avis° among Americans: an adult who has lived nearly her entire life in the same house. This fact makes her stories particularly valuable to Reese, who has been studying the changing food landscape in Deanwood, a historically black neighborhood across the Anacostia River from most of the city.

When Chandler was growing up, horse-drawn wagons delivered meat, fish, and vegetables to her doorstep. The neighborhood had a milkman, as did many U.S. communities in the mid-20th century. Her mother grew vegetables in a backyard garden and made wine from the fruit of their peach tree.

Food was shared across fence lines. "Your neighbor may have tomatoes and squash in their garden," Chandler says. "And you may have cucumbers in yours. Depending on how bountiful each one was, they would trade off." Likewise, when people went fishing, "they would bring back enough for friends in the neighborhood. That often meant a Saturday evening fish fry at home."

---

rara avis: Latin for "rare bird," indicating a rare or unique person or thing.

Around the corner was the Spic N Span Market, a grocery with penny 5
candy, display cases of fresh chicken and pork chops, and an old dog who
slept in the back. The owner, whom Chandler knew as "Mr. Eddie," was a
Jewish man who hired African-American cashiers and extended credit to
customers short on cash. Next door was a small farm whose owner used
to give fresh eggs to Chandler's mother.

Chandler was born into this architecturally eclectic neighborhood.
On the basis of oral histories found in archives, Reese mapped 11 different groceries that were open in Deanwood during its peak years, the
1930s and '40s. African-Americans owned five. Jews, excluded by restrictive covenants from living in some other D.C. neighborhoods, owned
six. For much of the mid-20th century, there was also a Safeway store.

Today there are exactly zero grocery stores. The only places for
Deanwood's 5,000 residents to buy food in their neighborhood are
corner stores, abundantly stocked with beer and Beefaroni but nearly
devoid of fruit, vegetables, and meat. At one of those stores, which I visited, a "Healthy Corners" sign promised fresh produce. Instead, I found
two nearly empty wooden shelves sporting a few sad-looking onions,
bananas, apples, and potatoes. The nearest supermarket, a Safeway, is a
hilly 30-minute walk away. A city council member who visited last year
found long lines, moldy strawberries, and meat that appeared to have
spoiled.

The common name for neighborhoods like these is "food deserts,"
which the U.S. Department of Agriculture defines as areas "where people
have limited access to a variety of healthy and affordable food." According to the USDA, food deserts tend to offer sugary, fatty foods; the department also says that poor access to fruits, vegetables, and lean meats could
lead to obesity and diabetes. A map produced by the nonpartisan D.C.
Policy Center puts about half of Deanwood into a desert.

But Reese, an assistant professor of anthropology at Spelman College
in Atlanta, Georgia, has joined a number of scholars who are pushing
back against the food desert model. She calls it a "lazy" shorthand to
describe both a series of corporate decisions and a complex human
ecosystem.

"Language matters," says Reese, who explores these issues in a new 10
book, *Black Food Geographies*, due out next year. Use the wrong words to
describe the problem and you end up with one-dimensional solutions
that don't address the root causes of poor diets. Both the U.S. and British
governments have emphasized supermarket-building as a way out of
their country's nutrition woes. Yet there's "limited causal evidence" that
this strategy improves diets, according to a 2017 report by economists
from New York University, Stanford University, and the University of

Chicago. They analyzed food-purchase data to understand the complex reasons why affluent Americans eat healthier than their poorer counterparts and concluded that leveling the grocery field would "reduce nutritional inequality by only 9 percent."

Reese adds that people often inaccurately think of deserts as lifeless. "The desert metaphor [implies] there's really nothing of value," she says. "When we use 'food desert,' we don't see the people and businesses and networks and thoughts and desires and hopes. This metaphor wipes all of that off the map." By looking past the label, she argues, we can finally understand and address the decades of disinvestment that have depleted neighborhoods of healthy retail options—and we can finally appreciate the resilience of current residents.

How communities feed themselves has been a theme running through Reese's life. Now 33 years old, she grew up in Porter Springs, Texas, whose population was (and is) 50, on a red-clay dirt road where everyone was family, "biological or not." Her uncles raised goats, hogs, and poultry for slaughter, and Reese remembers her grandfather wringing chickens' necks to process them for consumption. She and the other children picked wild blackberries, which her grandmother baked into what Reese recalls as "soulful" cobblers.

After college, in 2008, while Reese was teaching social studies and coaching track and field at an all-girls public school in Atlanta, she had a conversation with two young athletes that would inspire her later research. Reese had taken the girls to a clinic for a physical exam and was planning to cook dinner for them afterward. They went shopping together in suburban Cobb County. The girls marveled over Reese's neighborhood store, leading her to realize that even though they lived just a few miles away, they had never seen such bounty.

That same year, after Reese had taught her students about civil disobedience, they proposed a boycott of the cafeteria to protest its scant offerings. Reese's one condition was that no classmate went hungry. "If someone can't bring their lunch, then someone needs to bring an extra lunch," she remembers telling them. The students' efforts eventually led to a meeting with a school district representative, after which the school got a salad bar.

Those stories—about the power of food to widen inequalities *and* to 15 bring people together—were on Reese's mind when she entered graduate school at American University in Washington, D.C., and began studying Deanwood. It was 2012, and Reese was interested in how the neighborhood's food geography affected people's diets. Her first impulse was to ask neighbors about the contents of their pantries. That's not, however, what they wanted to talk about.

Instead, they began with history: the time when they had several grocery options, walked to shops, gardened in their yards, and bought produce from "hucksters" selling from wagons and trucks. "There were some gendered memories, too, around women and cooking, and remembering a time when mothers were home to do that," Reese says. (Chandler, for instance, recalls how rigorously she learned to cook: "That shucking of the corn—you had to do it precisely. You had to snap the peas in a given way.")

Throughout Reese's interviews, "the theme of community ran through quite strongly," she says. This was, and is, part of Deanwood's identity. The neighborhood took shape in the late 19th and early 20th centuries, as African-American architects, drafters, and carpenters designed and built single-family wood-frame houses on farmland once worked by slaves. It was also home to the Suburban Gardens Amusement Park, a destination for African-American families who were barred from whites-only parks. On the historical markers that dot its streets, Deanwood residents are described as "a self-reliant people."

This self-reliance is communal, not individualistic. "One of the elders was telling me about how he didn't remember there being homelessness in Deanwood in the past like there is now," Reese says. "It wasn't because people weren't transient. It's just that someone would always take them in."

Shortly after Reese began her fieldwork, she attended a conference where, for the first time, she heard scholars criticize the food desert model. Their arguments, along with Reese's Deanwood interviews, forced her to reconsider some of the assumptions she had brought into graduate school.

The food desert concept originated in Great Britain in the 1990s. 20 According to the *BMJ* (formerly the *British Medical Journal*), a public housing resident in Scotland reputedly first used the phrase, presumably to describe their surrounding neighborhood. Prime Minister Tony Blair's government adopted the term—despite warnings of thin data.

Much like his U.S. counterpart, President Bill Clinton, Blair advocated a moderate, market-driven political approach that he called the Third Way. The concept of food deserts fit neatly into his script: Incentives and public-private partnerships could "solve" the problem by helping to build groceries in depressed areas.

The metaphor found fans in the United States, too, as an alternative to blaming poor and working-class people for conditions like obesity. "Many of the debates over food and health disparities, especially if you look at the pop-culture debates, they're so individualistic," says Alison Alkon, a sociologist at the University of the Pacific in Stockton,

California. "They're focused on 'Why do you not have the willpower to put down the McDonald's and go exercise?'" (Even health professionals share these biases: In a 2003 survey of U.S. physicians, 44 percent called obese people "weak-willed" and 30 percent described them as "lazy.")

The desert metaphor challenged these stereotypes about individual behavior. "'Food deserts' makes it a structural issue that has to do with urban development and redlining and economic history," Alkon says. "Obviously, it's a step forward."

In 2010, U.S. President Barack Obama launched the Healthy Food Financing Initiative, designed to "eliminate food deserts" in part by using grants and low-interest loans to build supermarkets. The initiative was later incorporated into the 2014 Farm Bill.

But by then many academics, includ-25 ing Alkon, and activists were calling the metaphor inadequate and misleading. Yes, swaths of urban America have been abandoned by the supermarket industry. But that doesn't explain the link between wealth and nutrition.

The real explanations are multilayered and complicated. They're partly financial: Healthy food costs more (perhaps, some critics suggest, because U.S. farm policies subsidize commodity crops like corn and soy, which are used to make processed foods), and even small price differences can break the budget of a low-income family. In addition, the complications of poverty and racism—crowded housing, job discrimination, longer commutes, diminished educational opportunities, and greater overall emotional stress, to name a few—make it harder to act on public health messages.

The factors are partly geographic, too, but not just in terms of supermarkets. During her studies, Reese discovered the work of Naa Oyo A. Kwate, an associate professor of human ecology and Africana studies at Rutgers University in New Brunswick, New Jersey. Kwate has mapped the distribution of cheap, unhealthy fast food in New York and found an overabundance in black neighborhoods. "Segregation fosters a weak retail climate and a surplus of low-wage labor, both of which make the proliferation of fast food probable," Kwate wrote in a 2008 paper.

It's no surprise, then, that several studies have drawn the same conclusion: Introducing a supermarket to a depressed area does little to improve people's diets. Two food-policy scholars, Nathan Rosenberg and Nevin Cohen, argue that the real solutions lie in "upstream interventions" that address inequality: a higher minimum wage, stronger labor protections, more generous government benefits, and universal free school lunches. "There are no shortcuts to eliminating food poverty," they wrote in a recent article in the *Fordham Urban Law Journal*.

On the afternoon that we visit Deanwood, Reese cuts an elegant, fluorescent figure: lime-green nail polish, blue lipstick, and red-highlighted Marley twists piled into a bun. Because the neighborhood has so few restaurants, we first meet for lunch six miles away, near the Catholic University of America. Over shrimp and grits, she tells me about her fieldwork.

While interviewing residents, Reese says, she heard a consistent racial 30 critique. "No matter what age, [they] felt that Deanwood doesn't have as many options because it is predominantly black," she says. "Almost everyone articulated that."

She also found that Deanwood's residents talked about how they *continue* to eat well by working together. Reese tells me about a community garden at a public housing complex just outside the neighborhood's boundaries that produced vegetables such as kale, eggplant, and peppers. "They're growing in these six raised beds on city land, which they may or may not have permission to do," she says. Unlike many other such gardens, this one didn't have individual plots. "There was no lock on the gate. People could come in and take whatever they wanted. . . . There was one man who would use stuff from the garden to make big pots of soup at the end of the month, when people's money was low, and just share it."

Other ways people discussed self-reliance were more mundane. They patronized the one black-owned corner store in Deanwood that sold deli meats, canned beans, and some fresh produce. They organized ride shares, especially for elders, to supermarkets outside their neighborhood. They turned old automobiles into unlicensed cabs, which they parked outside the Safeway to spare shoppers a 30-minute walk with heavy bags. (Not many taxis served the area.)

Such self-reliant solutions often become invisible in discussions of food deserts. Semantically, the word "desert" is loaded; it's often paired with "barren" or "wasteland." One study from Australia noted that desert dwellers are often viewed as "marginalized" people who live off subsidies from the mainstream.

In her research, Reese met scholars and activists who argued that the food desert metaphor is equally freighted. Monica White, an assistant professor of environmental justice at the University of Wisconsin, Madison, points out that, even though the term has reduced the tendency to blame poor nutrition on individuals and their "lack of willpower," it's also shifted culpability to the neighborhood as a whole. "Somehow the community is at fault," she says.

That fault-finding can come from within. Reese discovered that 35 some Deanwood residents pointed to generational failings. I remembered that finding when Chandler talked about her own youth: "Soups, dumplings—women made things from scratch. And these young women barely know how to open the microwave."

On the flip side, food deserts wrongly imply a geographical determinism — an inevitable surrender to processed and fast food, says Dara Cooper, an organizer for the National Black Food and Justice Alliance, who has influenced Reese's scholarship. "So often, black communities are referenced" — by policymakers and even liberal advocates—"as passive, empty receptacles . . . completely ignoring what communities are doing themselves to drive solutions."

The solutions Reese witnessed in Deanwood are relatively modest. Elsewhere, communities have mounted more ambitious responses. In Oakland, California, Mandela Grocery, a worker-owned market, sources food from local farmers and offers deep discounts to families that use food stamps. Freedom Farmers' Market, also in Oakland, specializes in traditional foods grown by African-Americans.

But self-reliance has its limits. It's rare that local fixes meet the needs of an entire community, in part because they don't eradicate those big upstream woes. That's why it's also important to document the way African-American communities have been abandoned. "Supermarket executives know that people are resilient, because people need food and they're going to get food no matter what," Reese says. "Just because I'm focusing on the ways that people are able to get food despite corporate failures does not let corporations off the hook."

What happened in Deanwood was both city-specific and part of a larger exodus occurring in black neighborhoods around the country. After World War II, restrictive covenants, like the one barring home sales to "negroes" and to "Jews, Hebrews, Armenians, Persians, and Syrians," began easing up in the District—aided, in part, by a 1948 Supreme Court ruling that declared the covenants unenforceable. That opened up more of the city to Jewish grocery owners. Then, in 1972, the District Grocery Stores co-op, formed in 1921 to strengthen the Jewish community's buying power and fight anti-Semitism in the food industry, shut down. Merchants blamed competition from supermarkets, which had extended their hours to evenings and Sundays, along with a spike in crime.

"The small stores used to stay in business by staying open late at 40 night," one grocer told *The Washington Post*. "Now the only thing to wait for at night is someone with a gun."

Meanwhile, supermarket executives were plotting their exodus from minority neighborhoods nationwide. Reese studied industry trade publications and discovered discussion of "embattled cities" as early as the 1960s. "Several chains have 'had it,'" said a 1967 article in *Modern Grocer*, explaining that "chronic lawlessness" was forcing company executives to "reduce or eliminate entirely stores in . . . riot torn areas."

Deanwood's Safeway closed in 1980. For a few years, a black-owned grocery chain called Super Pride operated in the same building, drawing shoppers from around the region with traditional offerings like collards and hog maws (stomachs). It struggled, however, in the mid-1980s, when the nearby public housing complex was emptied for renovation. A few years later, the store was gone. (Another followed, Chandler says, but only briefly.)

By then, supermarket planners were coming to favor the ample square footage and easy parking of suburban strip malls. Stores were disappearing from urban neighborhoods, particularly those with large African-American populations. In 1984, *Mother Jones* reported that Safeway had closed 600 stores, many of them in inner cities, over the previous five years. Hartford, Connecticut, the same article noted, had lost 11 of its 13 chains since 1968.

Store locations, Reese concluded from her research, reflect larger patterns of racial segregation. (Even well-off African-American neighborhoods have fewer stores than their white counterparts, she noted.) "Want to know how/what inequality looks like in your city?" she wrote in a Twitter thread in January. "Trace the opening and closing of supermarkets."

"Welcome to Deanwood," Reese says after lunch, as I steer my rental 45 car onto Nannie Helen Burroughs Avenue. The road's namesake emblematizes the neighborhood's self-reliance: In 1909, Burroughs founded the National Training School for Women and Girls, which educated its mostly working-class black students in everything from power-machine operation to missionary work and didn't solicit funds from white donors.

We park in front of the black-owned corner store that residents had regarded fondly. This was Reese's first visit to Deanwood since the owner died three months earlier. She enters first, without me, and comes out crestfallen. The new management has gotten rid of the small vegetable section and erected a shield of Plexiglas in front of the cash register. The shelves offer little more than beer, canned soup, and snack foods, plus a few errant bags of flour.

"It looks like what we think of as a corner store now, in a way that it didn't look before," she says. "That catches me completely off-guard." She lets out a long, audible sigh.

We continue on to the public housing community. It's a vast complex of brick buildings laid out in hilly tiers. Outside, young men play basketball and an ice cream truck ("which may or may not be a real ice cream truck," Reese says) makes slow rounds. The complex is slated for demolition, and many of its buildings are boarded up. Despite policy efforts intended to "eliminate food deserts," no new stores have come to this neighborhood. In truth, interventions would need to target the damage of structural inequality, poverty, and racism to make meaningful change. In the meantime, the people of Deanwood have to find their own fixes.

We climb some concrete steps to view the garden Reese had described over lunch. All that remain are a single fallow bed and a waterlogged patch of dandelions and grass.

"I'm sorry," I say.   50

Reese laughs sadly. She uses the moment to reflect on what she calls the "limits of self-reliance." Even the Freedom Farm Cooperative, she observes, which civil rights leader Fannie Lou Hamer founded in Mississippi in 1969 as a model of community-based economic development, shut down after four years as external funding dried up.

Reese isn't totally surprised by this outcome. But it still hurts to see it on her return visit. "I am just going to get my heart broken in a bunch of different ways today," she says, surveying the ruins.

Understanding the Text

1. According to Yeoman, why is Ashanté Reese interested in Alice Chandler's story?
2. What is a "food desert," and why is it called this?
3. Why do some scholars (like Ashanté Reese) reject the term "food desert" to describe particular communities? What do they think it ignores?

Reflection and Response

4. How was Alice Chandler's upbringing similar to or different from your own? Compare her family's relationships with food production and consumption to your family's. What do you learn about yourself from this comparison?
5. According to Yeoman, why is it important for researchers to "document the way African American communities have been abandoned" (par. 38)? How does he use this example to discuss the relationship between food and race?
6. Yeoman emphasizes that Ashanté Reese values describing the problem of food access accurately: "'Language matters,' says Reese" (par. 10). Why is Reese so passionate about this? What problems occur when the wrong words are used to describe a problem?

Making Connections

7. Compare Yeoman's use of scholarly research with Joe Pinsker's ("Why So Many Rich Kids Come to Enjoy the Taste of Healthier Foods," p. 97). Why do you think they use the studies that they do? How do the various studies problematize conventional views about poverty, food access, and food culture?

8. Describe the early life experiences that inspired the direction of Ashanté Reese's research. Then think about how Stephen Satterfield ("I'm a Black Food Writer. Here's Why We Need More Like Me," p. 131) would see these experiences. What would Satterfield value? And why?

9. Yeoman suggests that we must consider "upstream interventions" (par. 28) to counter the negative influences of poverty and racism on food culture, food access, and health. What are "upstream interventions" and why is it so difficult and complex to implement them? Use Yeoman's argument and the work of Margaret Mead ("The Changing Significance of Food," p. 138), Joe Pinsker ("Why So Many Rich Kids Come to Enjoy the Taste of Healthier Foods," p. 97), Stephen Satterfield ("I'm a Black Food Writer. Here's Why We Need More Like Me," p. 131), and David H. Freedman ("How Junk Food Can End Obesity," p. 75) to support your response.

10. What is self-reliance, and why do you think Yeoman focuses on its role in the food culture of the neighborhoods discussed in this essay? What role does Yeoman suggest that self-reliance can play in improving food access and public health? Why is this solution powerful? What are its limitations? Explore the relationship between self-reliance and food culture by contrasting Yeoman's representation of this relationship with Taffy Brodesser-Akner's ("Why I've Never Learned How to Cook," p. 124).

Liver and Opinions: Why We Eat What We Eat and Despise the Rest

Mary Roach

Mary Roach is known for her lively, humorous, and illuminating treatment of taboo subjects about the human body. She graduated from Wesleyan with a degree in psychology before heading to San Francisco, where she worked as a freelance copy editor and a public relations consultant for the San Francisco Zoological Society. Eventually she began writing humor pieces and first-person essays in a variety of popular magazines, including *Vogue*, *National Geographic*, *Outside Magazine*, and *The New York Times Magazine*. She has published six highly regarded books, including *Grunt: The Curious Science of Humans at War* (2016), *Gulp: Adventures on the Alimentary Canal* (2013), *Packing for Mars: The Curious Science of Life in the Void* (2010), and *Stiff: The Curious Lives of Human Cadavers* (2003). Roach's gift as a writer is her ability to turn complex subjects into something average readers can understand and enjoy reading about, despite her having no formal academic background in science. In this excerpt from *Gulp*, Roach does just that.

The Northern Food Tradition and Health Resource Kit contains a deck of forty-eight labeled photographs of traditional Inuit foods. Most are meat, but none are steaks. Seal Heart, one is labeled. Caribou Brain, says another. The images, life-size where possible, are printed on stiff paper and die-cut, like paper dolls that you badly want to throw some clothes on. The kit I looked through belonged to Gabriel Nirlungayuk, a community health representative from Pelly Bay, a hamlet in Canada's Nunavut territory. Like me, he was visiting Igloolik—a town on a small island near Baffin Island—to attend an Arctic athletic competition.* With him was Pelly Bay's mayor at the time, Makabe Nartok. The three of us met by chance in the kitchen of Igloolik's sole lodgings, the Tujormivik Hotel.

Nirlungayuk's job entailed visiting classrooms to encourage young Inuit "chip-aholics and pop-aholics" to eat like their elders. As the number of Inuit who hunt has dwindled, so has the consumption of organs (and

---

*The Inuit Games. Most are indoor competitions originally designed to fit in igloos. Example: the Ear Lift: "On a signal, the competitor walks forward lifting the weight off the floor and carrying it with his ear for as far a distance as his ear will allow." For the Mouth Pull, opponents stand side by side, shoulders touching and arms around each other's necks as if they were dearest friends. Each grabs the outside corner of his opponent's mouth with his middle finger and attempts to pull him over a line drawn in the snow between them. As so often is the case in life, "strongest mouth wins."

other anatomy not available for purchase at the Igloolik Co-op: tendons, blubber, blood, head).

I picked up the card labeled Caribou Kidney, Raw. "Who actually eats this?"

"I do," said Nirlungayuk. He is taller than most Inuit, with a prominent, thrusting chin that he used to indicate Nartok. "He does."

Anyone who hunts, the pair told me, eats organs. Though the Inuit 5 (in Canada, the term is preferred over *Eskimo*) gave up their nomadic existence in the 1950s, most adult men still supplemented the family diet with hunted game, partly to save money. In 1993, when I visited, a small can of Spork, the local Spam, cost $2.69. Produce arrives by plane. A watermelon might set you back $25. Cucumbers were so expensive that the local sex educator did his condom demonstrations on a broomstick.

I asked Nartok to go through the cutouts and show me what he ate. He reached across the table to take them from me. His arms were pale to the wrist, then abruptly brown. The Arctic suntan could be mistaken, at a glance, for gloves. He peered at the cutouts through wire-rim glasses. "Caribou liver, yes. Brain. Yes, I eat brain. I eat caribou eyes, raw and cooked." Nirlungayuk looked on, nodding.

"I like this part very much." Nartok was holding a cutout labeled Caribou Bridal Veil. This is a prettier way of saying "stomach membrane." It was dawning on me that eating the whole beast was a matter not just of economics but of preference. At a community feast earlier in the week, I was offered "the best part" of an Arctic char. It was an eye, with fat and connective tissue dangling off the back like wiring on a headlamp. A cluster of old women stood by a chain-link fence digging marrow from caribou bones with the tilt-headed focus nowadays reserved for texting.

For Arctic nomads, eating organs has, historically, been a matter of survival. Even in summer, vegetation is sparse. Little beyond moss and lichen° grows abundantly on the tundra. Organs are so vitamin-rich, and edible plants so scarce, that the former are classified, for purposes of Arctic health education, both as "meat" and as "fruits and vegetables." One serving from the Fruits and Vegetables Group in Nirlungayuk's materials is "½ cup berries or greens, or 60 to 90 grams of organ meats."

Nartok shows me an example of Arctic "greens": cutout number 13, Caribou Stomach Contents. Moss and lichen are tough to digest, unless, like caribou, you have a multichambered stomach in which to ferment them. So the Inuit let the caribou have a go at it first. I thought of Pat Moeller and what he'd said about wild dogs and other predators eating

---

lichen: a plantlike organism that grows on rocks or walls in a symbiotic relationship.

the stomachs and stomach contents of their prey first. "And wouldn't we all," he'd said, "be better off."

If we could strip away the influences of modern Western culture and media and the high-fructose, high-salt temptations of the junk-food sellers, would we all be eating like Inuit elders, instinctively gravitating to the most healthful, nutrient-diverse foods? Perhaps. It's hard to say. There is a famous study from the 1930s involving a group of orphanage babies who, at mealtimes, were presented with a smorgasbord of thirty-four whole, healthy foods. Nothing was processed or prepared beyond mincing or mashing. Among the more standard offerings — fresh fruits and vegetables, eggs, milk, chicken, beef — the researcher, Clara Davis, included liver, kidney, brains, sweetbreads°, and bone marrow. The babies shunned liver and kidney (as well as all ten vegetables, haddock°, and pineapple), but brains and sweetbreads did *not* turn up among the low-preference foods she listed. And the most popular item of all? Bone marrow.

At half past ten, the sky was princess pink. There was still enough light to make out the walrus appliqués on the jacket of a young girl riding her bicycle on the gravel road through town. We were joined in the kitchen by a man named Marcel, just back from a hunting camp where a pod of narwhal° had been spotted earlier in the day. The narwhal is a medium-sized whale with a single tusk protruding from its head like a birthday candle.

Marcel dropped a white plastic bag onto the table. It bounced slightly on landing. "Muktuk," Nirlungayuk said approvingly. It was a piece of narwhal skin, uncooked. Nartok waved it off. "I ate muktuk earlier. Whole lot." In the air he outlined a square the size of a hardback book.

Nirlungayuk speared a chunk on the tip of a pocketknife blade and held it out for me. My instinct was to refuse it. I'm a product of my upbringing. I grew up in New Hampshire in the 1960s, when meat meant muscle. Breast and thigh, burgers and chops. Organs were something you donated. Kidney was a shape for coffee tables. It did not occur to my people to fix innards for supper, especially raw ones. Raw outards seemed even more unthinkable.

I pulled the rubbery chunk from Nirlungayuk's knife. It was cold from the air outside and disconcertingly narwhal-colored. The taste of muktuk is hard to pin down. Mushrooms? Walnut? There was plenty of time to think about it, as it takes approximately as long to chew narwhal as it does to hunt them. I know you won't believe me, because I didn't believe

10

---

sweetbreads: pancreas or thymus gland of a sheep or calf that is eaten as food.
haddock: a type of fish that is eaten as food, from the cod family.
narwhal: a medium-sized, toothed whale found in the Arctic; the males grow a large sword-like tusk.

Nartok, but muktuk is exquisite (and, again, healthy: as much vitamin A as in a carrot, plus a respectable amount of vitamin C).

I like chicken skin and pork rinds. Why the hesitation over muktuk? 15 Because to a far greater extent than most of us realize, culture writes the menu. And culture doesn't take kindly to substitutions.

What Gabriel Nirlungayuk was trying to do with organs for health, the United States government tried to do for war. During World War II, the U.S. military was shipping so much meat overseas to feed troops and allies that a domestic shortage loomed. According to a 1943 *Breeder's Gazette* article, the American soldier consumed close to a pound of meat a day. Beginning that year, meat on the homefront was rationed—but only the mainstream cuts. You could have all the organ meats you wanted. The army didn't use them because they spoiled more quickly and because, as *Life* put it, "the men don't like them."

> "To a far greater extent than most of us realize, culture writes the menu. And culture doesn't take kindly to substitutions."

Civilians didn't like them any better. Hoping to change this, the National Research Council (NRC) hired a team of anthropologists, led by the venerable Margaret Mead, to study American food habits. How do people decide what's good to eat, and how do you go about changing their minds? Studies were undertaken, recommendations drafted, reports published—including Mead's 1943 opus "The Problem of Changing Food Habits: Report of the Committee on Food Habits," and if ever a case were to be made for word-rationing, there it was.

The first order of business was to come up with a euphemism. People were unlikely to warm to a dinner of "offal" or "glandular meats," as organs were called in the industry.* "Tidbits" turned up here and there—as in *Life's* poetic "Plentiful are these meats called 'tidbits'"—but "variety meats" was the standout winner. It had a satisfactorily vague and cheery air, calling to mind both protein and primetime programming with dance numbers and spangly getups. In the same vein—ew! Sorry. Similarly, meal planners and chefs were encouraged "to give special attention to the naming" of new organ-meat entrées. A little French was thought to help things go down easier. A 1944 *Hotel Management* article included recipes for "Brains à la King" and "Beef Tongue Piquant."

---

*Among themselves, meat professionals speak a jolly slang. "Plucks" are thoracic viscera: heart, lungs, trachea. Spleens are "melts," rumens are "paunch," and unborn calves are "slunks." I once saw a cardboard box outside a New York meat district warehouse with a crude sign taped to it: FLAPS AND TRIANGLES.

A promotional poster by John E. Sheridan, sponsored by the United States Food Administration during war time.

Library of Congress, Prints & Photographs Division, [LC-USZC4-3177]

Another strategy was to target kids. "The human infant enters the world without information about what is edible and what is not," wrote psychologist Paul Rozin, who studied disgust for many years at the University of Pennsylvania. Until kids are around two, you can get them to try pretty much anything, and Rozin did. In one memorable study, he tallied the percentage of children aged sixteen to twenty-nine months who ate or tasted the following items presented to them on a plate: fish eggs (60 percent), dish soap (79 percent), cookies topped with ketchup (94 percent), a dead (sterilized) grasshopper (30 percent), and artfully coiled peanut butter scented with Limburger cheese and presented as "dog-doo" (55 percent). The lowest-ranked item, at 15 percent acceptance, was a human hair.*

---

*The children were wise to be wary. Compulsive hair-eaters wind up with trichobezoars — human hairballs. The biggest ones extend from stomach into intestine and look like otters or big hairy turds and require removal by stunned surgeons who run for their cameras and publish the pictures in medical journal articles about "Rapunzel syndrome." Bonus points for reading this footnote on April 27, National Hairball Awareness Day.

By the time children are ten years old, generally speaking, they've 20
learned to eat like the people around them. Once food prejudices are set,
it is no simple task to dissolve them. In a separate study, Rozin presented
sixty-eight American college students with a grasshopper snack, this
time a commercially prepared honey-covered variety sold in Japan. Only
12 percent were willing to try one.

So the NRC tried to get elementary schools involved. Home economists were urged to approach teachers and lunch planners. "Let's do more
than say 'How do you do' to variety meats; let's make friends with them!"
chirps Jessie Alice Cline in the February 1943 *Practical Home Economics*.
The War Food Administration pulled together a *Food Conservation Education* brochure with suggested variety-meat essay themes ("My Adventures in Eating New Foods"). Perhaps sensing the futility of trying to get
ten-year-olds to embrace brains and hearts, the administration focused
mainly on not wasting food. One suggested student activity took the
form of "a public display of wasted edible food actually found in the garbage dump," which does more than say "How do you do" to a long night
of parental phone calls.

The other problem with classroom-based efforts to change eating habits
was that children don't decide what's for dinner. Mead and her team soon
realized they had to get to the person they called the "gatekeeper"—Mom.
Nirlungayuk reached a similar conclusion. I tracked him down, seventeen
years later, and asked him what the outcome of his country-foods campaign had been. "It didn't really work," he said, from his office in the
Nunavut department of wildlife and environment. "Kids eat what parents
make for them. That's one thing I didn't do is go to the parents."

Even that can flop. Mead's colleague Kurt Lewin, as part of the NRC
research, gave a series of lectures to homemakers on the nutritional benefits of organ meats, ending with a plea for patriotic cooperation.* Based
on follow-up interviews, just 10 percent of the women who'd attended
had gone home and prepared a new organ meat for the family. Discussion
groups were more effective than lectures, but guilt worked best of all. "They
said to the women, 'A lot of people are making a lot of sacrifices in this
war,'" says Brian Wansink, author of "Changing Eating Habits on the Home
Front." " 'You can do your part by trying organ meats.' All of a sudden, it
was like, 'Well, I don't want to be the only person not doing my part.'"

Also effective: pledges. Though it now seems difficult to picture it,
Wansink says government anthropologists had PTA members stand up

---

*Meat and patriotism do not fit naturally together, and sloganeering proved a
challenge. The motto "Food Fights for Freedom" would seem to inspire cafeteria
mayhem more than personal sacrifice.

and recite, "I will prepare organ meats at least ___ times in the coming two weeks." "The act of making a public commitment," said Wansink, "was powerful, powerful, powerful." A little context here: The 1940s was the heyday of pledges and oaths.* In Boy Scout halls, homerooms, and Elks lodges, people were accustomed to signing on the dotted line or standing and reciting, one hand raised. Even the Clean Plate Club—dreamed up by a navy commander in 1942—had an oath: "I, ___, being a member in good standing . . . , hereby agree that I will finish all the food on my plate . . . and continue to do so until Uncle Sam has licked the Japs and Hitler"—like, presumably, a plate.

To open people's minds to a new food, you sometimes just have to get them to open their mouths. Research has shown that if people try something enough times, they'll probably grow to like it. In a wartime survey conducted by a team of food-habits researchers, only 14 percent of the students at a women's college said they liked evaporated milk. After serving it to the students sixteen times over the course of a month, the researchers asked again. Now 51 percent liked it. As Kurt Lewin put it, "People like what they eat, rather than eat what they like."   25

The phenomenon starts early. Breast milk and amniotic fluid° carry the flavors of the mother's foods, and studies consistently show that babies grow up to be more accepting of flavors they've sampled while in the womb and while breastfeeding. (Babies swallow several ounces of amniotic fluid a day.) Julie Mennella and Gary Beauchamp of the Monell Chemical Senses Center have done a great deal of work in this area, even recruiting sensory panelists to sniff† amniotic fluid° (withdrawn during

amniotic fluid: liquid in the womb of a pregnant woman that surrounds and provides nutrients to the fetus.

---

*Pledge madness peaked in 1942. The June issue of *Practical Home Economics* reprinted a twenty-item Alhambra, California, Student Council anti-waste pledge that included a promise to "drive carefully to conserve rubber" and another to "get to class on time to save paper on tardy slips." Perhaps more dire than the shortages in metal, meat, paper, and rubber was the "boy shortage" mentioned in an advice column on the same page. "Unless you do something about it, this means empty hours galore!" Luckily, the magazine had some suggestions. An out-of-fashion bouclé suit could be "unraveled, washed, tinted and reknitted" to make baby clothes. Still bored? "Take two worn rayon dresses and combine them to make one Sunday-best that looks brand new"—and fits like a dream if you are a giant insect or person with four arms.

†They are to be excused for not tasting it too. Amniotic fluid contains fetal urine (from swallowed amniotic fluid) and occasionally meconium: baby's first feces, composed of mucus, bile, epithelial cells, shed fetal hair, and other amniotic detritus. The *Wikipedia* entry helpfully contrasts the tarry, olive-brown smear of meconium—photographed in a tiny disposable diaper—with the similarly posed yellowish excretion of a breast-fed newborn, both with an option for viewing in the magnified resolution of 1,280 × 528 pixels.

amniocentesis) and breast milk from women who had and those who hadn't swallowed a garlic oil capsule. Panelists agreed: the garlic-eaters' samples smelled like garlic. (The babies didn't appear to mind. On the contrary, the Monell team wrote, "Infants . . . sucked more when the milk smelled like garlic.")

As a food marketing consultant, Brian Wansink was involved in efforts to increase global consumption of soy products. Whether one succeeds at such an undertaking, he found, depends a great deal on the culture whose diet you seek to change. Family-oriented countries where eating and cooking are firmly bound by tradition — Wansink gives the examples of China, Colombia, Japan, and India — are harder to infiltrate. Cultures like the United States and Russia, where there's less cultural pressure to follow tradition and more emphasis on the individual, are a better bet.

Price matters too, though not always how you think it would. Saving money can be part of the problem. The well-known, long-standing cheapness of offal, Mead wrote, condemned it to the wordy category "edible for human beings but not by own kind of human being." Eating organs, in 1943, could degrade one's social standing. Americans preferred bland preparations of muscle meat partly because for as long as they could recall, that's what the upper class ate.

So powerful are race- and status-based disgusts that explorers have starved to death rather than eat like the locals. British polar exploration suffered heavily for its mealtime snobbery. "The British believed that Eskimo food . . . was beneath a British sailor and certainly unthinkable for a British officer," wrote Robert Feeney in *Polar Journeys: The Role of Food and Nutrition in Early Exploration*. Members of the 1860 Burke and Wills expedition to cross Australia fell prey to scurvy or starved in part because they refused to eat what the indigenous Australians ate. Bugong-moth abdomen and witchetty grub may sound revolting, but they have as much scurvy-battling vitamin C as the same size serving of cooked spinach, with the additional benefits of potassium, calcium, and zinc.

Of all the so-called variety meats, none presents a steeper challenge to 30 the food persuader than the reproductive organs. Good luck to Deanna Pucciarelli, the woman who seeks to introduce mainstream America to the culinary joys of pig balls. "I am indeed working on a project on pork testicles," said Pucciarelli, director of the Hospitality and Food Management Program at — fill my heart with joy! — Ball State University. Because she was bound by a confidentiality agreement, Pucciarelli could not tell me who would be serving them or why or what form they would take. Setting aside alleged fertility enhancers and novelty dare items (for example, "Rocky Mountain oysters"), the reproductive equipment seem to have managed to stay off dinner plates world-wide. Neither I nor Janet

Riley, spokesperson for the American Meat Institute, could come up with a contemporary culture that regularly partakes of ovaries, uterus, penis, or vagina simply as something good to eat.

Historically, there was ancient Rome. Bruce Kraig, president of the Culinary Historians of Chicago, passed along a recipe from *Apicius*, for sow uterus sausage. For a cookbook, *Apicius* has a markedly gladiatorial style. "Remove the entrails° by the throat before the carcass hardens immediately after killing," begins one recipe. Where a modern recipe might direct one to "salt to taste," the uterus recipe says to "add cooked brains, as much as is needed." Sleeter Bull,* the author of the 1951 book *Meat for the Table*, claims the ancient Greeks had a taste for udders. Very specifically, "the udders of a sow just after she had farrowed but before she had suckled her pigs." That is either the cruelest culinary practice in history or so much Sleeter bull.

I would wager that if you look hard enough, you will find a welcoming mouth for any safe source of nourishment, no matter how unpleasant it may strike you. "If we consider the wide range of foods eaten by all human groups on earth, one must . . . question whether any edible material that provides nourishment with no ill effects can be considered inherently disgusting," writes the food scientist Anthony Blake. "If presented at a sufficiently early age with positive reinforcement from the childcarer, it would become an accepted part of the diet." As an example, Blake mentions a Sudanese condiment made from fermented cow urine and used as a flavor enhancer "very much in the way soy sauce is used in other parts of the world."

The comparison was especially apt in the summer of 2005, when a small-scale Chinese operation was caught using human hair instead of soy to make cheap ersatz° soy sauce. Our hair is as much as 14 percent L-cysteine, an amino acid commonly used to make meat flavorings and to elasticize dough in commercial baking. How commonly? Enough to merit debate among scholars of Jewish dietary law, or kashrut.° "Human hair, while not particularly appetizing, is Kosher," states Rabbi Zushe Blech, the author of *Kosher Food Production*, on Kashrut.com. "There is no 'guck' factor," Blech maintained, in an e-mail. Dissolving hair in hydrochloric acid, which creates the L-cysteine, renders it unrecognizable and

---

entrails: internal organs of an animal.
ersatz: artificial or inferior imitation or copy.
kashrut: the state of being kosher, in accordance with Jewish dietary laws.

---

*Bull was chief of the University of Illinois Meats Division and founding patron of the Sleeter Bull Undergraduate Meats Award. Along with meat scholarship, Bull supported and served as grand registrar of the Alpha Gamma Rho fraternity, where they knew a thing or two about undergraduate meats.

sterile. The rabbis' primary concern had not to do with hygiene but with idol worship. "It seems that women would grow a full head of hair and then shave it off and offer it to the idol," wrote Blech. Shrine attendants in India have been known to surreptitiously collect the hair and sell it to wigmakers, and some in kashrut circles worried they might also be selling it to L-cysteine* producers. This proved not to be the case. "The hair used in the process comes exclusively from local barber shops," Blech assures us. *Phew.*

---

*The other common source of L-cysteine is feathers. Blech has a theory that this might explain the medicinal value of chicken soup, a recipe for which can be found in the Gemorah (shabbos 145b) portion of the Talmud. L-cysteine, he says, is similar to the mucus-thinning drug acetylcysteine. And it is found, albeit in lesser amounts, in birds' skin. "Chicken soup and its L-cysteine," Blech said merrily, may indeed be "just what the doctor ordered."

Understanding the Text

1. Why did Arctic nomads eat organs?
2. What does research suggest is the best way to get people to be open to a new food?
3. According to Roach, where do our food preferences come from?

Reflection and Response

4. Locate three places in her essay where Roach comments on the relationship between our food choices and culture, and analyze them. What conclusions can you draw about Roach's understanding of this relationship?
5. Would you try a "grasshopper snack" (par. 20) if you were offered one? Why or why not? What does your answer say about who you are?

Making Connections

6. Look up the study conducted by Clara Davis that Mary Roach mentions. What does it suggest about the relationship between what we eat and who we are? Why do you think Roach finds it so compelling? Do you?
7. Roach discusses a research project led by anthropologist Margaret Mead. Consider Mead's project that Roach mentions and Mead's essay in this book ("The Changing Significance of Food," p. 138). What contributions can anthropology make to our understanding of the expression "we are what we eat"?
8. Roach is known for humor writing in which she writes about taboo subjects using raunchy, distasteful, and unpleasant descriptions to draw readers into her explanations of complex scientific descriptions of bodily functions. Consider the use of humor as a rhetorical strategy. When and why is it useful? Compare Roach's use of humor to Jill McCorkle's ("Her Chee-to Heart," p. 30) and Barbara Kingsolver's ("You Can't Run Away on Harvest Day," p. 150).

Why I've Never Learned How to Cook

Taffy Brodesser-Akner

Taffy Brodesser-Akner was born with the name Stephanie, but her childhood nickname Taffy stuck, and she continues to use it in her professional life. Brodesser-Akner worked as a freelance journalist for a range of publications before becoming a full-time staff writer for *The New York Times* in 2017. While she is mostly known for her writing of celebrity profiles, she published her first novel, *Fleishman is in Trouble*, in 2019. She has won many awards for her celebrity profiles, including multiple New York Press Club awards. In this piece, originally published in *Bon Appétit*, she recalls her experiences learning to cook with a celebrity chef to explore her own relationship with cooking, food, motherhood, and gender expectations.

People have always told me I'm too literal, so in fairness, you should keep that in mind, but here's how it happened: My mother told me, sometime in the early 1980s, as she cleaned breadcrumbs off the table and snot off our faces, that you could have it one way, but not all the ways. You could be someone who cooked, or you could be someone who worked. She was someone who cooked. She made chicken schnitzel and spaghetti and meatballs and fried flounder with creamed spinach, all on rotate. She didn't appear to enjoy cooking for her daughters very much, but we four weren't a rewarding group to cook for. We complained and nagged and fought with each other at the table. She smoked her Kents over the frying pan and talked in Hebrew to her sister and her mother on the phone and just got through it.

She probably meant something else when she said that. She was probably just telling me that there were different categories of existence, and likely she didn't mean for me to take it to heart quite so exactly, but here I am, 41 years old, and I don't cook. I didn't cook after I got married when I was 30, which people told me would magically happen. I didn't cook after I had two kids. I didn't cook after my mother, on a visit after I had a baby, kept the Food Network on nonstop for six weeks, hoping it would take. I didn't cook.

Now, I didn't not cook well. I didn't ever transform foods from their state into other states, or combine them, or pour things on them, or heat them, or mash them. I literally don't even know what other words to use to describe how you treat food when you're cooking it because I don't know how to cook. People would say to me, "How do you get so much done?" And I would say, "Because I don't cook." People would laugh, thinking surely I could cook something, but no. I later learned from my exasperated husband, who does cook (and cooks everything) and says he doesn't really cook, that people who say they don't cook usually cook some stuff. They at least try.

Then a few things happened. I went on a cruise to write a story about Paula Deen, and she asked me what I cook for my children. I told her I didn't cook, and she said, "Then how are your children going to have any memories of you?" I went back to my stateroom and cried. Then, several weeks ago, my seven-year-old son came home from school and asked if I knew who Talya was and if I knew that Talya had two mommies. "Sure," I told him. "I know both of them." He said, "How do they have dinner if there's no daddy in the house? Like, who makes it for them?"

My legend has carried far, and so on occasion, people will cross- 5 examine me to ask if I really don't cook or if I just don't cook anything to brag about. A nice editor at this magazine did the same, and when I told him, he looked at me the way the scientists looked at E.T. when they first found him. He asked if he could set me up with a cooking lesson, maybe with a famous chef. I said I would consider it. I told my husband "what a sexist world we live in where people hear that a woman doesn't cook and the first thing they do is try to fix it." My husband was cooking while I was telling him this, and he threw down a spatula so that it made a great clanking noise. He turned around to me. "So someone is going to pay you to learn how to cook from a famous chef, and you are not going to do it?" People have always told me I'm too literal.

> "What a sexist world we live in where people hear that a woman doesn't cook and the first thing they do is try to fix it."

I called the editor back, and here I was with April Bloomfield, who did not know my legend. (A note on my legend: I have a friend who never saw *The Godfather*, and she would tell people that, and they would say, "You never saw *The Godfather*?" And after all that, after all her years on Earth, it would have been reasonable for her to just stream it one day or watch any of the thousand times per day it's on cable. But now it was something like her brand that she had never seen *The Godfather*, and so she continued not to see it. This is not that. It is important to me that you know that I was never proud of not cooking.)

We were on the top floor of the Spotted Pig, April's restaurant in New York's West Village, in a room where they hold events. I told her the story: my mother, and then the people who told me that after you get married you just magically learn to cook, then my kids. Cooking just didn't seem rewarding to me. Look at the business I was in, I told her. I dealt in words that were put onto parchment that would exist forever.

Her business seemed ephemeral° to me: We would cook this, and it would be gone, and we'd have nothing to show for it. And then, just a little later, we'd be hungry again. I couldn't bear it.

She gave me a funny look and some suggestions for why learning how to cook wouldn't be so bad, how it could become permanent. "Well, you know, your kids will grow up, and they'll realize how hard you work in the kitchen."

"And what good will that do?"

She gave me another funny look. "You really don't know how to 10 cook?" It would be about 30 minutes and 17,000 of my stupid questions before she realized I wasn't messing with her.

There were two dead chickens on the counter, ready for us to season and roast. They had been fed marigolds and bugs in their life, which, she explained to me, would help them make the best possible chicken for us to eat.

We talked about tastes that went well together: "You know, like onions and sage, or anchovy and lamb, they're all kind of classic combinations." I took notes and nodded. How did you learn that? Just from "eating and cooking, you know," she said. Same funny look.

We tied up the chicken, which we did so that it wouldn't look like a crime-scene chicken, splayed° out lasciviously.° Then she pointed out parts of the chicken. She showed me the parson's nose. The what's nose, I asked. "Maybe in America you guys call it the pope's nose?" she said. Again I tried to explain to her that I was not a candidate for knowing what a certain piece of chicken was called beyond what you could specify in a bucket order.

She showed me further around the animal, the wishbone and the wings and the top of the neck and where you should put everything, how you should tuck it in together so it makes the smallest ball it could. She used phrases like "pull the skin" and "push the thighs." Me, I enjoyed euphemism.° I preferred cuts of meat that were called "hamburger" or "steak" and that didn't acknowledge the living existence of the thing. We were going to have one whole chicken and cut the other into parts, but she saw that talking about the chicken with such intimacy had caused me to break out into a light layer of sweat. She looked at me looking at the chicken.

She had always loved butchery, she told me. She'd happened into all 15 of this cooking as an accident. Growing up in Birmingham, England,

ephemeral: lasting only a very short time.
splayed: spread out and displayed.
lasciviously: overtly and offensively.
euphemism: an indirect or mild substitution of one word for another that is considered harsh or distasteful.

she'd wanted to be a policewoman, patrolling a community, but she missed the deadline on some forms and followed her sisters to cooking school instead.

She took a look at me and told me the chickens would go into the oven whole. "We'll take it easy," she said, because she is extraordinarily kind.

We preheated the oven to 350°, though sometimes if your oven isn't hot enough, you have to heat it to 375°. I asked her how I would know if the oven was hot enough. She said I should buy a thermometer. We seasoned the chickens with salt. You could put lemons or garlic in there too, she said. You can chop them up and stick them right up the chicken's ass with bay leaf and fennel. Later, when the chicken finished cooking, we would extract these things and turn them into sauce, so the chicken would be cooked in a form of auto-cannibalism that I think is what others just call "in its own juices."

Our goal was to make an entire meal, so we got to work cutting vegetables: carrots and parsnips and fennel. We shoved some into the chicken's ass (there's probably a word for this, but I didn't think to ask), but only enough so that the vegetables could breathe. Ideally, everything would turn out maximally chicken-y; to do that, the vegetables had to have a real moment with the chicken while we distilled the chicken to its most essential chickeniness. April loves chickeniness. Every time we tasted something or smelled something, April would say, "See how chicken-y?" And it was. But more than that, there was her pride for being able to make it so.

I asked her what size the vegetables should be cut into. "Well, medium," she said. If they're too big they won't cook well, and you don't want to start with "pissy little bits of veg."

But how big is medium, I wanted to know. Was there a way to quan- 20 tify it? Can I take a picture? I needed to have a skill when this was done. Maybe they were the size of my two thumbs put together. Would that be a good way to remember? How much time, and what do you do if this goes wrong, and how did she know that she could use Madeira instead of Marsala and olive oil instead of butter?

I was hot and overwhelmed. When I was young I could bear not knowing things. Now I realized that something as basic as roast chicken was going to be my undoing. She answered all of my questions gamely, but in the end, she said this: "Yes, but you know how it goes with practice. The practice is necessary." She was being gentle. "You should feel comfortable making mistakes because that's how you learn." She was saying that I shouldn't be afraid to start without knowing everything. There was no way to do this without screwing it up first. Look at her, all these years, and look at the burn marks on her arms. Look at the chickens she sometimes still has to throw away.

We continued to cut fennel in silence. Did she understand how endless this was? Did she understand how often children, particularly seven- and nine-year-old boys, needed to eat? If I somehow proved competent at cooking, did she realize how much I'd be on the hook for it? Children, people, need to eat every few hours, the most extraordinary inefficiency that the human body has. This would become my life. I could bear some of that. What I couldn't bear was that time plus the mistake time. The chickens in the garbage. The time with nothing to show for it.

I didn't feel like I had time to make mistakes; I was too old. I now had a keen sense of just how short life is. April went to cooking school on a lark when she was 16. She had time to figure it out. She had had time to make mistakes before she knew that time wasn't endless. I would just be starting.

We roasted more vegetables that weren't inside the chicken until they had a char on one side that extracted some sugar and made them sweet. The parsnips went into the pan too, but the fennel was an entirely different animal and had to go in later. The first time I bought a parsnip it was because it looked like something that belonged in soup. Yes, now I remembered. When I was young and lived out of my house for the first time, I used to try to make vegetable soup. I tried to make soup two or three times a week in my dorm. Sometimes it was okay, and sometimes it wasn't. That wasn't so bad. Eventually we pulled the chickens out briefly so we could give them a vegetablectomy and add those maximally chicken-y vegetables to the others in the pan.

The chickens went back into the oven, and every few minutes, April 25 would open the door and pull them out and turn them. "Look at that skin," she said. It was browning in some parts. It smelled incredible. This chicken, just a chicken made for demonstrative purposes. It wouldn't be served at a restaurant. I would take some home to my husband and children. Then it would be gone. And still, look how much she cared. Look how much pride she took in her work. There was no name on it and it wouldn't last forever, but right then it was the most important food. I was so moved by that. I was so moved at the care and devotion for the food of just one meal.

When we were done, we ate some of it. We couldn't believe how good it was. There is nothing like watching a chef eat her own food. I told her that and she said, "No, this is your food. You made it." I told her I would invite her over to my house when I figured out how to make this on my own after a few tries. She said that she would be there, and she hugged me goodbye and asked an assistant to bring me a cappuccino. "It's been a long day so far," she said. It was 2 p.m.

Ten days later I would stand over another dead, naked chicken, not quite remembering how we did it all: How we wiped sweat from our brows with our hands full of chicken, how the chicken was made into its most manifest chickeniness, which way you were supposed to tie it, how I had a goal and I achieved it in the space of two hours. I would drop the chicken by accident and google whether or not I could still eat it, then realize my hands were full of chicken afterlife when I typed and so googled how to clean a keyboard. I would burn the parsnip, unable to find the sweetness. But then 24 days later, I would do this again, this time just with chicken parts and some carrots, and I was able to remember how the carrots were supposed to turn out: bright orange, brighter than they had been raw, but soft without being mushy.

On that day, my kids sat down at the table. I served them the food. They ate a couple of bites of the carrots. My older son said they were too hard. The younger one said he didn't like the "burny" parts. Then they ate the chicken. They put it in the sauce and mindlessly put it in their mouths. They said nothing qualitative about it. I asked what they thought. They didn't answer me because they were fighting about Minecraft, how important it is to procure iron before nightfall. The older one ate a breast; the younger one had a drumstick. They left the table to play basketball. Mom: I'm sorry.

But at the Spotted Pig that afternoon, that hadn't happened yet. No, that afternoon, having said goodbye to April, I sat at the counter, drinking that cappuccino. Her assistants came in to clean up our mess and set up for whatever was going to happen next. As they did, they took giant hunks of chicken with their hands and ate them, and they popped carrots and fennel into their mouths. The food made its way into their bodies, where it became a part of them forever.

Understanding the Text

1. Why did Brodesser-Akner never learn to cook?
2. How has Brodesser-Akner's identity as someone who does not cook shaped her life?

Reflection and Response

3. What does Paula Deen suggest about the relationship between motherhood, cooking, food, and memory when she responds to Brodesser-Akner's statement that she doesn't cook for her children by saying, "Then how are your children going to have any memories of you?" (par. 4)? Does this resonate with you? Why or why not?

4. What does Brodesser-Akner learn about herself while cooking with a famous chef? Can you empathize with her reflections? Why or why not?

5. Brodesser-Akner was moved by the devotion that April Bloomfield put into the preparation of one meal. Track the various emotional states that Brodesser-Akner describes in her narrative. What role do they play in the story?

Making Connections

6. Michael Pollan ("Eat Food: Food Defined," p. 10) argues that we should not eat anything that our great grandmothers would not recognize as food. Why do you think he calls out grandmothers instead of grandfathers? What does this say about the gendered nature of food culture? How do the comments made by Brodesser-Akner's children complicate our gendered cultural expectations around food?

7. Brodesser-Akner and Stephen Satterfield ("I'm a Black Food Writer. Here's Why We Need More Like Me," p. 131) both write about food to comment on larger cultural expectations and social conditions. Go online and research the history and genre of food writing. What role does writing play in food culture? What does the variety and abundance of food writing suggest about U.S. culture more widely?

I'm a Black Food Writer. Here's Why We Need More Like Me

Stephen Satterfield

Stephen Satterfield worked as a restaurant manager and a sommelier before he became a food writer, activist, and media producer interested in how people connect to food systems and food culture. He was the 2016 Culinary Trust Fellow for *Civil Eats*, a nonprofit news organization covering issues that connect sustainable agriculture, social justice, and our food system, and is cofounder of Whetstone Media, a multimedia company that uses the stories of food to expand human empathy. The following essay explores Satterfield's identity as a black food writer and reflects on what his experiences teach us about U.S. food culture more generally.

"Outside-the-perimeter" is Atlanta nomenclature for the burbs. It refers to a 60ish-mile looping interstate that encircles the city. On the eastern side of the loop is Clarkston, Georgia, where I grew up: a modest multicultural town of thousands that, even among Atlantans, is not well known. Refugees from all over the world settled there in the nineties, so we were always flanked by Ethiopians and Somalis, Jamaicans with their heavily-spiced grilled chicken. I recall sour foods in unfamiliar packages at the Teyf household, who were from Russia.

Things changed in middle school. Against my wishes, I was sent to The Westminster Schools: a mostly-white, Christian school whose campus and endowment would humble most universities. There was no bus to Westminster, just my father driving us all the way across town, to the wealthy Northwest corner of the city. It was there that I really learned all the ways in which black was different. Even as I tried to assimilate, the reminders of otherness were strewn everywhere: in sports (where I was expected to excel), in finance, in social strata, in educational background, in music, and so on.

That's a common thing for minorities, I suspect. In mostly-white communities, you become an ambassador° for your race. The stakes are high, and you try hard not to screw it up for the ones behind you. This was how it felt to be a black student, and later, as a black restaurant manager, sommelier,° and now, as a food writer. Whether you hate it or embrace it, the conflict is impossible to divorce. Even if you don't acknowledge it, you are bound to it.

ambassador: an authorized representative.
sommelier: the waiter in a restaurant who is in charge of wine selections.

I left Atlanta just about as soon as I could. I was so eager, I moved to Oregon—a state I'd never been to, but whose Douglas fir-lined roads satisfied the primary criteria of getting as far away from home as possible. By 19, I had enrolled in culinary school in Portland. Every Saturday morning, I'd spend hours walking in circles at the Portland Farmers Market. It was in Oregon that I was exposed to the most defining revelation of my life: witnessing the connection between restaurant and agriculture. Before long, I had a sommelier certification and started managing restaurants. My youthfulness, and certainly my race, consistently baffled patrons asking for someone in charge, an expert.

A common part of the black experience is once you've reached any level of authority, it is often met with skepticism or surprise. Black chefs know this well: we must validate our presence, where others exist unquestioned. And what does it mean to be a black food writer? It means that you'll never just be a food writer, you'll be a black food writer. It will come up lots of times, maybe not every time, but in lots of ways, the way race does in just about every other facet of our lives.

People make all kinds of assumptions about food writers, but fundamentally, that they are academic, learned, polished. I am academic, learned, polished. But when people construct this image, they don't see a black person, because, when they look around in real life, there are not that many black people writing about food. It then becomes even more important that I do—if only so those who feel unwelcome in this space see someone who looks like them and are compelled to go forth.

The state of food culture in this country makes it a unique time to talk about all this. Undoubtedly we're living in a golden era of food, exemplified by knowledge, interest, and access, fanned by technology and travel. Over the last three decades, restaurants have evolved from convenience to fringe cultural interest to a primary form of entertainment for urbanites and millennials. Chefs, and to some degree, food professionals at every rung of the restaurant experience, have all been the beneficiary of expanding social capital and adoration. Working in food doesn't mean what it used to—though, with a $2.13 federal hourly wage for tipped workers, there are reminders.

Working in food doesn't look like it used to, either: from the 17th century until the latter part of the 20th, the notion of a white male as a professional cook was not only dishonorable, it was unfathomable. Many African-Americans left the kitchen because earning their civil rights meant they could pursue other careers, not just the one they'd been confined to.

In a matter of decades, restaurants have gone from the domain of the diminished—who couldn't even enter the same door as the guests at the place they worked—to the domain of the revered. The exodus of black kitchen labor necessitated a supplemental workforce, and it doesn't require intimate knowledge of food service to understand that many of those workers are from Mexico and other parts of Central America. As Anthony Bourdain famously said in 2007, "The bald fact is that the entire restaurant industry in America would close down overnight, would never recover, if current immigration laws were enforced quickly and thoroughly across the board."

It's made for a complicated convergence.° U.S. kitchens staff much   11 fewer African-Americans, though many of our nation's formative foods and traditions come from their recent ancestors. Latino workers, we know, are the fulcrum of the kitchen. Without them, there would be no kitchen, no ingredients. Wedged uncomfortably in the mix is the ascent of European-trained chefs and their ultimate influence as arbiters of food culture. When the gaze of celebrity does not extend to all national or cultural boundaries, we are left to assume one of these ancestries is superior to the others. Even the most benevolent analysis of this imbalance leaves us with a gloomy conclusion.

Diversity improves culture. This is particularly true with food. But when a chef becomes an authority on a cuisine and does not resemble the people or place that brought it forth, we struggle, because it's a perpetuation of painful erasure.°

It's often said that race is a difficult subject—and it is. But that doesn't mean it shouldn't be talked about. It should be talked with appropriate empathy. Empathy, along with understanding the far-reaching implications of race in our past and present, helps us grow together. Understanding and eating the food of a particular culture is one way to achieve it. In seeing ourselves and our identities so thoroughly cloaked in our diets, food is a fantastic medium to keep us closely attached to a resilient and sometimes tortured ancestry. It is a visceral way to see oneself in a history you may not have realized was your own.

> "In seeing ourselves and our identities so thoroughly cloaked in our diets, food is a fantastic medium to keep us closely attached to a resilient and sometimes tortured ancestry."

It is equally important to acknowledge the history being made in real time. To celebrate the vision of chefs like Nyesha Arrington, or Eduardo Jordan, or Therese Nelson. Preston Clark, Matthew Raiford, Bryant Terry. Tanya Holland, Nelson German.

---

convergence: common result.
erasure: act of ignoring, removing, or obliterating.

Black history is human history. It is all of ours. And like the herring 15
deftly reeled in by slaves on coastal plantations, destined for its
salt-cure—preservation is essential to survival.

Understanding the Text

1. According to Satterfield, why do we need more black food writers?
2. Where and how was Satterfield made to feel "an ambassador" for his race?
3. According to Satterfield, what is the "power of representation," and why does he concentrate on it?

Reflection and Response

4. Why is the "connection between restaurant and agriculture" (par. 5) so meaningful and important to Satterfield? Does this connection resonate with you? Why or why not?
5. How are Satterfield's experiences as a black food writer connected to the state of food culture in the United States?
6. Why does Satterfield argue that it is essential that we talk about the complex connections between race and food?

Making Connections

7. In what way does the history of food culture in the United States mirror the struggle of underrepresented minorities? Consider the work of Satterfield, Lily Wong ("Eating the Hyphen," p. 54), Abaki Beck ("How One Tribe Is Fighting for Their Food Culture in the Face of Climate Change," p. 279), Richard Marosi ("Hardship on Mexico's Farms, a Bounty for U.S. Tables," p. 306), and Selina Wang ("The Future of Farming Is Looking Up," p. 331) to develop your response.
8. Various authors in this collection explore how race, class, and gender affect food culture in the United States. Think about the potential intersections among these categories suggested by various authors. Select two or three authors that you can use to illustrate why we need to think about the intersections among race, class, and gender to better understand U.S. food culture. Write an essay that explores the intersections that you identify.

Claudia Totir/Moment/Getty Images

3 | What Does It Mean to Eat Ethically?

Although larger political, cultural, and socioeconomic factors play a significant role in determining what we eat, we do make our own food choices. And thus, what we eat is at least partially a moral choice, whether we are cognizant of it or not. What are our ethical responsibilities when we make food choices? Does it matter *morally* what we choose to eat? What does it mean to eat ethically? What moral principles should guide our food choices and ways of eating?

In this section, various authors weigh in on what it means to eat ethically and raise issues that can play a role in the ethics of food: animal rights, environmental concerns, world hunger, and farmer rights. These authors offer varied and sometimes conflicting views on the obligations we necessarily take on when we make dietary choices and offer a range of potential responsibilities — social, political, personal, environmental, spiritual, and global. They force us to consider the ethical dilemmas created by disputes between corporations. And they make suggestions about what principles and priorities should affect our ethical obligations related to food.

Beginning with a focus on global hunger and its relation to food production, Margaret Mead encourages Americans to develop a "world conscience" and to think of the ways that our ability to produce enough food to feed the world changes the ethical position of those who can or do overconsume. Barbara Kingsolver offers moral perspectives on the ethics of eating meat, suggesting varying and complex views on human responsibility in animal consumption. Bill McKibben brings environmental factors into the equation, and Donald Barlett and James Steele ask us to think through the ethical dilemmas created by corporations and the courts in food production and food availability. And while Yuval Noah Harari suggests that the treatment of domesticated animals on industrial farms is among the worst crimes in history, Blake Hurst takes issue with critiques of industrial farming by proponents of organic farming. On top of all of this, Amanda Little explores the complexities of food waste — a problem humans have created and one that we must find a way to solve that takes economics, social

photo: Claudia Totir/Moment/Getty Images

justice, and the environment into account. By making arguments in support of various ethical positions, the authors in this section argue for the moral principles they think should motivate our choices.

We do not eat in isolation. An ethics of eating, then, must take into account a variety of factors: what we eat, its ability to nourish us, how much we eat, where and how it is produced, who produces it, how they are compensated, and how food production and consumption affect our environment and natural resources. Moral obligations and responsibilities related to an ethics of food exist for consumers, producers, farmers, law and policy makers, regulators, corporations, and communities. They exist for the affluent and the poor. This chapter asks us to consider what it means to declare that eating is necessarily a moral act.

The Changing Significance of Food

Margaret Mead

Margaret Mead (1901–1978) was a highly respected, often controversial, cultural anthropologist. She is best known for her book *Coming of Age in Samoa* (1928), which she wrote after conducting fieldwork there. She received her doctoral degree from Columbia University and served as curator of ethnology at the American Museum of Natural History in New York and executive secretary of the National Research Council's Committee on Food Habits. She popularized anthropological discoveries through her extensive writing and speaking engagements, in which she sometimes shared her view that small groups of committed individuals could, in fact, change the world. President Jimmy Carter awarded Mead the Presidential Medal of Freedom posthumously in 1979. In this essay, originally published in *American Scientist*, Mead provides a historical look at our relationship with food, examining how it has changed over time and been affected by economic, political, and cultural trends. She argues that Americans need to think about the relationship between the American diet and their capacity to feed the poor and the hungry both at home and abroad.

We live in a world today where the state of nutrition in each country is relevant and important to each other country, and where the state of nutrition in the wealthy industrialized countries like the United States has profound significance for the role that such countries can play in eliminating famine and providing for adequate nutrition throughout the world. In a world in which each half knows what the other half does, we cannot live with hunger and malnutrition in one part of the world while people in another part are not only well nourished, but over-nourished. Any talk of one world, of brotherhood, rings hollow to those who have come face to face on the television screen with the emaciation° of starving children and to the people whose children are starving as they pore over month-old issues of glossy American and European magazines, where full color prints show people glowing with health, their plates piled high with food that glistens to match the shining textures of their clothes. Peoples who have resolutely tightened their belts and put up with going to bed hungry, peoples who have seen their children die because they did not have the strength to resist disease, and called it fate or the will of God, can no longer do so, in the vivid visual realization of the amount and quality of food eaten—and wasted—by others.

emaciation: extreme thinness.

Through human history there have been many stringent taboos on watching other people eat, or on eating in the presence of others. There have been attempts to explain this as a relationship between those who are involved and those who are not simultaneously involved in the satisfaction of a bodily need, and the inappropriateness of the already satiated watching others who appear—to the satisfied—to be shamelessly gorging. There is undoubtedly such an element in the taboos, but it seems more likely that they go back to the days when food was so scarce and the onlookers so hungry that not to offer them half of the little food one had was unthinkable, and every glance was a plea for at least a bite.

In the rural schools of America when my grandmother was a child, the better-off children took apples to school and, before they began to eat them, promised the poor children who had no apples that they might have the cores. The spectacle of the poor in rags at the rich man's gate and of hungry children pressing their noses against the glass window of the rich man's restaurant have long been invoked to arouse human compassion. But until the advent of the mass media and travel, the sensitive and sympathetic could protect themselves by shutting themselves away from the sight of the starving, by gifts of food to the poor on religious holidays, or perpetual bequests for the distribution of a piece of meat "the size of a child's head" annually. The starving in India and China saw only a few feasting foreigners and could not know how well or ill the poor were in countries from which they came. The proud poor hid their hunger behind a façade that often included insistent hospitality to the occasional visitor; the beggars flaunted their hunger and so, to a degree, discredited the hunger of their respectable compatriots.

> "We cannot live with hunger and malnutrition in one part of the world while people in another part are not only well nourished, but over-nourished."

But today the articulate cries of the hungry fill the air channels and there is no escape from the knowledge of the hundreds of millions who are seriously malnourished, of the periodic famines that beset whole populations, or of the looming danger of famine in many other parts of the world. The age-old divisions between one part of the world and another, between one class and another, between the rich and the poor everywhere, have been broken down, and the tolerances and insensitivities of the past are no longer possible.

But it is not only the media of communication which can take a man 5 sitting at an overloaded breakfast table straight into a household where some of the children are too weak to stand. Something else, something even more significant, has happened. Today, for the first time in the history of mankind, we have the productive capacity to feed everyone in the world, and the technical knowledge to see that their stomachs are not only filled but that their bodies are properly nourished with the essential ingredients for growth and health. The progress of agriculture—in all its complexities of improved seed, methods of cultivation, fertilizers and pesticides, methods of storage, preservation, and transportation—now make it possible for the food that is needed for the whole world to be produced by fewer and fewer farmers, with greater and greater certainty. Drought and flood still threaten, but we have the means to prepare for and deal with even mammoth shortages—if we will. The progress of nutritional science has matched the progress of agriculture; we have finer and finer-grained knowledge of just which substances—vitamins, minerals, proteins—are essential, especially to growth and full development, and increasing ability to synthesize many of them on a massive scale.

These new twentieth-century potentialities have altered the ethical position of the rich all over the world. In the past, there were so few who lived well, and so many who lived on the edge of starvation, that the well-to-do had a rationale and indeed almost a necessity to harden their hearts and turn their eyes away. The jewels of the richest rajah° could not have purchased enough food to feed his hungry subjects for more than a few days; the food did not exist, and the knowledge of how to use it was missing also. At the same time, however real the inability of a war-torn and submarine-ringed Britain to respond to the famine in Bengal, this inability was made bearable in Britain only by the extent to which the British were learning how to share what food they had among all the citizens, old and young. "You do not know," the American consul, who had come to Manchester from Spain, said to me: "you do not know what it means to live in a country where no child has to cry itself to sleep from hunger." But this was only achieved in Britain in the early 1940s. Before, the well-fed turned away their eyes, in the feeling that they were powerless to alleviate the perennial poverty and hunger of most of their own people and the peoples in their far-flung commonwealth. And such turning away the eyes, in Britain and in the United States and elsewhere, was accompanied by the rationalizations, not only of the inability of the well-to-do—had they given all their wealth—to feed the poor, but of the undeservingness of the poor, who had they only been industrious and saving would have had enough, although of course of a lower quality, to keep "body and soul together."

When differences in race and in cultural levels complicated the situation, it was only too easy to insist that lesser breeds somehow, in some

rajah: a ruler in India or the East Indies.

divinely correct scheme, would necessarily be less well fed, their alleged idleness and lack of frugality combining with such matters as sacred cows roaming over the landscapes—in India—or nights spent in the pub or the saloon—at home in Britain or America—while fathers drank up their meager pay checks and their children starved. So righteous was the assumed association between industriousness and food that, during the Irish famine, soup kitchens were set up out of town so that the starving could have the moral advantage of a long walk to receive the ration that stood between them and death. (The modern version of such ethical acrobatics can be found in the United States, in the mid-1960s, where food stamps were so expensive, since they had to be bought in large amounts, that only those who had been extraordinarily frugal, saving, and lucky could afford to buy them and obtain the benefits they were designed to give.)

The particular ways in which the well-to-do of different great civilizations have rationalized the contrast between rich and poor have differed dramatically, but ever since the agricultural revolution, we have been running a race between our capacity to produce enough food to make it possible to assemble great urban centers, outfit huge armies and armadas, and build and elaborate the institutions of civilization and our ability to feed and care for the burgeoning population which has always kept a little, often a great deal, ahead of the food supply.

In this, those societies which practiced agriculture contrasted with the earlier simpler societies in which the entire population was engaged in subsistence activities. Primitive peoples may be well or poorly fed, feasting seldom, or blessed with ample supplies of fish or fruit, but the relations between the haves and the have-nots were in many ways simpler. Methods by which men could obtain permanent supplies of food and withhold them from their fellows hardly existed. The sour, barely edible breadfruit mash which was stored in breadfruit pits against the ravages of hurricanes and famines in Polynesia was not a diet for the table of chiefs but a stern measure against the needs of entire communities. The chief might have a right to the first fruits, or to half the crop, but after he had claimed it, it was redistributed to his people. The germs of the kinds of inequities that later entered the world were present: there was occasional conspicuous destruction of food, piled up for prestige, oil poured on the flames of self-glorifying feasts, food left to rot after it was offered to the gods. People with very meager food resources might use phrases that made it seem that each man was the recipient of great generosity on the part of his fellows, or on the other hand always to be giving away a whole animal, and always receiving only small bits.

The fear of cannibalism that hovered over northern peoples might 10 be elaborated into cults of fear, or simply add to the concern that each member of a group had for all, against the terrible background that extremity might become so great that one of the group might in the end be sacrificed. But cannibalism could also be elaborated into a rite of vengeance or the celebration of victories in war, or even be used to provision an army in the field. Man's capacity to elaborate man's inhumanity to man existed before the beginning of civilization, which was made possible by the application of an increasingly productive technology to the production of food.

With the rise of civilizations, we also witness the growth of the great religions that made the brotherhood of all men part of their doctrine and the gift of alms or the life of voluntary poverty accepted religious practices. But the alms were never enough, and the life of individual poverty and abstinence was more efficacious for the individual's salvation than for the well-being of the poor and hungry, although both kept alive an ethic, as yet impossible of fulfillment, that it was right that all should be fed. The vision preceded the capability.

But today we have the capability. Whether that capability will be used or not becomes not a technical but an ethical question. It depends, in enormous measure, on the way in which the rich, industrialized countries handle the problems of distribution, of malnutrition and hunger, within their own borders. Failure to feed their own, with such high capabilities and such fully enunciated statements of responsibility and brotherhood, means that feeding the people of other countries is almost ruled out, except for sporadic escapist pieces of behavior where people who close their eyes to hunger in Mississippi can work hard to send food to a "Biafra." The development of the international instruments to meet food emergencies and to steadily improve the nutrition of the poorer countries will fail, unless there is greater consistency between ideal and practice at home.

And so, our present parlous° plight in the United States, with the many pockets of rural unemployment, city ghettos, ethnic enclaves, where Americans are starving and an estimated tenth of the population malnourished, must be viewed not only in its consequences for ourselves, as a viable political community, but also in its consequences for the world. We need to examine not only the conditions that make this possible, to have starving people in the richest country in the world, but also the repercussions of American conditions on the world scene.

---

parlous: full of danger, perilous.

Why, when twenty-five years ago we were well on the way to remedying the state of the American people who had been described by presidential announcement as "one third ill-housed, ill-clothed, and ill-fed," when the vitamin deficiency diseases had all but vanished, and a variety of instruments for better nutrition had been developed, did we find, just two short years ago, due to the urgent pleading of a few crusaders, that we had fallen so grievously behind? The situation is complex, closely related to a series of struggles for regional and racial justice, to the spread of automation and resulting unemployment, to changes in crop economies, as well as to population growth and the inadequacy of many of our institutions to deal with it. But I wish to single out here two conditions which have, I believe, seriously contributed to our blindness to what was happening: the increase in the diseases of affluence and the growth of commercial agriculture.

In a country pronounced only twenty years before to be one third   15
ill-fed, we suddenly began to have pronouncements from nutritional specialists that the major nutritional disease of the American people was overnutrition. If this had simply meant overeating, the old puritan ethics against greed and gluttony might have been more easily invoked, but it was over-nutrition that was at stake. And this in a country where our ideas of nutrition had been dominated by a dichotomy which distinguished food that was "good for you, but not good" from food that was "good, but not good for you." This split in man's needs, into our cultural conception of the need for nourishment and the search for pleasure, originally symbolized in the rewards for eating spinach or finishing what was on one's plate if one wanted to have a dessert, lay back of the movement to produce, commercially, nonnourishing foods. Beverages and snacks came in particularly for this demand, as it was the addition of between-meal eating to the three square, nutritionally adequate meals a day that was responsible for much of the trouble.

We began manufacturing, on a terrifying scale, foods and beverages that were guaranteed not to nourish. The resources and the ingenuity of industry were diverted from the preparation of foods necessary for life and growth to foods nonexpensive to prepare, expensive to buy. And every label reassuring the buyer that the product was not nourishing increased our sense that the trouble with Americans was that they were too well nourished. The diseases of affluence, represented by new forms of death in middle-age, had appeared before we had, in the words of Jean Mayer, who has done so much to define the needs of the country and of the world, conquered the diseases of poverty—the ill-fed pregnant women and lactating women, sometimes resulting in irreversible damage to the ill-weaned children, the school children so poorly fed that they could not learn.

It was hard for the average American to believe that while he struggled, and paid, so as not to be over-nourished, other people, several millions, right in this country, were hungry and near starvation. The gross contradiction was too great. Furthermore, those who think of their country as parental and caring find it hard to admit that this parental figure is starving their brothers and sisters. During the great depression of the 1930s, when thousands of children came to school desperately hungry, it was very difficult to wring from children the admission that their parents had no food to give them. "Or what man is there of you, whom, if his son ask bread, will he give a stone?"

So today we have in the United States a situation not unlike the situation in Germany under Hitler, when a large proportion of the decent and law-abiding simply refuse to believe that what is happening can be happening. "Look at the taxes we pay," they say, or they point to the millions spent on welfare; surely with such quantities assigned to the poor, people can't be really hungry, or if they are, it is because they spend their money on TV sets and drink. How can the country be overnourished and undernourished at the same time?

A second major shift, in the United States and in the world, is the increasing magnitude of commercial agriculture, in which food is seen

Spanish children begging in the 1950s.
Three Lions/Hulton Archive/Getty Images

not as food which nourishes men, women, and children, but as a staple crop on which the prosperity of a country or region and the economic prosperity — as opposed to the simple livelihood — of the individual farmer depend. This is pointed up on a world scale in the report of the Food and Agriculture Organization of the United Nations for 1969, which states that there are two major problems in the world: food deficits in the poor countries, which mean starvation, hunger, and malnutrition on an increasing scale, and food surpluses in the industrialized part of the world, serious food surpluses.

On the face of it, this sounds as foolish as the production of foods 20 guaranteed not to nourish, and the two are not unrelated. Surpluses, in a world where people are hungry! Too much food, in a world where children are starving! Yet we lump together all *agricultural* surpluses, such as cotton and tobacco, along with food, and we see these surpluses as threatening the commercial prosperity of many countries, and farmers in many countries. And in a world politically organized on a vanishing agrarian basis, this represents a political threat to those in power. However much the original destruction of food, killing little pigs, may have been phrased as relieving the desperate situation of little farmers or poor countries dependent upon single crop exports, such situations could not exist if food as something which man needs to provide growth and maintenance had not been separated from food as a cash crop, a commercial as opposed to a basic maintenance enterprise. When it becomes the task of government to foster the economic prosperity of an increasingly small, but politically influential, sector of the electorate at the expense of the well-being of its own and other nations' citizens, we have reached an ethically dangerous position.

And this situation, in the United States, is in part responsible for the grievous state of our poor and hungry and for the paralysis that still prevents adequate political action. During the great depression, agriculture in this country was still a viable way of life for millions. The Department of Agriculture had responsibility, not only for food production and marketing, but also for the well-being from the cradle to the grave, in the simplest, most human sense, of every family who lived in communities under 2,500. Where the needs of urban man were parceled out among a number of agencies — Office of Education, Children's Bureau, Labor Department — there was still a considerable amount of integration possible in the Department of Agriculture, where theory and practices of farm wives, the education of children and youth, the question of small loans for small landowners, all could be considered together. It was in the Department of Agriculture that concerned persons found, during the depression, the kind of understanding of basic human needs which they sought.

There were indeed always conflicts between the needs of farmers to sell crops and the needs of children to be fed. School lunch schemes were tied to the disposal of surplus commodities. But the recognition of the wholeness of human needs was still there, firmly related to the breadth of the responsibilities of the different agencies within the Department of Agriculture. Today this is no longer so. Agriculture is big business in the United States. The subsidies used to persuade farmers to withdraw their impoverished land from production, like the terrible measures involving the slaughter of little pigs, are no longer ways of helping the small farmer on a family farm. The subsidies go to the rich commercial farmers, many of them the inheritors of old exploitive plantation traditions, wasteful of manpower and land resources, often in the very counties where the farm workers, displaced by machinery, are penniless, too poor to move away, starving. These subsidies exceed the budget of the antipoverty administration.

So today, many of the reforms which are suggested, in the distribution of food or distribution of income from which food can be bought, center on removing food relief programs from the Department of Agriculture and placing them under the Department of Health, Education, and Welfare. In Britain, during World War II, it was necessary to have a Ministry of Food, concerned primarily in matching the limited food supplies with basic needs.

At first sight, this proposal is sound enough. Let us remove from an agency devoted to making a profit out of crops that are treated like any other manufactured product the responsibility for seeing that food actually feeds people. After all, we do not ask clothing manufacturers to take the responsibility for clothing people, or the house-building industry for housing them. To the extent that we recognize them at all, these are the responsibilities of agencies of government which provide the funds to supplement the activities of private industry. Why not also in food? The Department of Health, Education, and Welfare is concerned with human beings; they have no food to sell on a domestic or world market and no constituents to appease. And from this step it is simply a second step to demand that the whole system of distribution be re-oriented, that a basic guaranteed annual income be provided each citizen, on the one hand, and that the government police standards, on behalf of the consumer, on the other.

But neither of these changes, shifting food relief programs from 25 Agriculture to Health, Education, and Welfare, or shifting the whole welfare program into a guaranteed income, really meet the particular difficulties that arise because we are putting food into two compartments with disastrous effects; we are separating food that nourishes people from food out of which some people, and some countries, derive their incomes. It does not deal with the immediacy of the experience of food by the well-fed, or with the irreparability of food deprivation during prenatal and postnatal growth, deprivation that can never be made up. Human beings have maintained their dignity in incredibly bad conditions of housing and clothing, emerged triumphant from huts and log cabins, gone from ill-shod childhood to Wall Street or the Kremlin. Poor housing and poor clothing are demeaning to the human spirit when they contrast sharply with the visible standards of the way others live.

But food affects not only man's dignity but the capacity of children to reach their full potential, and the capacity of adults to act from day to day. You can't eat either nutrition or part of a not yet realized guaranteed annual income, or political promises. You can't eat hope. We know that hope and faith have enormous effects in preventing illness and enabling people to put forth the last ounce of energy they have. But energy is ultimately dependent upon food. No amount of rearrangement of priorities in the future can provide food in the present. It is true that the starving adult, his efficiency enormously impaired by lack of food, may usually be brought back again to his previous state of efficiency. But this is not true of children. What they lose is lost for good.

What we do about food is therefore far more crucial, both for the quality of the next generation, our own American children, and children everywhere, and also for the quality of our responsible action in every field. It is intimately concerned with the whole problem of the pollution and exhaustion of our environment, with the danger that man may make this planet uninhabitable within a short century or so. If food is grown in strict relationship to the needs of those who will eat it, if every effort is made to reduce the costs of transportation, to improve storage, to conserve the land, and there, where it is needed, by recycling wastes and water, we will go a long way toward solving many of our environmental problems also. It is as a responsible gardener on a small, limited plot, aware of the community about him with whom he will face adequate food or famine, that man has developed what conserving agricultural techniques we have.

Divorced from its primary function of feeding people, treated simply as a commercial commodity, food loses this primary significance; the land is mined instead of replenished and conserved. The Food and Agriculture Organization, intent on food production, lays great stress on the increase in the use of artificial fertilizers, yet the use of such fertilizers with their diffuse runoffs may be a greater danger to our total ecology than the industrial wastes from other forms of manufacturing. The same thing is true of pesticides. With the marvels of miracle rice and miracle wheat, which have brought the resources of international effort and scientific resources together, go at present prescriptions for artificial fertilizer and pesticides. The innovative industrialized countries are exporting, with improved agricultural methods, new dangers to the environment of the importing countries. Only by treating food, unitarily, as a substance necessary to feed people, subject first to the needs of people and only second to the needs of commercial prosperity—whether they be the needs of private enterprise or of a developing socialist country short of foreign capital—can we hope to meet the ethical demands that our present situation makes on us. For the first time since the beginning of civilization, we can feed everyone, now. Those who are not fed will die or, in the case of children, be permanently damaged.

We are just beginning to develop a world conscience. Our present dilemma is due to previous humanitarian moves with unanticipated effects. Without the spread of public health measures, we would not have had the fall in infant death rates which has resulted in the population explosion. Without the spread of agricultural techniques, there would not have been the food to feed the children who survived. The old constraints upon population growth—famine, plague, and war—are no longer acceptable to a world whose conscience is just barely stirring on behalf of all mankind. As we are groping our way back to a new version of the full fellow-feeling and respect for the natural world which the primitive Eskimo felt when food was scarce, so we are trembling on the edge of a new version of the sacrifice to cannibalism of the weak, just as we have the technical means to implement visions of responsibility that were very recently only visions.

The temptation is to turn aside, to deny what is happening to the environment, to trust to the "green revolution" and boast of how much rice previously hungry countries will export, to argue about legalities while people starve and infants and children are irreparably damaged, to refuse to deal with the paradoxes of hunger in plenty, and the coincidences of starvation and overnutrition. The basic problem is an ethical one; the solution of ethical problems can be solved only with a full recognition of reality. The children of the agricultural workers of the rural South, displaced by the machine, are hungry; so are the children in the Northern cities to which black and white poor have fled in search of food. On our American Indian reservations, among the Chicanos of California and the Southwest, among the seasonally employed, there is hunger now. If this hunger is not met now, we disqualify ourselves, we cripple ourselves, to deal with world problems.

We must balance our population so that every child that is born can be well fed. We must cherish our land, instead of mining it, so that food produced is first related to those who need it; and we must not despoil the earth, contaminate, and pollute it in the interests of immediate gain. Behind us, just a few decades ago, lies the vision of André Mayer and John Orr, the concepts of a world food bank, the founding of the United Nations Food and Agriculture Organization; behind us lie imaginative vision and deep concern. In the present we have new and various tools to make that vision into concrete actuality. But we must resolve the complications of present practice and present conceptions if the very precision and efficiency of our new knowledge is not to provide a stumbling block to the exercise of fuller humanity.

Understanding the Text

1. Mead points out that though we now have the technical ability to produce enough food to feed everyone in the world, we still do not do so. Why not, according to Mead?

2. What are some ways that people in the past have justified the contrast between the rich's easy access to food and the poor's lack of access to proper nourishment?

Reflection and Response

3. How has the capacity to feed all peoples in the world "altered the ethical position of the rich all over the world," according to Mead? (par. 6). Do you agree? Why or why not?

4. What are some solutions to the world's hunger problem proposed by Mead? Do you think they would work if pursued today? Why or why not?

5. What is a "world conscience"? What does Mead's call for a "world conscience" tell us about the ethical position she adopts? Why does she think this is the only morally legitimate path to take?

Making Connections

6. How might Frances Moore Lappé's essay ("Biotechnology Isn't the Key to Feeding the World," p. 317) be said to "update" the argument Mead makes here? In what ways does Lappé pick up where Mead left off? What would Mead say about the state of affairs described by Lappé?

7. What is the changing significance of food? Mead wrote this essay more than five decades ago. Do you think her conclusions are still useful for thinking about an ethics of eating? Why or why not? Locate two outside sources to help you support your response.

8. What is Mead's primary ethical concern? What other authors in this collection share this concern? Use textual examples from at least three other sources to support your response.

You Can't Run Away on Harvest Day

Barbara Kingsolver

Barbara Kingsolver studied biology before becoming a prolific and award-winning author. Her books have been translated into more than twenty languages, and her stories and essays have been published in major literary anthologies and most major U.S. newspapers and magazines. Best known for her novels and short stories, including *The Bean Trees* (1988), *Animal Dreams* (1990), *The Poisonwood Bible* (1998), *Prodigal Summer* (2000), and *Flight Behavior* (2012), she has also written about her experiences raising and harvesting her own food. Her 2007 memoir *Animal, Vegetable, Miracle: A Year of Food Life* chronicles her family's year devoted to eating locally — to eating food produced on their family farm or in their southern Appalachian community. In this essay excerpt from *Animal, Vegetable, Miracle*, Kingsolver provides an introspective and moving account of her experience slaughtering chickens and turkeys — and the moral principles that guide her ethics of eating.

The Saturday of Labor Day weekend dawned with a sweet, translucent bite, like a Golden Delicious apple. I always seem to harbor a child-like hope through the berry-stained months of June and July that summer will be for keeps. But then a day comes in early fall to remind me why it should end, after all. In September the quality of daylight shifts toward flirtation. The green berries on the spicebush shrubs along our lane begin to blink red, first one and then another, like faltering but resolute holiday lights. The woods fill with the restless singing of migrant birds warming up to the proposition of flying south. The cool air makes us restless too: jeans and sweater weather, perfect for a hike. Steven and I rose early that morning, looked out the window, looked at each other, and started in on the time-honored marital grumble: Was this *your* idea?

We weren't going on a hike today. Nor would we have the postsummer Saturday luxury of sitting on the porch with a cup of coffee and watching the farm wake up. On the docket instead was a hard day of work we could not postpone. The previous morning we'd sequestered half a dozen roosters and as many tom turkeys in a room of the barn we call "death row." We hold poultry there, clean and comfortable with water but no food, for a twenty-four-hour fast prior to harvest. It makes the processing cleaner and seems to calm the animals also. I could tell you it gives them time to get their emotional affairs in order, if that helps. But they have limited emotional affairs, and no idea what's coming.

We had a lot more of both. Our plan for this gorgeous day was the removal of some of our animals from the world of the living into the realm of food. At five months of age our roosters had put on a good harvest weight, and had lately opened rounds of cockfighting, venting their rising hormonal angst against any moving target, including us. When a rooster flies up at you with his spurs, he leaves marks. Lily now had to arm herself with a length of pipe in order to gather the eggs. Our barnyard wasn't big enough for this much machismo. We would certainly take no pleasure in the chore, but it was high time for the testosterone-reduction program. We sighed at the lovely weather and pulled out our old, bloody sneakers for harvest day.

There was probably a time when I thought it euphemistic to speak of "harvesting" animals. Now I don't. We calculate "months to harvest" when planning for the right time to start poultry. We invite friends to "harvest parties," whether we'll be gleaning° vegetable or animal. A harvest implies planning, respect, and effort. With animals, both the planning and physical effort are often greater, and respect for the enterprise is substantially more complex. It's a lot less fun than spending an autumn day picking apples off trees, but it's a similar operation on principle and the same word.

Killing is a culturally loaded term, for most of us inextricably tied up 5 with some version of a command that begins, "Thou shalt not." Every faith has it. And for all but perhaps the Jainists of India, that command is absolutely conditional. We know it does not refer to mosquitoes. Who among us has never killed living creatures on purpose? When a child is sick with an infection we rush for the medicine spoon, committing an eager and purposeful streptococcus massacre. We sprinkle boric acid or grab a spray can to rid our kitchens of cockroaches. What we mean by "killing" is to take a life cruelly, as in murder—or else more accidentally, as in "Oops, looks like I killed my African violet." Though the results are incomparable, what these different "killings" have in common is needless waste and some presumed measure of regret.

Most of us, if we know even a little about where our food comes from, understand that every bite put into our mouths since infancy (barring the odd rock or marble) was formerly alive. The blunt biological truth is that we animals can only remain alive by eating other life. Plants are inherently more blameless, having been born with the talent of whipping up their own food, peacefully and without noise, out of sunshine, water, and the odd mineral ingredient sucked up through their toes. Strangely enough, it's the animals to which we've assigned some rights,

gleaning: gathering, collecting.

while the saintly plants we maim and behead with moral impunity. Who thinks to beg forgiveness while mowing the lawn?

The moral rules of destroying our fellow biota° get even more tangled, the deeper we go. If we draw the okay-to-kill line between "animal" and "plant," and thus exclude meat, fowl, and fish from our diet on moral grounds, we still must live with the fact that every sack of flour and every soybean-based block of tofu came from a field where countless winged and furry lives were extinguished in the plowing, cultivating, and harvest. An estimated 67 million birds die each year from pesticide exposure on U.S. farms. Butterflies, too, are universally killed on contact in larval form by the genetically modified pollen contained in most U.S. corn. Foxes, rabbits, and bobolinks are starved out of their homes or dismembered by the sickle mower. Insects are "controlled" even by organic pesticides; earthworms are cut in half by the plow. Contrary to lore, they won't grow into two; both halves die.

To believe we can live without taking life is delusional. Humans may only cultivate nonviolence in our diets by degree. I've heard a Buddhist monk suggest the *number* of food-caused deaths is minimized in steak dinners, which share one death over many meals, whereas the equation is reversed for a bowl of clams. Others of us have lost heart for eating any steak dinner that's been shoved through the assembly line of feedlot life—however broadly we might share that responsibility. I take my gospel from Wendell Berry, who writes in *What Are People For*, "I dislike the thought that some animal has been made miserable in order to feed me. If I am going to eat meat, I want it to be from an animal that has lived a pleasant, uncrowded life outdoors, on bountiful pasture, with good water nearby and trees for shade. And I am getting almost as fussy about food plants."

I find myself fundamentally allied with a vegetarian position in every way except one: however selectively, I eat meat. I'm unimpressed by arguments that condemn animal harvest while ignoring, wholesale, the animal killing that underwrites vegetal foods. Uncountable deaths by pesticide and habitat removal—the beetles and bunnies that die collaterally for our bread and veggie-burgers—are lives plumb wasted. Animal harvest is at least not gratuitous, as part of a plan involving labor and recompense. We raise these creatures for a reason. Such premeditation may be presumed unkind, but without it our gentle domestic beasts in their picturesque shapes, colors, and finely tuned purposes would never have had the distinction of existing. To envision a vegan version of civilization, start by erasing from all time the Three Little Pigs, the boy who

biota: living things, both plant and animal.

cried wolf, *Charlotte's Web*, the golden calf, *Tess of the d'Urbervilles*. Next, erase civilization, brought to you by the people who learned to domesticate animals. Finally, rewrite our evolutionary history, since *Homo sapiens* became the species we are by means of regular binges of carnivory.

Most confounding of all, in the vegan revision, are the chapters 10 addressing the future. If farm animals have civil rights, what aspect of their bondage to humans shall they overcome? Most wouldn't last two days without it. Recently while I was cooking eggs, my kids sat at the kitchen table entertaining me with readings from a magazine profile of a famous, rather young vegan movie star. Her dream was to create a safe-haven ranch where the cows and chickens could live free, happy lives and die natural deaths. "Wait till those cows start bawling to be

> "I find myself fundamentally allied with a vegetarian position in every way except one: however selectively, I eat meat."

milked," I warned. Having nursed and weaned my own young, I can tell you there is no pain to compare with an overfilled udder. We wondered what the starlet might do for those bursting Jerseys, not to mention the eggs the chickens would keep dropping everywhere. What a life's work for that poor gal: traipsing about the farm in her strappy heels, weaving among the cow flops, bending gracefully to pick up eggs and stick them in an incubator where they would maddeningly *hatch*, and grow up bent on laying *more* eggs. It's dirty work, trying to save an endless chain of uneaten lives. Realistically, my kids observed, she'd hire somebody.

Forgive us. We know she meant well, and as fantasies of the super-rich go, it's more inspired than most. It's just the high-mindedness that rankles; when moral superiority combines with billowing ignorance, they fill up a hot-air balloon that's awfully hard not to poke. The farm-liberation fantasy simply reflects a modern cultural confusion about farm animals. They're human property, not just legally but biologically. Over the millennia of our clever history, we created from wild progenitors° whole new classes of beasts whose sole purpose was to feed us. If turned loose in the wild, they would haplessly starve, succumb to predation, and destroy the habitats and lives of most or all natural things. If housed at the public expense they would pose a more immense civic burden than our public schools and prisons combined. No thoughtful person really wants those things to happen. But living at a remove from the actual workings of a farm, most humans no longer learn appropriate modes of thinking about animal harvest. Knowing that our family raises meat animals, many

progenitor: ancestor.

friends have told us—not judgmentally, just confessionally—"I don't think I could kill an animal myself." I find myself explaining: It's not what you think. It's nothing like putting down your dog.

Most nonfarmers are intimate with animal life in only three categories: people; pets (i.e., junior people); and wildlife (as seen on nature shows, presumed beautiful and rare). Purposely beheading any of the above is unthinkable, for obvious reasons. No other categories present themselves at close range for consideration. So I understand why it's hard to think about harvest, a categorical act that includes cutting the heads off living lettuces, extended to crops that blink their beady eyes. On our farm we don't especially enjoy processing our animals, but we do value it, as an important ritual for ourselves and any friends adventurous enough to come and help, because of what we learn from it. We reconnect with the purpose for which these animals were bred. We dispense with all delusions about who put the *live* in livestock, and who must take it away.

A friend from whom we buy pasture-grazed lamb and poultry has concurred with us on this point. Kirsty Zahnke grew up in the U.K., and observes that American attitudes toward life and death probably add to the misgivings. "People in this country do everything to cheat death, it seems. Instead of being happy with each moment, they worry so much about what comes next. I think this gets transposed to animals—the preoccupation with 'taking a life.' My animals have all had a good life, with death as its natural end. It's not without thought and gratitude that I slaughter my animals, it is a hard thing to do. It's taken me time to be able to eat my own lambs that I had played with. But I always think of Kahlil Gibran's words:

When you kill a beast, say to him in your heart:

By the same power that slays you, I too am slain, and I too shall be consumed.
For the law that delivers you into my hand shall deliver me into a mightier hand.
Your blood and my blood is naught but the sap that feeds the tree of heaven."

Kirsty works with a local environmental organization and frequently hosts its out-of-town volunteers, who camp at her farm while working in the area. Many of these activists had not eaten meat for many years before arriving on the Zahnkes' meat farm—a formula not for disaster, she notes, but for education. "If one gets to know the mantras of the farm owners, it can change one's viewpoint. I would venture to say that seventy-five percent of the vegans and vegetarians who stayed at least a week here began to eat our meat or animal products, simply because they see what I am doing as right—for the animals, for the environment, for humans."

I respect every diner who makes morally motivated choices about consumption. And I stand with nonviolence, as one of those extremist moms who doesn't let kids at her house pretend to shoot each other, *ever*, or make any game out of human murder. But I've come to different conclusions about livestock. The ve-vangelical pamphlets showing jam-packed chickens and sick downer-cows usually declare, as their first principle, that all meat is factory-farmed. That is false, and an affront to those of us who work to raise animals humanely, or who support such practices with our buying power. I don't want to cause any creature misery, so I won't knowingly eat anything that has stood belly deep in its own poop wishing it was dead until *bam*, one day it was. (In restaurants I go for the fish, or the vegetarian option.)

But meat, poultry, and eggs from animals raised on open pasture are the traditional winter fare of my grandparents, and they serve us well here in the months when it would cost a lot of fossil fuels to keep us in tofu. Should I overlook the suffering of victims of hurricanes, famines, and wars brought on this world by profligate fuel consumption? Bananas that cost a rain forest, refrigerator-trucked soy milk, and prewashed spinach shipped two thousand miles in plastic containers do not seem cruelty-free, in this context. A hundred different paths may lighten the world's load of suffering. Giving up meat is one path; giving up bananas is another. The more we know about our food system, the more we are called into complex choices. It seems facile to declare one single forbidden fruit, when humans live under so many different kinds of trees.

To breed fewer meat animals in the future is possible; phasing out those types destined for confinement lots is a plan I'm assisting myself, by raising heirloom breeds. Most humans could well consume more vegetable foods, and less meat. But globally speaking, the vegetarian option is a luxury. The oft-cited energetic argument for vegetarianism, that it takes ten times as much land to make a pound of meat as a pound of grain, only applies to the kind of land where rain falls abundantly on rich topsoil. Many of the world's poor live in marginal lands that can't support plant-based agriculture. Those not blessed with the fruited plain and amber waves of grain must make do with woody tree pods, tough-leaved shrubs, or sparse grasses. Camels, reindeer, sheep, goats, cattle, and other ruminants are uniquely adapted to transform all those types of indigestible cellulose into edible milk and meat. The fringes of desert, tundra, and marginal grasslands on every continent—coastal Peru, the southwestern United States, the Kalahari, the Gobi, the Australian outback, northern Scandinavia—are inhabited by herders. The Navajo, Mongols, Lapps, Masai, and countless other resourceful tribes would starve without their animals. . . .

After many meatless years it felt strange to us to break the taboo, but over time our family has come back to carnivory. I like listening to a roasting bird in the oven on a Sunday afternoon, following Julia Child's advice to "regulate the chicken so it makes quiet cooking noises" as its schmaltzy aroma fills the house. When a friend began raising beef cattle entirely on pasture (rather than sending them to a CAFO° as six-month-olds, as most cattle farmers do), we were born again to the idea of hamburger. We can go visit his animals if we need to be reassured of the merciful cowness of their lives.

As meat farmers ourselves we are learning as we go, raising heritage breeds: the thrifty antiques that know how to stand in the sunshine, gaze upon a meadow, and munch. (Even mate without help!) We're grateful these old breeds weren't consigned to extinction during the past century, though it nearly did happen. Were it not for these animals that can thrive outdoors, and the healthy farms that maintain them, I would have stuck with tofu-burgers indefinitely. That wasn't a bad life, but we're also enjoying this one.

Believing in the righteousness of a piece of work, alas, is not what gets   20
it done. On harvest day we pulled on our stained shoes, sharpened our knives, lit a fire under the big kettle, and set ourselves to the whole show: mud, blood, and lots of little feathers. There are some things about a chicken harvest that are irrepressibly funny, and one of them is the feathers; in your hair, on the backs of your hands, dangling behind your left shoe the way toilet paper does in slapstick movies. Feathery little white tags end up stuck all over the chopping block and the butchering table like Post-it notes from the chicken hereafter. Sometimes we get through the awful parts on the strength of black comedy, joking about the feathers or our barn's death row and the "dead roosters walking."

But today was not one of those times. Some friends had come over to help us, including a family that had recently lost their teenage son in a drowning accident. Their surviving younger children, Abby and Eli, were among Lily's closest friends. The kids were understandably solemn and the adults measured all our words under the immense weight of grief as we set to work. Lily and Abby went to get the first rooster from the barn while I laid out the knives and spread plastic sheets over our butchering table on the back patio. The guys stoked a fire under our 50-gallon kettle, an antique brass instrument Steven and I scored at a farm auction.

CAFO: Concentrated Animal Feed Operation.

The girls returned carrying Rooster #1 upside down, by the legs. Inversion has the immediate effect of lulling a chicken to sleep, or something near to it. What comes next is quick and final. We set the rooster gently across our big chopping block (a legendary fixture of our backyard, whose bloodstains hold visiting children in thrall), and down comes the ax. All sensation ends with that quick stroke. He must then be held by the legs over a large plastic bucket until all the blood has run out. Farmers who regularly process poultry have more equipment, including banks of "killing cones" or inverted funnels that contain the birds while the processor pierces each neck with a sharp knife, cutting two major arteries and ending brain function. We're not pros, so we have a more rudimentary setup. By lulling and swiftly decapitating my animal, I can make sure my relatively unpracticed handling won't draw out the procedure or cause pain.

What you've heard is true: the rooster will flap his wings hard during this part. If you drop him he'll thrash right across the yard, unpleasantly spewing blood all around, though the body doesn't *run*—it's nothing that well coordinated. His newly detached head silently opens and closes its mouth, down in the bottom of the gut bucket, a world apart from the ruckus. The cause of all these actions is an explosion of massively firing neurons without a brain to supervise them. Most people who claim to be running around like a chicken with its head cut off, really, are not even close. The nearest thing might be the final convulsive seconds of an All-Star wrestling match.

For Rooster #1 it was over, and into the big kettle for a quick scald. After a one-minute immersion in 145-degree water, the muscle tissue releases the feathers so they're easier to pluck. "Easier" is relative—every last feather still has to be pulled, carefully enough to avoid tearing the skin. The downy breast feathers come out by handfuls, while the long wing and tail feathers sometimes must be removed individually with pliers. If we were pros we would have an electric scalder and automatic plucker, a fascinating bucket full of rotating rubber fingers that does the job in no time flat. For future harvests we might borrow a friend's equipment, but for today we had a pulley on a tree limb so we could hoist the scalded carcass to shoulder level, suspending it there from a rope so several of us could pluck at once. Lily, Abby, and Eli pulled neck and breast feathers, making necessary observations such as "Gag, look where his head came off," and "Wonder which one of these tube thingies was his windpipe." Most kids need only about ninety seconds to get from *eeew gross* to solid science. A few weeks later Abby would give an award-winning, fully illustrated 4-H presentation entitled "You Can't Run Away on Harvest Day."

Laura and Becky and I answered the kids' questions, and also talked   25
about Mom things while working on back and wing feathers. (Our hus-
bands were on to the next beheading.) Laura and I compared notes on
our teenage daughters—relatively new drivers on the narrow country
roads between their jobs, friends, and home—and the worries that come
with that territory. I was painfully conscious of Becky's quiet, her ache for
a teenage son who never even got to acquire a driver's license. The accident that killed Larry could not have been avoided through any amount
of worry. We all cultivate illusions of safety that could fall away in the
knife edge of one second.

I wondered how we would get through this afternoon, how *she* would
get through months and years of living with impossible loss. I wondered
if I'd been tactless, inviting these dear friends to an afternoon of ending lives. And then felt stupid for that thought. People who are grieving
walk with death, every waking moment. When the rest of us dread that
we'll somehow remind them of death's existence, we are missing their
reality. Harvesting turkeys—which this family would soon do on their
own farm—was just another kind of work. A rendezvous with death, for
them, was waking up each morning without their brother and son.

By early afternoon six roosters had lost their heads, feathers, and
viscera, and were chilling on ice. We had six turkeys to go, the hardest piece of our work simply because the animals are larger and heavier.
Some of these birds were close to twenty pounds. They would take center
stage on our holiday table and those of some of our friends. At least one
would be charcuterie—in the garden I had sage, rosemary, garlic, onions,
everything we needed for turkey sausage. And the first two roosters we'd
harvested would be going on the rotisserie later that afternoon.

We allowed ourselves a break before the challenge of hoisting, pluck-
ing, and dressing the turkeys. While Lily and her friends constructed
feather crowns and ran for the poultry house to check in with the living,
the adults cracked open beers and stretched out in lawn chairs in the
September sun.

Our conversation turned quickly to the national preoccupation of
that autumn: Katrina, the hurricane that had just hit southern Louisiana
and Mississippi. We were horrified by the news that was beginning to
filter out of that flooded darkness, the children stranded on rooftops, the
bereaved and bewildered families slogging through streets waist-deep in
water, breaking plate glass windows to get bottles of water. People drowning and dying of thirst at the same time.

It was already clear this would be an epic disaster. New Orleans and   30
countless other towns across southern Louisiana and Mississippi were
being evacuated and left for dead. The news cameras had focused solely
on urban losses, sending images of flooded streets, people on rooftops,

broken storefronts, and the desperate crises of people in the city with no resources for relocating or evacuating. I had not seen one photograph from the countryside—a wrecked golf course was the closest thing to it. I wondered about the farmers whose year of work still lay in the fields, just weeks or days away from harvest, when the flood took it all. I still can't say whether the rural victims of Katrina found their support systems more resilient, or if their hardships simply went unreported.

The disaster reached into the rest of the country with unexpected tentacles. Our town and schools were already taking in people who had lost everything. The office where I'd just sent my passport for renewal was now underwater. Gasoline had passed $3 a gallon, here and elsewhere, leaving our nation in sticker shock. U.S. citizens were making outlandish declarations about staying home. Climate scientists were saying, "If you warm up the globe, you eventually pay for it." Economists were eyeing our budget deficits and predicting collapse, mayhem, infrastructure breakdown. In so many ways, disaster makes us take stock. For me it had inspired powerful cravings about living within our means. I wasn't thinking so much of my household budget or the national one but the *big* budget, the one that involves consuming approximately the same things we produce. Taking a symbolic cue from my presumed-soggy passport, I suddenly felt like sticking very close to home, with a hand on my family's production, even when it wasn't all that easy or fun—like today.

Analysts of current events were mostly looking to blame administrators. Fair enough, but there were also, it seemed, obvious vulnerabilities here—whole populations, depending on everyday, long-distance lifelines, supplies of food and water and fuel and everything else that are acutely centralized. That's what we consider normal life. Now nature had written a hugely abnormal question across the bottom of our map. I wondered what our answers might be. . . .

Understanding the Text

1. What influences Kingsolver's decision to eat meat? What makes her see this as a morally defensible position?

2. What is animal harvest, and why does Kingsolver think it is important for her family to participate in it?

Reflection and Response

3. Describe your own reactions to the events described by Kingsolver. Why do you think she depicts "harvest day" the way she does? What images does she want us to come away with? What emotional reaction do you think she hopes to elicit?

4. Kingsolver argues that "*Killing* is a culturally loaded term" and that "To believe we can live without taking life is delusional" (par. 5; par. 8). How and why does she draw these conclusions? Do you agree with her? Why or why not?

Making Connections

5. Imagine growing up in Kingsolver's household. How would daily life resemble or differ from your upbringing? Compare the relationship between her children's upbringing and food values to the relationship between your upbringing and food values. What, if anything, does your upbringing reveal about your ethics of eating?

6. Reflect on Kingsolver's, Yuval Noah Harari's ("Industrial Farming Is One of the Worst Crimes in History," p. 177), and Bill McKibben's ("The Only Way to Have a Cow," p. 161) arguments regarding the ethics of meat eating in relation to your own life experiences and moral choices. Do you eat meat? Have you harvested it? Worked with farm animals? Hunted? If you eat meat, does it matter to you if the animals you eat roam freely? Were treated humanely? Lived a good life? Do you think it is wrong to kill animals for consumption? What moral principles guide your thinking? How do the views of Kingsolver, Harari, and McKibben inform your position? Describe what influences your own position on eating meat. Which authors speak to your concerns or moral principles? How?

7. Kingsolver claims that she follows Wendell Berry's beliefs about human responsibility in animal consumption. Analyze Berry's essay "The Pleasures of Eating" (p. 46). What principles do Kingsolver and Berry share? Do you find potential points of disagreement? Locate textual examples to support your analysis.

The Only Way to Have a Cow

Bill McKibben

Bill McKibben wrote *The End of Nature* in 1989, a book often described as the first book on climate change written for a popular audience. McKibben is an environmentalist and widely published author and journalist who writes extensively on the environment, nature, food policy, economic policy, and the impact of climate change. In his book *Deep Economy: The Wealth of Communities and the Durable Future* (2007), he argues for the value of local economies and documents his year of eating locally in Middlebury, Vermont. His most recent book, *Falter: Has the Human Game Begun to Play Itself Out?* (2019), augments his earlier warnings as it wonders if humans are capable of combatting the bleak future we face. He is a frequent contributor to various publications, including *The New York Times*, *The Atlantic*, *Mother Jones*, and *Rolling Stone*. He has received many awards, fellowships, and honorary degrees and is the Schumann Distinguished Scholar at Middlebury College and a leader of the climate campaign group 350.org. In this essay, originally published in *Orion* in 2010, McKibben calls on his readers to take environmental factors into account when deciding on the ethics of eating meat.

May I say—somewhat defensively—that I haven't cooked red meat in many years? That I haven't visited a McDonald's since college? That if you asked me how I like my steak, I'd say I don't really remember? I'm not a moral abstainer—I'll eat meat when poor people in distant places offer it to me, especially when they're proud to do so and I'd be an ass to say no. But in everyday life, for a series of reasons that began with the dietary scruples of the woman I chose to marry, hamburgers just don't come into play.

I begin this way because I plan to wade into one of the most impassioned fracases now underway on the planet—to meat or not to meat—and I want to establish that I Do Not Have A Cow In This Fight. In recent years vegetarians and vegans have upped their attack on the consumption of animal flesh, pointing out not only that it's disgusting (read Jonathan Safran Foer's new book) but also a major cause of climate change. The numbers range from 18 percent of the world's greenhouse gas emissions to—in one recent study that was quickly discredited—51 percent. Whatever the exact figure, suffice it to say it's high: there's the carbon that comes from cutting down the forest to start the farm, and from the fertilizer and diesel fuel it takes to grow the corn, there's the truck exhaust from shipping cows hither and yon, and most of all the methane that emanates from the cows themselves (95 percent of it from the front end, not the hind, and these millions of feedlot cows would prefer if you used the word *eructate* in place of *belch*). This news has led to an almost endless series of statistical calculations: going vegan is 50 percent more effective in reducing greenhouse gas emissions than switching to a hybrid car according to a University of Chicago study; the UN Food and Agriculture Organization finds that a half pound of ground beef has the same effect on climate change as driving an SUV 10 miles. It has led to a lot of political statements: the British health secretary last fall called on Englishmen to cut their beefeating by dropping at least a sausage a week from their diets, and Paul McCartney has declared that "the biggest change anyone could make in their own lifestyle to help the environment would be to become vegetarian." It has even led to the marketing of a men's flip-flop called the Stop Global Warming Toepeeka that's made along entirely vegan lines.

Industrial livestock production is essentially indefensible—ethically, ecologically, and otherwise. We now use an enormous percentage of our arable land to grow corn that we feed to cows who stand in feedlots and eructate until they are slaughtered in a variety of gross ways and lodge in our ever-larger abdomens. And the fact that the product of this exercise "tastes good" sounds pretty lame as an excuse. There are technofixes—engineering the corn feed so it produces less methane, or giving the cows shots so they eructate less violently. But this type of tailpipe fix only works around the edges, and with the planet warming fast that's not enough. We should simply stop eating factory-farmed meat, and the effects on climate change would be but one of the many benefits.

> "We should simply stop eating factory-farmed meat, and the effects on climate change would be but one of the many benefits."

Still, even once you've made that commitment, there's a nagging ecological question that's just now being raised. It goes like this: long before humans had figured out the whole cow thing, nature had its own herds of hoofed ungulates. Big herds of big animals—perhaps 60 million bison ranging across North America, and maybe 100 million antelope. That's considerably more than the number of cows now resident in these United States. These were noble creatures, but uncouth—*eructate* hadn't been coined yet. They really did just belch. So why weren't they filling the atmosphere with methane? Why wasn't their manure giving off great quantities of atmosphere-altering gas?

The answer, so far as we can tell, is both interesting and potentially 5 radical in its implications. These old-school ungulates weren't all that different in their plumbing—they were methane factories with legs too. But they used those legs for something. They didn't stand still in feedlots

waiting for corn, and they didn't stand still in big western federal allot-
ments overgrazing the same tender grass. They didn't stand still at all.
Maybe they would have enjoyed stationary life, but like teenagers in a
small town, they were continually moved along by their own version of
the police: wolves. And big cats. And eventually Indians. By predators.

As they moved, they kept eating grass and dropping manure. Or, as
soil scientists would put it, they grazed the same perennials once or twice
a year to "convert aboveground biomass to dung and urine." Then dung
beetles buried the results in the soil, nurturing the grass to grow back.
These grasslands covered places that don't get much rain—the Southwest and the Plains, Australia, Africa, much of Asia. And all that grassland
sequestered stupendous amounts of carbon and methane from out of the
atmosphere—recent preliminary research indicates that methane-loving
bacteria in healthy soils will sequester more of the gas in a day than cows
supported by the same area will emit in a year.

We're flat out of predators in most parts of the world, and it's hard
to imagine, in the short time that we have to deal with climate change,
ending the eating of meat and returning the herds of buffalo and packs
of wolves to all the necessary spots. It's marginally easier to imagine
mimicking those systems with cows. The key technology here is the
single-strand electric fence—you move your herd or your flock once
or twice a day from one small pasture to the next, forcing them to eat
everything that's growing there but moving them along before they
graze all the good stuff down to bare ground. Now their manure isn't a
problem that fills a cesspool, but a key part of making the system work.
Done right, some studies suggest, this method of raising cattle could put
much of the atmosphere's oversupply of greenhouse gases back in the
soil inside half a century. That means shifting from feedlot farming to
rotational grazing is one of the few changes we could make that's on the
same scale as the problem of global warming. It won't do away with the
need for radically cutting emissions, but it could help get the car exhaust
you emitted back in high school out of the atmosphere.

Oh, and grass-fed beef is apparently much better for you—full of
Omega 3s, like sardines that moo. Better yet, it's going to be more expensive, because you can't automate the process the same way you can feedlot agriculture. You need the guy to move the fence every afternoon.
(That's why about a billion of our fellow humans currently make their
livings as herders of one kind or another—some of them use slingshots,
or dogs, or shepherd's crooks, or horses instead of electric fence, but the
principle is the same.) More expensive, in this case, as in many others,
is good; we'd end up eating meat the way most of the world does—as a
condiment, a flavor, an ingredient, not an entrée.

I doubt McDonald's will be in favor. I doubt Paul McCartney will be in favor. It doesn't get rid of the essential dilemma of killing something and then putting it in your mouth. But it's possible that the atmosphere would be in favor, and that's worth putting down your fork and thinking about.

Understanding the Text

1. Why does McKibben conclude that it is impossible to defend industrial livestock production?

2. What is the relationship between factory farming and climate change?

3. What is rotational grazing, and why does McKibben advocate a return to it?

4. Why does McKibben almost never eat meat? When does he eat meat, and why?

Reflection and Response

5. What is the significance of the title? Why do you think McKibben selected it?

6. Why does McKibben think that it is good that grass-fed beef will be or is more expensive?

Making Connections

7. McKibben concludes that neither extreme (not McDonald's and not Paul McCartney's) will favor his position. Why not? How does McKibben position himself in relation to various other positions in this debate? How would Margaret Mead ("The Changing Significance of Food," p. 138), David Biello ("Will Organic Food Fail to Feed the World?" p. 288), and Rowan Jacobsen ("The Biography of a Plant-Based Burger," p. 232) evaluate his position? Use textual evidence to support your answer.

8. McKibben suggests that an ethics of eating must concern itself with environmental factors. Does he make a good case for why this particular issue should take the forefront? Who in this collection might disagree with his position, and on what grounds? What do their positions tells us about their ethical concerns?

9. Compare the arguments made by McKibben and Yuval Noah Harari ("Industrial Farming Is One of the Worst Crimes in History," p. 177). Consider both their main conclusions and the ways they go about communicating their conclusions to readers. What kinds of evidence do they use? What kinds of rhetorical strategies do they rely on? Which argument would be more likely to motivate you to change your behavior, and why?

Monsanto's Harvest of Fear

Donald L. Barlett and James B. Steele

Donald L. Barlett and James B. Steele have reported and written together for more than four decades. As a widely acclaimed and award-winning investigative reporting team, these two American journalists have wowed audiences with their in-depth reporting and careful research and analysis of the complex issues and institutions of their times. They began working together in the 1970s at the *Philadelphia Inquirer*, then moved to *Time*, and were contributing editors at *Vanity Fair*. They have won many prominent journalism awards, including the Pulitzer Prize (twice) and the National Magazine Award (twice). They have also coauthored eight books, including *The Betrayal of the American Dream* (2012). In this selection from a longer article that first appeared in *Vanity Fair* in May 2008, Barlett and Steele investigate the role of the Monsanto corporation and the legal system in American food production.

G ary Rinehart clearly remembers the summer day in 2002 when the stranger walked in and issued his threat. Rinehart was behind the counter of the Square Deal, his "old-time country store," as he calls it, on the fading town square of Eagleville, Missouri, a tiny farm community 100 miles north of Kansas City.

The Square Deal is a fixture in Eagleville, a place where farmers and townspeople can go for lightbulbs, greeting cards, hunting gear, ice cream, aspirin, and dozens of other small items without having to drive to a big-box store in Bethany, the county seat, 15 miles down Interstate 35.

Everyone knows Rinehart, who was born and raised in the area and runs one of Eagleville's few surviving businesses. The stranger came up to the counter and asked for him by name.

"Well, that's me," said Rinehart.

As Rinehart would recall, the man began verbally attacking him, say- 5 ing he had proof that Rinehart had planted Monsanto's genetically modified (G.M.) soybeans in violation of the company's patent. Better come clean and settle with Monsanto, Rinehart says the man told him — or face the consequences.

Rinehart was incredulous, listening to the words as puzzled customers and employees looked on. Like many others in rural America, Rinehart knew of Monsanto's fierce reputation for enforcing its patents and suing anyone who allegedly violated them. But Rinehart wasn't a farmer. He wasn't a seed dealer. He hadn't planted any seeds or sold any seeds. He owned a small—a *really* small—country store in a town of 350 people. He was angry that somebody could just barge into the store and embarrass him in front of everyone. "It made me and my business look bad," he says. Rinehart says he told the intruder, "You got the wrong guy."

When the stranger persisted, Rinehart showed him the door. On the way out the man kept making threats. Rinehart says he can't remember the exact words, but they were to the effect of: "Monsanto is big. You can't win. We will get you. You will pay."

Scenes like this are playing out in many parts of rural America these days as Monsanto goes after farmers, farmers' co-ops, seed dealers—anyone it suspects may have infringed its patents of genetically modified seeds. As interviews and reams of court documents reveal, Monsanto relies on a shadowy army of private investigators and agents in the American heartland to strike fear into farm country. They fan out into fields and farm towns, where they secretly videotape and photograph farmers, store owners, and co-ops; infiltrate community meetings; and gather information from informants about farming activities. Farmers say that some Monsanto agents pretend to be surveyors. Others confront farmers on their land and try to pressure them to sign papers giving Monsanto access to their private records. Farmers call them the "seed police" and use words such as "Gestapo" and "Mafia" to describe their tactics.

When asked about these practices, Monsanto declined to comment specifically, other than to say that the company is simply protecting its patents. "Monsanto spends more than $2 million a day in research to identify, test, develop, and bring to market innovative new seeds and technologies that benefit farmers," Monsanto spokesman Darren Wallis wrote in an e-mailed letter to *Vanity Fair*. "One tool in protecting this investment is patenting our discoveries and, if necessary, legally defending those patents against those who might choose to infringe upon them." Wallis said that, while the vast majority of farmers and seed dealers follow the licensing agreements, "a tiny fraction" do not, and that Monsanto is obligated to those who do abide by its rules to enforce its patent rights on those who "reap the benefits of the technology without paying for its use." He said only a small number of cases ever go to trial.

Some compare Monsanto's hard-line approach to Microsoft's zealous   10 efforts to protect its software from pirates. At least with Microsoft the buyer of a program can use it over and over again. But farmers who buy Monsanto's seeds can't even do that.

The Control of Nature

For centuries — millennia — farmers have saved seeds from season to season: they planted in the spring, harvested in the fall, then reclaimed and cleaned the seeds over the winter for re-planting the next spring. Monsanto has turned this ancient practice on its head.

Monsanto developed G.M. seeds that would resist its own herbicide, Roundup, offering farmers a convenient way to spray fields with weed killer without affecting crops. Monsanto then patented the seeds. For nearly all of its history the United States Patent and Trademark Office had refused to grant patents on seeds, viewing them as life-forms with too many variables to be patented. "It's not like describing a widget," says Joseph Mendelson III, the legal director of the Center for Food Safety, which has tracked Monsanto's activities in rural America for years.

Indeed not. But in 1980 the U.S. Supreme Court, in a five-to-four decision, turned seeds into widgets, laying the groundwork for a handful of corporations to begin taking control of the world's food supply. In its decision, the court extended patent law to cover "a live human-made microorganism." In this case, the organism wasn't even a seed. Rather, it was a *Pseudomonas* bacterium developed by a General Electric scientist to clean up oil spills. But the precedent was set, and Monsanto took advantage of it. Since the 1980s, Monsanto has become the world leader in genetic modification of seeds and has won 674 biotechnology patents, more than any other company, according to U.S. Department of Agriculture data.

Farmers who buy Monsanto's patented Roundup Ready seeds are required to sign an agreement promising not to save the seed produced after each harvest for re-planting, or to sell the seed to other farmers. This means that farmers must buy new seed every year. Those increased sales, coupled with ballooning sales of its Roundup weed killer, have been a bonanza for Monsanto.

This radical departure from age-old practice has created turmoil in 15 farm country. Some farmers don't fully understand that they aren't supposed to save Monsanto's seeds for next year's planting. Others do, but ignore the stipulation rather than throw away a perfectly usable product. Still others say that they don't use Monsanto's genetically modified seeds, but seeds have been blown into their fields by wind or deposited by birds. It's certainly easy for G.M. seeds to get mixed in with traditional varieties when seeds are cleaned by commercial dealers for re-planting. The seeds look identical; only a laboratory analysis can show the difference. Even if a farmer doesn't buy G.M. seeds and doesn't want them on his land, it's a safe bet he'll get a visit from Monsanto's seed police if crops grown from G.M. seeds are discovered in his fields.

Most Americans know Monsanto because of what it sells to put on our lawns — the ubiquitous weed killer Roundup. What they may not know is that the company now profoundly influences — and one day may virtually control — what we put on our tables. For most of its history Monsanto was a chemical giant, producing some of the most toxic substances ever created, residues from which have left us with some of the most polluted sites on earth. Yet in a little more than a decade, the company has sought to shed its polluted past and morph into something much different and more far-reaching — an "agricultural company" dedicated to making the world "a better place for future generations." Still, more than one Web log claims to see similarities between Monsanto and the fictional company "U-North" in the movie *Michael Clayton*, an agribusiness giant accused in a multibillion-dollar lawsuit of selling an herbicide that causes cancer.

Monsanto's genetically modified seeds have transformed the company and are radically altering global agriculture. So far, the company has produced G.M. seeds for soybeans, corn, canola, and cotton. Many more products have been developed or are in the pipeline, including seeds for sugar beets and alfalfa. The company is also seeking to extend its reach into milk production by marketing an artificial growth hormone for cows that increases their output, and it is taking aggressive steps to put those who don't want to use growth hormone at a commercial disadvantage.

> "Most Americans know Monsanto because of what it sells to put on our lawns — the ubiquitous weed killer Roundup. What they may not know is that the company now profoundly influences — and one day may virtually control — what we put on our tables."

Even as the company is pushing its G.M. agenda, Monsanto is buying up conventional-seed companies. In 2005, Monsanto paid $1.4 billion for Seminis, which controlled 40 percent of the U.S. market for lettuce, tomatoes, and other vegetable and fruit seeds. Two weeks later it announced the acquisition of the country's third-largest cottonseed company, Emergent Genetics, for $300 million. It's estimated that Monsanto seeds now account for 90 percent of the U.S. production of soybeans, which are used in food products beyond counting. Monsanto's acquisitions have fueled explosive growth, transforming the St. Louis–based corporation into the largest seed company in the world.

In Iraq, the groundwork has been laid to protect the patents of Monsanto and other G.M.-seed companies. One of L. Paul Bremer's last acts as head of the Coalition Provisional Authority was an order stipulating that "farmers shall be prohibited from re-using seeds of protected varieties." Monsanto has said that it has no interest in doing business in Iraq, but should the company change its mind, the American-style law is in place.

To be sure, more and more agricultural corporations and individ- 20 ual farmers are using Monsanto's G.M. seeds. As recently as 1980, no genetically modified crops were grown in the U.S. In 2007, the total was 142 million acres planted. Worldwide, the figure was 282 million acres. Many farmers believe that G.M. seeds increase crop yields and save money. Another reason for their attraction is convenience. By using Roundup Ready soybean seeds, a farmer can spend less time tending to his fields. With Monsanto seeds, a farmer plants his crop, then treats it later with Roundup to kill weeds. That takes the place of labor-intensive weed control and plowing.

Monsanto portrays its move into G.M. seeds as a giant leap for mankind. But out in the American countryside, Monsanto's no-holds-barred tactics have made it feared and loathed. Like it or not, farmers say, they have fewer and fewer choices in buying seeds.

And controlling the seeds is not some abstraction. Whoever provides the world's seeds controls the world's food supply.

Under Surveillance

After Monsanto's investigator confronted Gary Rinehart, Monsanto filed a federal lawsuit alleging that Rinehart "knowingly, intentionally, and willfully" planted seeds "in violation of Monsanto's patent rights." The company's complaint made it sound as if Monsanto had Rinehart dead to rights:

During the 2002 growing season, Investigator Jeffery Moore, through surveillance of Mr. Rinehart's farm facility and farming operations, observed Defendant planting brown bag soybean seed. Mr. Moore observed the Defendant take the brown bag soybeans to a field, which was subsequently loaded into a grain drill and planted. Mr. Moore located two empty bags in the ditch in the public road right-of-way beside one of the fields planted by Rinehart, which contained some soybeans. Mr. Moore collected a small amount of soybeans left in the bags which Defendant had tossed into the public right-of-way. These samples tested positive for Monsanto's Roundup Ready technology.

Faced with a federal lawsuit, Rinehart had to hire a lawyer. Monsanto eventually realized that "Investigator Jeffery Moore" had targeted the wrong man, and dropped the suit. Rinehart later learned that the company had been secretly investigating farmers in his area. Rinehart never heard from Monsanto again: no letter of apology, no public concession that the company had made a terrible mistake, no offer to pay his attorney's fees. "I don't know how they get away with it," he says. "If I tried to do something like that it would be bad news. I felt like I was in another country."

Gary Rinehart is actually one of Monsanto's luckier targets. Ever 25 since commercial introduction of its G.M. seeds, in 1996, Monsanto has launched thousands of investigations and filed lawsuits against hundreds of farmers and seed dealers. In a 2007 report, the Center for Food Safety, in Washington, D.C., documented 112 such lawsuits, in 27 states.

Even more significant, in the Center's opinion, are the numbers of farmers who settle because they don't have the money or the time to fight Monsanto. "The number of cases filed is only the tip of the iceberg," says Bill Freese, the Center's science-policy analyst. Freese says he has been told of many cases in which Monsanto investigators showed up at a farmer's house or confronted him in his fields, claiming he had violated the technology agreement and demanding to see his records. According to Freese, investigators will say, "Monsanto knows that you are saving Roundup Ready seeds, and if you don't sign these information-release forms, Monsanto is going to come after you and take your farm or take you for all you're worth." Investigators will sometimes show a farmer a photo of himself coming out of a store, to let him know he is being followed.

Lawyers who have represented farmers sued by Monsanto say that intimidating actions like these are commonplace. Most give in and pay Monsanto some amount in damages; those who resist face the full force of Monsanto's legal wrath. . . .

The Milk Wars

Jeff Kleinpeter takes very good care of his dairy cows. In the winter he turns on heaters to warm their barns. In the summer, fans blow gentle breezes to cool them, and on especially hot days, a fine mist floats down to take the edge off Louisiana's heat. The dairy has gone "to the ultimate end of the earth for cow comfort," says Kleinpeter, a fourth-generation dairy farmer in Baton Rouge. He says visitors marvel at what he does: "I've had many of them say, 'When I die, I want to come back as a Kleinpeter cow.' "

Monsanto would like to change the way Jeff Kleinpeter and his family do business. Specifically, Monsanto doesn't like the label on Kleinpeter

Dairy's milk cartons: "From Cows *Not* Treated with rBGH." To consumers, that means the milk comes from cows that were not given artificial bovine growth hormone, a supplement developed by Monsanto that can be injected into dairy cows to increase their milk output.

No one knows what effect, if any, the hormone has on milk or the 30 people who drink it. Studies have not detected any difference in the quality of milk produced by cows that receive rBGH, or rBST, a term by which it is also known. But Jeff Kleinpeter—like millions of consumers—wants no part of rBGH. Whatever its effect on humans, if any, Kleinpeter feels certain it's harmful to cows because it speeds up their metabolism and increases the chances that they'll contract a painful illness that can shorten their lives. "It's like putting a Volkswagen car in with the Indianapolis 500 racers," he says. "You gotta keep the pedal to the metal the whole way through, and pretty soon that poor little Volkswagen engine's going to burn up."

Kleinpeter Dairy has never used Monsanto's artificial hormone, and the dairy requires other dairy farmers from whom it buys milk to attest that they don't use it, either. At the suggestion of a marketing consultant, the dairy began advertising its milk as coming from rBGH-free cows in 2005, and the label began appearing on Kleinpeter milk cartons and in company literature, including a new Web site of Kleinpeter products that proclaims, "We treat our cows with love . . . not rBGH."

The dairy's sales soared. For Kleinpeter, it was simply a matter of giving consumers more information about their product.

But giving consumers that information has stirred the ire of Monsanto. The company contends that advertising by Kleinpeter and other dairies touting their "no rBGH" milk reflects adversely on Monsanto's product. In a letter to the Federal Trade Commission in February 2007, Monsanto said that, notwithstanding the overwhelming evidence that there is no difference in the milk from cows treated with its product, "milk processors persist in claiming on their labels and in advertisements that the use of rBST is somehow harmful, either to cows or to the people who consume milk from rBST-supplemented cows."

Monsanto called on the commission to investigate what it called the "deceptive advertising and labeling practices" of milk processors such as Kleinpeter, accusing them of misleading consumers "by falsely claiming that there are health and safety risks associated with milk from rBST-supplemented cows." As noted, Kleinpeter does not make any such claims—he simply states that his milk comes from cows not injected with rBGH.

Monsanto's attempt to get the F.T.C. to force dairies to change their 35 advertising was just one more step in the corporation's efforts to extend its reach into agriculture. After years of scientific debate and public controversy, the F.D.A. in 1993 approved commercial use of rBST, basing its decision in part on studies submitted by Monsanto. That decision allowed the company to market the artificial hormone. The effect of the hormone is to increase milk production, not exactly something the nation needed then—or needs now. The U.S. was actually awash in milk, with the government buying up the surplus to prevent a collapse in prices.

Monsanto began selling the supplement in 1994 under the name Posilac. Monsanto acknowledges that the possible side effects of rBST for cows include lameness, disorders of the uterus, increased body temperature, digestive problems, and birthing difficulties. Veterinary drug reports note that "cows injected with Posilac are at an increased risk for mastitis," an udder infection in which bacteria and pus may be pumped out with the milk. What's the effect on humans? The F.D.A. has consistently said that the milk produced by cows that receive rBGH is the same as milk from cows that aren't injected: "The public can be confident that milk and meat from BST-treated cows is safe to consume." Nevertheless, some scientists are concerned by the lack of long-term studies to test the additive's impact, especially on children. A Wisconsin geneticist, William von Meyer, observed that when rBGH was approved the longest study on which the F.D.A.'s approval was based covered only a 90-day laboratory test with small animals. "But people drink milk for a lifetime," he noted. Canada and the European Union have never approved the commercial sale of the artificial hormone. Today, nearly 15 years after the F.D.A. approved rBGH, there have still been no long-term studies "to determine the safety of milk from cows that receive artificial growth hormone," says Michael Hansen, senior staff scientist for Consumers Union. Not only have there been no studies, he adds, but the data that does exist all comes from Monsanto. "There is no scientific consensus about the safety," he says.

However F.D.A. approval came about, Monsanto has long been wired into Washington. Michael R. Taylor was a staff attorney and executive assistant to the F.D.A. commissioner before joining a law firm in Washington in 1981, where he worked to secure F.D.A. approval of Monsanto's artificial growth hormone before returning to the F.D.A. as deputy commissioner in 1991. Dr. Michael A. Friedman, formerly the F.D.A.'s deputy commissioner for operations, joined Monsanto in 1999 as a senior vice president. Linda J. Fisher was an assistant administrator at the E.P.A. when she left the agency in 1993. She became a vice president of Monsanto, from 1995 to 2000, only to return to the E.P.A. as deputy administrator the next year. William D. Ruckelshaus, former E.P.A.

administrator, and Mickey Kantor, former U.S. trade representative, each served on Monsanto's board after leaving government. Supreme Court justice Clarence Thomas was an attorney in Monsanto's corporate-law department in the 1970s. He wrote the Supreme Court opinion in a crucial G.M.-seed patent-rights case in 2001 that benefited Monsanto and all G.M.-seed companies. Donald Rumsfeld never served on the board or held any office at Monsanto, but Monsanto must occupy a soft spot in the heart of the former defense secretary. Rumsfeld was chairman and C.E.O. of the pharmaceutical maker G. D. Searle & Co. when Monsanto acquired Searle in 1985, after Searle had experienced difficulty in finding a buyer. Rumsfeld's stock and options in Searle were valued at $12 million at the time of the sale.

From the beginning some consumers have consistently been hesitant to drink milk from cows treated with artificial hormones. This is one reason Monsanto has waged so many battles with dairies and regulators over the wording of labels on milk cartons. It has sued at least two dairies and one co-op over labeling.

Critics of the artificial hormone have pushed for mandatory labeling on all milk products, but the F.D.A. has resisted and even taken action against some dairies that labeled their milk "BST-free." Since BST is a natural hormone found in all cows, including those not injected with Monsanto's artificial version, the F.D.A. argued that no dairy could claim that its milk is BST-free. The F.D.A. later issued guidelines allowing dairies to use labels saying their milk comes from "non-supplemented cows," as long as the carton has a disclaimer saying that the artificial supplement does not in any way change the milk. So the milk cartons from Kleinpeter Dairy, for example, carry a label on the front stating that the milk is from cows not treated with rBGH, and the rear panel says, "Government studies have shown no significant difference between milk derived from rBGH-treated and non-rBGH-treated cows." That's not good enough for Monsanto.

The Next Battleground

As more and more dairies have chosen to advertise their milk as "No 40 rBGH," Monsanto has gone on the offensive. Its attempt to force the F.T.C. to look into what Monsanto called "deceptive practices" by dairies trying to distance themselves from the company's artificial hormone was the most recent national salvo. But after reviewing Monsanto's claims, the F.T.C.'s Division of Advertising Practices decided in August 2007 that a "formal investigation and enforcement action is not warranted at this time." The agency found some instances where dairies had made "unfounded health and safety claims," but these were mostly on Web sites, not on milk cartons. And the F.T.C. determined that the dairies Monsanto had singled out all carried disclaimers that the F.D.A. had found no significant differences in milk from cows treated with the artificial hormone.

Blocked at the federal level, Monsanto is pushing for action by the states. In the fall of 2007, Pennsylvania's agriculture secretary, Dennis Wolff, issued an edict prohibiting dairies from stamping milk containers with labels stating their products were made without the use of the artificial hormone. Wolff said such a label implies that competitors' milk is not safe, and noted that non-supplemented milk comes at an unjustified higher price, arguments that Monsanto has frequently made. The ban was to take effect February 1, 2008.

Wolff's action created a firestorm in Pennsylvania (and beyond) from angry consumers. So intense was the outpouring of e-mails, letters, and calls that Pennsylvania governor Edward Rendell stepped in and reversed his agriculture secretary, saying, "The public has a right to complete information about how the milk they buy is produced."

On this issue, the tide may be shifting against Monsanto. Organic dairy products, which don't involve rBGH, are soaring in popularity. Supermarket chains such as Kroger, Publix, and Safeway are embracing them. Some other companies have turned away from rBGH products, including Starbucks, which has banned all milk products from cows treated with rBGH. Although Monsanto once claimed that an estimated 30 percent of the nation's dairy cows were injected with rBST, it's widely believed that today the number is much lower.

But don't count Monsanto out. Efforts similar to the one in Pennsylvania have been launched in other states, including New Jersey, Ohio, Indiana, Kansas, Utah, and Missouri. A Monsanto-backed group called AFACT—American Farmers for the Advancement and Conservation of Technology—has been spearheading efforts in many of these states. AFACT describes itself as a "producer organization" that decries "questionable labeling tactics and activism" by marketers who have convinced some consumers to "shy away from foods using new technology." AFACT reportedly uses the same St. Louis public-relations firm, Osborn & Barr, employed by Monsanto. An Osborn & Barr spokesman told the *Kansas City Star* that the company was doing work for AFACT on a pro bono basis.

Even if Monsanto's efforts to secure across-the-board labeling changes 45 should fall short, there's nothing to stop state agriculture departments from restricting labeling on a dairy-by-dairy basis. Beyond that,

Monsanto also has allies whose foot soldiers will almost certainly keep up the pressure on dairies that don't use Monsanto's artificial hormone. Jeff Kleinpeter knows about them, too.

He got a call one day from the man who prints the labels for his milk cartons, asking if he had seen the attack on Kleinpeter Dairy that had been posted on the Internet. Kleinpeter went online to a site called StopLabelingLies, which claims to "help consumers by publicizing examples of false and misleading food and other product labels." There, sure enough, Kleinpeter and other dairies that didn't use Monsanto's product were being accused of making misleading claims to sell their milk.

There was no address or phone number on the Web site, only a list of groups that apparently contribute to the site and whose issues range from disparaging organic farming to downplaying the impact of global warming. "They were criticizing people like me for doing what we had a right to do, had gone through a government agency to do," says Kleinpeter. "We never could get to the bottom of that Web site to get that corrected."

As it turns out, the Web site counts among its contributors Steven Milloy, the "junk science" commentator for FoxNews.com and operator of junkscience.com, which claims to debunk "faulty scientific data and analysis." It may come as no surprise that earlier in his career, Milloy, who calls himself the "junkman," was a registered lobbyist for Monsanto.

Understanding the Text

1. What are genetically modified seeds? What are Roundup Ready seeds?
2. Why is Monsanto trying to protect its patent?
3. How has Monsanto changed farming practices? What ancient practices are being eliminated?

Reflection and Response

4. What's at stake in the legal battles between Monsanto and the farmers accused of misusing patented seeds? Why is Monsanto trying to protect its interests so vigorously? Why and how are some farmers fighting back?
5. Barlett and Steele's investigative reporting is aimed at exposing Monsanto's ruthless tactics, legal and otherwise. How do they do this? What rhetorical strategies do they employ? How and why are their strategies effective?
6. Why does Monsanto care about how dairy farmers advertise their products? Should Monsanto have a say? Who should decide? And whose position is morally defensible, and why?

Making Connections

7. Describe Monsanto's tactics for protecting its own interests. Are they ethically justified? Why or why not? Which authors in this collection would critique Monsanto's tactics? Would any defend them? Use textual evidence to support your answers.

8. Barlett and Steele claim that Monsanto "profoundly influences — and one day may virtually control — what we put on our tables" (par. 16). How do they support this argument? Using your campus library resources, locate at least two other sources that discuss the impact of Monsanto on food production to develop your response to these questions. Use textual evidence to support your responses.

Industrial Farming Is One of the Worst Crimes in History

Yuval Noah Harari

Yuval Noah Harari is a prolific and award-winning writer and professor of history. He was born in Israel, where he attended college before moving to Oxford to complete his doctoral work at Jesus College. He has published numerous books and articles, both for academic and general audiences, and won many prestigious honors for his work. He is most known for his books *Sapiens: A Brief History of Humankind* (2011) and *21 Lessons for the 21st Century* (2018); video clips of his lectures on this material and free online courses that cover it can be found on the internet. Harari is proud to be a vegan and is known for writing about the plight of domesticated animals raised under industrial farming. The essay included here, originally published in the *Guardian*, looks to history to explore the state of industrial farming and our ethical obligations to the animals that live and die in its grasp.

Animals are the main victims of history, and the treatment of domesticated animals in industrial farms is perhaps the worst crime in history. The march of human progress is strewn with dead animals. Even tens of thousands of years ago, our stone age ancestors were already responsible for a series of ecological disasters. When the first humans reached Australia about 45,000 years ago, they quickly drove to extinction 90% of its large animals. This was the first significant impact that Homo sapiens had on the planet's ecosystem. It was not the last.

About 15,000 years ago, humans colonised America, wiping out in the process about 75% of its large mammals. Numerous other species disappeared from Africa, from Eurasia and from the myriad islands around their coasts. The archaeological record of country after country tells the same sad story. The tragedy opens with a scene showing a rich and varied population of large animals, without any trace of Homo sapiens. In scene two, humans appear, evidenced by a fossilized bone, a spear point, or perhaps a campfire. Scene three quickly follows, in which men and women occupy center-stage and most large animals, along with many smaller ones, have gone. Altogether, sapiens drove to extinction about 50% of all the large terrestrial mammals of the planet before they planted the first wheat field, shaped the first metal tool, wrote the first text or struck the first coin.

The next major landmark in human-animal relations was the agricultural revolution: the process by which we turned from nomadic hunter-gatherers into farmers living in permanent settlements.

It involved the appearance of a completely new life-form on Earth: domesticated animals. Initially, this development might seem to have been of minor importance, as humans only managed to domesticate fewer than 20 species of mammals and birds, compared with the countless thousands of species that remained "wild." Yet, with the passing of the centuries, this novel life-form became the norm. Today, more than 90% of all large animals are domesticated ("large" denotes animals that weigh at least a few kilograms). Consider the chicken, for example. Ten thousand years ago, it was a rare bird that was confined to small niches of South Asia. Today, billions of chickens live on almost every continent and island, bar Antarctica. The domesticated chicken is probably the most widespread bird in the annals of planet Earth. If you measure success in terms of numbers, chickens, cows and pigs are the most successful animals ever.

Alas, domesticated species paid for their unparalleled collective success with unprecedented individual suffering. The animal kingdom has known many types of pain and misery for millions of years. Yet the agricultural revolution created completely new kinds of suffering, ones that only worsened with the passing of the generations.

At first sight, domesticated animals may seem much better off than   5 their wild cousins and ancestors. Wild buffaloes spend their days searching for food, water and shelter, and are constantly threatened by lions, parasites, floods and droughts. Domesticated cattle, by contrast, enjoy care and protection from humans. People provide cows and calves with food, water and shelter, they treat their diseases, and protect them from predators and natural disasters. True, most cows and calves sooner or later find themselves in the slaughterhouse. Yet does that make their fate any worse than that of wild buffaloes? Is it better to be devoured by a lion than slaughtered by a man? Are crocodile teeth kinder than steel blades?

What makes the existence of domesticated farm animals particularly cruel is not just the way in which they die but above all how they live. Two competing factors have shaped the living conditions of farm animals: on the one hand, humans want meat, milk, eggs, leather, animal muscle-power and amusement; on the other, humans have to ensure the long-term survival and reproduction of farm animals. Theoretically, this should protect animals from extreme cruelty. If a farmer milks his cow without providing her with food and water, milk production will dwindle, and the cow herself will quickly die. Unfortunately, humans can cause tremendous suffering to farm animals in other ways, even while ensuring their survival and reproduction. The root of the problem is that domesticated animals have inherited from their wild ancestors many physical, emotional and social needs that are redundant in farms.

Pigs being transported to the slaughterhouse.
paul prescott/Shutterstock

Farmers routinely ignore these needs without paying any economic price. They lock animals in tiny cages, mutilate their horns and tails, separate mothers from offspring, and selectively breed monstrosities. The animals suffer greatly, yet they live on and multiply.

Doesn't that contradict the most basic principles of Darwinian evolution? The theory of evolution maintains that all instincts and drives have evolved in the interest of survival and reproduction. If so, doesn't the continuous reproduction of farm animals prove that all their real needs are met? How can a cow have a "need" that is not really essential for survival and reproduction?

It is certainly true that all instincts and drives evolved in order to meet the evolutionary pressures of survival and reproduction. When these pressures disappear, however, the instincts and drives they had shaped do not evaporate instantly. Even if they are no longer instrumental for survival and reproduction, they continue to mold the subjective experiences of the animal. The physical, emotional and social needs of present-day cows, dogs and humans don't reflect their current conditions but rather the evolutionary pressures their ancestors encountered tens of thousands of years ago. Why do modern people love sweets so much? Not because in the early 21st century we must gorge on ice cream and chocolate in order to survive. Rather, it is because if our stone age ancestors came across sweet, ripened fruits, the most sensible thing to do was to eat as many of them as they could as quickly as possible. Why do young men drive recklessly, get involved in violent rows, and hack confidential internet sites? Because they are obeying ancient genetic decrees. Seventy thousand years ago, a young hunter who risked his life chasing a mammoth outshone all his competitors and won the hand of the local beauty – and we are now stuck with his macho genes.

Exactly the same evolutionary logic shapes the life of cows and calves in our industrial farms. Ancient wild cattle were social animals. In order to survive and reproduce, they needed to communicate, cooperate and compete effectively. Like all social mammals, wild cattle learned the necessary social skills through play. Puppies, kittens, calves and children all love to play because evolution implanted this urge in them. In the wild, they needed to play. If they didn't, they would not learn the social skills vital for survival and reproduction. If a kitten or calf was born with some rare mutation that made them indifferent to play, they were unlikely to survive or reproduce, just as they would not exist in the first place if their ancestors hadn't acquired those skills. Similarly, evolution implanted in puppies, kittens, calves and children an overwhelming desire to bond with their mothers. A chance mutation weakening the mother-infant bond was a death sentence.

"Tragically, the agricultural revolution gave humans the power to ensure the survival and reproduction of domesticated animals while ignoring their subjective needs. In consequence, domesticated animals are collectively the most successful animals in the world, and at the same time they are individually the most miserable animals that have ever existed."

What happens when farmers now take a young calf, separate her from her mother, put her in a tiny cage, vaccinate her against various diseases, provide her with food and water, and then, when she is old enough, artificially inseminate her with bull sperm? From an objective perspective, this calf no longer needs either maternal bonding or playmates in order to survive and reproduce. All her needs are being taken care of by her human masters. But from a subjective perspective, the calf still feels a strong urge to bond with her mother and to play with other calves. If these urges are not fulfilled, the calf suffers greatly.

This is the basic lesson of evolutionary psychology: a need shaped thousands of generations ago continues to be felt subjectively even if it is no longer necessary for survival and reproduction in the present. Tragically, the agricultural revolution gave humans the power to ensure the survival and reproduction of domesticated animals while ignoring their subjective needs. In consequence, domesticated animals are collectively the most successful animals in the world, and at the same time they are individually the most miserable animals that have ever existed.

The situation has only worsened over the last few centuries, during which time traditional agriculture gave way to industrial farming. In traditional societies such as ancient Egypt, the Roman empire or medieval China, humans had a very partial understanding of biochemistry, genetics, zoology and epidemiology°. Consequently, their manipulative powers were limited. In medieval villages, chickens ran free between the houses, pecked seeds and worms from the garbage heap, and built nests in the barn. If an ambitious peasant tried to lock 1,000 chickens inside a crowded coop, a deadly bird-flu epidemic would probably have resulted, wiping out all the chickens, as well as many villagers. No priest, shaman or witch doctor could have prevented it. But once modern science had deciphered the secrets of birds, viruses and antibiotics, humans could begin to subject animals to extreme living conditions. With the help of vaccinations, medications, hormones, pesticides, central air-conditioning systems and automatic feeders, it is now possible to cram tens of thousands of chickens into tiny coops, and produce meat and eggs with unprecedented efficiency.

The fate of animals in such industrial installations has become one of the most pressing ethical issues of our time, certainly in terms of the numbers involved. These days, most big animals live on industrial farms. We imagine that our planet is populated by lions, elephants, whales and penguins. That may be true of the National Geographic channel, Disney movies and children's fairytales, but it is no longer true of the real world. The world contains 40,000 lions but, by way of contrast, there are around 1 billion domesticated pigs; 500,000 elephants and 1.5 billion domesticated cows; 50 million penguins and 20 billion chickens.

In 2009, there were 1.6 billion wild birds in Europe, counting all species together. That same year, the European meat and egg industry raised 1.9 billion chickens. Altogether, the domesticated animals of the world weigh about 700m tons, compared with 300m tons for humans, and fewer than 100m tons for large wild animals.

This is why the fate of farm animals is not an ethical side issue. 15 It concerns the majority of Earth's large creatures: tens of billions of sentient beings, each with a complex world of sensations and emotions, but which live and die on an industrial production line. Forty years ago,

---

epidemiology: the study of causes, effects, and patterns of health and disease across defined populations.

the moral philosopher Peter Singer published his canonical book *Animal Liberation*, which has done much to change people's minds on this issue. Singer claimed that industrial farming is responsible for more pain and misery than all the wars of history put together.

The scientific study of animals has played a dismal role in this tragedy. The scientific community has used its growing knowledge of animals mainly to manipulate their lives more efficiently in the service of human industry. Yet this same knowledge has demonstrated beyond reasonable doubt that farm animals are sentient beings, with intricate social relations and sophisticated psychological patterns. They may not be as intelligent as us, but they certainly know pain, fear and loneliness. They too can suffer, and they too can be happy.

It is high time we take these scientific findings to heart, because as human power keeps growing, our ability to harm or benefit other animals grows with it. For 4 billion years, life on Earth was governed by natural selection. Now it is governed increasingly by human intelligent design. Biotechnology, nanotechnology° and artificial intelligence will soon enable humans to reshape living beings in radical new ways, which will redefine the very meaning of life. When we come to design this brave new world, we should take into account the welfare of all sentient beings, and not just of Homo sapiens.

nanotechnology: the science of manipulating matter on a very small (atomic or molecular) scale.

Understanding the Text

1. How are domesticated animals treated on industrial farms?
2. What is Darwinian evolution? What is there about industrial animal farming that contradicts its basic principles?
3. How do most industrial farm animals reproduce?

Reflection and Response

4. Harari describes the origin and fate of the chicken — from rare to the most widespread bird on the planet. Recount his story, reflect on what it illustrates, and comment on the role it plays in his argument.
5. How and why does Harari use evolutionary psychology to help support his argument?
6. According to Harari, what role does science play in causing the pain and misery suffered by industrial farm animals?
7. Describe your personal reaction to the staggering statistics offered by Harari. Why do you think you have the reactions that you do? What does your reaction say about your values?

Making Connections

8. Harari claims that industrial farming might be the worst crime in history and is a pressing ethical concern. Consider the arguments made by Barbara Kingsolver ("You Can't Run Away on Harvest Day," p. 150) and Bill McKibben ("The Only Way to Have a Cow," p. 161). To what extent do they each agree with Harari? Compare how they support their positions — the kinds of reasons they provide, the assumptions they rely on, what they count as evidence, and what they each emphasize.

9. Margaret Mead ("The Changing Significance of Food," p. 138) credits the Industrial Revolution with increasing our capacity to produce food such that we can now feed the world's population. She argues that this changes the moral obligations of those who live in countries where food is abundant. Harari argues that this technological capability has brought with it other ethical dilemmas — most notably the welfare of all animals, not just humans. Drawing on three or four other sources from this book, make an argument for how you think we should weigh these various ethical obligations. For example, you may want to consider Blake Hurst's view of the Industrial Revolution ("The Omnivore's Delusion," p. 184) in your analysis.

The Omnivore's Delusion: Against the Agri-intellectuals

Blake Hurst

Blake Hurst has farmed for more than 30 years, first as a hog farmer and now as a grower of corn, soybeans, and flowers on his family farm in northwest Missouri. He also serves as president of the Missouri Farm Bureau. As a freelance writer, Hurst has published many articles on food and farming in the *Wall Street Journal*, *The New York Times*, *Wilson Quarterly*, and the *American*, among other periodicals. In this oft-quoted essay, originally published in 2009 in the *American* (the online magazine of the American Enterprise Institute), Hurst questions various ethical arguments against farming practices. He blasts the way intellectuals criticize industrial farming, arguing that their critiques are unfair and reliant on ignorance.

I'm dozing, as I often do on airplanes, but the guy behind me has been broadcasting nonstop for nearly three hours. I finally admit defeat and start some serious eavesdropping. He's talking about food, damning farming, particularly livestock farming, compensating for his lack of knowledge with volume.

I'm so tired of people who wouldn't visit a doctor who used a stethoscope instead of an MRI demanding that farmers like me use 1930s technology to raise food. Farming has always been messy and painful, and bloody and dirty. It still is.

But now we have to listen to self-appointed experts on airplanes frightening their seatmates about the profession I have practiced for more than 30 years. I'd had enough. I turned around and politely told the lecturer that he ought not believe everything he reads. He quieted and asked me what kind of farming I do. I told him, and when he asked if I used organic farming, I said no, and left it at that. I didn't answer with the first thought that came to mind, which is simply this: I deal in the real world, not superstitions, and unless the consumer absolutely forces my hand, I am about as likely to adopt organic methods as the *Wall Street Journal* is to publish their next edition by setting the type by hand.

He was a businessman, and I'm sure spends his days with spreadsheets, projections, and marketing studies. He hasn't used a slide rule in his career and wouldn't make projections with tea leaves or soothsayers. He does not blame witchcraft for a bad quarter, or expect the factory that makes his product to use steam power instead of electricity, or horses and wagons to deliver his products instead of trucks and trains. But he expects me to farm like my grandfather, and not incidentally, I suppose, to live like him as well. He thinks farmers are too stupid to farm sustainably, too cruel to treat their animals well, and too careless to worry about their communities, their health, and their families. I would not presume to criticize his car, or the size of his house, or the way he runs his business. But he is an expert about me, on the strength of one book, and is sharing that expertise with captive audiences every time he gets the chance. Enough, enough, enough.

Industrial Farming and Its Critics

Critics of "industrial farming" spend most of their time concerned   5
with the processes by which food is raised. This is because the results of organic production are so, well, troublesome. With the subtraction of every "unnatural" additive, molds, fungus, and bugs increase. Since it is difficult to sell a religion with so many readily quantifiable bad results, the trusty family farmer has to be thrown into the breach, saving the whole organic movement by his saintly presence, chewing on his straw, plodding along, at one with his environment, his community, his neighborhood. Except that some of the largest farms in the country are organic—and are giant organizations dependent upon lots of hired stoop labor doing the most backbreaking of tasks in order to save the sensitive conscience of my fellow passenger the merest whiff of pesticide contamination. They do not spend much time talking about that at the Whole Foods store.

The most delicious irony is this: the parts of farming that are the most "industrial" are the most likely to be owned by the kind of family farmers that elicit such a positive response from the consumer. Corn farms are almost all owned and managed by small family farmers. But corn farmers salivate at the thought of one more biotech breakthrough, use vast amounts of energy to increase production, and raise large quantities of an indistinguishable commodity to sell to huge corporations that turn that corn into thousands of industrial products.

Most livestock is produced by family farms, and even the poultry industry, with its contracts and vertical integration°, relies on family farms to contract for the production of the birds. Despite the obvious change in scale over time, family farms, like ours, still meet around the kitchen table, send their kids to the same small schools, sit in the same church pew, and belong to the same civic organizations our parents and grandparents did. We may be industrial by some definition, but not our

---

vertical integration: a style of management where different companies working on different parts of a process all have the same owner.

own. Reality is messier than it appears in the book my tormentor was reading, and farming more complicated than a simple morality play.

On the desk in front of me are a dozen books, all hugely critical of present-day farming. Farmers are often given a pass in these books, painted as either naïve tools of corporate greed, or economic nullities° forced into their present circumstances by the unrelenting forces of the twin grindstones of corporate greed and unfeeling markets. To the farmer on the ground, though, a farmer blessed with free choice and hard-won experience, the moral choices aren't quite so easy. Biotech crops actually cut the use of chemicals, and increase food safety. Are people who refuse to use them my moral superiors? Herbicides cut the need for tillage, which decreases soil erosion by millions of tons. The biggest environmental harm I have done as a farmer is the topsoil (and nutrients) I used to send down the Missouri River to the Gulf of Mexico before we began to practice no-till farming, made possible only by the use of herbicides. The combination of herbicides and genetically modified seed has made my farm more sustainable, not less, and actually reduces the pollution I send down the river.

Finally, consumers benefit from cheap food. If you think they don't, just remember the headlines after food prices began increasing in 2007 and 2008, including the study by the Food and Agriculture Organization of the United Nations announcing that 50 million additional people are now hungry because of increasing food prices. Only "industrial farming" can possibly meet the demands of an increasing population and increased demand for food as a result of growing incomes.

> "Farming [is] more complicated than a simple morality play."

So the stakes in this argument are even higher. Farmers can raise food   10 in different ways if that is what the market wants. It is important, though, that even people riding in airplanes know that there are environmental and food safety costs to whatever kind of farming we choose.

Pigs in a Pen

In his book *Dominion*, author Mathew Scully calls "factory farming" an "obvious moral evil so sickening and horrendous it would leave us ashen." Scully, a speechwriter for the second President Bush, can hardly

---

nullity: nothingness, nonentity.

be called a man of the left. Just to make sure the point is not lost, he quotes the conservative historian Paul Johnson a page later:

The rise of factory farming, whereby food producers cannot remain competitive except by subjecting animals to unspeakable deprivation, has hastened this process. The human spirit revolts at what we have been doing.

Arizona and Florida have outlawed pig gestation crates, and California recently passed, overwhelmingly, a ballot initiative doing the same. There is no doubt that Scully and Johnson have the wind at their backs, and confinement raising of livestock may well be outlawed everywhere. And only a person so callous as to have a spirit that cannot be revolted, or so hardened to any kind of morality that he could countenance an obvious moral evil, could say a word in defense of caging animals during their production. In the quote above, Paul Johnson is forecasting a move toward vegetarianism. But if we assume, at least for the present, that most of us will continue to eat meat, let me dive in where most fear to tread.

Lynn Niemann was a neighbor of my family's, a farmer with a vision. He began raising turkeys on a field near his house around 1956. They were, I suppose, what we would now call "free range" turkeys. Turkeys raised in a natural manner, with no roof over their heads, just gamboling around in the pasture, as God surely intended. Free to eat grasshoppers, and grass, and scratch for grubs and worms. And also free to serve as prey for weasels, who kill turkeys by slitting their necks and practicing exsanguination. Weasels were a problem, but not as much a threat as one of our typically violent early summer thunderstorms. It seems that turkeys, at least young ones, are not smart enough to come in out of the rain, and will stand outside in a downpour, with beaks open and eyes skyward, until they drown. One night Niemann lost 4,000 turkeys to drowning, along with his dream, and his farm.

Now, turkeys are raised in large open sheds. Chickens and turkeys raised for meat are not grown in cages. As the critics of "industrial farming" like to point out, the sheds get quite crowded by the time Thanksgiving rolls around and the turkeys are fully grown. And yes, the birds are bedded in sawdust, so the turkeys do walk around in their own waste. Although the turkeys don't seem to mind, this quite clearly disgusts the various authors I've read who have actually visited a turkey farm. But none of those authors, whose descriptions of the horrors of modern poultry production have a certain sameness, were there when Niemann picked up those 4,000 dead turkeys. Sheds are expensive, and it was easier to raise turkeys in open, inexpensive pastures. But that type of production really was hard on the turkeys. Protected from the weather and predators, today's turkeys may not be aware that they are a part of a morally reprehensible system.

Like most young people in my part of the world, I was a 4-H member. 15 Raising cattle and hogs, showing them at the county fair, and then sending to slaughter those animals that we had spent the summer feeding, washing, and training. We would then tour the packing house, where our friend was hung on a rail, with his loin eye measured and his carcass evaluated. We farm kids got an early start on dulling our moral sensibilities. I'm still proud of my win in the Atchison County Carcass competition of 1969, as it is the only trophy I have ever received. We raised the hogs in a shed, or farrowing (birthing) house. On one side were eight crates of the kind that the good citizens of California have outlawed. On the other were the kind of wooden pens that our critics would have us use, where the sow could turn around, lie down, and presumably act in a natural way. Which included lying down on my 4-H project, killing several piglets, and forcing me to clean up the mess when I did my chores before school. The crates protect the piglets from their mothers. Farmers do not cage their hogs because of sadism, but because dead pigs are a drag on the profit margin, and because being crushed by your mother really is an awful way to go. As is being eaten by your mother, which I've seen sows do to newborn pigs as well.

I warned you that farming is still dirty and bloody, and I wasn't kidding. So let's talk about manure. It is an article of faith amongst the agri-intellectuals that we no longer use manure as fertilizer. To quote Dr. Michael Fox in his book *Eating with a Conscience*, "The animal waste is not going back to the land from which the animal feed originated." Or Bill McKibben, in his book *Deep Economy*, writing about modern livestock production: "But this concentrates the waste in one place, where instead of being useful fertilizer to spread on crop fields it becomes a toxic threat."

In my inbox is an email from our farm's neighbor, who raises thousands of hogs in close proximity to our farm, and several of my family members' houses as well. The email outlines the amount and chemical analysis of the manure that will be spread on our fields this fall, manure that will replace dozens of tons of commercial fertilizer. The manure is captured underneath the hog houses in cement pits, and is knifed into the soil after the crops are harvested. At no time is it exposed to erosion, and it is an extremely valuable resource, one which farmers use to its fullest extent, just as they have since agriculture began.

In the southern part of Missouri, there is an extensive poultry industry in areas of the state where the soil is poor. The farmers there spread the poultry litter on pasture, and the advent of poultry barns made cattle production possible in areas that used to be waste ground. The "industrial" poultry houses are owned by family farmers, who have then used the byproducts to produce beef in areas where cattle couldn't survive before. McKibben is certain that the contracts these farmers sign with companies like Tyson are unfair, and the farmers might agree. But they like those cows, so there is a waiting list for new chicken barns. In some areas, there is indeed more manure than available cropland. But the trend in the industry, thankfully, is toward a dispersion of animals and manure, as the value of the manure increases, and the cost of transporting the manure becomes prohibitive.

We Can't Change Nature

The largest producer of pigs in the United States has promised to gradually end the use of hog crates. The Humane Society promises to take their initiative drive to outlaw farrowing crates and poultry cages to more states. Many of the counties in my own state of Missouri have chosen to outlaw the building of confinement facilities. Barack Obama has been harshly critical of animal agriculture. We are clearly in the process of deciding that we will not continue to raise animals the way we do now. Because other countries may not share our sensibilities, we'll have to withdraw or amend free trade agreements to keep any semblance of a livestock industry.

We can do that, and we may be a better society for it, but we can't 20 change nature. Pigs will be allowed to "return to their mire," as Kipling had it, but they'll also be crushed and eaten by their mothers. Chickens will provide lunch to any number of predators, and some number of chickens will die as flocks establish their pecking order.

In recent years, the cost of producing pork dropped as farmers increased feed efficiency (the amount of feed needed to produce a pound of pork) by 20 percent. Free-range chickens and pigs will increase the price of food, using more energy and water to produce the extra grain required for the same amount of meat, and some people will go hungry. It is also instructive that the first company to move away from farrowing crates is the largest producer of pigs. Changing the way we raise animals will not necessarily change the scale of the companies involved in the industry. If we are about to require more expensive ways of producing food, the largest and most well-capitalized farms will have the least trouble adapting.

The Omnivores' Delusions

Michael Pollan, in an 8,000-word essay in the *New York Times Magazine*, took the expected swipes at animal agriculture. But his truly radical prescriptions had to do with raising of crops. Pollan, who seemed to be aware of the nitrogen problem in his book *The Omnivore's Dilemma*, left nuance behind, as well as the laws of chemistry, in his recommendations. The nitrogen problem is this: without nitrogen, we do not have life. Until we learned to produce nitrogen from natural gas early in the last century, the only way to get nitrogen was through nitrogen produced by plants called legumes, or from small amounts of nitrogen that are produced by lightning strikes. The amount of life the earth could support was limited by the amount of nitrogen available for crop production.

In his book, Pollan quotes geographer Vaclav Smil to the effect that 40 percent of the people alive today would not be alive without the ability to artificially synthesize nitrogen. But in his directive on food policy, Pollan damns agriculture's dependence on fossil fuels, and urges the president to encourage agriculture to move away from expensive and declining supplies of natural gas toward the unlimited sunshine that supported life, and agriculture, as recently as the 1940s. Now, why didn't I think of that?

Well, I did. I've raised clover and alfalfa for the nitrogen they produce, and half the time my land is planted to soybeans, another nitrogen-producing legume. Pollan writes as if all of his ideas are new, but my father tells of agriculture extension meetings in the late 1950s entitled "Clover and Corn, the Road to Profitability." Farmers know that organic farming was the default position of agriculture for thousands of years, years when hunger was just around the corner for even advanced societies. I use all the animal manure available to me, and do everything I can to reduce the amount of commercial fertilizers I use. When corn genetically modified to use nitrogen more efficiently enters the market, as it soon will, I will use it as well. But none of those things will completely replace commercial fertilizer.

Norman Borlaug, founder of the green revolution, estimates that the 25 amount of nitrogen available naturally would only support a worldwide population of 4 billion souls or so. He further remarks that we would need another 5 billion cows to produce enough manure to fertilize our present crops with "natural" fertilizer. That would play havoc with global warming. And cows do not produce nitrogen from the air, but only from the forages they eat, so to produce more manure we will have to plant more forages. Most of the critics of industrial farming maintain the contradictory positions that we should increase the use of manure as a fertilizer, and decrease our consumption of meat. Pollan would solve the problem with cover crops, planted after the corn crop is harvested, and with mandatory composting. Pollan should talk to some actual farmers before he presumes to advise a president.

Pollan tells of flying over the upper Midwest in the winter, and seeing the black, fallow soil. I suppose one sees what one wants to see, but we have not had the kind of tillage implement on our farm that would produce black soil in nearly 20 years. Pollan would provide our nitrogen by planting those black fields to nitrogen-producing cover crops after the cash crops are harvested. This is a fine plan, one that farmers have known about for generations. And sometimes it would even work. But not last year, as we finished harvest in November in a freezing rain. It is hard to think of a legume that would have done its thing between then and corn planting time. Plants do not grow very well in freezing weather, a fact that would evidently surprise Pollan.

And even if we could have gotten a legume established last fall, it would not have fixed any nitrogen before planting time. We used to plant corn in late May, plowing down our green manure and killing the first flush of weeds. But that meant the corn would enter its crucial growing period during the hottest, driest parts of the summer, and that soil erosion would be increased because the land was bare during drenching spring rains. Now we plant in early April, best utilizing our spring rains, and ensuring that pollination occurs before the dog days of August.

A few other problems come to mind. The last time I planted a cover crop, the clover provided a perfect habitat in early spring for bugs, bugs that I had to kill with an insecticide. We do not normally apply insecticides, but we did that year. Of course, you can provide nitrogen with legumes by using a longer crop rotation, growing clover one year and corn the next. But that uses twice as much water to produce a corn crop, and takes twice as much land to produce the same number of bushels. We are producing twice the food we did in 1960 on less land, and commercial nitrogen is one of the main reasons why. It may be that we decide we would rather spend land and water than energy, but Pollan never mentions that we are faced with that choice.

His other grand idea is mandatory household composting, with the compost delivered to farmers free of charge. Why not? Compost is a valuable soil amendment, and if somebody else is paying to deliver it to my farm, then bring it on. But it will not do much to solve the nitrogen problem. Household compost has somewhere between 1 and 5 percent nitrogen, and not all that nitrogen is available to crops the first year. Presently, we are applying about 150 pounds of nitrogen per acre to corn, and crediting about 40 pounds per acre from the preceding year's soybean crop. Let's assume a 5 percent nitrogen rate, or about 100 pounds of nitrogen per ton of compost. That would require 3,000 pounds of compost per acre. Or about 150,000 tons for the corn raised in our county. The average truck carries about 20 tons. Picture 7,500 trucks traveling from New York City to our small county here in the Midwest, delivering compost. Five million truckloads to fertilize the country's corn crop. Now, that would be a carbon footprint!

Pollan thinks farmers use commercial fertilizer because it is easier, and because it is cheap. Pollan is right. But those are perfectly defensible reasons. Nitrogen quadrupled in price over the last several years, and farmers are still using it, albeit more cautiously. We are using GPS monitors on all of our equipment to ensure that we do not use too much, and our production of corn per pound of nitrogen is rapidly increasing. On our farm, we have increased yields about 50 percent during my career, while applying about the same amount of nitrogen we did when I began farming. That fortunate trend will increase even faster with the advent of new GMO hybrids. But as much as Pollan might desire it, even President Obama cannot reshuffle the chemical deck that nature has dealt. Energy may well get much more expensive, and peak oil production may have been reached. But food production will have a claim on fossil fuels long after we have learned how to use renewables and nuclear power to handle many of our other energy needs.

Farming and Connectedness

Much of farming is more "industrial," more technical, and more complex than it used to be. Farmers farm more acres, and are less close to the ground and their animals than they were in the past. Almost all critics of industrial agriculture bemoan this loss of closeness, this "connectedness," to use author Rod Dreher's term. It is a given in most of the writing about agriculture that the knowledge and experience of the organic farmer is what makes him so unique and so important. The "industrial farmer," on the other hand, is a mere pawn of Cargill, backed into his ignorant way of life by forces too large, too far from the farm, and too powerful to resist. Concern about this alienation, both between farmers and the land, and between consumers and their food supply, is what drives much of the literature about agriculture.

The distance between the farmer and what he grows has certainly increased, but, believe me, if we weren't closely connected, we wouldn't still be farming. It's important to our critics that they emphasize this alienation, because they have to ignore the "industrial" farmer's experience and knowledge to say the things they do about farming.

But farmers have reasons for their actions, and society should listen to them as we embark upon this reappraisal of our agricultural system. I use chemicals and diesel fuel to accomplish the tasks my grandfather used to do with sweat, and I use a computer instead of a lined notebook and a pencil, but I'm still farming the same land he did 80 years ago, and the fund of knowledge that our family has accumulated about our small part of Missouri is valuable. And everything I know and I have learned tells me this: we have to farm "industrially" to feed the world, and by using those "industrial" tools sensibly, we can accomplish that task and leave my grandchildren a prosperous and productive farm, while protecting the land, water, and air around us.

Understanding the Text

1. Why does Hurst think it is a bad idea to allow pigs free range to wander as they please?
2. What is the nitrogen problem?
3. Why does Hurst object to the way critics of industrial farming make their cases?

Reflection and Response

4. What is Hurst so angry about? How does he communicate this emotion in writing?
5. Hurst suggests that critics of "industrial farming" do not realize that they cannot have it "both ways" — organic and local. What evidence does he use to support his position? Does he make a good case?

Making Connections

6. How does Hurst position his argument in relation to ones made by Michael Pollan ("Eat Food: Food Defined," p. 10), Bill McKibben ("The Only Way to Have a Cow," p. 161), and Paul Greenberg ("Heartland," p. 256)? What are the fundamental differences in how they view the environmental impact of "industrial farming"? What moral principles do they each privilege? Is there any shared terrain?
7. Consider the arguments made by Hurst and David Biello ("Will Organic Food Fail to Feed the World?" p. 288), and analyze the positions they take on the impact of organic farming. Then, do some research of your own. Explain the debate over organic versus commercially grown food. Why do organic proponents support it? How does Hurst argue against their position? Which argument makes the most sense to you? Why? What does your position say about your values?
8. Compare Hurst's representation of the Green Revolution to those offered by at least two other authors in this book. Then, research the Green Revolution on your own and select three distinct perspectives on the revolution. Make a presentation that describes all three, and then explain which one you think is most compelling and why. Use at least three sources from this book and at least two other sources.

Stop the Rot

Amanda Little

Amanda Little works as an investigative journalist focusing on environmental issues and science. Her award-winning writing on energy, technology, and the environment has appeared in the *Washington Post*, *The New York Times*, *Rolling Stone*, and many other prominent publications. She is a professor of science writing and investigative journalism at Vanderbilt University, and the author of *Power Trip: The Story of America's Love Affair with Energy* (2009) and *The Fate of Food: What We'll Eat in a Bigger, Hotter, Smarter World* (2019). This essay, excerpted from *The Fate of Food*, explores why we waste so much food and what some companies and people are doing about it.

It's a drizzly March morning in Nashville, and the sky looks like the garbage dump beneath it — a vast gray-brown morass. Against this backdrop, Georgann Parker appears like a Mad Max desperado. She's wearing safety glasses and surgical gloves, tall rubber wellies over her jeans, a bright orange vest over her jacket, and a hard hat over her cropped gray-blond hair. "We can be glad it's not hot," she says, smiling behind her respiration mask. Parker is uncannily upbeat for a woman about to perform a diagnostic exercise that's technically called a waste audit but in Kroger inner circles is referred to as a "Dumpster dive." Parker is Kroger's corporate chief of perishable donations, a role that occasionally involves ripping into hundreds of garbage bags to manually investigate their rotting contents.

Parker has come with two Kroger employees and two officials from Waste Management, the company that collects and dumps all of Kroger's trash. They stand and watch as a compactor truck unloads on the ground in front of them. The trash mound has been generated over the previous six days by a Kroger supermarket located a few miles from my house — one of 117 Krogers in the Tennessee division and one of 2800 Kroger supermarkets nationwide. In all, Kroger's stores serve 9 million individual American shoppers per day and 60 million American families per year,[1] more than a third of the U.S. population. Each store produces many tons of trash a week — most of it perishable fruits, vegetables, meats, dairy, and deli products that have passed their prime or reached their sell-by dates but are still safe to eat.

It's Parker's job to help rescue Kroger's sizable trove of safe-but-unsellable food across its many stores. She oversees the 120 division heads nationwide who manage the company's food rescue operations. Annually Parker and her team capture about 75 million pounds of fresh meats, produce, and baked goods before they get thrown out, and donate them to local food banks and pantries.[2] The number is big, but it's a fraction of Kroger's total fresh-foods waste stream. The company has pledged to donate more than ten times that amount as part of the Zero Hunger, Zero Waste campaign it launched in 2018. The goal is to eliminate food waste from its stores by 2025, and alleviate hunger in the communities surrounding these stores in the same time frame.

"Crazy-big" is how Parker describes the scope of Kroger's goal, "and, yeah, a little daunting. The logistics of food rescue are very complex." For a company as big as Kroger it means not only rescuing the food before it goes bad but coordinating the donations with tens of thousands of food banks and soup kitchens across the country.

Parker, who has round cheeks and pale blue eyes, grew up in a town 5 in Minnesota—in the same region as Garrison Keillor's Lake Wobegon, the fictional place "where it's always pleasant." Parker is that rare person who manages to come off as both effusively and effortlessly friendly. In her colorful midwestern patois, people are "folks," soda is "pop," a lot of something is "a crud-load," and excitement is often expressed as a rhetorical question: "How cool is that?" In other words, she's a gold mine of enthusiasm about things that many of us have trouble caring about—but should.

In the decade before her move to Kroger, Parker clerked for a federal judge in Minnesota, and then spent several years serving as a federal probation officer. In this role, she wrote the sentencing recommendations for convicted felons, and she did her best to be positive about even this. "I appreciated the responsibility I had to be sure everybody gets a fair shake under the law, but after a good long run of it, the job beat me down." She sees a continuity between her past and current jobs—"I'm still trying to help fix broken systems," she says. Her law-and-order training has also inspired the moniker she's been given by Kroger colleagues: "food waste sheriff."

Whether because of her chipper disposition or because she's seen more sobering circumstances in her professional past, Parker is unfazed by the disgusting conditions at the garbage dump. Odorous° methane emanates up from the depths of landfill below; dozens of overfed vultures circle heavily in the sky above as Parker and her team paw through the mountain of waste. They find bags of potatoes and cabbages that look perfectly fresh, heads of lettuce that look less so, heaps of boxed salads and spinach, serving trays of cut fruit, countless crates of cracked

---

odorous: giving off a smell.

eggs, dozens of meal kits filled with prepped fresh ingredients for cooking shrimp scampi and chicken à la king, packages of sliced salami and cheese, cracked bottles of tomato sauce, dented tubs of icing and ice cream, and cans of Gravy Train dog food marked "Reclaim."

Eventually, Parker becomes sullen. "Gosh, it turns your stomach—I mean not the garbage, the *waste*," she says. It's the many gallons of milk lying on the ground that upset her most. She checks their sell-by date—eight days left before they expire. "There's no good reason for this." Next to the milk is the carrion the vultures are after: packages of breakfast meats and pork chops, steaks, ground beef, a ham hock, and a heap of twenty or so rotisserie chickens, roasted the color of the mud in which they rest.

Parker and her team separate the waste into categories, weighing and photographing the contents of each. Later, they'll crunch the numbers and find that more than half—52 percent—of the waste produced by the supermarket could have been donated, recycled, or composted. They will assemble the data into graphs and charts with crime-sceneesque photos. "You can see which departments in the store are doing their job of food rescue, and which are not," Parker grumbles when we discuss the results. "A lot of this should have been given a second chance."

Fifty-two million tons of food are sent to U.S. garbage dumps annually, and another 10 million are discarded or left to rot on farms, according to Darby Hoover, a waste researcher with the San Francisco office of the environmental group Natural Resources Defense Council (NRDC).[3] Put another way, Americans waste enough food to fill a 90,000-seat stadium every day, and that's about 25 percent more per capita than we were wasting in the 1970s.[4] Most of the food waste in the United States, about 35 percent, is generated by households. The average American throws out more than a pound of food a day—some 400 pounds per year each.[5] Restaurants and retailers like Kroger are close behind, generating another third of it. The value of the food wasted in America each year has been estimated at between $162 billion and $218 billion.[6]

Hoover sees the problem from an environmental angle. "Wasting food also means wasting all the water, energy, agricultural chemicals, labor, and other resources we put into growing, processing, packaging, distributing, washing, and refrigerating it," she observes. The nonprofit group ReFed estimates that food waste consumes 21 percent of all freshwater, 19 percent of fertilizer, 18 percent of cropland, and 21 percent of landfill volume in the United States.[7] Add to that the methane problem: only 5 percent of food waste in America gets composted into soil fertilizer,

10

using a controlled process in which bacteria and heat decompose food scraps into rich plant nutrients. The other 95 percent of food waste goes to landfill and rots in an uncontrolled way, emitting methane, a potent greenhouse gas. "If food waste around the world was a country, it would rank third behind China and the U.S. in terms of greenhouse gas emissions," says Hoover.

To Georgann Parker, the problem is a social injustice: "Wasting food — especially healthy perishables — becomes an ethical problem when you consider that there's about forty million folks in this country living in poverty who don't have reliable access to nutritious food." Less than a third of the food we're tossing would be enough to feed this underserved population.

Kroger has half a million employees, many of whom are paid minimum wage and themselves face food insecurity. Parker says, "Having a larger purpose that sustains low-income communities — that builds employee morale and it honors the company's traditions." Kroger's founder, Barney Kroger, started with a bakery business and he used to hand out day-old bread and pastries every evening to low-income neighbors. "Our brand and core values hinge on food accessibility," Parker maintains.

Kroger's Zero Hunger, Zero Waste campaign is also a bottom-line opportunity for the company, which has to pay increasingly steep "tipping fees" — the costs imposed by some state governments on the loads of waste that a company or institution dumps. Kroger can also collect millions of dollars in federal tax breaks annually for its food donations. Pressure to cut waste is also coming from Kroger's investors. Nearly every major brand in food retail, including Publix, Walmart, Costco, Target, and Whole Foods, has introduced waste-reduction programs in the past five years. In a recent assessment of these programs by the Center for Biological Diversity, a nonprofit based in Tucson, Arizona, Kroger was the third-highest performer in the not-very-high-performing bunch — it scored a C on the overall grading scale.[8]

Food retailers have historically been lax on waste management, but 15 they're under increasing pressure to reform. When Amazon, for example, resisted efforts to address the food-waste problem within Whole Foods and its other retailers, top investors said they'd pull out if the company didn't start reining in waste.[9] Kroger CEO Rodney McMullen got similar prodding from BlackRock, his biggest investor. Jessica Edelman, Kroger's director of sustainability, says, "You gotta believe when our largest shareholder tells my boss: If you don't have a social-impact proposition then we're not going to continue to invest in you — that resonates."

Edelman enlisted World Wildlife Fund (WWF), which conducts a large food-waste research program (on the grounds that agriculture is the world's biggest threat to wildlife habitat), to help Kroger devise a strategy for food-waste prevention and donation. WWF encouraged the Dumpster dives and other rigorous waste-stream analysis. "There's a misconception that the answer to food waste is composting," says Pete Pearson, WWF's director of food-waste research. "The real emphasis—whether you're a company, or a household, or a city—needs to be on prevention first, then rescue and donation, then composting as a last resort."

What makes solving food waste so difficult, says Pearson, is that "there's no single technology or policy intervention that can nip this thing in the bud." He continues, "The problem occurs upstream and downstream, in fields, warehouses, packaging, distribution, supermarkets, restaurants, and homes." It will require participation not just from a few "food waste sheriffs" like Georgann Parker in the corporate trenches, but from an army of them at many levels of the private and public sectors: academics and federal policy makers who are trying to standardize expiration dates and incentivize food rescue; players in city and state government building curbside composting programs and increasing "tipping fees" to discourage waste; software developers building apps that connect people with food surpluses to people with food deficits; materials scientists finding new ways to preserve perishable foods and extend shelf life; engineers designing machines to accelerate large-scale composting; and activists leading campaigns to transform public consciousness on this issue.

Over several weeks, I ventured behind the scenes of Kroger to try to understand the nuts and bolts of a zero-waste strategy, following that process through the three stages—prevention, rescue and donation, and ultimately composting. First I needed context—a better understanding of why we squander so much food in the first place.

"There isn't any waste in nature. Anything that dies in nature becomes food for something else," Darby Hoover tells me. "Humans have created waste as a concept, and we should be able to *uncreate* waste as a concept."

"'Humans have created waste as a concept, and we should be able to uncreate waste as a concept.'"

Hoover recently conducted a two-year study exploring and comparing food-waste patterns in three U.S. cities—Denver, New York City, and, coincidentally, my hometown, Nashville. "There's surprisingly little hard data about who's wasting what, where, and why, and that makes it harder for cities and companies and households to solve this problem," she asserts.

To run her analysis, Hoover worked with Tetra Tech, a San Francisco–based engineering company that specializes in waste logistics. They recruited 1150 residents in the three cities to participate, all of whom agreed to offer up their trash for inspection. More than half kept "kitchen diaries," noting when they threw out their food and why. The foods most often dumped in the trash or poured down the drain included brewed coffee and coffee grounds, bananas, chicken, apples, bread, oranges, potatoes, and milk. Hoover noted the conspicuous absence of things like Doritos, Spam, and Twinkies on this list. "Food waste is riddled with unexpected contradictions, and one of them is that healthier diets tend to be the most wasteful diets," she says. "Our current cultural obsession with eating fresh foods is a great thing from a health perspective, but not so great from a waste perspective."

Hoover also found that in Denver and New York, which both have municipal composting programs, the participants who regularly composted their leftovers tossed out significantly more food than non-composters,[10] presumably because they felt better about the outcome of the waste. "Prevention is the holy grail of waste work," says Hoover. "*Not* generating waste is far better for the planet than recycling food scraps." She also found that parents with young kids generated waste in their efforts, however hopeful and virtuous, to expose their kids to new flavors and healthy offerings—only to have the kids refuse to eat it. The upshot: food waste at the consumer level "is often tangled up with good intentions—and that makes it particularly tricky to solve," Hoover observes.

I'll admit that too much of the food in my own household goes uneaten. My husband distrusts anything that's been in the fridge for more than two days. I like to buy those big bundles of fresh spinach and large bunches of bananas in hopes of plying my family with nutrient-dense foods, only to have the bananas brown and the spinach molder. I chronically overcook for guests and get excited about new recipes for which I buy too many esoteric ingredients—only to use a teaspoon of this and a quarter cup of that. Weeks later, when no one's looking, I guiltily throw the neglected remainders away.

Beyond good intentions, several other factors pave the road to the local dump here in the United States. For one thing, there's what Hoover calls "our conformist standards of beauty." American shoppers have a very rigid idea of what fruits and vegetables should look like, she says, and it "doesn't include produce that's marred° or that's grown in irregular

---

marred: blemished.

shapes, or that's gotten bruised, browned, bumped, wilted, or discolored during their journeys from field to market." The average American shopper has aesthetic° standards not unlike Tony Zhang,* chucker° of gnarled carrots: we reflexively snub irregularities. The problem lies both with the shoppers who demand perfect-looking foods, and with the grocers who behind the scenes reject the nonconformist fruits and vegetables. "Unthinkable quantities of fresh produce grown in the U.S. never make it to the store because they don't make the aesthetic cut," Hoover asserts. A recent study in Minnesota found that about 20 percent of all the fruit and vegetables produced in the state get trashed because they don't meet our narrow aesthetic standards.[11]

Common victims: table grapes that don't grow as a wedge-shaped 25 bunch are left to rot in the field or hauled directly from field to landfill. The same goes for lopsided bell peppers, gnarled carrots, blemished apples, and so forth. (Think back to Andy Ferguson's frostbitten apples—perfectly healthy and delicious, but the ones with frost rings won't sell.*) Large organic vegetable farmers, said Hoover, routinely toss more than conventional growers because their products are less uniform. The unfortunate irony is that marred produce is often more nutritious and flavorful than unmarred produce—fruits and vegetables in fact produce flavors and antioxidants when they're under stress from insects, heat, frost, or blight.[12]

Hoover, who built Stanford University's first recycling program as a student there in the early 1980s, wrote her thesis in graduate school on the psychology of waste. The desire for perfect produce has been around since long before the emperor Tiberius was demanding perfect, year-round snake melons, but Hoover maintains it reached a new level of intensity in the United States in the 1950s, as housewives adapted to widespread refrigeration, new packaged products, and internationally shipped fruits and vegetables. "Suddenly, you could eat pineapples in Maine and strawberries in January. It was the era of Wonder Bread, and TV dinners," she says. "Perfect, rote foods came to represent safety and innovation." Today, this obsession has reached still further heights owing in part to

---

aesthetic: concerned with beauty or a pleasing appearance.
chucker: person who throws something away carelessly or casually.

---

*Tony Zhang, a Chinese entrepreneur formerly involved in a subscription delivery model of sustainable food production in China, is discussed earlier in Little's *The Fate of Food.* [Ed.]
*Andy Ferguson's apple orchards appear in Chapter 1 of Little's *The Fate of Food.* [Ed.]

the "camera cuisine" trends on social media. Hoover and I discuss the Instagramming of golden fresh-baked pies and arty restaurant entrées—a feel-good phenomenon that, to her mind, reinforces a cultural obsession with perfect food and a tendency to reject anything less.

Even as Americans blithely ogle #foodporn, Europeans are learning to think in more realistic terms about food value. Selina Juul isn't a politician, yet according to the Danish government she's largely responsible for reducing that country's food waste by 25 percent in five years.[13] Juul was born in Russia and moved to Denmark in 1995, when she was thirteen. "I come from a country where there were food shortages. We had the collapse of infrastructure, communism collapsed, we were not sure we could get food on the table," Juul told the BBC. "Then I was really shocked to see a lot of food getting wasted."

She had an interest in graphic design and began waging clever public campaigns. Juul founded Stop Spild Af Mad (Stop Wasting Food) as a Facebook group in 2008; it now has tens of thousands of followers and has shown up in supermarket boardrooms, on the TED stage, and in the European Union Parliament advocating for waste reform. "Food waste is the lack of respect for our nature, for our society, for the people who produce the food, for the animals, and a lack of respect for your time and your money," says Juul. She helped rebrand restaurant doggy bags as "goodie bags," and distributed sixty thousand of them across the country. Denmark's supermarkets started selling bananas with single-item discounts under a sign that read TAKE ME I'M SINGLE, reducing banana waste by 90 percent.[14]

The trend caught on: Wefood, a Danish charity, opened what it called "the world's first food-waste supermarket" in Copenhagen, selling rejected produce and food nearing its best-by date. Nine months later it opened a second branch. The country's major supermarket chains stopped offering quantity discounts that entice shoppers to overbuy; many have added "stop food waste" sections, where they aggregate the older, cut-rate offerings.

The Danish momentum rippled elsewhere. In London, activist Adam   30 Smith founded the Real Junk Food Project and opened the country's first food-waste supermarket along with a chain of "pay as you feel" cafés that cook up soups and sandwiches from ingredients that would've been tossed at no fixed price. Similar cafés have sprung up in Australia and Israel.

Another promising London-based effort is "Olio," a "food-sharing app" that connects not just businesses and food banks but also individual neighbors to one another to off-load their excess food. "Ever cooked too much for dinner? Ever bought a pack of onions and only need 1? Going on a holiday and your fridge is full of food?" reads the Olio website. The endeavor was slow-going when the app debuted in 2016, but by 2019 it had over half a million members—mostly neighbors sharing the contents of their fridges. A Copenhagen-based app, Too Good to Go, has also had success selling users discounted just-before-closing bakery and restaurant food. The chain Tesco (an English version of Walmart) has pledged to be zero-waste by 2019 and eliminated best-by dates on its products altogether, encouraging its customers to trust their own judgment.

Not to be outdone, France recently passed a law banning grocery stores from throwing away unsold food, threatening fines of up to $4500 for an infraction.[15] In some French cities, a fleet of "food ambulances" collects waste from grocers and stores and delivers it to churches and synagogues. The shift in public consciousness has pushed the European Union to establish a goal of cutting per capita food waste in half among retailers and consumers by 2030.[16]

We may be a long way from seeing this kind of shift occur in the United States. For one thing, everything is bigger here—our shopping carts, plates, portions, appetites, and of course our people. "If you're willing to indulge a little food-waste psychoanalysis," says Hoover. "Americans irrationally associate the size and quantity of food we consume—and the waste we generate—with the extent of our freedom and power." We get away with this in part because food is relatively cheap in America (aided by subsidies to crops like corn and soybeans). Middle- and upper-income families in the United States spend a much smaller portion of their household budgets on food than nearly anywhere else in the world.[17] When I ask Hoover for some advice that could help us prevent household food waste, she gives me marching orders.

First, leftovers should be fine to eat for at least a week (she stretches hers to ten or more days and has never gotten sick). "Use your eyes and nose," she exhorts. "If it looks and smells fine, eat it." If you can, use glass storage containers, which keep food fresher for longer than plastic. Buy mottled° or misshapen produce: it tastes just as good and it's probably better for you than the perfect-looking stuff. Choose frozen fruits and veggies over their fresh counterparts—they won't go bad and they're no less nutritious (some nutrients do get lost when foods are blanched before freezing, but others are preserved because the foods get frozen right after harvest and don't deteriorate in transit to market).

mottled: having spots or patches of irregular color.

Lastly, "channel your grandmother and reimagine your leftovers," says Hoover: Sunday's roast chicken can become Monday's chicken tacos and Tuesday's tortilla soup.

Pete Pearson of WWF, for his part, supports both traditional and tech-forward approaches to food waste prevention. He cites the example of Opal apples, a non-GMO version of the contentious Arctic apples that are gene edited to eliminate browning of the flesh.[18] There are also CRISPR-edited nonbrowning mushrooms coming onto the market, and potatoes that have been edited to be less prone to browning, bruising, and black spots—meaning fewer will end up in landfills.

"Here's where we put the uglies," says Georgann Parker as she walks me through the produce section of a Kroger supermarket outside of Indianapolis, Indiana—one of the largest stores in the chain. I've come to get a crash course in supermarket logistics and a glimpse into the company's waste-prevention efforts. I'd never noticed these particular offerings in my local Kroger before. There, tucked into the side of an island bearing those iconic pyramids of supermarket fruit—perfect orbs of red, orange, green, and yellow—is a four-tiered shelf topped with a sign MARKDOWN! BEAUTY IS ONLY SKIN DEEP. The shelves bear mostly empty straw baskets of gnarled bell peppers, arthritic-looking carrots, too-small cantaloupes, and cucumbers curved like pistols.

While fresh produce accounts for less than 15 percent of Kroger's profits, it's in the company's interest to sell every last misshapen product. "We want everything that comes in the back door to go out the front, but of course it doesn't," says Parker. Most of the ugly produce is rejected before it gets to a store and left to farms to dispose of, but inevitably some misshapen fruits and vegetables make their way into the shipments. "They used to get immediately tagged for donation to food banks, but now we're selling them at a steep discount, and they almost always sell out," she tells me. There's some waste they simply can't sell—because stores overorder, or because refrigerators fail, or because customer purchasing patterns shift and aren't what buyers predict.

Kroger introduced the "uglies" section into its stores in early 2017, around the time that activists and entrepreneurs were embracing cast-off produce. A start-up called Imperfect Produce launched a subscription delivery service for "funky fruits and vegetables" in the San Francisco Bay Area and began selling its irregular products in Whole Foods. Hungry Harvest, Ugly Mugs, and Food Cowboy are among other new enterprises that have been building markets for millions of tons of rejected produce. "These efforts are seeing gradual success, but they're rerouting only a small fraction of the rejected produce that's still safe to eat," says Pete Pearson. "It'll take the big players to really move the needle."

Pearson is working with Kroger on a plan to capture the aberrant° produce earlier in the waste stream, not for direct sales but rather for the enormous amount of prepared and packaged foods—potato and macaroni salads, coleslaws, pizzas, frozen fruits and vegetables, and so forth—that Kroger makes and sells through its eponymous° and private-label brands.

The ugly produce program works in tandem with Kroger's regular 40 markdown programs. If meats don't sell within a day of their sell-by dates, they get pulled from shelves, slapped with a "WooHoo! *MARKDOWN*" sticker, and placed in the sale area of the meat section. If the discounted products still don't sell, they're supposed to be yanked the night before their sell-by date, scanned out of the system as a loss, and put in a back-room freezer for donation. A similar process is supposed to be followed for bakery items and dairy products. The company policy is to pull milk from the dairy case ten days before its expiration date, at which point it can be donated fresh, or frozen and then thawed for donation. "There's no good reason any milk products sold in a Kroger store should ever be dumped," says Parker.

Confusing sell-by labeling is another major barrier to waste prevention both in supermarkets and in homes. The dates printed on the perishable products you buy are not federally regulated and do not represent any technical or standardized measure of food safety. The Food and Drug Administration, which has the power to regulate date labels, has chosen not to do so because no food-safety outbreak in the United States has ever been traced to a food being consumed past date. (They've been traced instead to certain pathogens that may have contaminated the food during processing; or to "temperature abuse," like leaving raw chicken in a hot car; or to air exposure that encourages mold.) "You're far more likely to get sick from something because it's contaminated or gone unrefrigerated than because it's past-date," says Parker.

Milk has the most inconsistent labeling, state to state. Most milk is pasteurized, a process that eliminates the risk of food-borne illness, even after the sell-by or use-by date. The sell-by date that dairies generally print is twenty-one to twenty-four days after pasteurization. However, Parker tells me, "milk that's been properly refrigerated is safe to drink well after that." Some states like Montana impose even stricter time limitations,

---

aberrant: abnormal, different from the accepted norm.
eponymous: giving its name to someone or something.

requiring sell-by dates of just twelve days after pasteurization, and ban the sale or donation of milk after that date, which wastes countless gallons of good milk.

"Supermarkets have to juggle dozens of different date-labeling laws and they lose about $1 billion a year from food that expires in theory—but not in reality—before it's sold," says Emily Broad Leib, director of the Food Policy Program at Harvard Law School. "Date label confusion harms consumers and food companies, and it wastes massive amounts of food." Leib helped develop the Food Date Labeling Act, proposed federal legislation that would standardize labels to "best if used by," a phrase indicating that a product may not be optimally fresh but is still safe to eat. The bill will also prohibit states from preventing stores or manufacturers from donating products that have passed their peak-quality periods but remain edible and nutritious.

The date-labeling effort is part of a broader Food Recovery Act legislation, which was introduced in the Senate in 2017 and would standardize date-labeling and food-rescue laws throughout the fifty states.[19] It would also incentivize public schools and government institutions to make use of ugly fruits and veggies that never make it to market.

Georgann Parker says Kroger is throwing its lobbying weight behind 45 these laws while also pushing for better food packaging. Materials scientists are now finally beginning to break new ground in food packaging and preservation techniques. The challenge in preserving freshness of perishable foods comes down to sealing out oxygen. It's a seemingly benign gas, but when it penetrates food packaging it feeds mold growth and speeds the proliferation of microorganisms and enzymes. Especially in foods untreated with chemical preservatives, oxidation can degrade the flavors, pigments, and textures, and the quality of nutrients, oils, and fats.

Kroger has partnered with Apeel Sciences, a Silicon Valley start-up founded in 2012 by a young materials scientist, James Rogers. Rogers studied the casings—skin, rinds, and peels—that fruits and vegetables naturally create to seal out oxygen and protect themselves from decay. The big idea, he says, is "using food to protect food." He found a way to recycle organic ingredients, like grape skins left over after wine pressings, to create a natural sealant that can be sprayed on fruits and vegetables and extend the shelf life of produce up to three times longer than conventional produce. The film is transparent, flavorless, and completely natural, and debuted in 2018 as a protective casing on avocados in the produce sections of Krogers throughout the Midwest. It's a good example of third way thinking: "We don't need to go into a lab and create new chemistries to solve old problems," says Rogers. "We can draw inspiration from plants."

Chemists in labs are also making important progress. Parker tells me that researchers are developing oxygen-absorbing films that can be incorporated into either flexible or rigid packaging materials, and reduce the oxygen concentration within to less than 0.01 percent—more than doubling shelf life. The problem is cost. Food manufacturers are still packaging bread in the same plastic bags and eggs in the same cardboard cartons they've been using for aeons because it's cheap. Kroger's investment arm is funding start-ups that are developing new packaging technologies, but Parker maintains we need a coordinated industry-wide R&D effort on this front.

Pearson of WWF is optimistic about advances in data-management tools that consumers can't see. Using product ID codes and tracking systems like Blockchain, Kroger can monitor the movement of each one of the billions of products that flow through its stores, as well as the shopping habits of 60 million families. All this data is managed with the goal of synchronizing each store's supply with its shoppers' demand—thereby shrinking the volume of unwanted and expired products.

There will always be some amount of oversupply and therefore waste in supermarkets, says Pearson, "until the day we create a Star Trek replicator"—which would enable food to materialize upon demand. In the meantime, digital tools will get ever-better at tracking the life cycle of a product from conception to sale, which will go a long way to helping supermarkets reduce their excess inventory and donate far more of it.

Notes

1. "The Kroger Family of Companies 2018 Sustainability Report," Kroger, 2018, https://tinyurl.com/y8v7tcpr.

2. Ibid.

3. "27 Solutions to Food Waste," ReFED, 2018, https://tinyurl.com/y9ar7rha.

4. Jonathan Bloom, *American Wasteland: How America Throws Away Nearly Half of Its Food (and What We Can Do About It)* (Cambridge, Mass.: Da Capo Press, 2010). See also U.S. Environmental Protection Agency, "Municipal Solid Waste Generation, Recycling, and Disposal in the United States: Facts and Figures for 2012," Feb. 2014, https://tinyurl.com/y8ec8k6j.

5. Zach Conrad, Meredith T. Niles, Deborah A. Neher, Eric D. Roy, Nicole E. Tichenor, Lisa Jahns, "Relationship Between Food Waste, Diet Quality, and Environmental Sustainability," *PLOS ONE* 13 (2018).

6. "Frequently Asked Questions," U.S. Department of Agriculture, 2010, https://tinyurl.com/y82prs50. See also Jonathan Bloom, "A New Roadmap for Fighting Food Waste," *National Geographic,* Mar. 14, 2016, https://tinyurl.com/y9uu6wp7.

7. "27 Solutions to Food Waste," ReFED.

8. Jennifer Molidor and Jordan Figueiredo, "Checked Out: How U.S. Supermarkets Fail to Make the Grade in Reducing Food Waste," Center for Biological Diversity, Apr. 2018, https://tinyurl.com/yc7d8ut8.

9. Heather Haddon and Laura Stevens, "Investors Want to Talk Food Waste with Amazon," *Wall Street Journal,* Mar. 1, 2018.

10. Darby Hoover, "Estimating Quantities and Types of Food Waste at the City Level," National Resources Defense Council, 2017, https://tinyurl.com/y9zm7ax9.

11. JoAnne Berkenkamp, "Beyond Beauty: The Opportunities and Challenges of Cosmetically Imperfect Produce," Minnesota Institute for Sustainable Agriculture, May 2015, https://tinyurl.com/ybncfs6c.

12. Jo Robinson, *Eating on the Wild Side: The Missing Link to Optimum Health* (New York: Little, Brown, 2013).

13. Zlata Rodionova, "Denmark Reduces Food Waste by 25% in Five Years with the Help of One Woman—Selina Juul," *Independent,* Feb. 28, 2017.

14. Ibid.

15. Eleanor Beardsley, "French Food Waste Law Changing How Grocery Stores Approach Excess Food," NPR, Feb. 24, 2018.

16. "EU Actions Against Food Waste," European Commission, https://tinyurl.com/ya36hlhy.

17. Alex Morrell and Andy Kiersz, "Seeing How the Highest and Lowest-Earners Spend Their Money Will Make You Think Differently About 'Rich' vs. 'Poor,'" *Business Insider,* Dec. 4, 2017, https://tinyurl.com/y75rt906.

18. "How'd We 'Make' a Nonbrowning Apple?" Arctic Apples, https://tinyurl.com/ybgpqz83.

19. Food Recovery Act of 2017, S. 1680, 115th Congress (2017–2018).

Understanding the Text

1. What is "food rescue"?

2. What is the makeup of Kroger's tons of trash?

3. What are some food waste prevention strategies happening in Europe?

Reflection and Response

4. Why do you think Kroger launched its "Zero Hunger, Zero Waste" campaign? Who or what entities does it help?

5. Review how Little describes the amount of food Americans waste (par. 10–11). Why do you think Little describes American food waste in terms, for example, of how many stadiums a day it will fill? What reactions do you think she hopes to elicit? Did it work with you? Why or why not?

6. What are the various layers of the food waste problem that Little explores, and how does she demonstrate their interconnectedness?

7. What is "camera cuisine," and why do people participate in it? How does it contribute to the food waste problem Little describes?

Making Connections

8. Little juxtaposes the massive amount of food waste (particularly healthier foods) with the reality that many Americans face food insecurity and do not have enough to eat. Explore this American contradiction and the ethical dilemma it poses: while some go hungry, others toss perfectly good food into the trash. Using Barry Yeoman ("The Hidden Resilience of 'Food Desert' Neighborhoods," p. 104) and Joe Pinsker ("Why So Many Rich Kids Come to Enjoy the Taste of Healthier Foods" p. 97), consider how best to apply the solutions offered by Little and Margaret Mead ("The Changing Significance of Food," p. 138) to communities with differing needs. What strategies do you think are most effective for reducing both food waste and food insecurity?

9. Research food rescue programs in your local community. Do they exist? Who supports them? Who are they designed to help, and why? How are they similar to or different from the programs Little describes? How do they address the ethical, economic, social, aesthetic, and environmental layers of the problem that Little explores? Using textual support from Little and other selections in this collection, write an argument that analyzes the ethics of food rescue in your community.

10. Review the high-tech solutions that Little describes at the end of her essay. How can new technologies be used to help solve the food waste problem? How could these high-tech solutions complicate or worsen the problem? Using Little, David H. Freedman ("How Junk Food Can End Obesity," p. 75), Frances Moore Lappé ("Biotechnology Isn't the Key to Feeding the World," p. 317), Alejandra Borunda ("Grocery Stores Are Packed with Plastic," p. 222), and Selina Wang ("The Future of Farming Is Looking Up," p. 331), make an argument about if and how new technologies can help decrease and perhaps even solve the food waste problem.

Claudia Totir/Moment/Getty Images

4

How Does Our
Food System
Contribute to the
Climate Crisis?

Although there may be disagreement about how to respond to climate change and the environmental impacts it brings, experts widely agree that food production worldwide both affects and is affected by the climate crisis — and that we need to make meaningful changes to how we produce and consume food. The writers in this chapter all address the complex connections between the climate crisis and our food system, offering both global and local ways of understanding the problems and identifying solutions to them. They help us understand various aspects of the conversation that experts are currently engaged in, as they explore potential changes that should be made to our food system and who ought to make those changes.

Jonathan Foley draws on the work of a team of international scientists to lay out the most important aspects of the problem and to present a five-step plan for global food production that takes climate change into account. While he offers large, global recommendations, others look at more specific issues and problems. Alejandra Borunda writes about plastic packaging of food and its impact on the environment, as Georgina Gustin examines how eating meat and dairy products contributes to the climate crisis and Rowan Jacobsen offers a glimpse into the world of plant-based burgers and how scientific advancements might allow us to enjoy the flavor of meat without actually consuming animal products.

Nicole Walker takes a more creative approach, offering object lessons around the egg to raise important issues about climate change and to provoke us to think about how and what we consume in new ways. Paul Greenberg helps us see how our relationship to the fish we eat is connected to U.S. agriculture, as Bren Smith adds to our understanding of the politics of seafood. Together, they show us what it means to eat sustainably and in ways that allow those who produce our food to make a fair profit. Finally, Abaki Beck explores how climate change negatively affects the food

photo: Claudia Totir/Moment/Getty Images

culture of indigenous peoples, reminding us of the complex human relationships among food, the environment, culture, and the economy. These are relationships we must consider as we discuss and debate how to best feed ourselves (and the planet) as we face the realities of the climate crisis.

Together, the authors in this chapter ask us to confront difficult questions about how our eating habits, culinary choices, and food culture are connected to the current climate crisis. They force us to rethink what we eat, where it comes from, how it is packaged and delivered. They also challenge us to consider our role in potential solutions, asking us how far we are willing to go (what we are willing to give up and also what we are willing to eat) to reverse the direction of climate change.

Can We Feed the World and Sustain the Planet?

Jonathan A. Foley

Jonathan Foley has won multiple prestigious awards in science because of the many ways he has contributed to our understanding of the sustainability of our biosphere, the behaviors that endanger life on our planet, and what we can do to improve how humans interact with the complex global environmental systems that we rely on. After establishing himself as an important figure in sustainability studies at the University of Wisconsin, Foley joined the University of Minnesota faculty and served as the director of the Institute on the Environment and a professor and McKnight Presidential Chair in the department of Ecology, Evolution, and Behavior. Later, he became the executive director of the California Academy of Sciences, a scientific and educational institution in San Francisco that brings together experts who study and explore ways to sustain life on earth. Currently, he serves as the executive director of Project Drawdown, a global research organization that focuses on finding and promoting the best solutions to the climate crisis. Foley's more-than-130 scientific articles and numerous popular articles have made an enormous impact on science and beyond. Foley is passionate about finding ways to use new technologies to solve our biggest global environmental problems — problems like climate change, food and water security, human health, and sustainability. The essay included here presents the findings of a team of international experts that Foley assembled to study ways that we can dramatically increase food production and decrease environmental damage simultaneously.

Right now about one billion people suffer from chronic hunger. The world's farmers grow enough food to feed them, but it is not properly distributed and, even if it were, many cannot afford it, because prices are escalating. But another challenge looms. By 2050 the world's population will increase by two billion or three billion, which will likely double the demand for food, according to several studies. Demand will also rise because many more people will have higher incomes, which means they will eat more, especially meat. Increasing use of cropland for biofuels will put additional demands on our farms. So even if we solve today's problems of poverty and access — a daunting task — we will also have to produce twice as much to guarantee adequate supply worldwide. And that's not all.

By clearing tropical forests, farming marginal lands, and intensifying industrial farming in sensitive landscapes and watersheds, humankind has made agriculture the planet's dominant environmental threat. Agriculture already consumes a large percentage of the earth's land surface and is destroying habitat, using up freshwater, polluting rivers and oceans, and emitting greenhouse gases more extensively than almost any other human activity. To guarantee the globe's long-term health, we must dramatically reduce agriculture's adverse impacts.

The world's food system faces three incredible, interwoven challenges. It must guarantee that all seven billion people alive today are adequately fed; it must double food production in the next 40 years; and it must become truly environmentally sustainable—all at the same time.

Could these simultaneous goals possibly be met? An international team of experts, which I coordinated, has settled on five steps that, if pursued together, could increase by more than 100 percent the food available for human consumption globally while substantially reducing greenhouse gas emissions, biodiversity° losses, water use and water pollution. Tackling the triple challenge will be one of the most important tests humanity has ever faced. It is fair to say that our response will determine the fate of our civilization.

Bumping up against Barriers

At first blush, the way to feed more people seems clear: grow more 5 food, by expanding farmland and improving yield (crops harvested per hectare). Unfortunately, the world is running into significant barriers on both counts.

Society already uses about 37 percent of the earth's land surface, not counting Greenland or Antarctica, for farms or pastures. Agriculture is by far the biggest human use of land on the planet; nothing else comes close. And most of that 37 percent covers the *best* farmland. Much of the remainder is covered by deserts, mountains, tundra, ice, cities, parks and other unsuitable growing areas. The few remaining frontiers are mainly in tropical forests and savannas, which are vital to the stability of the globe, especially as stores of carbon and biodiversity. Expanding into those areas is not a good idea, yet five million to 10 million hectares° of cropland have been created in each of the past 20 years, with a signif-icant portion of that land conversion happening in the tropics. These additions enlarged the net area of cultivated land by only 3 percent, however, because of farmland losses caused by urban development and other forces, particularly in temperate zones.

Improving yield also sounds enticing. Yet our research team found that average global crop yield increased by just 20 percent from 1985 to 2005—far less than had been reported. Cereals yield has been rising at

---

biodiversity: biological diversity, usually used to refer to the variety of life on earth.
hectares: a metric unit of area equal to 10,000 square meters, or about 2.47 acres.

less than 2 percent a year since 2000 and yields of pulses (beans, lentils) and root crops by less than 1 percent — rates that are nowhere near enough to double food production by midcentury.

Feeding more people would be easier if all the food we grew went into human hands. But only 60 percent of the world's crops are meant for people: mostly grains, followed by pulses, oil plants, vegetables and fruits. Another 35 percent is used for animal feed, and the final 5 percent goes to biofuels° and other industrial products. Meat is the biggest issue here. Even with the most efficient meat and dairy systems, feeding crops to animals reduces the world's potential food supply. Grain-fed cattle operations typically use at least 100 kilograms of grain to make one kilogram of edible, boneless beef protein. Chicken and pork are more efficient, and grass-fed beef converts nonfood material into protein. Overall, grain-fed meat production systems are a drain on the global food supply.

> "To guarantee the globe's long-term health, we must dramatically reduce agriculture's adverse impacts."

Another deterrent to growing more food is damage to the environment, which is already extensive. Only our use of energy, with its profound impacts on climate and ocean acidification, rivals the sheer magnitude of agriculture's environmental footprint. Our research team has estimated that by 2010 agriculture had already cleared or radically transformed 70 percent of the world's prehistoric grasslands, 50 percent of the savannas, 45 percent of the temperate deciduous forests and 25 percent of the tropical forests. Since the last ice age, nothing has disrupted ecosystems more. Agriculture's physical footprint is nearly 60 times that of the world's pavements and buildings.

Freshwater is another casualty. Humans use an astounding 4,000 cubic kilometers of water per year, mostly withdrawn from rivers and aquifers.° Irrigation accounts for 70 percent of the draw. If we count only consumptive water use—water that is used and not returned to the watershed—irrigation climbs to 80 or 90 percent of the total. As a result, many large rivers, such as the Colorado, have diminished flows, some have dried up altogether, and many places have rapidly declining water tables, including regions of the U.S. and India.

Water is not only disappearing, it is being contaminated. Fertilizers, herbicides and pesticides are being spread at incredible levels and are found in nearly every ecosystem. The flows of phosphorus and nitrogen

10

---

biofuels: fuels produced through biological processes instead of geological processes; ethanol and biodiesel are the most common of these.
aquifers: huge storehouses of water underground from which groundwater can be extracted using wells.

through the environment have more than doubled since 1960, causing widespread water pollution and enormous hypoxic° "dead zones" at the mouths of many of the world's major rivers. Ironically, fertilizer run-off from farmland—in the name of growing more food—compromises another crucial source of nutrition: coastal fishing grounds. Fertilizer certainly has been a key ingredient of the green revolution that has helped feed the world, but when nearly half the fertilizer we apply runs off rather than nourishes crops, we clearly can do better.

Farming also accounts for 10 to 12 percent of the warming effects of greenhouse gases released by human activity—a contribution equal to that of all the road vehicles on the planet. Most of the direct emissions from farming come from methane produced by animals and rice paddies and from nitrous oxide released by over-fertilized soils. Add in the effects of tropical deforestation and other land clearing, and agriculture's share of global emissions rises to 24 percent of the total.

Five Solutions

Modern agriculture has been an incredibly positive force in the world, but we can no longer ignore its dwindling ability to expand or the mounting environmental harm it imposes. Previous approaches to solving food issues were often at odds with environmental imperatives. We could boost food production by clearing more land or using more water and chemicals but only at a cost to forests, streams and wetlands. Or we could restore ecosystems by taking farmland out of cultivation but only by reducing food production. This either-or approach is no longer acceptable. We need truly integrated solutions.

After months of research and deliberation—based on analysis of newly generated global agricultural and environmental data—our international team settled on a five-point plan that deals with food and environmental challenges together.

Stop expanding agriculture's footprint. Our first recommenda-   15
tion is to slow and ultimately stop the expansion of agriculture, particularly into tropical forests and savannas°. The demise of these ecosystems has far-reaching impacts on the environment, especially through lost biodiversity and increased carbon dioxide emissions (from clearing land).

Slowing deforestation would dramatically reduce environmental damage while imposing only minor constraints on global food

---

hypoxic: deprived of oxygen.
savannas: tropical grasslands; a grassland ecosystem with some scattered shrubs and isolated trees.

production. The resulting dip in farm capacity could be offset by reducing the displacement of more productive croplands by urbanization, degradation and abandonment.

Many proposals have been made to reduce deforestation. One of the most promising has been the Reducing Emissions from Deforestation and Degradation (REDD) mechanism. Under REDD, rich nations pay tropical nations to protect their rain forests, in exchange for carbon credits. Other mechanisms include developing certification standards for agricultural products so that supply chains can be assured that crops were not grown on lands created by deforestation. Also, better biofuel policy—one that relies on nonfood crops such as switchgrass instead of food crops—could make vital farmland newly available.

Close the world's yield gaps. To double global food production without expanding agriculture's footprint, we must significantly improve yields of existing farmlands. Two options exist. We can boost the productivity of our best farms—raising their "yield ceiling" through improved crop genetics and management. Or we can improve the yields of the world's least productive farms—closing the "yield gap" between a farm's current yield and its higher potential yield. The second option provides the largest and most immediate gain, especially in regions where hunger is most acute.

Our research group analyzed global patterns of crop yields and found significant yield gaps in many regions: most notably parts of Africa, Central America and eastern Europe. In these regions, better seeds, more effective fertilizer application and more efficient irrigation could produce much more food without increasing the amount of land under cultivation. Our analysis suggests that closing the yield gap for the world's top 16 crops could increase total food production by 50 to 60 percent, without causing much additional environmental damage.

Reducing yield gaps in the least productive agricultural lands may 20 often require the use of additional chemicals and water. Farmers will have to irrigate and fertilize in responsible ways. They can also make use of other yield-lifting techniques, such as reduced tillage°, which disturbs less soil and thus minimizes erosion. Cover crops planted between food-crop seasons suppress weeds and add nutrients and nitrogen to the soil when plowed under. Lessons from organic and agroecological° systems can also be adopted, such as leaving crop

---

tillage: digging and overturning soil to prepare it for growing crops.
agroecological: agricultural systems that consider ecological processes and are resource conserving.

residues on fields so that they decompose into nutrients. To close the world's yield gaps, we also have to overcome serious economic and social challenges, including better distribution of fertilizer and seed varieties to farms in impoverished regions and improved access to global markets for many regions.

Use resources much more efficiently. To reduce the environmental impacts of agriculture, low- and high-yield regions alike must practice agriculture in ways that produce vastly greater output of crops per unit input of water, fertilizer and energy.

On average, it takes about one liter of irrigation water to grow one calorie of food. Some places use much more, however. Our analysis found that farms can significantly curb water use without much reduction in food production, especially in dry climates. Primary strategies include drip irrigation (where water is applied directly to the plant's base and not wastefully sprayed into the air); mulching (covering the soil with organic matter to retain moisture); and reducing water lost from irrigation systems (by lessening evaporation from canals and reservoirs).

With fertilizers, we face a kind of Goldilocks problem. Some places have too few nutrients and therefore poor crop production, whereas others have too much, leading to pollution. Almost no one uses fertilizers "just right." Amazingly, only 10 percent of the world's cropland generates 30 to 40 percent of agriculture's fertilizer pollution. Our analysis identified hotspots on the planet—particularly in the central U.S., China, northern India and western Europe—where farmers could substantially reduce fertilizer use with little or no impact on food production.

Among the actions that can fix wasteful overfertilization are policy and economic incentives, such as payments to farmers for: promoting watershed stewardship and protection, reducing excessive fertilizer use, improving manure management (especially manure storage, so that less runs off into the watershed during a storm), capturing excess nutrients through recycling, and instituting other conservation practices. In addition, wetlands could be restored to enhance their capacity to act as natural sponges that filter out nutrients in runoff.

Here again, reduced tillage can help nourish the soil, as can precision 25 agriculture (applying fertilizer and water only when and where they are needed and most effective) and organic farming techniques.

Shift diets away from meat. We can dramatically increase global food availability and environmental sustainability by using more of our crops to feed people directly and less to fatten livestock.

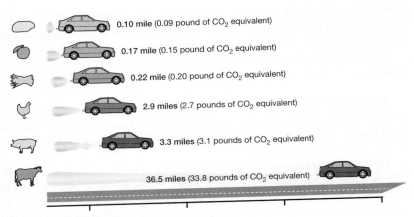

Eating and Driving: An Atmospheric Comparison

Greenhouse gas emissions per half pound of food grown (represented as comparable number of miles driven and pounds of CO_2 equivalent).

Sources: U.S. Environmental Protection Agency; "Seattle Food System Enhancement Project: Greenhouse Gas Emissions Study," University of Washington, 2007; "Tackling Climate Change Through Livestock," by P.J. Gerber et al., U.N. FAO, 2013.

Lucy Reading-Ikkanda

Globally, humans could net up to three quadrillion additional calories every year—a 50 percent increase from our current supply—by switching to all-plant diets. Naturally, our current diets and uses of crops have many economic and social benefits, and our preferences are unlikely to change completely. Still, even small shifts in diet, say, from grain-fed beef to poultry, pork or pasture-fed beef, can pay off handsomely.

Reduce food waste. A final, obvious but often neglected recommendation is to reduce waste in the food system. Roughly 30 percent of the food produced on the planet is discarded, lost, spoiled or consumed by pests.

In rich countries, much of the waste takes place at the consumer end of the system, in restaurants and trash cans. Simple changes in our daily consumption patterns—reducing oversize portions, the food thrown in the garbage, and the number of takeout and restaurant meals—could significantly trim losses, as well as our expanding waistlines. In poorer countries, the losses are similar in size but occur at the producer end, in the form of failed crops, stockpiles ruined by pests or spoilage, or food that is never delivered because of bad infrastructure and markets. Improved storage, refrigeration and distribution systems can cut waste appreciably. Moreover, better market tools can connect people who have crops to those who need them, such as cell-phone systems in Africa that link suppliers, traders and purchasers.

Although completely eliminating waste from farm to fork is not 30 realistic, even small steps would be extremely beneficial. Targeted efforts—especially reducing waste of the most resource-intensive foods such as meat and dairy—could make a big difference.

Moving toward a Networked Food System

In principle, our five-point strategy can address many food security and environmental challenges. If they were done together, the steps could increase the world's food availability by 100 to 180 percent while significantly lowering green-house gas emissions, biodiversity losses, water use and water pollution.

It is important to emphasize that all five points (and perhaps more) must be pursued simultaneously. No single strategy is sufficient to solve all our problems. Think silver buckshot, not a silver bullet. We have tremendous successes from the green revolution and industrial-scale agriculture to build on, along with innovations in organic farming and local food systems. Let's take the best ideas and incorporate them into a new approach—a sustainable food system that focuses on nutritional, social and environmental performance, to bring responsible food production to scale.

> "Feeding nine billion people in a truly sustainable way will be one of the greatest challenges our civilization has had to confront."

We can configure this next-generation system as a network of local agricultural systems that are sensitive to nearby climate, water resources, ecosystems and culture and that are connected through efficient means of global trade and transport. Such a system could be resilient and pay farmers a living wage.

One device that would help foster this new food system would be the equivalent of the Leadership in Energy and Environmental Design program now in place for constructing new commercial buildings sustainably. This LEED program awards increasingly higher levels of certification based on points that are accumulated by incorporating any of a wide range of green options, from solar power and efficient lighting to recycled building materials and low construction waste.

For sustainable agriculture, foods would be awarded points based on 35 how well they deliver nutrition, food security and other public benefits, minus their environmental and social costs. This certification would help us get beyond current food labels such as "local" and "organic," which really do not tell us much about what we are eating. Instead we can look at the whole performance of our food—across nutritional, social and environmental dimensions—and weigh the costs and benefits of different farming approaches.

Imagine the possibilities: sustainable citrus and coffee from the tropics, connected to sustainable cereals from the temperate zone, supplemented by locally grown greens and root vegetables, all grown under transparent, performance-based standards. Use your smartphone and the latest sustainable food app, and you will learn where your food came from, who grew it, how it was grown, and how it ranks against various social, nutritional and environmental criteria. And when you find food that works, you can tweet about it to your social network of farmers and foodies.

The principles and practices of our different agricultural systems—from large-scale commercial to local and organic—provide the foundation for grappling with the world's food security and environmental needs. Feeding nine billion people in a truly sustainable way will be one of the greatest challenges our civilization has had to confront. It will require the imagination, determination and hard work of countless people from all over the world. There is no time to lose.

Understanding the Text

1. What is the relationship between the world's population and the global demand for food?

2. What do we need to do to increase the global food supply by so much?

3. What specific human actions have made agriculture the dominant environmental threat on earth?

4. How does Foley describe the relationship between farming and climate change?

Reflection and Response

5. If you had to draw conclusions about the future of food based on Foley's essay, what would you conclude? Is he convincing? Are you optimistic that a plan like his could or will work? If so, why? If not, why not?

6. According to Foley, since the last ice age, agriculture has disrupted the earth's ecosystems more than any other factor. What evidence does he use to support this assertion?

7. Foley and his team of experts make five policy recommendations that we can use to feed the world's population while also adopting sustainable practices. These are aimed at policy makers and government leaders. Having read about them, what kinds of actions do you think you could take to improve sustainability? Are there local or personal measures you can adopt that might help achieve the goals of the five recommendations Foley makes?

Making Connections

8. Foley agrees with Margaret Mead ("The Changing Significance of Food," p. 138) that modern agriculture has had positive effects in the world. Compare their arguments. How does Foley's argument update Mead's? On what points do they agree? On what issues might they disagree? Use textual evidence to support your responses.

9. Foley claims that agriculture uses an astounding amount of water and is largely responsible for both the disappearance and the contamination of our freshwater supply. Research the relationship between our growing "food problem" and "water problem." Find several sources that discuss the relationship. Evaluate what they say as you work to identify ways we might rethink the future of food and the future of water together. Consider using Paul Greenberg's "Heartland" (p. 256) as a starting point for your research.

10. "Let's take the best ideas," Foley writes, "and incorporate them into a new approach — a sustainable food system that focuses on nutritional, social and environmental performance, to bring responsible food production to scale" (par. 32). Identify which authors in this book suggest ideas that might help create the kind of responsible global food system that Foley envisions. Use them to support your ideas and create a multimodal argument that presents at least three potential solutions, ideas, or innovations that we might consider. You may decide to make a podcast, short video, or slide presentation and include photos, video clips, graphics, or other visual elements to help support your ideas.

Grocery Stores Are Packed with Plastic. Some Are Changing

Alejandra Borunda

Alejandra Borunda is a PhD candidate in Earth Science at Columbia University who also writes on environmental science and the climate crisis as a freelance journalist. Borunda is a Ford Foundation fellow and was chosen as a 2018 Mass Media Science and Engineering fellow. As part of this fellowship, she worked at *National Geographic* writing essays, including this one, which draw on her academic research to explain complex scientific issues to the public. In this essay, she zeroes in on a specific issue — plastic packaging — to help us better understand the complex effects of our food choices on the environment.

A t Precycle, an airy grocery store in Brooklyn's Bushwick neighborhood, shoppers can find spices and fruit, grains and pastas, fresh olives and tofu, toothbrushes and floss, and many other household basics. What they won't find? Plastic.

Precycle is one in an expanding cohort of grocery stores that use little, if any, plastic packaging. As awareness of our ever-growing plastic pollution problem has swelled, some shoppers have looked for places where they can buy food free from the cling wrap and Styrofoam trays that fill many modern grocery stores.

In the last few years, more and more plastic-free food stores have opened their doors, springing up from Hong Kong to Germany to Ecuador. These stores are testing the models that grocers have long relied on, searching for ways to de-plasticize both the food supply chain and their customers' carts.

"I opened the store because I had this little blister on my brain telling me there was a different way to do things," says Katerina Bogatireva, the founder and owner of Precycle. Once she saw how pervasive plastic was in her life, she wanted to do something to help herself and others break free from it.

"It was like I was dropped in the middle of the sea and I couldn't see 5 the coast, but I had to swim forward toward a solution," she says. And what she came up with was a plastic-free grocery store.

Does That Avocado Need to Be Wrapped in Plastic?

Plastic is ubiquitous° in most grocery stores, so common it's almost invisible.

ubiquitous: present everywhere; found everywhere.

But the moments when its presence is felt can be dramatic. The internet erupted in outrage in 2016 when Whole Foods packed pre-peeled oranges in plastic containers. A few months later, it erupted again when a Canadian company marketed pre-halved avocados, the green hemispheres individually vacuum-sealed in a thick layer of plastic. "The avocado comes in its own NATURAL PACKAGING," typed commenters on Reddit. "What kind of person would do this?" typed others.

Others defended the moves, saying, like plastic straws, the pre-peeled oranges and avocados can be important resources for people with disabilities and mobility issues. People with arthritic hands often struggle to peel oranges, for example.

But avocado fiasco was, in some ways, the logical outcome of a long, complicated story about something else: Food waste.

Plastic food packaging established its reign over the modern grocery 10
store because it served a crucial purpose in preserving perishable food items for much longer than their natural life.

A cucumber, picked even a little early, only lasts about two weeks maximum. But wrap that same cucumber in an impermeable plastic sleeve and the decay slows down. In the cutthroat world of grocery stores, where profit margins are thin and every bruised apple that doesn't sell represents a loss, that extended life makes a big difference.

Plastic took over because it was cheap, light, and convenient. As supply chains daisy-linked longer and longer, the weight and size of a package became more critical, so a quart of milk encased in a few-ounce plastic jug was better, shipping-costs-wise, than that same quart glugging in a hefty, breakable glass bottle. Produce, carefully nestled into specially molded plastic trays, stacked in light, sturdy plastic crates, and loaded on cheap, sturdy plastic pallets, could survive weeks rather than days.

At the same time, consumer behavior also changed. With the advent of refrigerators, shoppers shifted away from buying just what they needed for a day or two and started shopping for a week or more. And where cars were abundant, shoppers could buy more—not just what they could carry but what they could load into trunks and backseats.

Taken together, it meant that consumers were looking for products that would last longer. Airtight plastic packaging helped that happen.

The trickle of plastic food packaging, though, is now a deluge. Packag- 15
ing makes up nearly a quarter of all the trash that goes to U.S. landfills,

according to the EPA—and much, if not most of that waste, was at some point attached to a food or beverage item.

But, "packaging plays an important role in helping to protect food, so getting rid of it all is not the answer," says Liz Goodwin, the director of the food loss and waste program at the World Resources Institute. "Unfortunately, it's not as simple as that."

Plastic-free Grocery Stores Experiment with Solutions

What's a shopper—or a store manager—to do?

"Like with almost anything sustainability related, the model is both something very new and innovative and also something that draws from things that have been around for a long time," says Elizabeth Balkan, the director of the food waste program at the Natural Resources Defense Council. "There have been local health food stores and co-ops around the country for 30 or 40 years that have been placing bulk food at the center of their commerce."

For Bogatireva of Precycle, the challenge was to figure out how much plastic snaked through normal supply chains and into the hands of consumers—and then get rid of it. Providing bulk foods that customers can scoop into their own containers to take home was a central concept.

But she also looked upstream.° It wasn't enough for her that customers 20 didn't see the plastic, if it was just lurking behind the scenes, secretly peeled off before their eyes could land on it.

Plastic-wrapped fruits and veggies were a no-no, so produce would have to come from local sources who could deliver bushels of apples in reusable crates. Then, she tried to find tofu that didn't come in a throw-away plastic container. No luck, for individually sized blocks. Eventually, she linked up with a manufacturer who will deliver big blocks of tofu in a five-gallon bucket that they'll pick up after it's emptied and refill. So there's still some plastic in the chain—but it's far from single-use.

The other part of the challenge was helping her customers maintain a sense of ease and convenience. It's better if they come in with their own empty jars to fill or egg cartons to re-stock, but if they don't, she has ones they can pick up. Since the produce options she has are often dependent on what the farmers bring in, there's a shelf of cookbooks to browse for ideas.

upstream: relating to a previous stage in the process.

"It's learning to think about shopping in a different way," she says.

Big Stores Tackle the Issue

At bigger stores, the drive to slim down the plastic footprint is also taking hold, if less comprehensively.

Kroger, which operates over 2,700 grocery stores across the U.S., 25 recently began to phase out plastic bags from their various chains. The impact adds up fast, says Jessica Adelman, the vice president of corporate affairs for Kroger. The company calculated that they handed out about 6 billion plastic bags a year, about six percent of the total number of bags distributed annually across the country. That's the equivalent of about 32,000 tons of plastic, or enough to fill over 3,000 moving trucks jam packed with bags.

Trader Joe's has also begun the process of peering into its supply chain to peel away unnecessary plastic use. Matt Sloan, VP of marketing for Trader Joe's, is realistic about how much work it will take to de-plasticize the grocery business. Think about a tea bag, he explains. There's plastic in that packaging that lets the tea stay fresh for months. But the biodegradable or bio-sourced plastic alternatives aren't yet good enough to maintain that same freshness, so changing the packaging would disrupt the product, and lead to more waste.

> "Plastic is ubiquitous in most grocery stores, so common it's almost invisible."

Each change seems like it should be simple, Sloan says. But, "we're at a point where we understand the practical realities to be so under-developed" for both alternatives to traditional plastic packaging and to recycling solutions that even the smallest changes can generate big, cascading challenges.

"We're often running down this path and then hitting the proverbial wall, and I think we're getting to the fascinating and frustrating point where we're understanding there's no simple thing that has in it the all-encompassing solution."

But more awareness and pressure from consumers will keep the projects moving forward, says Balkan of NRDC.

"There's been some really powerful shifts in consumer awareness 30 around single-use items, straws and bags lately," says Balkan. "People are starting to see that the dependence we've formed on these things—we can undo it, if we wish to. And not having them—it might not make our lives any harder or more complicated; it could even make them much better."

Understanding the Text

1. What are the benefits of plastic packaging? What are the problems with it?

2. What roles have consumers played in eliminating plastic packaging and plastic waste?

Reflection and Response

3. Why is the relationship between plastic packaging and food waste so complicated?

4. Do an inventory of the food you have stored at home — in the refrigerator, in the cupboards, and/or the pantry. How much plastic is there? What is it being used for? What would it take to eliminate it completely? Would your eating habits have to change? If so, how and why?

5. Plastic use can greatly increase the quality of life for some people with disabilities (par. 8). Do these benefits outweigh the climate repercussions of plastic? How could we cut back the prevalence of single-use plastic without further disadvantaging people with disabilities?

Making Connections

6. Borunda describes Precycle, a business aiming to eliminate plastic packaging from its shelves and from the food chain of its customers. What makes this goal complicated? Discuss the complications presented by this local effort by referring to the global problems described by Jonathan Foley ("Can We Feed the World and Sustain the Planet?," p. 212).

7. Research local regulations where you live and shop. Are there restrictions on plastic, single-use bags, plastic straws, or packaging? If so, what are the restrictions aiming to accomplish? Are there signs that they are working? If not, why do you think this is the case? Are there restrictions you would advocate for? Why or why not?

8. Much of the plastic used in grocery stores is to help prevent food waste. Amanda Little, in "Stop the Rot" (p. 194), discusses actions grocery stores can — and are — taking to cut down food waste. Using Borunda and Little, brainstorm steps your nearest market could take to combat climate change and food waste. What would need to happen to put these steps into effect?

Can a Climate Conscious Diet Include Meat or Dairy?

Georgina Gustin

As a journalist based in Washington, DC, Georgina Gustin has covered food policy and the environment for more than a decade and written extensively about the relationship between food production and the climate crisis. At the *St. Louis Post-Dispatch*, she launched the "food beat," then went on to cover food policy and governmental agencies that regulate food at *CQ Roll Call*. Currently, she reports for *InsideClimate News*, a news organization that covers climate change. Her writing covers food production's impact on the climate, seeking to answer the question of how to produce enough food without destroying the planet. Her articles have appeared in various publications including *The New York Times*, *Washington Post*, and *National Geographic*. In this essay, first published by *InsideClimate News*, Gustin discusses two studies that help us understand the impacts of eating meat and dairy on the climate crisis.

Two new studies are making the case that people in high-income countries need to cut back on livestock-based foods, but they're also suggesting that one-size-fits-all recommendations won't work in all cases.

Though each advocates a major transformation in how the world eats and produces food in order to slow climate change — including a shift toward plant-based diets — they also say that consuming meat and dairy products in certain parts of the world, by certain populations, is critical for meeting nutritional goals.

One report explores the economic case for changing current food production and consumption habits, estimating that they cause about $12 trillion a year in damage to the environment, human health and development. If countries invested just half of 1 percent of global GDP in carbon-friendly agriculture, food waste reduction, reforestation and prescribing more plant-focused diets, among other measures, the world could sustainably feed itself and reduce the climate-related damage, the authors found.

"What over 9 billion people choose to eat and how they make these choices are at the heart of how our food and land use systems evolve," the report finds, adding: "The right animals, in the right places and raised in the right conditions can continue to play an important role in sustainable food and land use systems."

In a second report, published in August 2019 in the journal *Global Environmental Change*, researchers at Johns Hopkins University found that modest shifts toward plant-based diets globally could cancel out the

5

"If countries invested just half of 1 percent of global GDP in carbon-friendly agriculture, food waste reduction, reforestation and prescribing more plant-focused diets, among other measures, the world could sustainably feed itself and reduce the climate-related damage."

increase in greenhouse gas emissions from helping undernourished populations get adequate nutrition, including protein. The number of malnourished people in the world — roughly 820 million — remains stubbornly high.

"So many countries are dealing with under-nourishment. They're going to have to increase food consumption, and accordingly their carbon footprints are going to have to go up," said Keeve Nachman, director of the Food Production and Public Health Program at Johns Hopkins' Center for a Livable Future and one of the report's authors. "We have a responsibility as a global community to make sure they have enough food. What that means is that high-income countries that typically consume more animal products are going to have to more rapidly consider some of these plant-forward dietary shifts."

Their study took nine different plant-focused diets and determined what the carbon impacts of each would be for 140 different countries around the world. The idea, Nachman explained, was to help policy makers in those countries understand how potential dietary shifts might impact nutritional needs and their carbon footprints.

The study comes in the wake of a series of reports, including one from the United Nations, calling for a global shift toward plant-based diets. During the negotiations on that report's language, some developing countries argued that it was unfair to call for a broad, global reduction in meat consumption when some populations still lack enough protein.

"We recognize that every country has its own complex set of situations and priorities, so we're presenting these nine plant-forward diets in the hopes that we're giving decision makers options that are benchmarked to these climate and water footprints," Nachman said. "If we come barreling in with statements about how we need to reduce animal products, that could fall on deaf ears. All countries can be part of the solution."

Different Plant-Based Diets, Different Impacts

Nachman and his colleagues analyzed common, recognizable diets 10 including "lacto-ovo vegetarian," in which people eschew meat and fish but eat dairy and eggs; a "two-thirds" vegan diet, in which people consume one-third of their diets in animal-based protein; strictly vegan diets; and diets in which people ate mostly plant-based foods but also some proteins low on the food chain, like mollusks and small fish.

They found that a shift to vegan diets reduced per capita greenhouse gas footprints by 70 percent, having the lowest per capita carbon impact in 97 percent of the countries.

They also found that lacto-ovo vegetarian diets had a higher carbon footprint than diets in which vegans consumed meat in moderation but avoided dairy, largely because of the greenhouse gas emissions from dairy production. And they found that low-food-chain diets had less than half the greenhouse gas emissions of lacto-ovo vegetarians in more than 90 percent of the countries.

"These findings suggest populations could do far more to reduce their climate impact by eating mostly plants with a modest amount of low-impact meat than by eliminating meat entirely and replacing a large share of the meat's protein and calories with dairy," the report said.

It added: "The country-specific results presented here could provide nutritionally viable pathways for high-meat-consuming countries, as well as transitioning countries that might otherwise adopt the Western dietary pattern."

Overhauling a Food System

In the economics-focused report released September 2019, the Land and 15 Food Use Coalition, a group of scientists, economists and environmental groups that formed in 2017 to help overhaul food and land use systems with the goal of achieving global climate targets, lays out 10 strategies for transforming food and land use systems, including a more diverse diet that's lower in livestock-based foods, particularly in high-income countries.

It recommends that global consumption of meat from cattle and sheep "should be halted and gradually reduced," but "in some cases this means people will need to eat more meat, and in others less." For example, the report says, children and women of childbearing years in sub-Saharan Africa who are among the world's undernourished populations, will need more protein to meet their nutritional needs, while people in high-income countries will need to cut back for both health and climate reasons.

The coalition found that if governments and societies invested about $350 billion a year—about 0.5 percent of GDP—in carbon-friendly agriculture and other sustainable food and farming measures, the world could save $10.5 trillion annually in environmental and health costs by 2050.

"The productive potential of the earth is plenty big enough to return 1.2 billion hectares of land to nature and produce healthy food for a growing population," said Per Pharo, the report's lead author and director of Norway's Climate and Forest Initiative. "There are no technical, financial or biophysical barriers to doing this."

Farmers Have Important Roles to Play

There are, however, political and systemic barriers.

"The goal of this report is to say this can be done, it should be done," Pharo said. "We haven't been able to mobilize the political will."   20

The report points out that governments spend about $700 billion supporting agriculture globally, but only about 1 percent of that is directed toward beneficial environmental practices. Governments need to substantially increase their support for farmers in ways that incentivize regenerative and carbon-friendly farming, the authors write.

"We are extremely aware that [farmers] will be part of solving this," Pharo said. "We have asked them to deliver and they've delivered. . . . This is not about blaming farmers. It's a question of aligning more people behind the mission of transformative change."

Understanding the Text

1. What is a climate-conscious diet?
2. According to the research presented by Gustin, why should most of us move toward plant-based diets?
3. Why don't "one-size-fits-all" recommendations work when we attempt to lessen the impacts of climate change on food choices?

Reflection and Response

4. Consider the factors that affect how we should decide what to eat — and who should eat what. Based on the factors discussed in the studies Gustin describes, what should you eat? Which diet would be healthiest for you and the planet?
5. Why is it difficult to make the kinds of changes recommended by the studies that Gustin cites? How difficult would it be for you to follow what the research indicates is necessary to lessen the impacts of your food choices on the climate crisis? Does the research convince you to change? If so, why? If not, what would have to happen to convince you?

Making Connections

6. Gustin draws attention to the many different stakeholders that have a role or that will be impacted by changes in the consumption of meat and dairy products — including consumers, politicians, farmers, those living with food insecurity, and those whose daily lives are already impacted by climate change. Use Gustin; Eric Schlosser ("Why the Fries Taste Good," p. 20); Dhruv Khullar ("Why Shame Won't Stop Obesity," p. 71); Barry Yeoman ("The Hidden Resilience of 'Food Desert' Neighborhoods," p. 104); Donald Barlett and James Steele ("Monsanto's Harvest of Fear," p. 165); Blake Hurst ("The Omnivore's Delusion," p. 184); Joon Yun, David Kessler, and Dan Glickman ("We Need Better Answers on Nutrition," p. 301); and/or Richard Marosi ("Hardship on Mexico's Farms, a Bounty for U.S. Tables," p. 306) to identify two stakeholders that have competing interests in this discussion. Then use two to three of these sources to help you understand the problem from each stakeholder's position. Put their views into conversation with each other. Are there areas of agreement? What specifically do they disagree on? What would it take to mediate between the views and find solutions that might satisfy both stakeholders?

7. For many of us, embracing the dietary changes that are suggested by the research presented by Gustin would require big dietary changes — ones that might require us to give up foods that are connected to our family traditions or cultural identity. Drawing on Wendell Berry ("The Pleasure of Eating," p. 46) and Michael Pollan ("Eat Food: Food Defined," p. 10), explain the dilemma. Then propose one potential compromise. Use two to three other readings in this collection to help you argue for your compromise.

8. Gustin argues that we have the capability to make the kinds of changes necessary for lessening the negative effects of food production on climate change and feeding the world's population, but that there are "political and systemic barriers" that keep us from doing this. Select two to three readings in Chapters 4 and 5 to help you explain what these political barriers are and how we might address them. Which solution do you think is most likely to work? Support your response with evidence from the texts.

The Biography of a Plant-Based Burger: One Man's Mission to Make Meat Obsolete

Rowan Jacobsen

Rowan Jacobsen is an award-winning science, nature, and travel writer. He has written for many magazines and news-papers, including *The New York Times*, *Huffington Post*, *Outside*, *Harper's*, and *Medium*. He has authored several books, includ-ing *A Geography of Oysters* (2007), for which he won a James Beard Award; *Fruitless Fall* (2008); *The Living Shore* (2009); and *Apples of Uncommon Character* (2014). As a Knight Science Journalism Fellow at MIT and a McGraw Center for Business Journalism Fellow, he wrote about plant-based proteins and synthetic biology, issues related to the piece included here. Originally published by *Pacific Standard*, the essay that follows combines Jacobsen's story-telling acumen with his interest in science and food as it tells the story of one man's attempt to create the perfect plant-based burger, one that looks, tastes, smells, and feels just like meat.

I'm sitting in a Silicon Valley conference room, gazing at a burger on a plate and thinking about its past. This sort of speculation has been something of a national pastime since 2002, when Michael Pollan wrote a seminal feature for the *New York Times Magazine* called "Power Steer." The essay was, as Pollan put it, "the biography of my cow," and it traced the journey of No. 534, an eight-month-old steer he had purchased, from its birth on a South Dakota prairie, through branding and castration, weaning from its mother, forced conversion to a diet of corn and antibi-otics, confinement in a manure-caked Kansas feedlot, and up to its inev-itable end in a slaughterhouse, where it would be stunned, skinned, and eviscerated.

"Power Steer" illuminated not just the misery of industrial meat production, but also the extraordinary sums of chemical fertilizer, oil, pharmaceuticals, and land required to keep the system afloat—all of which remained invisible at the meat counter. "What grocery-store item is more silent about its origins than a shrink-wrapped steak?" Pollan asked. "If I was going to continue to eat red meat, then I owed it to myself, as well as to the animals, to take more responsibility for the invisible but crucial transaction between ourselves and the animals we eat."

It's easy to forget what a radical idea this was, and what an impact the piece had on American food culture. It must have launched a thou-sand grass-fed farms and farm-to-table bistros. In a sense, it also helped produce the burger before me, now oozing an ocher jus* onto its bottom bun. Because the more attention consumers paid to the realities of feed-lot farming, the more they wanted out. But organic, grass-fed, and local meat is expensive, and vegetarianism appeals to surprisingly few Americans—just 2 percent, almost all of whom lapse at some point. Meat happens to be incredibly tasty and convenient, and the substitutes we've been offered heretofore have done little to help us forget it.

But this burger before me, piled with pickles and onions and avocado and looking seriously meaty, may represent the first real solution to Pollan's dilemma. Which could make this piece a kind of bookend to "Power Steer." This is the biography of my burger—but it is a radically different story from No. 534's. Unlike poor 534, my burger actually has a name: It's called Griffin (which I'll explain shortly). And if Griffin delivers, then we may be able to close the book on the whole sad, ugly story of industrial meat sooner than anybody realizes, because Griffin happens to be entirely animal-free.

Patrick O. Brown, the creative force behind Griffin, likes to tell   5 the story of the 1830 race between *Tom Thumb*, one of the first steam locomotives, and a draft horse on a newly constructed segment of the Baltimore & Ohio Railroad. The race started, and *Tom Thumb* began to pull away from the horse, but then it threw a belt and the horse passed it. The takeaway from that story, Brown says, is not that the horse won. It's that the horse was never going to win again.

So what I'm wondering, as the first tendrils of beefiness fill the air of the conference room, is if this race is competitive. If this burger is as good as its inventors say—if it even comes close to tasting like a conventional hamburger—then the cow is never going to win again.

The biography of my burger begins in 2009—not on a ranch but in the mind of a graying, bespectacled, 62-year-old Stanford University professor. In the 1990s, Brown pioneered DNA microarrays, a technology used to measure gene expression and determine an individual gene's function, which made possible many of the genetic breakthroughs of the past 20 years. In 2000 he co-founded the Public Library of Science, a non-profit publisher of open-access science journals, as a way of disrupting the pay-per-view journal model. At Stanford, he had his own biochemistry lab for mapping the way genes respond to their environment, particularly in relation to cancer cells.

In 2009, Brown decided to devote an 18-month sabbatical to eliminating industrial meat production, which he determined at the time to be the world's largest environmental problem. A staggering one-third of

ocher jus: juice that is an earthy color like red or yellow.

the land on Earth is used to raise livestock and their food. The Midwest is a giant feed trough. Reducing meat consumption, Brown figured, would free up vast amounts of land and water, would greatly mitigate climate change, would alleviate the suffering of billions of animals, would eliminate mountains of chemical fertilizer, and would make people healthier. It seemed like a no-brainer.

Such a no-brainer, in fact, that at first Brown assumed all he had to do was a little education. "I started doing the typical misguided academic approach to the problem," he told me. He organized an A-list 2010 National Research Council workshop in Washington called "The Role of Animal Agriculture in a Sustainable 21st Century Global Food System," which caused not a ripple. Not long after, he determined that the only real way to impact meat production would be to beat it in the free market. "All you have to do is make a product that the current consumers of meat and dairy prefer to what they're getting now," he said. "It's easier to change people's behavior than to change their minds."

By the end of his sabbatical, Brown, who has been a vegetarian since   10
the 1970s and a vegan since 2004, had distilled his challenge: He would re-create meat, but with plants. All meat production is environmentally ruinous, but beef is by far the worst offender, so for his initial target, Brown chose ground beef, which accounts for 60 percent of all beef consumption.

Various companies have been trying for decades to concoct a veggie burger that is as juicy and toothsome as a fresh-cooked beef burger, but so far no one has come close. Plant stuff just doesn't act like animal stuff. But Brown thought it could. "I was exceedingly confident that we could make products that compete on an even playing field with anything the animal-farming industry makes," he told me as we toured Impossible Foods, his start-up. Brown is lean and owlish and very serious. "The food industry is decades behind the times," he said. "The stuff we're doing now that's new to the food system was old news 40 years ago in the biotech world." Brown knew he could extract certain ingredients from certain plants and make them do things they had never done before. He believed he could create a meat substitute that would act exactly like ground beef.

Convinced that the moment was right, Brown began to assemble the expensive equipment and tech-savvy minds needed for his burger moonshot project. And that meant turning to Silicon Valley. "If you live around here," he told me, "you can't walk down the block without tripping over a venture capitalist."

When Brown said this, Alison Davis, the 27-year-old manager of special projects for Impossible Foods, was with us. She immediately laughed and said, *"Pat Brown* can't walk down the street without tripping over a venture capitalist." That's because they all throw themselves at his feet and beg the Gandalf of Stanford to take their money. Brown regularly utters venture capital catnip like, "Our mission is not to make a decent burger, it's to make

> "[T]he only real way to impact meat production would be to beat it in the free market."

the best burger the world has ever seen." And as much as Silicon Valley loves Brown, he loves it right back. "There's this sense that there are all these things that are possible that you can't imagine," he told me, "that the world can be very different from the way it is today. Out here, you're more appreciated if you're doing something insanely ambitious, even if it doesn't work. There's a tolerance for swinging for the fences and striking out."

Brown met with three venture capital firms and came away with three offers. He chose Khosla Ventures because he felt Vinod Khosla best grasped the urgency of the problem, and because Khosla agreed that the company could never be sold to the meat industry, which could have made it disappear for pocket change, eliminating the competition.

Suddenly he had $3 million of seed money. And that meant it was time to leave Stanford. "I never imagined that I'd want to leave," he admitted. "My job description was: Follow your curiosity wherever it leads you and make discoveries. I was not at all looking for a change. But to do this project, I had to." 15

Picture, in your mind, a fat, juicy hamburger hot off the grill. It's sizzling, it's weeping a little grease, and it's pumping out some outrageously tasty aromas. Now raise it to your mouth and sink your teeth in. Hot, salty juice sprays across your palate, your mouth waters, and your brain is filled with smoky happiness.

Humans are hard-wired to go crazy for meat—one of our richest sources of sustenance. Plants are just a few percent protein, but meat is mostly protein, which our bodies use to build brains and biceps and enzymes and more. We crave meat on a visceral level.

"One of the first things we needed to do is to have a biochemical understanding of why meat tastes like meat," Brown told me as we stepped into the Impossible Foods research and development lab. I gazed at the gas chromatograph-mass spectrometer (GC-MS), a pile of white cabinets and flashing lights that looked as if it had been assembled by a Hollywood set designer. At one end, a lab-coated, safety-goggled guy named Alex was sniffing the end of a glass tube.

A GC-MS separates the aroma-carrying molecules in a food and boils them off one by one. Half the flow is directed to the mass spectrometer, which identifies the molecules by mass and charge, while the other half heads for the nose of somebody like Alex, who writes down what he smells. As I peeked over Alex's shoulder, he wrote: "Chemical. Astringent. Green veg. Sweet. Beef. Sulfur. Cedar bark."

"When you cook ground beef," Brown explained, "of the thousands 20 of compounds that come through, maybe 150 have a smell that you can detect. None of them smell like meat. They smell like butter, caramel, dust, garbage, a struck match, lilacs, but not meat. But they become meat"—he tapped his head—"up here."

In fact, the list of flavors and aromas that make up beef is pretty weird. The National Cattlemen's Beef Association primer on the subject lists the expected beefy, meaty, roasted, fatty, savory, and brothy flavors, but also nutty, mushroom, sweet, sour, bitter, dairy, waxy, buttery, green, grassy, musty, fruity, bell pepper, potato, pungent, metallic, earthy, beany, soapy, sulfurous, rancid, sweaty, and, my personal favorite, warmed over. It makes you realize that, when we know we've got a hunk of beef on the end of our fork, we're pretty forgiving about what it actually tastes like.

To choose a representative burger flavor to re-create, Impossible Foods sampled widely in the marketplace. "Some of the bad ones are really shitty," said Celeste Holz-Schietinger, Impossible Foods' lead flavor scientist. (And that is literally true: When *Consumer Reports* tested 300 samples of ground beef around the country, all 300 tested positive for fecal contamination.) On the other hand, in taste tests, top grades of beef like Kobe don't significantly outperform Safeway 80/20 ground beef, which is what Impossible Foods ended up choosing. "It's the most standard beef out there," she said. "It's a good reference point for most people's experience."

Most key beef aromas are generated through the alchemy of cooking, when heat transforms the proteins, fats, and sugars in raw beef into new compounds. Nailing the perfect raw-beef replacement doesn't mean mixing a cocktail of the final flavors; it means finding the right precursors. And this is what no veggie burger has ever been able to accomplish. The best try to maximize brothy flavors while suppressing cereal ones, but none has ever gone beyond a savory miso—not bad, but not beef.

What's missing is blood.

Beef contains hemoglobin, which, Impossible Foods researchers 25 found, is the secret catalyst that transforms raw flesh into yum.

If your blood were a start-up, you might say that its core technology is heme, an iron-containing molecule with the ability to grab oxygen from the lungs and deliver it through the bloodstream to your cells. Oxygen particularly loves to bind with iron (hence rust), and, when this happens, the resulting compound turns red. Heme is why hemoglobin is red, and it's also what separates red meat from white meat. Ground beef is about 10 parts per million heme, while chicken is only two parts per million heme. Pork is in the middle at three to eight parts per million. Add heme to raw chicken, cook it, and people start to think it tastes like beef. Add too much heme and it tastes like liver.

As soon as heme was added to the Impossible Foods formula, the classic beefy scents and tastes emerged. Which made the first challenge obvious: The meatless burger needed blood.

I'd always assumed the animal kingdom had a lock on hemoglobin, but it turns out that soy and other nitrogen-fixing legumes make it too. Dig up a soy plant and you'll find red marbles amid the roots. These are root nodules, which capture nitrogen (an essential component of protein) with the help of millions of symbiotic bacteria. Root nodules are red because of the presence of hemoglobin, which the plants use to maintain proper oxygen levels for the underground bacteria to do their work.

Initially, Impossible Foods hoped to source the heme for its burger from soy root nodules. But harvesting underground soy roots would have entailed developing a new supply chain, and would have released quite a lot of carbon into the atmosphere as well, so the company tried the Silicon Valley approach: taking the snippet of soy DNA that codes for heme and inserting it into a standard yeast strain.

Yeasts are the single-celled workhorses of biotechnology, so malleable 30 and undemanding that they can be genetically tweaked to make almost anything: alcohols, oils, proteins. Genetically modified yeasts have been used for years to produce things like pharmaceuticals and the animal-free rennet used in cheesemaking. Impossible Foods has invented a yeast that makes plant blood.

Inside the Impossible Foods pilot plant, 24 hours a day, five days a week, stainless steel fermentation tanks filled with this proprietary yeast crank out bright-red heme. If you were to sample it, you'd think you just bit your lip. It runs through tubes, is purified in a series of columns, and then is frozen in ice-cube trays until it's time to make burgers. (Though most of the yeast is filtered out of the heme—and no GMO crops are used—there are still trace amounts of genetically modified ingredients in the Impossible Burger, which, I suspect, may attract some level of antipathy from the natural foods crowd.)

Much of the company's first year was devoted to developing, patenting, and proving its heme technology. Then it was time to design the rest of the burger. Each significant burger iteration is codenamed after a bird, starting with A; both Anhinga and Blue-Footed Booby tasted more like "rancid polenta," in Brown's words, than beef, but he caught a glimpse of the path to success. He had 25 employees and counting, and was well on his way to beating meat. But there was just one problem. He was out of seed money. So he went back to the venture capitalists and raised another $75 million. He'd learned over time how to better frame his pitch. "I kind of hadn't realized how much businesspeople focus on money," he admitted to me. "Which sounds incredibly naive. But I'd go in and my pitch would be, 'This is such a huge problem for the world, and we have a solution.' And almost as a footnote, I'd say, 'Oh, and by the way, this is a trillion-dollar industry.' Over time, the footnote became the headline."

Heme may be the magic that manifests the Beef Experience, but a burger is mostly just a lump of flesh. All the carcass trimmings that don't fit neatly into one of the more valuable cuts of beef get dumped into meat grinders and extruded as the pink squiggles we know and love. Most of this tissue is fat and muscle, but there are also blood vessels, nerve tissue, and a lot of connective tissue—the membranes and collagen that hold the animal together. That connective tissue plays an important role in building a burger, contributing the slightly gristly chew that gives the thing its bounce, which is also something no veggie burger has been able to duplicate.

Inventing an analog for connective tissue was the job of the Protein Discovery Team. There's a lot to discover. Every plant species contains 20,000 to 40,000 proteins in its genome, any one of which could have surprising functions once separated from the rest of the plant.

"It's never-ending Christmas for a biochemist like me," declared Allen   35 Henderson, who was standing at a stainless steel table in the lab, wearing the Impossible Foods lab uniform—white lab coat, plastic gloves, safety goggles. He handed me a rubbery, beige hunk of mystery and said, "I just feel like I'm playing the whole time."

Soft-spoken, with kind eyes and a touch of professorial gray in his beard, Henderson embodies the Impossible Foods vibe. He was a postdoc at the University of California–San Francisco when the company found him. "I'd been building this career toward a professorship," he recalled. "But when I interviewed here, the culture and the scientific questions were so compelling that I actually walked away from everything. I spent a long weekend torturing over it, and the thing that tipped the scales was that I realized this was the one thing I could do as a scientist that would make the biggest impact on the world."

Henderson described what he does as protein speed dating. "I'm learning a lot about how proteins do or don't play well together." The rules are turning out to be very different than we thought. "They do things that are completely unexpected. I have over a decade of training as a biochemist, and I'm still like, *Why did that just happen?*" Impossible Foods has patents in the works for using proteins to bind, emulsify, gel, and stretch in novel ways. The hunk in my hand squeezed and tore like chicken breast, with noticeable muscle fiber striations, but was actually made from soy proteins.

For practicality, the Protein Discovery Team limits its experimentation to plants that are already part of the food system and can be sourced relatively inexpensively around the world. The muscle tissue in Griffin comes from select wheat and potato proteins, while the connective tissue comes from soybeans and wheat gluten. The fat is coconut oil, emulsified so that it mimics flecks of beef tallow, which partially melt during cooking. Together, these fats and proteins act like ground beef when heated, searing and cohering into a springy, moist matrix.

Griffin's predecessor, Falcon, chewed like beef and had the bloody savor of beef, but something was still missing. So it was back to the ol' gas chromatograph, which indicated that Falcon needed a touch of some sweet and fatty aldehydes and ketone molecules, many of which are common in the cucurbit family, which includes cucumbers and melons. Could that really transform Falcon into beef?

"A few weeks ago we had a melon party," Alison Davis told me. "We   40
had four people in the kitchen all day slicing and boiling melons. We had special melon music playing."

They tried mixing each one into the formulation. "Cantaloupe was a no-go for sure," Celeste Holz-Schietinger recalled with a shudder. "We tried watermelon. We tried some squashes." All weird. Then they tried honeydew. "It was a yay! We knew right away." With honeydew in the mix, they decided they were ready to take on beef.

But I get to be the judge of that. After watching a technician mix muscle tissue, connective tissue, heme, and a few flavor compounds into a pink patty, I follow her to the conference room, where she fries a burger on an electric griddle, plates it expertly on a cute bun with avocado, caramelized onions, egg-free dijonnaise, and cornichons, and presents it to me with a basket of chips on the side.

And now I lift the burger, and bite, and chew.

It is profoundly awkward to be chewing a burger in silence with the eyes of five Impossible Foodies fixed upon me. It's a tense moment. Their nervousness is palpable. They really, really want me to like this burger. And I really, really want to like it too. I want it to be the best burger I've ever eaten. I want *Tom Thumb* to leave the horse in the dust. I want steer No. 534 to be out of a job.

And it's...   45

Not quite there.

It's a solid burger, better than any veggie burger I've tried (and I've tried them all), but it's not a mindblower. The chew is right. The smell is right. What's missing is the joy. When you sink your teeth into a perfectly grilled burger with all your favorite fixings, there's a momentary sense of hitting the jackpot, of being the luckiest organism on Earth. And that, I think, will be hard to replicate.

Would I opt for this burger instead of the mind-blower, sacrificing a soupçon of taste for a generous helping of righteousness? Absolutely.

Would Joe Beef? Not likely.

I manage to utter some nice things about the burger, congratulate 50 them on strong work, and, soon after, my visit to Impossible Foods ends.

But that is not the end of this story. Because in Silicon Valley there is never an end. There is only a next. Honeydew proved hard to come by in the quantities needed, and so was withdrawn from the formula, while other ingredients were added along the road to refinement. After Griffin came Harpy. And Harpy begat Ibis, which begat Jailbird, which begat Kiwi, which led to Loon. And in May 2016, two little pink shrink-wrapped sliders arrive at my door in a foam box. It had taken some cajoling to convince the company to ship them to me. I even had to agree to a Skype tutorial on how to cook them (the upshot: fry in a little vegetable oil until brown, then flip).

The burgers are accompanied by three pages of instructions, their own buns, and tiny containers of chopped cornichons, caramelized onions, and homemade dijonnaise sauce, all of which I immediately discard. My plan is to fry a Loon slider alongside a slider of real ground beef in a separate pan.

The raw Loon burger looks unquestionably like ground beef, only slightly paler and more finely grained, and it even *smells* like raw meat, cool and dank. In the pan, it immediately begins to sizzle as fat melts out, though significantly less fat than the Walmart Special beside it, which is hissing and spitting like a Chinese sparkler.

Unlike ground beef, which becomes firmer during the cooking process, the Impossible Burger initially softens, which would make it difficult to grill. But soon I see a firm brown line creeping upward from the bottom of the burger and droplets of "blood" seeping out of the perimeter. I flip. The top has a gorgeous brown crust—much more so than the hamburger, thanks to those potato proteins—and the patty has firmed up nicely. It smells like steak and caramel. I let it cook another minute, then nestle it in a bun with ketchup and tomato, and chomp down while still standing there at the stove. Juice squirts out the back of the burger and hits the hot pan with a hiss. I know that sound, and it doesn't come from a veggie burger.

This time around, my world shifts a little. That semi-crispy crust is 55 a savory revelation, even if it's not entirely hamburger-like. The inside isn't overly homogenous, as veggie burgers tend to be. It's chewy without being gristly. It feels clean yet flavorful, and I can already see that any kid raised on the Impossible Burger would likely be repulsed by a greasy hamburger. To that generation, "Power Steer" may be nothing but a historical curiosity, the *Jungle* of its time.

In other words, if you own shares in livestock, it might be a good time to sell.

By the time you read this, the Impossible Burger will be making its debut at a handful of upscale burger joints, and the market will begin to decide its fate.

But this story doesn't end with Loon either, of course. "A cow will never get better at being meat," Brown says, "but we'll get better and better at understanding meat and using that information. When we get to the point where our burger is just as delicious as the best burger you've ever eaten, we don't have to stop there." I find myself fantasizing about Yellow-Bellied Sapsucker and Zebra Finch. Our kids may expect their burgers — and dogs and nuggets — to come in an audacious array of textures and flavors, none of them held back by the physical limitations of meat. To them, the prospect of making burgers out of something as bland as beef may be as appealing as riding from Baltimore to Ohio on a horse.

That moment is not yet here. The initial price of the burger will make it more alluring to sustainability freaks like me than to Joe Beef. But in a few years, once the company has its production plant up and running, the price will start to drop. At that point, Brown and his team will have their sights trained right on Safeway 80/20.

Those same economies of scale will reduce the burger's environmental 60 footprint, which already is a fraction of a hamburger's. The Impossible Burger uses one-ninth the water and one-twelfth the land and produces one-quarter of the greenhouse gases as a beef burger. "It isn't that our process is so brilliant or efficient," Brown says, "it's that when you're competing against cows, you'd have to be deliberately trying to fail to be as bad as they are."

The last time I saw Brown, we were hurtling down Highway 101 from South San Francisco, where Brown had inspected (and rejected) a defunct dried-soup facility that he had hoped to lease. Impossible Foods had grown from 25 employees to 125, Brown had a fresh $108 million from investors, and he was scrambling to find new digs before the insatiable Google snapped everything up. (He eventually found an industrial space in Oakland.) It was late in the day, the soup facility had been a bust, and I wondered if saving the world was turning out to be a bit of a grind.

Brown was undeterred. He told me that once the burger was launched, he'd be going after other foods. He mentioned bacon, sausage, cheese, and blue fin tuna, which also derives its meaty flavor from heme. That rubbery prototype I'd held in the lab was possibly on its way to being steak. Chicken and fish were also in the works. There were several patents pending.

It all sounded so Silicon Valley. Meanwhile, back on planet Earth, meat was still big business, with tremendous political and economic clout. I told Brown that he was taking on a very big opponent, one that wasn't going down without a fight, but he waved off my concern. "The livestock industry is intrinsically fragile," he suggested. "It's got small margins, it's got very long planning cycles, and it does not deal well with instability." His voice had the flat, declarative tones of somebody explaining the law of gravity. "The fundamental economics of it are completely unsuited to 2016," he said. "And that means it's not going to exist in several decades."

"You think so?" I asked skeptically.

"Absolutely. It's just a matter of time. Someone else was going to   65
outcompete it, if not us." Brown shrugged, and, for the first time all day, allowed himself a smile. "But as it happens, it *is* us."

Understanding the Text

1. What is Griffin? Why is it named this?
2. Why did Patrick O. Brown set out to create an animal-free burger?
3. What is heme? Where in nature is heme found?

Reflection and Response

4. What is the "alchemy of cooking" (par. 23)? Why is it important to Jacobsen's account of plant-based burgers and to the pleasure of eating?

5. Patrick Brown explained to Jacobsen that to create an animal-free burger that could compete with meat, one of the first things he needed to do was "to have a biochemical understanding of why meat tastes like meat" (par. 18). Have you thought about the flavor of the foods you eat in these ways before? How might knowing more about this change how you think about food? How might it change how you eat?

Making Connections

6. Think about Jacobsen's explanation of the development of animal-free meat products in relation to Barbara Kingsolver's ("You Can't Run Away on Harvest Day," p. 150) description of harvesting animals on her small family farm. Drawing on the other writers in this book who talk about the ethics of eating meat, make an argument that brings a discussion of animal-free meat substitutes into the debate over the ethics of meat eating.

7. Consider the philosophies of eating that Michael Pollan ("Eat Food: Food Defined," p. 10) and Wendell Berry ("The Pleasures of Eating," p. 46) offer. How would they react to scientific advancements that lead to the production of plant-based meat substitutes in a laboratory? How might these scientific advancements alter our definitions of "natural" or "food"? Do these products have the potential to change how we think about the natural world and our relationship to it? Describe at least three potential ways to think through these problems before drawing conclusions of your own.

8. Research the future of plant-based meat substitutes and other synthetic foods that are produced in laboratories. Why is there so much interest in producing them? Do they have the potential to solve some of the food shortages, water problems, and environmental crises that are described by writers in this book? Find at least four or five good sources that you can use to explore these questions. Make a presentation that teaches your audience about the potential benefits and possible drawbacks of producing food in the lab.

How to Cook a Planet

Nicole Walker

Nicole Walker attended Reed College as an undergraduate and then received her PhD in English Literature and Creative Writing from the University of Utah. She is currently a professor at Northern Arizona University in Flagstaff, Arizona. Walker is a prolific writer who blurs the line between fiction and nonfiction. In addition to her own creative work, Walker has written almost 100 letters to the governor of Arizona focused on public education in Arizona, many of which have appeared in the newspaper *Arizona Daily Sun*. The *Arizona Capitol Times* referred to her letters as a "one-way pen pal relationship." Her book *Egg* (2017) is part of the Bloomsbury's Object Lesson series. The following essay, excerpted from *Egg*, raises important issues about global warming and the climate crisis by focusing on *the egg*.

Experiment with Eggs by Making a Hollandaise in the Time of Global Warming

Lecithin is a protein in egg yolks that helps to make an emulsion. Emulsions are things like salad dressing and mayonnaise, gravies, and the five mother sauces: béchamel, velouté, hollandaise, tomato, and espagnole. The lecithin holds them together. Lecithin is a kind of leviathan. It is a fish of a molecule. A busybody of a protein that likes to put its nose in a cell of water and its tail in a cell of fat, bringing the sauce together. It's a matchmaker of water and oil, preventing the oil droplets from pooling together. Oil droplets are Romeo and Juliet. We have to keep them apart if we want this lemon juice to hold up its heavier, fatter lover with its tiny, slippery hands.

Of the mother sauces, only hollandaise uses eggs instead of a roux to bring things together. You have to break up the egg itself first, separate white from yolk. If you have a hard time separating eggs, the Internet provides a video of a water bottle sucking the yolk into its mouth, leaving the white behind. Picture a popping sound like the kind the fish make when they need a lot of oxygen and have to force the water faster over their gills, or the sound of a whale bringing to surface only his blowhole. In a hollandaise, air is not your friend (leave air and eggs for meringues and soufflés—the whites, the whites! Shut up. This is a yolk story, heavy as water). Try to ignore the fossil fuels it took to make your plastic bottle. Disregard that this plastic will, most likely, end up in the plastic garbage patch that spans the size of Texas, swirls in the Pacific Ocean. Maybe the plastic will meet its mate there. Who are you to keep them apart?

Remember, you're a matchmaker, trying to arrange the right marriage and hollandaise is, of all things, moral, truly righteous. You can add hollandaise to cold salmon or hot asparagus. You can double-dip your egg eating and make a Benedict over which you pour the hot hollandaise onto hot poached egg and the difference in egg here is more distinct than a Capulet or a Montague.

To make a good hollandaise, you need good balance more than a good story. Juliet and Romeo will not suffice. Hollandaise is the wisdom of the mother, not the rush of the youth. Separating the yolks takes balance. Producing the lecithin takes patience. Pouring the butter into the egg and lemon mixture is the kind of equation that makes for healthy, bountiful seas. Not too much lemony acid. Don't let the temperature get too hot. If you want hollandaise — and your ocean — to be productive, you have to know when too warm is too warm.

Hollandaise marries best with almost every kind of fish but, as Romeo 5 goes, so doth the bigeye tuna. The cod. The halibut. Even the salmon, whose own blend of water and fat make the fish canonical and invincible, a hollandaise itself, until it breaks into water and egg as hard and pliable as plastic.

How to Cook a Planet

Recipe for a Planet

1 singularity
1 expanding universe
1 pile of space dust
1 cup disobedience
4 cups punishment

Swirl ingredients around either big-bangily or invented Godily. Mix to combine. Shake to ensure combination. Fold in matter with antimatter, gas with gas, gravity with electronic charge. Proportion, balance, and chemical reactions are all it takes to make a cake — or, in this case, a primordial soup; a little more mixing, some surprising hydrogens catching some sweet carbons. A hook-up for the weekend resulting in an amoeba that is, in some ways, an egg. From the amoeba-egg hatches a two-celled chicken that produces another egg. It's always the egg that came first. Before the egg, there was only soup.

Recipe for Soufflé

4 large egg yolks
5 egg whites
1 package frozen spinach, defrosted
4 tablespoons butter
4 tablespoons flour
1 cup grated gruyère
1 cup scalded milk

Soufflé might be the best creation story. Like these myths, you have to separate the eggs, egg from ocean, wet from dry, hydrogen from oxygen, in order to make something new. To make soufflé you must separate at least four eggs. Maybe six. Make a bèchamel, which is really just a roux with milk (and onion poked with cloves if you're really serious, which I am not). Add the egg yolks and cheese to the roux. Whip the egg whites until frothy. Fold in the whites, an egg at a time. Put in oven and watch the creation lift toward the clouds. Turn on the oven light and watch the soufflé rise through the window of the oven door. This creation requires silence. It is pure and good, and therefore, wordless. Do not open the door or the soufflé will fall.

Recipe for Global Warming

1 planet
7 continents
5 oceans
400 parts per million of CO_2

It is as easy to crack a planet as to wreck an egg recipe. Putting too much baking powder in its oceans, turning it acidic, cracking its mountains to dig for coal, cooking that coal like a soufflé in an oven, making those broken eggs reach for the clouds, turning the crust golden brown. The temperature rises silently. We yap and yap at it like dogs at the back door, but the carbon is as invisible and as hard of hearing as glass.

Recipe for Turtle Extinction

1 female turtle
110 sea turtles
~~One shoreline from where the turtle came~~

We think of eggs as "of the air," or as "union between air and land." They are the material that conjoins the ethereal bird with her terrestrial nest, but eggs also marry marine to terrestrial — or they do for now. As temperatures warm across the globe and glaciers and sea ice continue to melt, the oceans will begin to rise. This is bad news for sea turtles. Sea turtles lay their eggs on the same beaches upon which they were born.

Imagine you are a young female turtle. You were hatched from an egg 10 buried in a nest of sand. You flip-flopped your way to the water, avoiding seagull and tsunami. You spent a year or two spinning around the ocean but then some male turtle swam by and knocked you up. No skin off his nose. He just keeps swimming. But now, in addition to your having to carry these fertilized eggs (as if your shell wasn't heavy enough), something inside you has been triggered and now you must swim in a certain direction, toward a certain beach, to lay these eggs. For the eggs to make it, they need crusty sand, hot air, whipping wind. You arrive at the general vicinity but nothing smells the same. You swim shoreward but instead of finding sand, your legs are still kicking in deep water. Your long-memory flickers: the waters shallow and see-through blue. These waters are still dark. The ocean floor is a Brontosaurus-height below. The part of you that remembers waters is the species memory that remembers brontosauri 165 million species-years ago. You swim around in circles like a dog looking for a place to lie down but you never find that place. The eggs stay inside. The turtle swims on. You have no say in the matter. Turtles have always been quiet creatures. Turtle birth, like egg cooking, is time-dependent. The female turtle can swim and swim and swim but eventually, like all women, her ovaries give out.

Recipe for Eggs Poached in Broth

There is no recipe. Poach the eggs in broth

I have read religiously the Julia Child recipe for omelets. I have seen Jacques Pépin make omelets with chopsticks. I have beaten eggs in a bowl and poured them into butter in a nonstick pan and moved the eggs around until it seemed I'd never get them flat again. I've rolled the omelet onto itself and then onto a plate, but I have never eaten an omelet so good as the one I made using beef consommé. I've looked and looked for the recipe but I can't find one. I thought beef consommé omelet was a thing but perhaps it is not a thing. Now, what I mostly end up with is something like egg drop soup, which is also delicious because the surface area of the broth matches the surface area of the stomach and the proteins in the egg pin down that immediate, surface satisfaction, with a deeper, more permanent satisfaction.

Sometimes, it's the simplest things that are the hardest. Like riding your bicycle, something most five-year-olds can accomplish. It is as easy as poaching an egg but it does take time and some skill and there are hills and also too-hard-boiling water, but eggs poached in water require no dead chickens and bicycles require no more carbon dioxide than a human naturally breathes out and no more energy than frying an egg, if you poach the egg in a reasonably small amount of water. If only we could eat poached eggs and ride bikes exclusively. Even the chickens, though still in service, would be grateful to keep their heads.

Recipe for Poached Eggs

fresh eggs
slightly, but not overly, boiling water

Proportion isn't as easy as it looks. "Slightly boiling" is an ineffable° phrase. How many bubbles per square inch? What percentage of the water should boil? When water reaches 212 degrees Fahrenheit does that mean the whole of the water is as hot as it can get, or just the bubbles that you can see?

It is important to ask questions of the water as much as it is to ask 15 questions of the egg. Remember, we're in this together—the chicken notwithstanding.

Science experiments are cooking, too. Remember, dear Generation Xers, we have missed the mark. The temperatures have arisen 2 degrees Celsius—the ceiling temperature increase scientists argue will set off catastrophic climate change. It's up to the Millennials now.

Zoe's science project is due. Zoe, who is going to save the planet with her solar oven, carbon scrubbing device, and slippers she will invent for easier floor mopping, is a fan of the science fair. She wanted to test to see if dogs' saliva killed other bacteria-like bacteria in boogers, mold, and human saliva but (a), we don't have a high-powered microscope, and (b), layering objects with saliva seemed kind of gross, so instead she turned her focus toward an egg-shrinking/egg-enlarging project that was awesome since I am immersed in all things egg.

---

ineffable: extreme, such that it cannot be expressed in words.

How to Shrink an Egg

> 2 boiled eggs.
> vinegar
> corn syrup
> 48 hours.

Soak the hard-boiled shell in vinegar. Overnight, the vinegar will react with the shell, turning the carbon of the shell into carbon dioxide. Watch the vinegar bubble. You will be left with a thick membrane you had no idea existed between the hard carbon shell and the egg white. This is NOT the thin membrane that sticks to a regular, I'm-just-going-to-eat-this hard-boiled egg. Take the now-squeezy egg, its pliability comparable to a stress ball, its resilience probably not so plastic. But it feels so stable.

Immerse one of these stable eggs in water, the other egg in corn syrup.

Overnight, the egg submerged in water expands. The one soaked in corn syrup shrinks. Why does the egg submerged in corn syrup shrink? The membrane is permeable enough to let the smaller-sized water molecule escape from the egg, but the larger-sized sugar molecules cannot get inside. The egg submerged in water allows the water molecules to travel back and forth, leaving that egg about the same size it was to start.

Here's a planet as egg, shrink-wrapped by carbon rather than corn 20 syrup but still losing water, at least the potable, egg-poaching kind, every day. The world gets smaller every year, they say; metaphorically, at Disneyland. No one thought that driving our cars and burning our goal would make it literal. Suffocating. Tight dress on a full stomach. Perhaps we could manufacture a few million more stress balls as the water evaporates, as the aquifer dries up, as the ice shelf melts?

The surface of the planet is 71 percent water; about 96 percent of that water is saline. The planet looks incredibly blue from space, but much of that water is good only for salt-water-living plants and animals. The octopi and the dolphins like it. The rest of us have to spend a lot of money to access potable water, walk a long way to get to the water, or rearrange the riverways, to get the water to come to us. It takes nearly fifty-three gallons of water to produce one egg in the mass-produced-egg industry. Chickens feed on grain that requires a lot of water to grow.

Would raising backyard chickens require as much water? Not if you were efficient about it. When you're rinsing the sprouts you're growing in your Mason jars, you can collect the water you used to soak and rinse them for the chickens to drink. And, although you may need to buy them some grain from the Tractor Supply store sometimes, you can also feed them leftovers. Chickens will eat anything — even chicken soup. The surface area of broth satisfies everyone. Homegrown chickens and solar-powered ovens: Save the planet, one egg at a time.

Scrambled Eggs

> Crack them in a bowl. Whisk them.
> Add a pinch of salt.
> A pinch of pepper.
> Put them in a pan. A pan on low heat. I know you're hungry.
> Low, though. Low.

Eggs react intensely to the pan. If you put eggs in a too-hot pan their proteins seize up. Heat is more of a killer than motion. Eggs withstand a good whipping. Harold McGee writes in *On Food and Cooking: The Science and Lore of the Kitchen,* "Scrambled eggs made in the usual quick, offhand way are usually hard and forgettable. The key to moist scrambled eggs is low heat and patience; they will take several minutes to cook."[1] A student, Gary Fish, in one of the first classes I taught as a professor, taught me, "Low and slow, let the pan hug the eggs with heat, but not strangle them." It takes a long time to learn how to teach writing, even longer to learn how to slow down to cook an egg.

Slow cooking is important for the egg. Slow cooking includes nearly everything you do to the egg. When you make custard, you want to add hot ingredients to the cold, putting in hot milk a little at a time to temper the eggs. If you add cold eggs to hot milk, the protein molecules separate from the water molecules and you get clumps of curdled eggs and a stringy liquid mass strewn throughout your would-have-been pudding. It is nearly as impossible to repair a mess of stringy egg as it is to repair a fractured rainforest or revise a pointless story.

"It is nearly as impossible to repair a mess of stringy egg as it is to repair a fractured rainforest or revise a pointless story."

But a little heat makes the molecules move around gently. By slow 25 cooking or adding the eggs slowly, you give the protein molecules time to adjust, inviting water molecules to bond with them. At a low, less panicky temperature, the proteins aren't xenophobic; they are friendly, diplomatic. A lot of heat freaks them out. The proteins cling together in fear, not allowing water molecules in. With a lot of heat you get fried eggs that become rubbery and custards that become lumpy and no one is getting along and everyone is hungry.

Recipe for How to Make Yourself Believe Everything Is Going to Be All Right

1 pound easy-migration imagination
3 pounds "I've seen polar bears adapt before" refrain
1.5 pounds bikini—who doesn't love warmer temps?
10 pounds strawberries. Everyone can live on strawberries
15 goose eggs to distract the bears that might think ringed seals and human seals taste pretty similar

Slowly. Slowly the planet warms. We can't all move north, at least not quickly. Our xenophobia˚ increases in correlation to time and space. Surely, we could get along if we met each under slower, less panicky circumstances.

Researcher Antero Järvinen from the University of Helsinki studied the effects of global warming on bird eggs.[2] One shouldn't be able to study the effects of global warming on bird eggs over nineteen years. That is too fast for a planet to warm. Adaptation is a slow, generational process. Most of us haven't even had kids by nineteen. When a planet warms, it should do so slowly, over eons. Two degrees Celsius in a human lifetime is a speed of warming that has never been witnessed on earth, unless you count the heat from the events caused by the asteroid that killed the dinosaurs. When you're talking about effects of global warming, you don't want to compare your age to that of the dinosaur extinction—a hard metaphor to live with.

Although Järvinen had only nineteen years to study the eggs, he found some significant changes in the amount of resources the pied fly-catcher, a long-distance migrating bird that winters in Africa, devoted to egg growth. He saw increases in egg volume, which "Warm weather during the egg laying period was the probable cause of an increase in egg volume" (109). Although the egg size increased overtime, overall success of the fledglings did not increase, most likely because although overall temperatures increased, cold spells occurred as often. Very cold spells, especially in northern Finland, can kill baby birds quickly. Still, Järvinen concludes that, "some of the results herein supported the hypothesis that global warming may have favourable effects on the reproduction of birds. This in turn may help them rapidly conquer new areas when

xenophobia: fear of, dislike of, or prejudice against people from another country.

they become available and compensate for rising mortality rates to be expected elsewhere where warming means desiccation" (110). The point here is that in northern areas, birds may have time to warm their eggs slowly. In the southern regions, eggs may warm too quickly to adapt, cooking the would-be babies inside.[3]

In northern countries, it might seem like a good thing that these eggs will be bigger. Maybe big eggs will save other species. Some climate change optimists have argued that polar bears can adapt their diet from sea-based to land-based. Goose eggs and berries abound — except, some argue, there are not enough goose eggs in all the land to feed the largest bears on earth. The protein content in an egg isn't the same as in a seal. Ringed seals, the primary diet for polar bears, are 34 percent fat. Goose eggs are also nearly 30 percent fat, and, as noted by Järvinen, northerly eggs are likely to grow bigger due to global warming, but that does not mean there will be enough eggs to feed all the bears. Earth Touch News reports in the article "Climate Change Will Scramble Polar Bears' Diets — and Eggs Aren't the Solution" reports that "Five of the major genetic differences between brown bears and polar bears involve metabolising lipids, which includes fats and fat-soluble vitamins. This means a land-based diet of proteins and carbohydrates may not suit the physical needs of polar bears."[4]

Likely too, the current brown bears in habitats of northern Alaska do 30 what they can to make a living off the land, right next to where the polar bears once thrived, living by the sea. These brown bears are the smallest and least well dispersed of all the brown bears. Now, as the polar bears turn toward their food, competition will abound. The geese have wings. They can leave that cold town, head south, even head north, further away from the hungry bears. Their fat eggs may ensure their own survival but now the bears are left with only berries that, if you check the USDA's Web site for nutrition content, have no fat content whatsoever. All those bears in the north aren't going to make it. I guess the climate change optimists might say that's all right. The humans will need to move there quickly to take over the ground, claim the berries, trap the geese, force them to leave their fat eggs with you.

Recipe for an Apocalyptic Novel

1. Viggo Mortensen — as either Aragorn, or the father in Cormac McCarthy's *The Road.*

2. Black and white film, or, barring that, a lot of ash strewn about.

3. A tank or a shopping cart.

4. Hard-boiled eggs. Portable and something you can pawn off on a chicken if you need to blame someone for the apocalypse.

5. Recipes for eggs for the future. Because an apocalypse always ends. Otherwise, they wouldn't make a movie out of your book.

There are a lot of egg recipes. Could you survive on eggs alone? Would your cholesterol get too high? Would you come down with scurvy? What if butter wasn't one of your free ingredients? Still, if you were allotted butter, lemon, flour, and spinach, you might be able to survive, happily, for a number of weeks, on eggs alone. Begin with eggs Benedict (You can make your own English muffins! You can borrow Canadian bacon from the Canadians. They're a sharing people). Spinach salad with hard-boiled eggs for lunch. You can make lemon curd for dessert, spinach soufflé for dinner. The next day, eggs scrambled in hollandaise sauce leftover from breakfast the day before. Egg salad sandwiches. Quiche for supper. Pancakes for breakfast, deviled eggs for lunch, egg drop soup for dinner. Eggs baked in ham cream with spinach on the side. Spinach covered with béarnaise. Cheesy poofs are easy to make. Make a béchamel (I know. You are forever making béchamel when you're talking to me). Whip an egg into the béchamel; wait until it's completely incorporated, whip in another. Add gruyère. Dollop onto sheet pan. Bake for 425 minutes. Cheesy cream puffs: a homemade, noncrunchy Cheeto. The apocalypse with cheese and eggs. If you can cook (and have access to cheese) maybe you will be the one to survive.

Funeral Potatoes

1 package hash browns
1 can Campbell's mushroom soup
1 can fried onions
There are no eggs in this recipe but if it is the end of the world/your funeral, you want nonperishable items anyway.

Every Mormon funeral boasts funeral potatoes served in the gym of the neighborhood ward house. I grew up with the end of the world. Mormon church. Wasatch Fault. Father's drinking. It lets me pretend I'm able to take these things in stride. The end of the bird. The end of the world. It's a tiny shaking, these minor household dramas. The glaciers that made the Little and Big Cottonwood canyons, those were big things. The earthquake they promise will liquefy the Salt Lake Valley and pull down the fancy houses on the foothills—that's a big thing. They have predicted that two tectonic plates in the bottom of the Pacific Ocean haven't released enough tension, that they're saving it up for the big one—a tsunami that could drown California. Small things include the white bird with black wings that has gone extinct. The goose that laid the golden egg was, after the hunter killed her, found to be just a regular, non-gold-on-the-inside goose. In this case, it's not what was literally inside the goose that counted; it was what the insides could make. The goose was an artist. Never kill the artists to scoop out the art, leave them alive but oppressed—they'll make millions of tiny, ornate metaphors for you. Now there are no more golden eggs, no more golden geese, no more passenger pigeons. Big and little apocalypses threaten every day.

As the living goose and living artist know, there is always a chance for revision. Once upon a time, bald eagles nearly went extinct. Then a clever ban on the pesticide DDT put an end to thin-shelled bald eagle eggs. The bald eagles may not think their whole world is restored—they have to sit on man-made telephone poles rather than snags. They dodge cars. They eat lead-filled bullets and die of lead poisoning like the much-less-well-off condors. But it is no small thing that the birds of which there were only seventy-six pairs left in the world have rebounded to numbers too big to count. Maybe there are no small things. Maybe the beginning of order is to count all the small things—each ant, each tree, each bird, each egg—to see how large things can be.

You would think that if humans can figure out how, with eggs, to puff 35 a soufflé, make meringues and divinity, balloon pâte choux, glue flour and sugar into cookies, surely you can undo this global warming. You don't need to know the exact science of how custard sets to set custard; you just need to get the proportion right. Eggs are excellent because they increase their surface area as you cook with them. Only a few other things do that: yeast for bread, baking powder and baking soda for cakes and cookies. Usually, cooking shrinks things but as there are more people on the planet who require more arable land and more potable water, a bigger planet is what we need. We need to think like an egg: add proper ingredients, the right amount of heat. We need patience and quiet footing. Don't stomp on the ground outside the oven. Let the soufflé rise.

Notes

1. Harold McGee, *On Food and Cooking: The Science and Lore of The Kitchen.* Scribner 2004.

2. Antero Järvinen, "Global Warming and Egg Size of Birds," *Ecography* 17, no. 1 (January to March, 1994): 108–10.

3. Stable URL: http://www.jstor.org/stable/3682938.

4. John Platt, *Climate Change Will Scramble Polar Bears Diets and Eggs Aren't the Solution,* Earth Touch NewsNetwork April 1, 2015, http://www.earthtouchnews.com/ conservation/human-impact/ climate-change-will-scramble-polar-bears-diets-andeggs-arent-the-solution.

Understanding the Text

1. What is an object lesson? How does Walker's piece on the egg function as one?

2. Make a list of the objects that Walker compares (or contrasts) to an egg (or eggs). Describe the comparisons in your own words.

Reflection and Response

3. Why do you think Walker uses the egg as a metaphor? What is it a metaphor for?

4. Why do you think Walker organizes her essay via "recipes"? What do you think she wants us to do with her recipes?

5. What is Walker's implicit argument? Why do you think she chose to make it this way?

Making Connections

6. Look at Walker's footnotes. Describe how (and why) she uses sources. Then compare her use of sources to two other readings in this chapter. Does each other author use sources similarly to Walker? Why might the sources be functioning differently in other readings? Consider starting with Paul Greenberg ("Heartland," p. 256), Georgina Gustin ("Can a Climate Conscious Diet Include Meat or Dairy?," p. 227), or Alejandra Borunda ("Grocery Stores Are Packed with Plastic. Some Are Changing," p. 222).

7. What would it require for us to, in Walker's words, "think like an egg"? What changes would we need to make in our behavior? Is Walker advocating for this type of thinking on an individual or societal level? Using at least two other readings in this chapter, brainstorm a list of changes you would make to your daily life if you were thinking like an egg. Compare your list to Jonathan Foley's ("Can We Feed the World and Sustain the Planet?," p. 212) five-point plan, which is aimed at policy makers. How much overlap is there? Is "thinking like an egg" a good thought process for world leaders?

Heartland

Paul Greenberg

Paul Greenberg writes about the science, history, and economics of the American interest in omega-3 oils, as he works to help explain how they affect us and how our interest in (or even our obsession with) fish oils affects the climate crisis and the health of our fish supplies. He has written articles for *The New York Times*, *National Geographic*, and *The Atlantic* and has authored three best-selling books: *Four Fish* (2010), *American Catch* (2014), and *The Omega Principle: Seafood and the Quest for a Long Life and a Healthier Planet* (2018). He also has received the James Beard Award for Writing and Literature and a Pew Fellowship in Marine Conservation. As a writer-in-residence at the Safina Center, he has continued to unpack the complexities of the politics of seafood. In this essay, excerpted from *The Omega Principle*, Greenberg helps us understand our relationship to the fish we eat and its relationship to farming in the Midwest.

Supplementism and reductionism are sibling industries of a sort. They rely on the same animals and ecosystems to bring product to market. They also share an ideology to justify the boiling down of complex life into marketable molecules. In the case of supplementism, that boiling down is meant to address an imbalance in our bodies where an industrialized Western diet has removed many natural forms of omega-3s from our food. In the case of reductionism, it came about to address a dietary deficit in the diets of the animals we raise—an imbalance that occurred after we removed livestock from the ALA omega-3-rich grasses with which they evolved.

But over and above supplementism and reductionism, there is a much larger nutritional issue that modern societies keep circling but never really change: the overproduction of commodity-crop-centered foods that today can be found as readily in our school cafeterias as in our cupboards at home. These foods comprise the majority of our calories. They trend toward high amounts of refined carbohydrates, high levels of saturated fats, and, yes, low omega-3s and high omega-6s. A perusal of the top ten sources of calories[1] in the American diet shows the general landscape:

1. Grain-based desserts (cakes, cookies, doughnuts, pies, crisps, cobblers, and granola bars)
2. Yeast breads
3. Chicken and chicken-mixed dishes
4. Soda, energy drinks, and sports drinks
5. Pizza

6. Alcoholic beverages

7. Pasta and pasta dishes

8. Mexican mixed dishes

9. Beef and beef-mixed dishes

10. Dairy desserts

The majority of these products are different expressions of three crops. The crop used to bring the meat-based products to market and create the sweeteners in those different desserts is corn. The lipid in all these high-calorie products is usually soy; 75 percent of the fat used in American processed food is soy, the second-largest commodity crop in the United States. Finally, the substrate used to make the more solid parts of all those cobblers and crumbles is wheat, 80 percent of these highly processed foods are so high in starch and sugar and so devoid of nutrients that, as the Mediterranean Diet scholar Walter Willett put it to me, "veterinarians would not feed it to their dogs."[2]

A recent study in the *Journal of the American Medical Association* found that commodity crops could be linked to high body mass index, glucose-related abnormalities such as diabetes, and cholesterol imbalances. In summary, the study's authors concluded that "overall better alignment of agricultural and nutritional policies may potentially improve population health."[3]

As of now, there is little sign of that realignment. Currently the federal government spends $15 billion annually propping up our current eating pattern. By comparison, Washington spends less than $1 billion on all fisheries program combined.[4] This persistent support of land food commodities translates into cost incentives that allow unhealthy eating patterns to persist. From 1985 to 2000, the cost of fruits and vegetables increased by 118 percent.[5] During this same period the price of commodity fats and oils rose by only 35 percent.

The competition between nutrient-rich, omega-3-leaning foods and nutrient-poor, omega-6-leaning commodity foods can be described in two different ways, one chemical, the other systemic. The chemical argument posits that on a cellular level, enzymes that are the first step in metabolizing both omega-6s and omega-3s are, as the biochemist William Lands put it, "promiscuous and indiscriminate":[6] they will work on an omega-6 just as easily as an omega-3, depending on what's most available. If there are a lot of 6s around, enzymes will favor them, which eventually produces compounds that are pro-inflammatory and linked to many Western diseases. If there are more 3s around, the enzymes will help produce compounds that slow the development of inflammatory compounds and lead to resolution.

The systemic argument, on the other hand, focuses on high-calorie/nutrient-poor food versus low-calorie/nutrient-rich food. The oversupply of carbohydrates and empty calories a commodity-based diet provides leads to excessive weight gain, which in turn underlies many of the same Western diseases the chemical argument attributes to an omega-6/omega-3 imbalance.

Take, for example, type 2 diabetes. Diabetes occurs when the body loses its ability to process sugar. Type 2 diabetes is part of a metabolic syndrome that is strongly linked with obesity. Roughly 80 percent of those with type 2 diabetes are overweight. And if the American diet with its carbo-loading cakes and crumbles, its saturated beef and dairy, is anything, it's calorie intensive.

Omega World suggests type 2 diabetes may be ameliorated by correcting a deficiency in omega-3 fatty acids. Omega-3s could address type 2 diabetes by increasing "good" cholesterol, HDL, and decreasing triglycerides (two outcomes trials of omega-3s have shown, albeit with some inconsistency). But also, once again, inflammation is at the center of the justification for omega-3s as treatment for diabetes. "Obesity is associated with low-grade chronic inflammation characterized by inflamed adipose tissue with increased macrophage infiltration," writes Dr. Dyerberg in *The Missing Wellness Factors—EPA and DHA*.[7] In other words, when a subject becomes obese fat cells release chemical signals that trigger the immune system to come to their aid, as if they were being attacked by pathogens. This in turn creates inflammation. All this has led Dyerberg and others to conclude that "inflammation is now widely believed to be the key link between obesity and development of insulin resistance." Okay, sure. But what is the link between diet and obesity? Too many calories. And where are those calories coming from in the United States? Commodity crops. At the end of the day, it almost doesn't matter whose argument you choose. The seemingly impregnable° position of commodity crops in the modern food portfolio means that corn, soy, and processed wheat time and again win in the battle for money from our wallets and caloric space in our stomachs. Foods like seafood and leafy greens that are lower in fats and sugars and higher in omega-3s continually lose and cost more at the supermarket.

> "Foods like seafood and leafy greens that are lower in fats and sugars and higher in omega-3s continually lose and cost more at the supermarket."

But what often goes unmentioned in the diagnosis of our food production disorder is an *environmental* competition that is being fought

10

impregnable: unable to be defeated or destroyed.

in the American heartland and in agricultural heartlands of countries around the world between commodity crop omega-6 systems and
omega-3 systems. To get an idea of how the nation's native omega-3 system is being impaired by the commodities behemoth,° it would be worth
taking a summertime trip to the mouth of the Mississippi River, where
most of the nation's fertilizer runoff exits into the sea. In certain places
in the delta in July, if the air is still and hot, an event will occur that the
residents of the Gulf Coast refer to as a "dead zone"—a blob of hypoxic°
water that has been forming in the Gulf since commodity crops started to
boom in the 1980s. The Gulf dead zone has increased yearly to the point
where in 2017 it exceeded eighty-seven hundred square miles, as big as
the state of New Jersey.[8] That this suffocation is taking place atop the
most important commercial fishing grounds in the continental United
States is indicative of this omega-3/omega-6 trade-off.

Dead zones begin when rivers carry nitrogen and phosphorus-based
nutrients, primarily agricultural fertilizers, into the ocean. In the case of
the Gulf of Mexico it is the Mississippi River that delivers nitrates and
phosphates from the American heartland into the Gulf at a rate of 1.7
million tons per year.[9] Once this stew of nutrients reaches the ocean,
algae bloom in prodigious amounts. When those algae die, bacteria consume them and draw oxygen out of the water in the process of
respiration. In this way, bacteria suck the oxygen out of nearshore fishing
grounds and suffocate the fish we like to eat.

The Gulf dead zone occurs far enough from shore that most people
never get a chance to see it. But localized smaller dead zones (known on
the coasts of Mississippi, Louisiana, and Alabama as jubilees) give an idea
of what's going on. The bottom-dwelling flounder kicks things off. Sensing that there is no oxygen available, they will grow increasingly agitated
as each successive gulp of water brings less and less refreshment across
their gills. In a panic, the fish will head shoreward to the only breathable
water they can find: the thinly oxygenated riffle the sea makes as it
bumps lazily against the beach. At the shoreline, they will find humans
waiting for them armed with "gigs," crude sticks with nails protruding
from them. With an easy stab, each gigger will impale a suffocating fish,
sometimes two at a time. Wading out farther, the fishermen will find
sluggish pods of blue crab and brown shrimp. As the area slowly asphyx-
iates° and the free-for-all reaches its climax the human *whoops* coming
from the darkness will give the impression of a happy time, a celebration
of the ocean's seemingly endless gifts.[10]

behemoth: something enormous, including a powerful organization.
hypoxic: condition in which a body is deprived of oxygen.
asphyxiate: to die from lack of oxygen.

As industrial agriculture and animal feedlots have spread around the globe, dead zones have been spreading exponentially along with them. According to a 2008 study published in the journal *Science,* dead zones now affect ninety-five thousand square miles of water in four hundred different systems.[11] They are as far-flung as the dozens of dead zones that have appeared off the coast of emerging Asia or as close to home as the Chesapeake Bay and Long Island Sound. But the place that tells the story of dead zones and the clash between seafood and land food is the Mississippi. A journey to those headwaters reveals the tensions contained within the river's twenty-five-hundred-mile journey to the sea.

The Mississippi River begins clear and cold at Minnesota's lovely Lake Itasca, a place where wild rice flutters in the shallows and giant stands of old-growth oak and maple give a hint of what the world looked like two centuries ago, a time when millions of acres of riverside forest and hundreds of millions of acres of native prairie covered the Mississippi valley. But soon after the Mississippi exits Itasca State Park, the river begins picking up tributaries. The water turns a milk-chocolate brown. The forests fall away and are replaced by tilled fields. Along one of these tributaries I encountered the corn and soybean farmer Brian Hicks of Tracy, Minnesota.[12]

Hicks is a kind and conscientious man who thinks a lot about his farm 15 and the impact it has on the surrounding environment. At the time of my visit, he tended to an orphaned deer on his property that ambled up and nuzzled me as I walked up his drive. He maintains stands of forest along the creeks that wend their way through his land, and his daughters are fond of pressing wildflowers they gather from the remnant patches of prairie that still dot the farm.

But along with his environmental responsibilities, Hicks has significant economic burdens. He is the father of ten children, and uppermost in his thinking is the agricultural machine that supports his family. "I tell lots of people that this farm is my factory," he said as we drove through his fifteen hundred acres that straddle the Cottonwood River, which feeds the Minnesota River, which in turn feeds the Mississippi. "Some factories make shoes. Mine makes corn and soybeans."

Hicks's Nettiewyynnt Farm has transitioned over the last 120 years from a diverse operation of livestock, vegetables, and grain to an operation that focuses exclusively on chemically fertilized, genetically modified corn and soy. Today these are the number one and two crops in the United States. Together the American land planted in soy and corn would cover nearly two Californias.[13] Much has already been written about the prominence of commodity crops in modern food systems. But what of the seascape and the food systems that existed before corn and soy took over the heartland? A look back to the time before the first pioneers reveals that water flowed quite differently.

"In Minnesota before settlers arrived we had eighteen million acres of wetlands," Jeff Strock, a professor at the University of Minnesota who works with Hicks on several agricultural experiments, told me.[14] Those wetlands slowed the rate at which water entered the soil and allowed plants to take up excess nutrients before they hit the main stem of the river.

Which is why after farmers plowed the native prairie throughout the nineteenth and early twentieth centuries, they were forced to introduce artificially produced nitrogen fertilizers. Today, something like 30 percent of a farmer's annual budget is spent on fertilizer.[15] And a huge amount of that fertilizer ends up in the Mississippi because of the way farmers have decided to deal with water.

Next time you fly over the Midwest, look down at the millions of acres of farmland planted in corn and soy below. Now imagine beneath all those acres a similarly expansive set of drainage tubes, funnels, and switches. This system is called tiling.[16] Corn's growth rate slows when the soil is too moist, and farmers are forever at war with the environment to move water off their land. Tiling has been the principal weapon in that war. Today something like forty-eight million acres of American cropland have been tiled.[17] In the Midwest, this extensive plumbing network often empties into tributaries of the Mississippi.

In some areas, farm runoff from tiling presents a major health risk. Since 2012, the city of Des Moines has been spending millions of dollars each summer so its utility can remove nitrate fertilizer—a pollutant that can be especially harmful to infants and small children—from drinking water.[18] Infants who drink water with nitrate levels as high as Des Moines' have suffered from something called blue baby syndrome, which can lead to asphyxiation.[19] Medical reviews at the University of Iowa have also linked nitrates to cancer and immune deficiencies. All this makes professionals opposed to the behavior of large agriculture operations throw up their hands in frustration as they watch untreated farm water flow out of pipes into the municipal drinking water supply. "Look at the culverts discharging agricultural runoff into the Raccoon River"—the main source of drinking water for half a million people—says Des Moines Water Works utility manager Bill Stowe. "This is a publicly subsidized private plumbing system. They have the exact same configuration as if they were coming out of a city sewer."[20] Unlike a city, though, agriculture has an exemption for storm-water discharge under the Clean Water Act. Stowe sued to block these upstream agricultural pollutants, but the closely watched suit was dismissed in federal court in March 2016. Nor is the Raccoon

River and the greater Mississippi drainage the only place where this is occurring. A few hundred miles to the northeast, fertilizer-driven algae blooms spread out of the Maumee River in Ohio and for the last three years turned nearly a third of Lake Erie a sickening bright green, at times shutting down the city of Toledo's municipal water supply.[21]

In spite of these increasing health concerns, the process of tiling and draining wetlands has only increased of late. And, again, it is the growth of a corn- and soy-driven food system that has put the pedal to the metal.

Perhaps the greatest cause of this acceleration is the shift of developing economies from native omega-3-based food systems to omega-6 ones. In China, beef consumption is trending sharply upward and is projected to nearly double in the period from 2010 to 2025.[22] Along with this has been the same rise in poor health. The average Chinese citizen is now eight to fifteen kilograms heavier than the average a generation ago. With so many more Asians entering the middle class, they are moving away from a traditional diet of vegetables and seafood and eating more land food meat.[23] Farmers in China and elsewhere in Asia have begun importing American corn and soy to feed their growing herds.

Corn prices have therefore trended consistently higher. By 2012, a China-driven spike put corn prices over 200 percent higher than a decade earlier.[24] Prices have declined slightly since then, but the hope for another big boom means that the default is always corn. As you travel through the agro-industrial Midwest, you have the impression that the Mississippi River has faded from the consciousness of a region that once depended upon it. A river-oblivious industrial infrastructure has been overlaid on the American heartland, where a golden river of corn flows east and west by rail or truck, servicing the ever-growing demands of Asia.

This redirected flow of money has affected how farmers treat their land and correspondingly how they treat the Mississippi. As the beating heart at the center of the country's circulatory system, the river needs to process and balance all the runoff from all the surrounding land. Sometimes this runoff is natural—silt and soil that come off the mountains and plains in the natural process of erosion. But increasingly this runoff is coming off agricultural territory and is laced with many forms of nitrogen- and phosphorus-based fertilizer. And the territory the river drains is vast. Stretching from the Appalachian Mountains to the east and the Rockies to the west, it covers 1.1 million square miles—a third of the area of the continental United States.

Up until corn's recent price surge, a U.S. Department of Agriculture initiative called the Conservation Reserve Program (CRP) did a lot to keep dead zone–forming fertilizers from flowing into the Mississippi. Growing out of the post–Dust Bowl soil bank program of the 1950s, the CRP was officially established as part of the 1985 farm bill and paid farmers *not* to farm wetlands that are critical to fish.[25] The price farmers were paid to refrain from farming these marginal lands usually bested what they could earn from planting them in corn. But today with Asian buyers competing for corn, crop prices are higher than any government conservation program can pay. Much of the land that was key to preventing nutrients from entering the Mississippi is now getting planted. A 2013 study in the *Proceedings of the National Academy of Sciences* revealed that from 2006 to 2011, farmers in the Dakotas, Minnesota, Nebraska, and Iowa plowed up 1.3 million acres of grassland and replaced it with corn and soybeans. That land-use change is of a similar magnitude as the deforestations taking place in the Amazon and is the fastest destruction of grasslands since the Great Plains were first plowed.[26]

By the time I caught up with him, Brian Hicks was desperately trying to find a compromise. His biggest attempt focused on the plumbing network that had been laid beneath his farm and that until recently was constantly sending fertilized runoff into the nearby river. As we cruised his fields in his four-by-four we came to a three-foot-high metal box that acts as a kind of switch to all the runoff that goes into the nearby river. While many farmers lack these control boxes and let their tiling flow continually, Hicks was proud to show me that he could time the opening and closing of his outflow, allowing water and fertilizers to be strategically retained in the soil and thereby not pollute the river.

He had other fixes. Back at his modest home tucked away in a copse of trees at the center of Nettiewyynnt Farm, he showed me his PowerPoint presentation with all of his stewardship ideas. Whether through GPS-based monitoring that allows him to pinpoint portions of his land that require less fertilizer or better tiling, or other ideas, it was in his interest to keep nutrients on his land because it makes his crops grow better.

"My feeling is that most farmers," he says, "they realize the dead zone is there, but I think they all feel like, 'You know, I'm one little farmer. . . . What I do can't really affect the Gulf of Mexico.' But what I'm reading and what I'm feeling and seeing is I know what we are doing as far as managing outflow is positively impacting the environment."

When you write about the environment, you always try to include 30 stories like Hicks's. The drumbeat of the death of the natural world is deafening to readers, and the writer feels ever compelled to bait the hook, so to speak, with a solution around the bend. And when I met Hicks I sensed a heartfelt sincerity. No one wants to destroy his own backyard.

But still one could not help but notice that behind Hicks stood this edifice—this multimillion-dollar industrialized farm with reams of bills to pay that spoke to him in the grinding drone of corn.

And the more I looked into it the more I found food system thinkers who believe that everything farmers like Hicks are doing is nothing more than a Band-Aid on a gaping hemorrhage that started the moment settlers began their free-for-all on the prairie and sliced into the Midwest's native sod. In other words, the problem of nutrient loading into the Mississippi isn't the *methods* of commodity crop farming but commodity crop farming itself: an open-ended wasteful approach to land use that destroys the way that water, soil, vegetation, and nutrients reach equilibrium in a naturally composed ecosystem. Chief among those critics is Wes Jackson, until recently the director of the Land Institute in Salina, Kansas, and an oftquoted spokesperson for the ending of farming as we know it.[27]

"The essential problem is this," Jackson told me. "Humans went from perennial° polyculture° to annual monocultures.° This in my view was the biblical fall."

Jackson's research has shown that the root structure of the perennial° and diverse prairie grasses of the primeval° Midwest extended more than a dozen feet down into the soil. When nutrients flowed toward the Mississippi and its tributaries they were intercepted by these root structures, processed, and dissipated. Indeed, Jackson's monitoring of a plot of prairie left in its native state on the Land Institute's grounds reveals that almost no nitrogen and phosphorus leave a field planted in native grasses.

This abandonment of native, deep-rooted grasslands that provided 35 forage to grazers like bison and the early cattle in the United States also appears to have a health consequence that circles back to omega-3s. When animals are taken off grass and confined to stalls and fed primarily a diet of corn, they can suffer profoundly. In their natural state cattle live off a diet that leans in the direction of omega-3. Animals fed on grass ingest high amounts of plant-based ALA fatty acids, which they in turn can elongate into EPA and DHA. One reason is perhaps some of the farmers who transitioned from corn to pasture have found that their vet bills dropped markedly.

polyculture: the practice of farming more than one crop in the same space at the same time.
monoculture: the practice of farming a single crop or plant.
perennial: plants that continue to grow year after year even if they are dormant in the winter.
primeval: based on primitive conditions, resembling early stages in the history of a place.

Indeed, when you look at how a grain-fed animal is twisted away from its grassland-based dietary norms and put on corn you literally see evolution turned against itself. Cattle have an organ called a rumen in which grass is fermented and broken down in a kind of predigestive process. A grazing animal typically has a neutral pH in its rumen. But as Michael Pollan noted in his *New York Times* feedlot beef investigation, corn causes the rumen to become acidic. Once this happens, animals have been known to go off their feed, chew dirt, paw at their undersides, and open sores in their hides. A corn-stuffed rumen can become overloaded with gas, producing far more methane than in a grass-fed animal.[28] It is of course possible to mitigate the effects of a corn diet, and animal feed science has made significant strides since Pollan reported on the matter in 2002. As the animal welfare expert Temple Grandin told *The Washington Post* in 2015, "Grain is fine as long as there's plenty of roughage. . . . The problems come when you push too hard."[29] Unfortunately the drive for cheaper and cheaper meat creates incentives for pushing hard, which can mean sicker cows and more methane. And methane as a greenhouse gas is ten times more potent than carbon dioxide.

In addition to chronic environmental damages like climate change, there are immediate health risks posed by CAFOs.[30] Collectively livestock in the United States generate more than five hundred million tons of excrement every year, much of it coming from CAFOs. The waste gathers under industrial feeding barns and is eventually routed downhill to collecting ponds that the industry euphemistically calls lagoons.[31] These stagnant stews of feces and urine pose a public health risk all on their own. True, some of it is used to fertilize crops, but there is far more of it than can be effectively spread on fields. Much of it lingers and in so doing pollutes the surrounding air with toxic chemicals like hydrogen sulfide and ammonia.

No one really cared about these sorts of things when the modern-day animal confinement system was created. What farmers transitioning from grass to corn noticed was the immense concentration of energy they could achieve by swapping grass with corn. But the large-scale replacement of prairie with row crops and CAFOs is just one aspect of land food's reworking of the country. A much more serious problem concerns the way agriculture has changed the very way that rivers flow—a direct and comprehensive reworking of the nation's very circulatory system.

Notes

1. U.S. Department of Agriculture and U.S. Department of Health and Human Services, *Dietary Guidelines for Americans, 2010*, 7th ed. (Washington, DC: Government Printing Office, 2010), 12, https://health.gov/dietaryguidelines/dga2010/DietaryGuidelines2010.pdf.

2. Walter Willett, interview with the author, August 14, 2017. When Willett made this statement he was referring to the generally low quality of all carbohydrates in the American diet, not just wheat. But since wheat comprises the bulk of our carbohydrate intake I've made this small elision.

3. For the full investigation, see Sonia M. Grandi and Caroline Franck, "Agricultural Subsidies: Are They a Contributing Factor to the American Obesity Epidemic?," *JAMA Internal Medicine* 172, no. 22, (2012): 1754–55.

4. "Overview of NOAA Fisheries' Budgets for Fiscal Years 2014 & 2015," a presentation to fisheries' stakeholders, NOAA Fisheries, national conference call and webinar, March 19, 2014, www.nmfs.noaa.gov/mb/budget/noaafisheries2014_2015budget.pdf. NOAA budget cuts are part of an overall 16 percent budget cut to the Department of Commerce, which oversees NOAA's fisheries and weather divisions. As *The Washington Post* reported in March 2017, "The Commerce cuts would eliminate $250 million in coastal research programs that prepare communities for rising seas and worsening storms, including the popular $73 million Sea Grant program, which works with universities in 33 states." Chris Mooney, "Proposed Budget for Commerce Would Cut Funds for NOAA," *The Washington Post,* March 16, 2017, www.washingtonpost.com/business/economy/proposed-budget-for-commerce-would-cut-funds-for-noaa/2017/03/15/6c93d864-09ad-11e7-93dc-00f9bdd74ed1_story.html?utm_term=.b6b65ecf1f00.

5. The relative price rises for fruits and vegetables and fats and oils can be found in Grandi and Franck, "Agricultural Subsidies," 1754. Similar price divergences are seen in emerging economies; a recent report of food prices in Brazil, Mexico, China, and South Korea found that fruits and vegetable prices increased by 91 percent while processed foods *declined* by 20 percent. Steve Wiggins and Sharada Keats, "The Rising Cost of a Healthy Diet: Changing Relative Prices of Foods in High-Income and Emerging Economies," Overseas Development Institute (ODI), May 2015, www.odi.org/rising-cost-healthy-diet. For an overall discussion of the low cost of high-energy diets versus the high cost of high-nutrient diets, see Nicole Darmon and Adam Drewnowski, "Contribution of Food Prices and Diet Cost to Socioeconomic Disparities in Diet Quality and Health: A Systematic Review and Analysis," *Nutrition Reviews* 73, no. 10 (October 2015): 643–60, www.ncbi.nlm.nih.gov/pmc/articles/PMC4586446/.

6. Dr. William Lands, interview with the author, May 17, 2017.

7. Jørn Dyerberg and Richard Passwater, *The Missing Wellness Factors—EPA and DHA: The Most Important Nutrients Since Vitamins?* (Laguna Beach, CA: Basic Health Publications, 2012), 206. It is important to note here that research into the omega-3 effect on ameliorating type 2 diabetes is inconclusive. Studies have yielded conflicting results regarding which cholesterols are raised (in some cases "bad," or LDL, increases), whether insulin resistance is reduced,

and which sources (fish, nuts, olive oil, supplements) of omega-3s might be helpful or might increase risks. See L. Azadbakht, M. H. Rouhani, and P. J. Surkan, "Omega-3 Fatty Acids, Insulin Resistance and Type 2 Diabetes," *Journal of Research in Medical Sciences* 16, no. 10 (October 2011): 1259–60. And for the explanation of how fat cells trigger an immune response that causes inflammation, see Methodist Hospital, Houston, "Obesity Makes Fat Cells Act Like They're Infected," *ScienceDaily*, March 5, 2013, www.sciencedaily.com/releases/2013/03/130305l45145.htm.

8. The Gulf of Mexico dead zone reached the record-breaking size of 8,776 square miles, as reported by NOAA. New Jersey is 8,771 square miles, including water area. "Gulf of Mexico 'Dead Zone' Is the Largest Ever Measured," NOAA, August 2, 2017, www.noaa.gov/media-release/gulf-of-mexico-dead-zone-is-largest-ever-measured.

9. I originally published these facts about dead zones and of the connections between agriculture, fertilizer, the Mississippi, and the Gulf dead zone in Paul Greenberg, "A River Runs Through It," *American Prospect*, May 22, 2013.

10. Ibid., 2.

11. Robert J. Diaz and Rutger Rosenberg, "Spreading Dead Zones and Consequences for Marine Ecosystems," *Science* 321, no. 5891 (August 15, 2008): 926–29. For a map that shows where these global dead zones exist, see "Dead Zones," Virginia Institute of Marine Science, www.vims.edu/research/topics/dead_zones/index.php.

12. My visit with Brian Hicks and his story appear throughout Greenberg, "A River Runs Through It."

13. Total estimated corn acreage in 2017 was 90.9 million acres. Total estimated soy acreage in 2017 was 89.5 million acres. "Acreage," U.S. Department of Agriculture (USDA), ISSN: 1949–1522, June 30, 2017, https://usda.mannlib.cornell.edu/usda/current/Acre/Acre-06 -30-2017.pdf. The total surface area of California is 155,779 square miles, which equals 99,698,560 acres. It should be noted, however, that farmers often rotate corn and soy in succession on the same piece of land.

14. Greenberg, "A River Runs Through It," 7.

15. Fertilizer cost varies depending on whether farmers are growing corn only, corn and soy, or more diverse systems. A representative chart for production in Iowa can be found from Iowa State's agriculture extension: "Estimated Costs of Crop Production in Iowa," Ag Decision Maker, Iowa State University, File A1-20, January 2017, www.extension.iastate.edu/agdm/crops/pdf/a1-20.pdf.

16. Greenberg, "A River Runs Through It," 7.

17. "Conservation," 2012 Census of Agriculture, USDA, July 2014, 2, www.agcensus.usda.gov/Publications/2012/Online_Resources/Highlights/Conservation/Highlights_Conservation.pdf.

18. The information about drinking water health issues, expenses, and pollution in the waters from agricultural fertilizer runoff in Des Moines, Iowa, is from Bill Stowe, interview with the author, October 18, 2017, Stowe is the Des Moines Water Works CEO and general manager and a fifth-generation native Iowan.

19. "Nutrient Pollution. The Effects—Human Health," EPA, www.epa.gov/nutrientpollution/effects-human-health.

20. Paul Greenberg, "How Your Diet Contributes to Water Pollution," *Eating Well*, July/August 2017, www.eatingwell.com/article/290358/how-your-diet-contributes-to-water-pollution/.

21. Jugal K. Patel and Yuliya Parshina-Kottas, "Miles of Algae Covering Lake Erie," *The New York Times*, October 3, 2017, www.nytimes.com/interactive/2017/10/03/science/earth/lake-erie.html.

22. S. Anderson et al., *Chinese Beef Consumption Trends: Implications for Future Trading Partners*, Kansas State University, Department of Agricultural Economics, April 2011.

23. Tom Levitt, "China Facing Bigger Dietary Health Crisis Than the U.S.," *Chinadialogue*, July 4, 2014.

24. Historical prices for commodity crops can be tracked with this tool presenting average U.S. farm prices from 1960 to the present: Darrel L. Good and Ping Li, "US Average Farm Price Received Database Tool," Farmdoc, University of Illinois, www.farmdoc.illinois.edu/manage/uspricehistory/us_price_history.html.

25. Greenberg, "A River Runs Through It," 6–7.

26. See Christopher K. Wright and Michael C. Wimberly, "Recent Land Use Change in the Western Corn Belt Threatens Grasslands and Wetlands." *PNAS* 110, no. 10 (March 5, 2013): 4134–39.

27. Ibid., 9–10.

28. Michael Pollan, "Power Steer." *The New York Times Magazine*, March 31, 2002.

29. Tamar Haspel, "Is Grass-Fed Beef Really Better for You, the Animal and the Planet?," *The Washington Post*, February 23, 2015, www.washingtonpost.com/lifestyle/food/is-grass-fed-beef-really-better-for-you-the-animal-and-the-planet/2015/02/23/92733524-b6d1-11e4-9423-f3d0a1ec335c_story.html?utm_term=.c694f5739ae7.

30. Julie Janovsky, "Industrial Animal Agriculture: A Broken System," PEW Charitable Trusts, June 2013, www.pewtrusts.org/~/media/assets/2011/07/19/pewindustrialanimalagriculturebrokensystemjuly2011.pdf.

31. Bill Field, "Beware of On-Farm Manure Storage Hazards," Rural Health and Safety Guide, Purdue University, S-82, www.extension.purdue.edu/extmedia/S/S-82.html.

Understanding the Text

1. In your own words, define supplementism, reductionism, and omega-3s.

2. What is a dead zone?

3. What are tiling and draining, and how and why do Midwestern farmers use them?

Reflection and Response

4. Review the list of the top ten sources of calories provided by Greenberg. How does your own diet add up? How much of what you eat falls into the categories he identifies?

5. Why is "Heartland" an appropriate name for this essay?

6. What do you think it would take to shift the American diet away from corn, soy, and wheat products and toward more leafy greens and seafood? How is this related to the difference between diets rich in omega-3s and diets rich in omega-6s?

7. How does American agriculture negatively affect fish supplies? Describe how Greenberg uses the Mississippi River to answer this question.

Making Connections

8. Imagine that Bren Smith ("The Least Deadly Catch," p. 270) and Brian Hicks (as represented by Greenberg) were sitting down at lunch to discuss the state of farming in America. What would they focus on? And what would they eat? If you were to join the discussion, what would you ask? Use specific textual references to support your responses.

9. Rowan Jacobsen ("The Biography of a Plant-Based Burger," p. 232) and Greenberg both refer to Michael Pollan's *New York Times* essay on cattle and beef. Look up the article they reference, and think about how it informs their work. What questions does Pollan raise? How do Jacobsen and Greenberg add to the conversation? What questions should we continue to raise and explore? Identify one question that they collectively raise and that you think is important. Write an exploratory essay that responds to the question you identify.

10. Greenberg advocates a realignment of agricultural and nutritional guidelines. How does this align with Joon Yun, David Kessler, and Dan Glickman's ("We Need Better Answers on Nutrition," p. 301) call for a National Institute of Nutrition? How could this proposed institute help not just with nutrition but also with climate-friendly food production practices? What do you think it would take to achieve an "overall better alignment of agricultural and nutritional policies" (par. 4)—one that could improve the health of most Americans?

The Least Deadly Catch: Ocean Farming in the Climate Change Era

Bren Smith

After working as a commercial fisherman and witnessing firsthand some of the ways commercial fishing destroys the ocean's ecosystem, Bren Smith became a restorative ocean farmer and established one of the first sustainable 3-D ocean farms in the country. His work aims to restore not deplete the ocean's ecosystem while also growing food sustainably and making a profit. He helped found GreenWave, an organization that supports people who want to start their own ocean farms and that provides new employment opportunities and start-up grants for those who have lost jobs in industrial fishing and farming. Smith wrote a book about his journey, titled *Eat Like a Fish: My Adventures as a Fisherman Turned Restorative Ocean Farmer* (2019). What follows is based on the transcript of a speech he gave in 2016 at a conference sponsored by Bioneers, a nonprofit organization that promotes just and sustainable innovations for restoring the planet and its people. In this speech, Smith discusses his ideas for sustainable solutions by telling the story of his own transformation.

My story is a story of ecological redemption. I was born and raised in Newfoundland, Canada, dropped out of high school when I was 14, and headed out to sea. I fished the Grand Banks and the Georges Banks — tuna, lobster. I headed out to the Bering Sea in the 80s and fished cod and crab.

Now, this was the height of industrialized fishing. We were tearing up entire ecosystems with our trawls, chasing fewer and fewer fish further and further out to sea. And most of the fish I was catching were going to McDonald's for their fish sandwich.

I was a kid producing some of the lowest, worst, most destructive food on the planet. But God, I loved that job. The sense of humility of being in 30-foot seas; the sense of solidarity being in the belly of a boat with 13 other people doing 20-hour shifts; and the sense of meaning, of helping feed my country. Those were some of the best days of my life. I've been on the water for 30 years, and I miss them so, so much.

Then the cod stocks crashed back home in Newfoundland. This was a real wake-up call. Thousands of fishermen thrown out of work, boats beached, canneries emptied. It is amazing that a culture and economy built up over a hundred years can disappear in a matter of weeks in the face of ecological crisis.

That's when I began to learn that ecological crisis has nothing to do 5
with the environment, it has to do with the economy. There will be no
jobs on a dead planet.

So, I started this search for sustainability, and I ended up in the aquaculture farms in Northern Canada, because aquaculture was supposed to
be the great answer to over fishing, job creation, and reduction of pressure on fish stocks. Instead, it was more of the same. We were polluting
local waters with antibiotics and pesticides. We were growing neither fish
nor food. These were Iowa pig farms at sea.

I kept searching, disillusioned, and I ended up in Long Island Sound.
I chased a woman down there. They were opening up shell fishing
grounds for the first time in 150 years to attract young fishers back
into the industry. I remade myself as an oysterman. I did that for a
couple years, and then the storms hit—Hurricane Irene, Hurricane
Sandy—barreling through, wiping out 90 percent of my crop. Most
of my gear washed out to sea two years in a row. Suddenly I found
myself on the front lines of a climate crisis that arrived 100 years earlier than expected. This was supposed to be a slow lobster boil. It's
here and now.

Facing ecological collapse means I can't work on the water. The goal
in my life is to work on the sea. My goal is to die on my boat one day.
That's going to be a measure of success. But we need to protect and save
the oceans for me to die that way.

I picked myself up and started redesigning my farm. I lifted it off the
bottom so it was resilient to storm surges, used the entire water column
and searching for new species to grow—species that were regenerative.
After 15 years of experimentation with sustainability, I ended up as the
first regenerative ocean farmer, growing a mix of seaweeds and shellfish
to create good local food, create jobs, and help fight the climate crisis.

Now, let's look at the farm, because it's hard to picture what I'm doing 10
under the water.

I had a kid draw this picture, and it's really simple. It's just hurricane-
proof anchors on the edges of the farm and then a rope eight feet
across the surface. From there, we grow our kelp vertically downward.
Next to that, we've got our scallops and lantern nets, mussels and mus-
sel socks. On the bottom, we have oysters in cages, and then clams
down in the mud.

So, kelp grows in post-hurricane season, and it's one of the fastest-
growing plants on Earth. Once we harvest the kelp, the mussels set. We
have mini-scallops and then we've got our oysters, which are Thimble
Island salts. It's like a splash of ocean when you eat it.

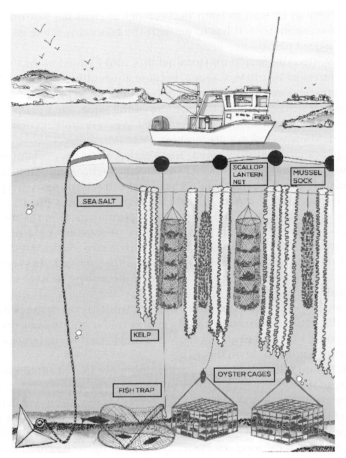

Illustration of GreenWave's regenerative ocean farming design.
Stephanie Stroud for GreenWave (www.greenwave.org)

From the surface, there's nothing of the farm to see. But that's such a good thing, right? It has a low aesthetic impact. Our oceans are these beautiful pristine places and we want to keep them that way.

Our farms have small footprints. My farm used to be 100 acres. It's down to 20 acres, and I'm growing way more food than before because we're vertical.

Anybody can boat, swim and fish on our farms. They're community 15 spaces where you can dive through our kelp forests. We don't own the property. All we own is the right to grow shellfish and seaweeds. We own a process, not a property. We're going to farm to protect our commons rather than privatize it like agriculture did.

Our goal was to take on three major challenges.

One was develop a delicious new seafood plate in this era of overfishing and food insecurity. We reject agriculture's obsession with monoculture.° We grow for polyculture.° Seaweeds, four kinds of shellfish, and we harvest salt as well.

But we've barely broken the surface. There are 10,000 edible plants in the ocean, and a couple hundred shellfish. I mean, imagine being a chef at this time and finding out there are arugulas, tomatoes, and rices that you've never cooked with before, tasted or seen. This is an exciting time to develop a culinary cuisine. What we're going to do is re-imagine a seafood plate. We'll move bivalves° and sea greens to the center, and wild fish to the edges.

Our kelp is the "gateway drug" to de-sushify sea greens. We're making kelp the new kale by doing barbecue kelp noodles with parsnips and bread crumbs. These are vegetables. This isn't seafood. We're doing sea green butters and umami bomb bullion cubes. Our new ocean dinner, it's going to be fun, it's going to be creative, and it's going to be delicious. It's time to eat like fish, because fish don't make omega 3's and all these things we need—they eat them. By eating like fish, we get the benefits while reducing pressure on fish stocks.

This isn't some little boutique, bearded Brooklyn bee farm. We can   20 grow huge amounts of crops in small areas—10 to 30 tons of seaweed, 250,000 shellfish per acre. If you were to take a network of our farms totaling the size of Washington state, you could feed the world. And this is zero-input food. It requires no freshwater, no fertilizer, no feed, no land, making it hands-down the most sustainable form of food production on the planet. In the era of climate change, as water prices and feed/ fertilizer prices go up, our food is going to be the most affordable food on the planet to grow, and the most affordable food on the planet to eat. We are going to be eating sea greens.

Climate change is going to force us to eat zero-input foods. Question is: Is it going to be delicious, or is it going to be like being force-fed cod liver oil? That's where the chefs come in. If chefs can't make what we

---

monoculture: the practice of farming a single crop or plant.
polyculture: the practice of farming more than one crop in the same space at the same time.
bivalves: an aquatic shellfish that has a compressed body enclosed within a hinged shell, such as oysters, clams, mussels, and scallops.

can grow delicious, they should quit their jobs. Developing this climate cuisine is what they're here on Earth to do.

The second goal of the farm is to transform fishers into regenerative ocean farmers. Mother Nature created these two technologies millions of years ago, designing them to mitigate our harm: shellfish and seaweeds. Oysters are these incredible agents of sustainability that filter out 50 gallons of water a day, pulling nitrogen out of our water column, which is the root cause of dead zones spreading through the globe. Our kelp soaks up five times more carbon than land-based plants. It's called the sequoia of the sea. *The New Yorker* recently called it the culinary equivalent of the electric car.

Our farms also function as storm surge protectors. Now that our coral reefs or oyster reefs are gone, our farms replace them. There are artificial reefs attracting over 150 species that come hide and thrive. My farm used to be a barren patch of ocean, and now it's a thriving ecosystem.

As fishermen, we're now climate farmers. Restoring rather than depleting, and really trying to tackle, in our own small way, the climate crisis we all face. We're also trying to use our zero-input crops to replace land-based inputs. We've got a program with the Yale Sustainable Food Program to use our kelp as fertilizer in their organic farm. As the nitrogen leaches off back into the waters, we capture it and close that nitrogen loop.

Cattle have been eating kelp for hundreds of years, until industrial feed pushed it off the farm. If you feed cattle a majority diet of kelp, you get up to a 90 percent reduction in methane, and you get this beautiful tasting, umami-filled beef. It's delicious stuff. When we bring this stuff into New York, I'm going to blow grass-fed beef off the table.   25

The idea is really to build a bridge between land and sea. Too often, our thinking about the food system stops at the water's edge. I go to food conferences. There are maybe 1,000 people, and there's this little break-off session about the ocean, and eight people attend. That's why I'm absolutely frightened.

"That's when I began to learn that ecological crisis has nothing to do with the environment, it has to do with the economy. There will be no jobs on a dead planet."

The last piece is building a foundation of a new economy that puts jobs, justice, and restoration at the center of the plate. Now, I'm not an environmentalist. I kill things for a living. You give me a gun, I'll shoot moose out of my kitchen window. I grew up with seal hunts. And I wouldn't be doing this unless it created jobs for the 40 percent of people that are unemployed in my community—unless it created opportunity for the millions of people that were left behind as we built the polluting industrial economy. That's why I'm here.

We built GreenWave, a nonprofit dedicated to training and supporting regenerative ocean farmers, to begin building this industry from the bottom up. We work to replicate and scale. We build the infrastructure necessary, and we develop new markets.

First thing we did was open-source our model. We don't franchise. That's a tool of the old economy. In a new economy, we make things accessible to everybody. Anybody with 20 acres and a boat and $20-50,000 can start their farm and be up and growing the first year. The key to replication is designing around simplicity, not complexity. Our farms require minimal capital costs and minimal skill. Think of it as the nail salon model of the sea.

And they're profitable. Because we don't have to feed and weed 30 these things, we're able to net up to $200,000 or $300,000 per farm and employ up to 10 people, and that's just on the farm, that doesn't count the processing centers.

As a farmer, you get some start-up grants. We give free seed, and we're keeping the hatchery under the nonprofit side, because three companies own 53 percent of the land-based seed supply, and seed is the most expensive input for farmers. We're going to look at our system and decide where profits can be extracted and where can't they. They're not going to come off the backs of new ocean farmers. It's hard to farm in the era of climate change and globalization. We're going to give people a stable platform so they can learn to grow.

We have requests flooding in. We've had requests to start farms in every coastal state in North America and 102 countries around the world. We have land-based farmers—young ones—just flooding in, because they can't afford land. We also have our first farmer here in California who's a Mexican American, second-generation plumber, and I'm really hoping he is going to be the new face on the West Coast, so I never have to fly here again.

We're also building a land-based infrastructure to scale. We have the largest hatchery network in the U.S., and we're building seafood hubs so farmers can capture more of that value chain. Our land-based infrastructure is designed to be an engine of food justice—a place where we embed good jobs and food access into the DNA of the new ocean economy. In practice, this means placing our seafood hubs in communities that need it most. Our first one was in one of the poorest neighborhoods on the East Coast. Our starting wages are minimum $15 an hour, and it's open employment, so don't you dare bring your resume. I don't care if you're a former felon or undocumented worker, we're going to figure out a way to work together.

This isn't just about jobs. This isn't about working in our processing factories. This is about agency. One of the major deficits in our society today is the feeling that you can make a difference—that you have to be an Amazon, you have to be a Google, in order to tackle the big problems. You don't.

Our goal is to make sure the folks who were left behind from the old economy own their own farms, that they don't have bosses, that they have self-directed lives. Giving people agency over their lives is a core value of this new ocean economy. 35

The last piece of the GreenWave program is innovation and market development. We're developing mobile hatcheries and data sensing. Data sensors make it so we can do pollution farming in places like the Bronx and measure our ecosystem services. We can use it for food, fertilizer, animal feed, bioplastics, and more. Kelp is the soy of the sea, except for it's not evil. The market power is that it has so many uses in so many sectors.

If you put this together, everybody asks me what does scale look like. It's not thousand-acre banana plantations. It's networks of 25 to 50 farms in a local region—a seafood hub, a hatchery on land, a ring of big institutional buyers (hospitals, colleges, companies like Google), and then a ring of entrepreneurs developing value-added products and doing the innovation.

Offshore, we want to embed our farms in wind farms. Why just harvest wind? We have that structure, let's do food, fuel, and fertilizer in those same spaces. Our oceans are huge places. There's a lot of room to play, as long as we do it the right way.

To close, turning GreenWave's vision into reality, I think, is a necessity. The land-based ag system is entering these cycles of escalating crisis. Climate change is expected to drive up corn prices up to 140 percent in the next 15 years. It is terrifying, the carbon and methane output from the ag sector. You throw in population rise, growing inequality in the U.S. and around the globe, and food insecurities emerging as the new normal, and if that's not enough, farmers can't even make a living—91 percent of farmers in the U.S. lose money year after year. This is just a system that's not working.

Climate change is going to force us into the ocean. I think that's one 40 of the real lessons of the droughts out here in California—we're going to be forced out to sea. But our wild fisheries can't handle it—85 percent of wild fish stocks are over-harvested, and we just can't expect our fish to bear that burden.

This is all what's so exciting: Climate change, at least out on the water, is breeding hope for those of us that are out there on our boats. Because this is our chance to do food right. For the first time in generations, to build an agricultural system from the bottom up. Our oceans are these blank slates. More of the U.S. is under water than above. This is our opportunity to protect rather than privatize our oceans, our seas, ensure beginning and low-income farmers have access to low-cost property, avoid all the mistakes made in industrial land-based ag and industrial aquaculture. Let's invent whole new occupations to feed the planet and lift communities out of poverty.

This is the new face of environmentalism. It's not just conservation and stopping pipelines. We have to do that, that is great stuff, but it's also about building alternative visions. It's about fighting climate change by creating jobs, and giving people meaning and agency. Wouldn't that be a beautiful environmental movement, if we were pushing for that? We could be building an economy of food and work, where fishermen like me are proud to write songs about it. We can create something so beautiful, so powerful and restorative out at sea. And we can eat together, we can work together, and figure out how to make a living on a living planet.

Understanding the Text

1. What is a regenerative ocean farm? How does it work?

2. How is regenerative ocean farming different from industrialized fishing?

Reflection and Response

3. After reading the transcript, locate the video of Bren Smith's speech online and watch it. How does your perception of the argument change when you watch him deliver it?

4. How and why does Smith use humor to connect to his audience? Find two to three uses of humor to analyze and discuss what makes them funny and why.

5. Why do you think Smith emphasizes that "Giving people agency over their lives is a core value of this new ocean economy" (par. 35)?

Making Connections

6. Compare Smith's 3-D ocean farm to the vertical farms described by Selina Wang ("The Future of Farming Is Looking Up," p. 331). What do they have in common — both in terms of physical factors and the values embedded in their creation? What is different? How do they each compare to land farming?

7. While Smith explains that he is helping to develop ocean farming because it helps create jobs for the unemployed and it helps provide meaning and agency to farmers and others who have been left behind by the "polluting industrial economy," (par. 27), others cite a tension between true climate solutions and economic factors. Does Smith offer a viable solution — one that protects the economy and the planet? Use the work of Jonathan Foley ("Can We Feed the World and Sustain the Planet?," p. 212), Richard Marosi ("Hardship on Mexico's Farms, a Bounty for U.S. Tables," p. 306), Frances Moore Lappé ("Biotechnology Isn't the Key to Feeding the World," p. 317), Blake Hurst ("The Omnivore's Delusion," p. 184), and Donald Bartlett and James Steele ("Monsanto's Harvest of Fear," p. 165) to support your response.

8. Compare Smith's stories of ocean farming to Hurst's ("The Omnivore's Delusion," p. 184) and Barbara Kingsolver's ("You Can't Run Away on Harvest Day," p. 150) stories of land farming. How and why do they each use their personal experiences to make a compelling argument for change? What do we learn about farms and farming that is similar to or different from third-person descriptions of farmers and farming such as Marosi's ("Hardship on Mexico's Farms, a Bounty for U.S. Tables," p. 306) or Paul Greenberg's ("Heartland," p. 256)?

How One Tribe Is Fighting for Their Food Culture in the Face of Climate Change

Abaki Beck

Abaki Beck is a graduate student in public health at Washington University where she conducts research on health equity and capacity building in tribal communities, using both data analysis and qualitative research. Beck also works as a freelance writer focusing on issues that connect social justice, science, and indigenous peoples. She is the founder and editor of POC Online Classroom and a coeditor of the Daughters of Violence zine. Her writing has appeared in *Bitch*, *Yes! Magazine*, *Aperture*, *TalkPoverty*, and *The Establishment*. The following essay, originally published by *TalkPoverty*, explores how climate change negatively impacts the food culture of the Swinomish indigenous tribe.

As in many tribal communities, the Swinomish relationship with the environment is complex. The Northwest coastal tribe not only uses the land for food, medicine, and material goods, but many cultural traditions like ceremonies are land-based.

The federal government has long attempted to sever tribes from the land—their source of knowledge, culture, and health. Through war and forced relocation, tribes were physically removed. Policies such as the 1887 General Allotment Act forced many to adopt sedentary lifestyles and use Western agricultural techniques. And contemporary legal restrictions on centuries-old fishing, hunting, and gathering techniques means that tribes are still limited in how they can gather foods and medicines.

Food sovereignty—efforts to re-create local, sustainable, and traditional food systems that prioritize community need over profits—has been one of the major ways tribal communities are combating disparities driven by colonial policies. Food sovereignty looks different in every tribe, as it is based on community need and tribal tradition, and it isn't just about food. Swinomish efforts have focused on the impacts of climate change, which is already threatening their community health.

History led many reservations to become food insecure, and federal support is limited. Hundreds of tribes utilize the Federal Distribution Program on Indian Reservations—which since 1973 has distributed bulk food items to rural Native Americans who don't have access to Supplemental Nutrition Assistance Program-eligible stores—but the food often doesn't meet basic dietary standards and sometimes arrives spoiled.

Loss of land and traditional foods has caused myriad health prob- 5
lems in tribal communities. Native Americans have the highest rates of
diabetes of any racial group, as well as disproportionately higher rates
of cancer, heart disease, and stroke. Mental wellbeing has also been
impacted: Some scholars argue that colonial violence like displacement
and spiritual disconnection from the land has led to cross-generational
trauma and unresolved grief for Native individuals and communities.

Climate change is making this worse.

Historically, the Swinomish harvesting calendar revolved around
13 moons. The calendar corresponds to seasonal shifts throughout the
year, with each moon bringing a new set of ceremonies and foods to be
collected and processed. The first moon of spring, moon when the frog
talks, is when herring and smelt are harvested and sitka spruce, red cedar,
and Oregon grape roots are collected. In the moon of the sacred time,
during the end of December and January, cultural traditions are passed
from elders to younger community members.

The seasonal changes associated with each moon are becoming less
predictable with climate change. Extreme heat waves in the normally
moderate climate stress plants and may stunt root development. Less
predictable or extreme tides (whether too high or too low) hamper clam
digging and other shorefront gathering.

Public health leaders, including the Centers for Disease Control and
Prevention and the World Health Organization, recognize that climate
change has direct impacts on human health. These impacts may be
even more acute for the Washington tribe: the reservation is 90 percent
surrounded by water, and salmon, crab, and clam are major sources of
food. The sea is of intimate importance.

Yet Western measurements of health and climate impact do not 10
take cultural history, interdependence, and connection to the land and
non-human world into consideration,
often focusing exclusively on individual, physiological health impacts. For
example, a toxicologist may look at
pollutants in seafood and advise the
Swinomish to eat less. Yet when taking into consideration food security,
ceremonial use, and transmission of
traditional knowledge, the removal
of seafood would be detrimental to
Swinomish conceptions of health; climate change is threatening the tribe's
autonomy.

> "Yet Western measure-
ments of health and climate
impact do not take cultural
history, interdependence,
and connection to the land
and non-human world into
consideration, often focusing exclusively on individual, physiological health
impacts."

To address this disconnect, in 2003, Dr. Jamie Donatuto, the environmental health analyst for the tribe, set out with elder Larry Campbell
to develop indigenous health indicators, which they hoped would bring
a more holistic and culturally relevant lens to public health policy, climate change predictions, environmental risk assessment, and the tribe's
food sovereignty work. After interviewing more than 100 community
members, they determined the Swinomish health indicators to be: self-
determination (healing and restoration, development and trust); cultural
use (respect and stewardship, sense of place); natural resource security
(quality, access, safety); resilience (self-esteem, identity, sustainability);
education (teachings, elders, youth); and community connection (work,
sharing, relations).

One of the first challenges they wanted to tackle using these indicators was climate change impacts. After gathering data on predicted storm
surge, sea-level rise, sediment movement and more, they led a series of
workshops with elders, youth, clam diggers, and fishers, to gauge which
beaches they should focus their limited resources on. They identified
several that were both culturally significant to the tribe and at high risk
for climate impacts, and focused their workshops on traditional foods to
contextualize these problems.

"It's not about outreach, it's not unidirectional. It's about really
engaging them," Donatuto reflected. Now, based on community input,
the tribe is developing clam gardens that are more resilient to climate
impacts such as sea level rise, storm surge, and possibly ocean acidification. Clam gardens are a traditional way of managing a beach ecosystem to create optimal habitat for clams while ensuring food security for
the tribe. Dr. Donatuto's team also shared community feedback with the
Swinomish Senate, who valued their priorities equally to scientific data
when constructing the tribe's climate change adaptation plan.

Beyond policy changes to address climate change impacts, elders were
also concerned about a generational disconnect in traditional ecological
knowledge. Using the 13 moons as a guide, in 2015 the tribe developed
an informal curriculum to educate youth on the lunar calendar and
traditional foods. Though it has attracted interest from local schools,
Donatuto stressed that it is a land-based, community-led curriculum. The
tribe hosts dinners and other events in which elders and educators lead
community members outside to learn, for example, tree identification,
how to collect tree resin, and how to process it. Participants not only
learn about traditional foods, but learn it through traditional methods of
knowledge transmission.

Swinomish food sovereignty and climate change adaptation efforts 15
are reflective of national movements in Indigenous reclamation and

resistance. Tribes recognize that in many cases, disparities that face Native communities are borne from and exacerbated by systemic colonial and racial violence, including the devaluation of Indigenous knowledge. So how could the same system that produced these disparities be a source of the solution?

Resistance and reclamation take many forms. The White Earth Band of Ojibwe recently recognized the "personhood" rights of wild rice in an effort to thwart oil pipeline construction through their habitat. Some tribal courts are beginning to draw from traditional gender and familial beliefs instead of U.S. federal law in domestic violence, divorce, and custody cases. And studies have found that Native students in schools that teach entirely in tribal languages are often higher performing than their counterparts that attend English-only schools, including on English language standardized tests.

As these and Swinomish efforts reflect: Revitalization of Indigenous knowledge, politics, and land relations is not just about remembering traditions, but solving urgent contemporary issues.

Understanding the Text

1. What is the 1887 General Allotment Act?
2. What is food sovereignty?
3. What is food insecurity?

Reflection and Response

4. Why is it important that we all care about how the climate crisis is affecting the Swinomish tribe — their food, health, culture, and identity?
5. Why is it necessary to understand the complex interdependence of culture and health for the Swinomish people? Why is it especially important in the face of climate change? And how might their story be a lesson for everyone?
6. How does a history of "systemic colonial and racial violence" (par. 15) make the Swinomish tribe more susceptible to the negative effects of climate change? What does Beck suggest to help mitigate or overcome these affects?

Making Connections

7. Many authors in this collection name seafood as a solution to both unhealthy lifestyles and to climate change. (You might refer to Paul Greenberg's "Heartland," p. 256, or Bren Smith's "The Least Deadly Catch," p. 270). How does the situation facing the Swinomish people exemplify the problems they identify? Do the values and culture of the Swinomish offer ideas for change?

8. How might Stephen Satterfield ("I'm a Black Food Writer," p. 131) respond to the problems that Beck identifies? What values do they share? How are their viewpoints connected to a history of racism in the United States?

9. Review what Beck, Joe Pinsker ("Why So Many Kids Come to Enjoy the Taste of Healthier Foods," p. 97), and Barry Yeoman ("The Hidden Resilience of 'Food Desert' Neighborhoods," p. 104) have written about food insecurity and how to overcome it. Then research food insecurity in your community. Is it a problem your community or particular groups in your community face? Are there organizations or programs working toward food security for those who do not have enough to eat?

5

What Is the Future of Food?

We never know what the future will bring, but we do know that we will need food. In this last chapter, authors weigh in on what they think will influence the future of food. They identify problems that will remain at the forefront — the climate crisis, global hunger, nutrition, labor injustice, and sustainability, to name a few. They also discuss potential changes that might lessen the negative impact of food production on the environment and that might actually promote global environmental sustainability. Still, even as we think of solutions to existing concerns, new problems will inevitably emerge.

While David Biello suggests ways to pursue food production that promote environmental sustainability and health, Robert Paarlberg complicates his view with a critique of the organic food movement and argues for a different kind of emphasis on solving world hunger. Together, they reveal the crisis of values that underlies much of the debate over organic versus conventional farming and the related environmental and health impacts.

Joon Yun, David Kessler, and Dan Glickman combine their experience and expertise to make a case for an institute that would support research to help us better understand the connections between health and nutrition, implicitly suggesting that the government must do more to support better eating habits and better access to nutritional foods.

Richard Marosi and Frances Moore Lappé further expand and question our understanding of the future of food by examining social, economic, and political inequities that affect food production and distribution. Marosi investigates the exploitation of laborers on the Mexican farms that supply much of the U.S. produce we eat. And Lappé suggests that a "scarcity of democracy" — and not food — is the real culprit behind world hunger. Together, then, they suggest that we have a lot of work to do to reduce social and political inequities that plague the global food system.

Finally, Bob Quinn, Liz Carlisle, and Selina Wang describe innovations in farming that could remake the future of farming as we know it. Quinn and Carlisle describe levels of innovations and partnerships that led to more

photo: Claudia Totir/Moment/Getty Images

sustainable and renewable energy sources for Quinn's farm and community, while Wang focuses on the possibilities for indoor, vertical farming. Both offer hope for the future of food production.

This chapter thus demonstrates that the future of food will be no less complex than the present. The authors also reveal that the ways we define food and determine its purpose will continue to change as other aspects of culture, science, business, politics, and society change. The factors that help determine what foods are available and what foods we choose to eat will continue to evolve, too.

The readings in this chapter, then, suggest as many questions as they answer. Here are some to consider: Is the future of food going to be organic? Will it rely on conventional, industrial approaches? Or will we adopt hybrid approaches? What ethical principles will guide food policy in the future? What kinds of moral choices will individuals make? Will they see food choices as moral choices more or less than they do now? What roles will innovative approaches and new technologies play in feeding the population? Should we focus on futuristic, potentially expensive, inventions or return to the basics? What roles will corporations and industrial farming play in the future of food? What roles will small-scale farming and local businesses play? Will worker justice, fair labor practices, and the impacts of food production on historically oppressed groups be considered? Will democracy emerge as a positive force in bringing about food equity? Will people care more or less about global hunger in the future than they do now? Will the global hunger crisis ever become a thing of the past? Will we succeed in finding a way to feed the world while sustaining the planet at the same time? Although these questions have yet to be answered, the readings in this chapter offer food for thought and ways for us to think critically about the future of food.

Will Organic Food Fail to Feed the World?

David Biello

David Biello is a journalist and author of *The Unnatural World: The Race to Remake Civilization in Earth's Newest Age* (2016). He writes frequently for *Scientific American*, as well as for *Yale Environment 360* and hosts the podcast *60-Second Earth*. He covers environmental issues in the United States and internationally. In 2009, he won the Internews Earth Journalism Award for his series *A Guide to Carbon Capture and Storage*. He continues to cover international climate negotiations and worked with Detroit Public Television on *Beyond the Light Switch*, a documentary on the future of electricity that won the duPont-Columbia University Award for journalistic excellence, and is the science curator for TED. In this article, first published in *Scientific American* in 2012, Biello suggests a hybrid approach to food production that takes environmental impact and yield into account.

Food for hungry mouths, feed for animals headed to the slaughter-house, fiber for clothing, and even, in some cases, fuel for vehicles—all derive from global agriculture. As a result, in the world's temperate climes human agriculture has supplanted 70 percent of grasslands, 50 percent of savannas, and 45 percent of temperate forests. Farming is also the leading cause of deforestation in the tropics and one of the *largest sources of greenhouse gas emissions*, a major contributor to the ongoing maul of species known as the sixth extinction, and a perennial source of nonrenewable groundwater mining and water pollution.

To restrain the environmental impact of agriculture as well as produce more wholesome foods, some farmers have turned to so-called organic techniques. This type of farming is meant to minimize environmental and human health impacts by avoiding the use of synthetic fertilizers, chemical pesticides, and hormones or antibiotic treatments for livestock, among other tactics. But the use of industrial technologies, particularly synthetic nitrogen fertilizer, has fed the swelling human population during the last century. Can organic agriculture feed a world of nine billion people?

In a bid to bring clarity to what has too often been an emotional debate, environmental scientists at McGill University in Montreal and the University of Minnesota performed an analysis of 66 studies comparing conventional and organic methods across 34 different crop species. "We found that, overall, organic yields are considerably lower than conventional yields," explains McGill's Verena Seufert, lead author of the study to be published in *Nature* on April 26. (*Scientific American* is part of

Nature Publishing Group.) "But, this yield difference varies across different conditions. When farmers apply best management practices, organic systems, for example, perform relatively better."

In particular, organic agriculture delivers just 5 percent less yield in rain-watered legume crops, such as alfalfa or beans, and in perennial crops, such as fruit trees. But when it comes to major cereal crops, such as corn or wheat, and vegetables, such as broccoli, conventional methods delivered more than 25 percent more yield.

The key limit to further yield increases via organic methods appears 5 to be nitrogen—large doses of synthetic fertilizer can keep up with high demand from crops during the growing season better than the slow release from compost, manure, or nitrogen-fixing cover crops. Of course, the cost of using 171 million metric tons of synthetic nitrogen fertilizer is paid in dead zones at the mouths of many of the world's rivers. These anoxic zones result from nitrogen-rich runoff promoting algal blooms that then die and, in decomposing, suck all the oxygen out of surrounding waters. "To address the problem of [nitrogen] limitation and to produce high yields, organic farmers should use best management practices, supply more organic fertilizers, or grow legumes or perennial crops," Seufert says.

In fact, more knowledge would be key to any effort to boost organic farming or its yields. Conventional farming requires knowledge of how to manage what farmers know as inputs—synthetic fertilizer, chemical pesticides, and the like—as well as fields laid out precisely via global-positioning systems. Organic farmers, on the other hand, must learn to manage an entire ecosystem geared to producing food—controlling pests through biological means, using the waste from animals to fertilize fields, and even growing one crop amidst another. "Organic farming is a very knowledge-intensive farming system," Seufert notes. An organic farmer "needs to create a fertile soil that provides sufficient nutrients at the right time when the crops need them. The same is true for pest management."

But the end result is a healthier soil, which may prove vital in efforts to make it more resilient in the face of climate change as well as conserve it. Organic soils, for example, retain water better than those farms that employ conventional methods. "You use a lot more water [in irrigation] because the soil doesn't have the capacity to retain the water you use," noted farmer Fred Kirschenmann, president of Stone Barns Center for Food and Agriculture at the "Feeding the World While the Earth Cooks" event at the New America Foundation in Washington, D.C., on April 12, [2012].

At the same time, a still-growing human population requires more food, which has led some to propose further intensifying conventional methods of applying fertilizer and pesticides to specially bred crops, enabling either a second Green Revolution or improved yields from farmlands currently under cultivation. Crops genetically modified to endure drought may also play a role as well as efforts to develop perennial versions of annual staple crops, such as wheat, which could help reduce environmental impacts and improve soil. "Increasing salt, drought, or heat tolerance of our existing crops can move them a little but not a lot," said biologist Nina Fedoroff of Pennsylvania State University at the New America event. "That won't be enough."

And breeding new perennial versions of staple crops would require compressing millennia of crop improvements that resulted in the high-yielding wheat varieties of today, such as the dwarf wheat created by breeder Norman Borlaug and his colleagues in the 1950s, into a span of years while changing the fundamental character of wheat from an annual crop to a perennial one. Then there is the profit motive. "The private sector is not likely to embrace an idea like perennial crop seeds, which do not require the continued purchase of seeds and thus do not provide a very good source of profit," Seufert notes.

> "The world already produces 22 trillion calories annually via agriculture, enough to provide more than 3,000 calories to every person on the planet. The food problem is one of distribution and waste."

Regardless, the world already produces 22 trillion calories annually via agriculture, enough to provide more than 3,000 calories to every person on the planet. The food problem is one of distribution and waste—whether the latter is food spoilage during harvest, in storage, or even after purchase. According to the Grocery Manufacturers Association, in the U.S. alone, 215 meals per person go to waste annually.

"Since the world already produces more than enough food to feed everyone well, there are other important considerations" besides yield, argues ecologist Catherine Badgley of the University of Michigan, who also compared yields from organic and conventional methods in a 2006 study that found similar results. Those range from environmental impacts of various practices to the number of people employed in farming. As it stands, conventional agriculture relies on cheap energy, cheap labor, and other unsustainable practices. "Anyone who thinks we will be using Roundup [a herbicide] in eight [thousand] to 10,000 years is foolish," argued organic evangelist Jeff Moyer, farm director of the Rodale Institute, at the New America Foundation event.

But there is unlikely to be a simple solution. Instead the best farming practices will vary from crop to crop and place to place. Building healthier soils, however, will be key everywhere. "Current conventional agriculture is one of the major threats to the environment and degrades the very natural resources it depends on. We thus need to change the way we produce our food," Seufert argues. "Given the current precarious situation of agriculture, we should assess many alternative management systems, including conventional, organic, other agro-ecological, and possibly hybrid systems to identify the best options to improve the way we produce our food."

Understanding the Text

1. What are some of the negative impacts of conventional farming methods that Biello names?

2. What did environment scientists at McGill University and the University of Minnesota find in their comparison study of conventional and organic farming methods?

Reflection and Response

3. What makes organic farming a "very knowledge-intensive" system? What are the benefits of this? What are its drawbacks?

4. What kind of hybrid approach to food production is suggested by Biello? What evidence does he present to support his argument in favor of this approach?

Making Connections

5. Biello and Margaret Mead ("The Changing Significance of Food," p. 138) both argue that we produce enough food to feed the world, but we fail to do so. Compare the evidence they each present and the solutions they recommend. Taken together, what do they suggest about the future of food?

6. Both Biello and Paul Greenberg ("Heartland," p. 256) discuss the effects of nitrogen fertilizer. Greenberg introduces us to Brian Hicks, a Minnesotan farmer who uses a variety of techniques to reduce fertilizer pollution. What would Biello think of Brian Hicks' techniques? Would he think they're the type of hybrid approach he's advocating? What else might Biello suggest Hicks attempt on his farm?

7. What concrete ways does Biello suggest we use to fight global hunger problems? Which authors in this collection would applaud his approach? Which would critique it? Where do you stand? Which positions do you find more compelling? Why? Use textual evidence to support your response.

Attention Whole Foods Shoppers

Robert Paarlberg

Robert Paarlberg is a professor emeritus of political science at Wellesley College and an adjunct professor of public policy at the John F. Kennedy School of Government at Harvard University, as well as an associate at Harvard's Weatherhead Center for International Affairs. He conducts research on public policy, with a specific interest in international food and agriculture policy. His research examines national policy responses to obesity and climate change, and he is particularly interested in the relationship between the failure of democratic governments to take action on such issues in the face of modern views of personal freedom and material abundance. He is the author of many scholarly articles and books, including *Food Politics: What Everyone Needs to Know* (2010). In this essay published in *Foreign Policy* in 2010, he draws connections between personal ideals about food and larger global realities of world hunger. He argues that we should prioritize finding effective ways to address world hunger over ideals that emphasize eating "organic, local, and slow" food.

From Whole Foods recyclable cloth bags to Michelle Obama's organic White House garden, modern eco-foodies are full of good intentions. We want to save the planet. Help local farmers. Fight climate change—and childhood obesity, too. But though it's certainly a good thing to be thinking about global welfare while chopping our certified organic onions, the hope that we can help others by changing our shopping and eating habits is being wildly oversold to Western consumers. Food has become an elite preoccupation in the West, ironically, just as the most effective ways to address hunger in poor countries have fallen out of fashion.

Helping the world's poor feed themselves is no longer the rallying cry it once was. Food may be today's cause célèbre, but in the pampered West, that means trendy causes like making food "sustainable"—in other words, organic, local, and slow. Appealing as that might sound, it is the wrong recipe for helping those who need it the most. Even our understanding of the global food problem is wrong these days, driven too much by the single issue of international prices. In April 2008, when the cost of rice for export had tripled in just six months and wheat reached its highest price in 28 years, a *New York Times* editorial branded this a "World Food Crisis." World Bank president Robert Zoellick warned that high food prices would be particularly damaging in poor countries, where "there is no margin for survival." Now that international rice prices are down 40 percent from their peak and wheat prices have fallen by more than half, we too quickly conclude that the crisis is over. Yet 850 million people in poor countries were chronically undernourished before the 2008 price spike, and the number is even larger now, thanks in part to last year's global recession. This is the real food crisis we face.

It turns out that food prices on the world market tell us very little about global hunger. International markets for food, like most other international markets, are used most heavily by the well-to-do, who are far from hungry. The majority of truly undernourished people—62 percent, according to the U.N. Food and Agriculture Organization—live in either Africa or South Asia, and most are small farmers or rural landless laborers living in the countryside of Africa and South Asia. They are significantly shielded from global price fluctuations both by the trade policies of their own governments and by poor roads and infrastructure. In Africa, more than 70 percent of rural households are cut off from the closest urban markets because, for instance, they live more than a 30-minute walk from the nearest all-weather road.

> "If we are going to get serious about solving global hunger, we need to de-romanticize our view of preindustrial food and farming."

Poverty—caused by the low income productivity of farmers' labor—is the primary source of hunger in Africa, and the problem is only getting worse. The number of "food insecure" people in Africa (those consuming less than 2,100 calories a day) will increase 30 percent over the next decade without significant reforms, to 645 million, the U.S. Agriculture Department projects.

What's so tragic about this is that we know from experience how to 5 fix the problem. Wherever the rural poor have gained access to improved roads, modern seeds, less expensive fertilizer, electrical power, and better schools and clinics, their productivity and their income have increased. But recent efforts to deliver such essentials have been undercut by deeply misguided (if sometimes well-meaning) advocacy against agricultural modernization and foreign aid.

In Europe and the United States, a new line of thinking has emerged in elite circles that opposes bringing improved seeds and fertilizers to traditional farmers and opposes linking those farmers more closely to international markets. Influential food writers, advocates, and celebrity restaurant owners are repeating the mantra that "sustainable food" in the future must be organic, local, and slow. But guess what: Rural Africa already has such a system, and it doesn't work. Few smallholder farmers in Africa use any synthetic chemicals, so their food is de facto organic. High transportation costs force them to purchase and sell almost all of their food locally. And food preparation is painfully slow. The result is nothing to celebrate: average income levels of only $1 a day and a one-in-three chance of being malnourished.

If we are going to get serious about solving global hunger, we need to de-romanticize our view of preindustrial food and farming. And that means learning to appreciate the modern, science-intensive, and highly capitalized agricultural system we've developed in the West. Without it, our food would be more expensive and less safe. In other words, a lot like the hunger-plagued rest of the world.

Original Sins

Thirty years ago, had someone asserted in a prominent journal or newspaper that the Green Revolution was a failure, he or she would have been quickly dismissed. Today the charge is surprisingly common. Celebrity author and eco-activist Vandana Shiva claims the Green Revolution has brought nothing to India except "indebted and discontented farmers." A 2002 meeting in Rome of 500 prominent international NGOs, including Friends of the Earth and Greenpeace, even blamed the Green Revolution for the rise in world hunger. Let's set the record straight.

The development and introduction of high-yielding wheat and rice seeds into poor countries, led by American scientist Norman Borlaug and others in the 1960s and 1970s, paid huge dividends. In Asia these new seeds lifted tens of millions of small farmers out of desperate poverty and finally ended the threat of periodic famine. India, for instance, doubled its wheat production between 1964 and 1970 and was able to terminate all dependence on international food aid by 1975. As for indebted and discontented farmers, India's rural poverty rate fell from 60 percent to just 27 percent today. Dismissing these great achievements as a "myth" (the official view of Food First, a California-based organization that campaigns globally against agricultural modernization) is just silly.

It's true that the story of the Green Revolution is not everywhere a   10 happy one. When powerful new farming technologies are introduced into deeply unjust rural social systems, the poor tend to lose out. In Latin America, where access to good agricultural land and credit has been narrowly controlled by traditional elites, the improved seeds made available by the Green Revolution *increased* income gaps. Absentee landlords in Central America, who previously allowed peasants to plant subsistence crops on underutilized land, pushed them off to sell or rent the land to commercial growers who could turn a profit using the new seeds. Many of the displaced rural poor became slum dwellers. Yet even in Latin America, the prevalence of hunger declined more than 50 percent between 1980 and 2005.

In Asia, the Green Revolution seeds performed just as well on small nonmechanized farms as on larger farms. Wherever small farmers had sufficient access to credit, they took up the new technology just as quickly as big farmers, which led to dramatic income gains and no increase in inequality or social friction. Even poor landless laborers gained, because more abundant crops meant more work at harvest time, increasing rural wages. In Asia, the Green Revolution was good for both agriculture and social justice.

And Africa? Africa has a relatively equitable and secure distribution of land, making it more like Asia than Latin America and increasing the chances that improvements in farm technology will help the poor. If Africa were to put greater resources into farm technology, irrigation, and rural roads, small farmers would benefit.

Organic Myths

There are other common objections to doing what is necessary to solve the real hunger crisis. Most revolve around caveats° that purist critics raise regarding food systems in the United States and western Europe. Yet such concerns, though well-intentioned, are often misinformed and counterproductive—especially when applied to the developing world.

Take industrial food systems, the current bugaboo of American food writers. Yes, they have many unappealing aspects, but without them food would be not only less abundant but also less safe. Traditional food systems lacking in reliable refrigeration and sanitary packaging are dangerous vectors for diseases. Surveys over the past several decades by the Centers for Disease Control and Prevention have found that the U.S. food supply became steadily safer over time, thanks in part to the introduction of industrial-scale technical improvements. Since 2000, the incidence of *E. coli* contamination in beef has fallen 45 percent. Today in the United States, most hospitalizations and fatalities from unsafe food come not from sales of contaminated products at supermarkets, but from the mishandling or improper preparation of food inside the home. Illness outbreaks from contaminated foods sold in stores still occur, but the fatalities are typically quite limited. A nationwide scare over unsafe spinach in 2006 triggered the virtual suspension of all fresh and bagged spinach sales, but only three known deaths were recorded. Incidents such as these command attention in part because they are now so rare. Food Inc. should be criticized for filling our plates with too many foods that are unhealthy, but not foods that are unsafe.

caveat: warning, caution.

Where industrial-scale food technologies have not yet reached into the developing world, contaminated food remains a major risk. In Africa, where many foods are still purchased in open-air markets (often uninspected, unpackaged, unlabeled, unrefrigerated, unpasteurized, and unwashed), an estimated 700,000 people die every year from food- and water-borne diseases, compared with an estimated 5,000 in the United States.

Food grown organically — that is, without any synthetic nitro- gen fertilizers or pesticides — is not an answer to the health and safety issues. The *American Journal of Clinical Nutrition* last year published a study of 162 scientific papers from the past 50 years on the health benefits of organically grown foods and found no nutritional advantage over conventionally grown foods. According to the Mayo Clinic, "No conclusive evidence shows that organic food is more nutritious than is conventionally grown food."

Health professionals also reject the claim that organic food is safer to eat due to lower pesticide residues. Food and Drug Administration sur- veys have revealed that the highest dietary exposures to pesticide residues on foods in the United States are so trivial (less than one one-thousandth of a level that would cause toxicity) that the safety gains from buying organic are insignificant. Pesticide exposures remain a serious problem in the developing world, where farm chemical use is not as well regu- lated, yet even there they are more an occupational risk for unprotected farmworkers than a residue risk for food consumers.

When it comes to protecting the environment, assessments of organic farming become more complex. Excess nitrogen fertilizer use on conven- tional farms in the United States has polluted rivers and created a "dead zone" in the Gulf of Mexico, but halting synthetic nitrogen fertilizer use entirely (as farmers must do in the United States to get organic certifi- cation from the Agriculture Department) would cause environmental problems far worse.

Here's why: Less than 1 percent of American cropland is under certi- fied organic production. If the other 99 percent were to switch to organic and had to fertilize crops without any synthetic nitrogen fertilizer, that would require a lot more composted animal manure. To supply enough organic fertilizer, the U.S. cattle population would have to increase roughly fivefold. And because those animals would have to be raised organically on forage crops, much of the land in the lower 48 states would need to be converted to pasture. Organic field crops also have lower yields per hectare. If Europe tried to feed itself organically, it would need an addi- tional 28 million hectares of cropland, equal to all of the remaining forest cover in France, Germany, Britain, and Denmark combined.

Mass deforestation probably isn't what organic advocates intend. 20 The smart way to protect against nitrogen runoff is to reduce synthetic fertilizer applications with taxes, regulations, and cuts in farm subsidies, but not try to go all the way to zero as required by the official organic standard. Scaling up registered organic farming would be on balance harmful, not helpful, to the natural environment.

Not only is organic farming less friendly to the environment than assumed, but modern conventional farming is becoming significantly more sustainable. High-tech farming in rich countries today is far safer for the environment, per bushel of production, than it was in the 1960s, when Rachel Carson criticized the indiscriminate farm use of DDT in her environmental classic *Silent Spring*. Thanks in part to Carson's devastating critique, that era's most damaging insecticides were banned and replaced by chemicals that could be applied in lower volume and were less persistent in the environment. Chemical use in American agriculture peaked soon thereafter, in 1973. This was a major victory for environmental advocacy.

And it was just the beginning of what has continued as a significant greening of modern farming in the United States. Soil erosion on farms dropped sharply in the 1970s with the introduction of "no-till" seed planting, an innovation that also reduced dependence on diesel fuel because fields no longer had to be plowed every spring. Farmers then began conserving water by moving to drip irrigation and by leveling their fields with lasers to minimize wasteful runoff. In the 1990s, GPS equipment was added to tractors, autosteering the machines in straighter paths and telling farmers exactly where they were in the field to within one square meter, allowing precise adjustments in chemical use. Infrared sensors were brought in to detect the greenness of the crop, telling a farmer exactly how much more (or less) nitrogen might be needed as the growing season went forward. To reduce wasteful nitrogen use, equipment was developed that can insert fertilizers into the ground at exactly the depth needed and in perfect rows, only where it will be taken up by the plant roots.

These "precision farming" techniques have significantly reduced the environmental footprint of modern agriculture relative to the quantity of food being produced. In 2008, the Organization for Economic Cooperation and Development published a review of the "environmental performance of agriculture" in the world's 30 most advanced industrial countries—those with the most highly capitalized and science-intensive farming systems. The results showed that between 1990 and 2004, food production in these countries continued to increase (by 5 percent in volume), yet adverse environmental impacts were reduced in every category. The land area taken up by farming declined 4 percent, soil erosion from both wind and water fell, gross greenhouse gas emissions from farming declined 3 percent, and excessive nitrogen fertilizer use fell 17 percent. Biodiversity also improved, as increased numbers of crop varieties and livestock breeds came into use.

Seeding the Future

Africa faces a food crisis, but it's not because the continent's population is growing faster than its potential to produce food, as vintage Malthusians such as environmental advocate Lester Brown and advocacy organizations such as Population Action International would have it. Food production in Africa is vastly less than the region's known potential, and that is why so many millions are going hungry there. African farmers still use almost no fertilizer; only 4 percent of cropland has been improved with irrigation; and most of the continent's cropped area is not planted with seeds improved through scientific plant breeding, so cereal yields are only a fraction of what they could be. Africa is failing to keep up with population growth not because it has exhausted its potential, but instead because too little has been invested in reaching that potential.

One reason for this failure has been sharply diminished assistance   25
from international donors. When agricultural modernization went out of fashion among elites in the developed world beginning in the 1980s, development assistance to farming in poor countries collapsed. Per capita food production in Africa was declining during the 1980s and 1990s and the number of hungry people on the continent was doubling, but the U.S. response was to withdraw development assistance and simply ship more food aid to Africa. Food aid doesn't help farmers become more productive—and it can create long-term dependency. But in recent years, the dollar value of U.S. food aid to Africa has reached 20 times the dollar value of agricultural development assistance.

The alternative is right in front of us. Foreign assistance to support agricultural improvements has a strong record of success, when undertaken with purpose. In the 1960s, international assistance from the Rockefeller Foundation, the Ford Foundation, and donor governments led by the United States made Asia's original Green Revolution possible. U.S. assistance to India provided critical help in improving agricultural education, launching a successful agricultural extension service, and funding advanced degrees for Indian agricultural specialists at universities in the United States. The U.S. Agency for International Development, with the World Bank, helped finance fertilizer plants and infrastructure projects, including rural roads and irrigation. India could not have done this on its own—the country was on the brink of famine at the time and dangerously dependent on food aid. But instead of suffering a famine in 1975, as some naysayers had predicted, India that year celebrated a final and permanent end to its need for food aid.

Foreign assistance to farming has been a high-payoff investment every-where, including Africa. The World Bank has documented average rates of return on investments in agricultural research in Africa of 35 percent a year, accompanied by significant reductions in poverty. Some research investments in African agriculture have brought rates of return estimated at 68 percent. Blind to these realities, the United States cut its assistance to agricultural research in Africa 77 percent between 1980 and 2006.

When it comes to Africa's growing hunger, governments in rich coun-tries face a stark choice: They can decide to support a steady new infusion of financial and technical assistance to help local governments and farm-ers become more productive, or they can take a "worry later" approach and be forced to address hunger problems with increasingly expensive shipments of food aid. Development skeptics and farm modernization critics keep pushing us toward this unappealing second path. It's time for leaders with vision and political courage to push back.

Understanding the Text

1. What is a crisis of values?
2. What do global food prices reveal about food availability and food production?
3. What is food security?

Reflection and Response

4. What does Paarlberg suggest about the future of the politics of food? What are at least two ways to respond to his position? What do you think is the best way? Explain your response.
5. Why do you think Paarlberg titles his essay "Attention Whole Foods Shoppers"? Why does Paarlberg single out this particular demographic? How does he characterize them? What do people who shop at Whole Foods represent for him?

Making Connections

6. Paarlberg critiques outright dismissals of the Green Revolution. What's at stake in this debate? And for whom? Find two credible online sources that argue in support of the Green Revolution, and two that argue against it. Compare their positions to Paarlberg's, and describe the differences in their fundamental assumptions.

7. Paarlberg criticizes organic food advocates, arguing that they romanticize preindustrial food and farming. How might he critique the ways that Wendell Berry ("The Pleasures of Eating," p. 46), Michael Pollan ("Eat Food: Food Defined," p. 10), and Barbara Kingsolver ("You Can't Run Away on Harvest Day," p. 150) talk about food? Would he argue that they are romanticizing food and farming? If so, in what ways? Explain your response with evidence from the texts.

8. Margaret Mead ("The Changing Significance of Food," p. 138), Jonathan Foley ("Can We Feed the World and Sustain the Planet?," p. 212), and Paarlberg all say they want to reduce world hunger. What values and ideas for doing so do they share? Where do they diverge? Whose approach to solving world hunger seems more realistic? Whose approach seems more ethical? Whose approach do you think has the potential to actually succeed? What role should moral considerations play in the solution?

We Need Better Answers on Nutrition

Joon Yun, David Kessler, and Dan Glickman

Joon Yun is a medical doctor specializing in radiology, the president and managing partner of a health-care hedge fund, and a trustee of the Salk Institute. He has written many scientific articles and has worked as a faculty member at Stanford University. David Kessler is a pediatrician, lawyer, and author. He studied medicine at Harvard University and law at the University of Chicago. Kessler has worked in politics and served as the Commissioner of the Food and Drug Administration under Presidents George H. W. Bush and Bill Clinton. Dan Glickman is a lawyer, politician, and nonprofit leader who served as the U.S. Secretary of Agriculture under President Bill Clinton. Prior to his position as secretary, he represented Kansas in Congress for 18 years. More recently, he has served as the vice president of the Aspen Institute, a nonpartisan public policy education and civility building program for members of Congress. Glickman has also served as the chairman of the Motion Picture Association of America, Inc. Together, these three leaders have worked to improve the health of the nation through their leadership in government, academia, and philanthropy. In this essay, they argue in favor of the creation of a National Institute of Nutrition that would encourage and support research on the science of nutrition.

Poor nutrition is a leading cause of poor health and spiraling health care spending. Research from the Tufts Friedman School suggests that poor eating causes nearly 1,000 deaths *each day* in the United States from heart disease, stroke or diabetes. In 2016, the direct and indirect costs of chronic diseases as a result of obesity were $1.72 trillion — almost 10 percent of the nation's gross domestic product.

Poor eating also contributes to disparities in well-being, especially among children: a vicious cycle of bad health, lost productivity, increased health costs and poverty. Poor nutrition and obesity are also a major threat to military readiness. A recent report from Mission: Readiness, a group of more than 700 retired admirals and generals, noted that obesity is the leading medical disqualifier that prevents otherwise qualified Americans from joining the military.

Yet many of the most fundamental questions about foods and health — especially their impact on the economy and the military — remain

"Yet many of the most fundamental questions about foods and health — especially their impact on the economy and the military — remain unanswered."

unanswered. There is also tremendous confusion about what constitutes a healthy diet. Despite the urgency of these questions, the sum of research funding for nutritional research across all federal agencies — like the agriculture department, Health and Human Services and Department Defense — is only about $1.5 billion annually. To put this into perspective, national spending on candy purchases is about $40 billion per year.

That is why our country needs an institute devoted to research on the top cause of poor health. We would call it the National Institute of Nutrition, and it would be part of the National Institutes of Health.

The institute will facilitate and help coordinate incisive research into 5 nutrients, foods and their relationships to better health. Some examples of its focus would include:

- How to leverage food and nutrition policy and public-private partnerships in a "food is medicine" effort to reduce health care costs.

- Optimal nutrition for military readiness.

- Optimal nutrition for treatment of battlefield consequences, including bodily injuries, brain injuries and post-traumatic stress.

- Relationships between the gut microbiome and health.

- Personalized nutrition based on life stage, metabolism, health state, health goals and genetics.

- Health and metabolic effects of major food groups for which effects remain unclear or controversial, such as cheese, yogurt, whole-fat milk, unprocessed red meat, coconut oil, fermented foods, organic foods and more.

- Optimal diets for weight loss and weight maintenance.

- Optimal diets to prevent and treat Type 2 diabetes and pre-diabetes.

- Optimal diets for cancer, both to reduce side effects of chemotherapy and radiation and also to directly target the cancer.

- Health effect of trace bioactives and phenolics, like those in extra-virgin olive oil, cocoa, green tea, coffee, red wine, blueberries and more.

- Effective behavior change and systems approaches for healthier eating.

- Effective approaches to reduce dietary and health disparities.

- Effects of foods on brain and mental health, from the developing brain in infants and children to protecting against memory loss, dementia and depression later in life.

- Effects of foods on allergies and autoimmune and inflammatory diseases.

- Coordinated new science for translation into national dietary guidelines and policies, such as the Dietary Guidelines for Americans.

Discoveries in these areas will help bring down health care costs and recover productivity loss as a result of diet-related diseases like obesity, diabetes, heart disease, many cancers and more.

They will also benefit our military readiness, including treatment of injuries. A new nutrition institute will not include regulatory or enforcement functions. Those will remain at the Food and Drug Administration and Department of Agriculture. As the convening body for research in the country, the National Institute of Nutrition would encourage the participation of a large group of stakeholders providing important input into the science of nutrition.

There are numerous precedents for creating a nutrition research institute at the N.I.H., which was created by an act of Congress in 1930. Several new institutes have been added there in the years since: For example, in 1937, Congress passed legislation to add a new National Cancer Institute. Ideally, Congress would draft and pass a bill to create and fund a nutrition institute.

Although their existence and benefits today are obvious in retrospect, we did not always have—and thus needed to create—institutions such as the Institutes of Health and F.D.A. But their contributions have far surpassed our imagination. The N.I.H.'s original founding vision was to detect cholera and yellow fever. Yet, it began to help train young physicians and now supports cutting-edge research that helps treat and cure many types of diseases. Similarly, the F.D.A.'s founding vision was to regulate contaminated foods; now it helps bring safe and effective drugs to market. None of these mandates or benefits were foreseeable at their founding, and the same is true for founding a nutrition institute today.

Establishing a place to research nutrition is also crucial to retain 10 American competitiveness. The governments of China, India and Japan fund similar institutions.

Improving the nation's health through better nutrition will pay large and direct economic dividends. An independent analysis concluded that

A promotional poster from the Works Progress
Administration (1935–1943) encouraging
Americans to eat well.

John Parrot/Stocktrek Images/Getty Images

every $1 spent on research by the N.I.H. has led to $3.20 in economic
gains, a return-on-investment of more than 200 percent.

Given the role of diet in health and well-being, the current challenges
to our military readiness and the spending of one in four federal dollars
and one in five dollars in our economy on health care, the right question to ask ourselves is, can we afford not having a National Institute of
Nutrition.

Understanding the Text

1. List the various costs of poor eating habits.
2. Why do we need to fund more and better nutritional research?
3. What are the potential financial advantages of a nutritional research institute?
4. What would be the positive effects of the proposed National Institute of
   Nutrition?

Reflection and Response

5. Why do you think that there is so much confusion about what constitutes healthy eating? What do you think would help lessen the confusion?

6. Which of the areas of focus for research proposed by Yun, Kessler, and Glickman seem the most important to you? Why?

7. Review the biographies of the three authors of this piece. Why is it significant that they are proposing this together?

Making Connections

8. Yun, Kessler, and Glickman are partially motivated by their belief that we need more research in the science of nutrition. Consider this claim in relation to the research described by Dhruv Khullar ("Why Shame Won't Stop Obesity," p. 71), Joe Pinsker ("Why So Many Rich Kids Come to Enjoy the Taste of Healthier Foods," p. 97), and Marion Nestle ("Eating Made Simple," p. 36). Then weigh in and argue for or against more research on nutrition. Whatever you argue, be sure to consider potential counterarguments to your position.

9. Yun, Kessler, and Glickman argue that poor nutrition and health problems related to poor eating habits are contributing to challenges to U.S. military readiness. Research this issue online. Develop a visual and written presentation to inform your local community about this problem.

Hardship on Mexico's Farms, a Bounty for U.S. Tables

Richard Marosi

Best known for his investigative reporting on the U.S.-Mexico border, Richard Marosi is a *Los Angeles Times* staff writer and a two-time Pulitzer Prize finalist. Marosi grew up in the San Francisco Bay Area but has lived for many years in Southern California, where he has written articles about a range of issues affecting the border region — ones that address the economy, immigration, the drug wars, agriculture, and national security. The following excerpt is part of his "Product of Mexico" series in the *LA Times*, for which he and photojournalist Don Bartletti traveled through nine Mexican states to observe working conditions and interview workers on farms that are some of the biggest suppliers of produce for the United States. In it, he carefully chronicles the lives of farm laborers, writing in a way that he hopes will make their plight real and important to his readers.

The tomatoes, peppers and cucumbers arrive year-round by the ton, with peel-off stickers proclaiming "Product of Mexico." Farm exports to the U.S. from Mexico have tripled to $7.6 billion in the last decade, enriching agribusinesses, distributors and retailers. American consumers get all the salsa, squash and melons they can eat at affordable prices. And top U.S. brands—Wal-Mart, Whole Foods, Subway and Safeway, among many others—profit from produce they have come to depend on. These corporations say their Mexican suppliers have committed to decent treatment and living conditions for workers. But a *Los Angeles Times* investigation found that for thousands of farm laborers south of the border, the export boom is a story of exploitation and extreme hardship.

The Times found:

- Many farm laborers are essentially trapped for months at a time in rat-infested camps, often without beds and sometimes without functioning toilets or a reliable water supply.

- Some camp bosses illegally withhold wages to prevent workers from leaving during peak harvest periods.

- Laborers often go deep in debt paying inflated prices for necessities at company stores. Some are reduced to scavenging for food when their credit is cut off. It's common for laborers to head home penniless at the end of a harvest.

- Those who seek to escape their debts and miserable living conditions have to contend with guards, barbed-wire fences and sometimes threats of violence from camp supervisors.

- Major U.S. companies have done little to enforce social responsibility guidelines that call for basic worker protections such as clean housing and fair pay practices.

The farm laborers are mostly indigenous° people from Mexico's poorest regions. Bused hundreds of miles to vast agricultural complexes, they work six days a week for the equivalent of $8 to $12 a day. The squalid° camps where they live, sometimes sleeping on scraps of cardboard on concrete floors, are operated by the same agribusinesses that employ advanced growing techniques and sanitary measures in their fields and greenhouses. The contrast between the treatment of produce and of people is stark. In immaculate greenhouses, laborers are ordered to use hand sanitizers and schooled in how to pamper the produce. They're required to keep their fingernails carefully trimmed so the fruit will arrive unblemished in U.S. supermarkets. "They want us to take such great care of the tomatoes, but they don't take care of us," said Japolina Jaimez, a field hand at Rene Produce, a grower of tomatoes, peppers and cucumbers in the northwestern state of Sinaloa. "Look at how we live." He pointed to co-workers and their children, bathing in an irrigation canal because the camp's showers had no water that day.

At the mega-farms that supply major American retailers, child labor has been largely eradicated. But on many small and mid-sized farms, children still work the fields, picking chiles, tomatillos and other produce, some of which makes its way to the U.S. through middlemen. About 100,000 children younger than 14 pick crops for pay, according to the Mexican government's most recent estimate. During The Times' 18-month investigation, a reporter and a photographer traveled across nine Mexican states, observing conditions at farm labor camps and interviewing hundreds of workers. At half the 30 camps they visited, laborers were in effect prevented from leaving because their wages were being withheld or they owed money to the company store, or both. Some of the worst camps were linked to companies that have been lauded by government and industry groups. Mexico's President Enrique Peña Nieto presented at least two of them with "exporter of the year" honors. The Times traced produce from fields to U.S. supermarket shelves using Mexican

---

indigenous: native, originally occurring in a particular place.
squalid: extremely foul, unpleasant, neglected, and dirty.

government export data, food safety reports from independent auditors, California pesticide surveys that identify the origin of imported produce, and numerous interviews with company officials and industry experts.

The practice of withholding wages, although barred by Mexican law, 5 persists, especially for workers recruited from indigenous areas, according to government officials and a 2010 report by the federal Secretariat of Social Development. These laborers typically work under three-month contracts and are not paid until the end. The law says they must be paid weekly. The Times visited five big export farms where wages were being withheld. Each employed hundreds of workers. Wal-Mart, the world's largest retailer, bought produce directly or through middlemen from at least three of those farms, The Times found. Bosses at one of Mexico's biggest growers, Bioparques de Occidente in the state of Jalisco, not only withheld wages but kept hundreds of workers in a labor camp against their will and beat some who tried to escape, according to laborers and Mexican authorities. Asked about its ties to Bioparques and other farms where workers were exploited, Wal-Mart released this statement:

We care about the men and women in our supply chain, and recognize that challenges remain in this industry. We know the world is a big place. While our standards and audits make things better around the world, we won't catch every instance when people do things that are wrong.

At Rene Produce in Sinaloa, The Times saw hungry laborers hunting for scraps because they could not afford to buy food at the company store. The grower, which exported $55 million in tomatoes in 2014, supplies supermarkets across the U.S., including Whole Foods, which recently took out full-page newspaper ads promoting its commitment to social responsibility. Asked for comment, Whole Foods said it did not expect to buy any more produce "directly" from Rene, which it described as a minor supplier. "We take the findings you shared VERY seriously, especially since Rene has signed our social accountability agreement," Edmund LaMacchia, a global vice president of procurement for Whole Foods, said in a statement. Rene Produce was named one of Mexico's exporters of the year in September. Jose Humberto Garcia, the company's chief operating officer, said Rene had consulted with outside experts about ways to enhance worker welfare. "We have tried in recent years to improve the lives of our workers," he said. "There's still room for improvement. There's always room for improvement."

Executives at Triple H in Sinaloa, another exporter of the year and a distributor for major supermarkets across the U.S., said they were surprised to hear about abusive labor practices at farms including one of their suppliers, Agricola San Emilio. "It completely violates our principles," said Heriberto Vlaminck, Triple H's general director. His son Heriberto Vlaminck Jr., the company's commercial director, added: "I find it incredible that people work under these conditions."

In northern Mexico, agro-industrial complexes stretch for miles across coastal plains and inland valleys, their white rows of tent-like hothouses so vast they can be seen from space. Half the tomatoes consumed in the U.S. come from Mexico, mostly from the area around Culiacan, the capital of Sinaloa. Many farms use growing techniques from Europe. Walls of tomato vines grow 10 feet tall and are picked by laborers on stilts. Agricola San Emilio raises crops on 370 acres of open fields and green-houses 20 miles west of Culiacan. In a tin-roofed packinghouse, tomatoes, bell peppers and cucumbers are boxed for the journey north to distributors for Wal-Mart, Olive Garden, Safeway, Subway and other retailers.

In 2014, the company exported more than 80 million pounds of tomatoes alone, according to government data. Every winter, 1,000 workers arrive at San Emilio by bus with backpacks and blankets, hoping to make enough money to support family members back home. Some simply want to stay fed. Behind the packing facility lies the company's main labor camp, a cluster of low-slung buildings made of cinder block or corrugated metal where about 500 laborers live. The shed-like structures are crudely partitioned into tiny rooms that house four to six people each. The floors are concrete. There are no beds or other furniture, nor any windows. The workers' day begins at 3 a.m. when a freight train known as "The Beast" rumbles past the dusty camp, rousting the inhabitants. They get coffee, a biscuit and a short stack of tortillas before heading to the fields.

When Times journalists visited the camp in March, Juan Ramirez, a 10 22-year-old with a toddler back home in Veracruz, had been working at San Emilio for six weeks and had yet to be paid. He and other laborers spent their days picking, packing and pruning, or scouring the plants for weevils. They lined up for their daily meals: a bowl of lentil soup for lunch, a bowl of lentil soup for dinner. Ramirez, wearing a stained white T-shirt, chatted with two young men who were recent arrivals. They complained of hunger and constant headaches. Ramirez knew the feeling. He had lost 20 pounds since starting work at the farm. "We arrive here fat, and leave skinny," he said.

Ramirez and several hundred others recruited by the same labor contractor earned $8 a day and were owed as much as $300 each. They said they wouldn't be paid until the end of their three-month contracts. That would be in six more weeks. Workers said they had been promised $8 in pocket money every two weeks but received it only sporadically.° If they left now, they would forfeit the wages they'd earned. The barbed-wire fence that ringed the camp was an added deterrent.° Farm owners say the barriers are meant to keep out thieves and drug dealers. They also serve another purpose: to discourage laborers from leaving before the crop has been picked and they've paid their debts to the company store.

Even if the workers at San Emilio jumped the fence, as some had, they wouldn't be able to afford a ride to Culiacan, let alone $100 for the bus ticket home. Juan Hernandez, a father of five from Veracruz, was worried about his wife, who had been injured in an accident back home. "I want to go," he said. "But if I leave, I lose everything." Hernandez slept atop packing crates padded with cardboard. A suitcase served as his dinner table. In another building, Jacinto Santiago hung a scrap of cardboard in the open doorway of his room, which he shared with his son, daughter and son-in-law. Santiago said that in some ways, he had been better off back home in the central state of San Luis Potosi. There, he had a thatched-roof house with windows and a hen that laid eggs.

Santiago, like the other laborers, said he was promised that he would be able to send money home. His family was still waiting, because he hadn't been paid. "My family isn't the only one that suffers. Anyone who has a family at home suffers," he said. Efrain Hernandez, 18, said recruiters told him his earnings would be held back so he wouldn't get robbed: "They said it was for my own good." Outside one of the buildings, a group of men gathered under a dim light. It was nearing the 9 p.m. curfew, when the camp's heavy metal gate rolls shut and workers retreat to their rooms. Their voices echoed across the compound as they swapped stories about conditions in various camps. There are at least 200 across Mexico, 150 in Sinaloa alone. Pedro Hernandez, 51, complained that unlike some other camps, San Emilio didn't offer beds or blankets. Then again, there were fewer rats, he said. The conversation attracted a camp supervisor, who was surprised to see a reporter and photographer. "When the people from Wal-Mart come," she said, "they let us know in advance." She walked the journalists to the exit. The pickers went back to their rooms. The gate rolled shut.

The road to labor camps like San Emilio begins deep in the indigenous regions of central and southern Mexico, where advertising jingles play endlessly on the radio, echoing from storefront speakers.

"Attention. Attention. We are looking for 400 peasants to pick tomatoes."
"You'll earn 100 pesos per day, three free meals per day and overtime."
"Vamonos a trabajar!"—Let's go work!

sporadically: happening irregularly.
deterrent: discouragement, something that discourages people from doing something.

On a warm January morning this year, dozens of indigenous people 15
looking for work descended from mud-hut villages in the steep mountains of the Huasteca region. Nahuatl men wore holstered machetes.
Women cradled children in their arms. Young men shouldered backpacks
stuffed with the clothes they would wear for the next few months. The
laborers approached a knot of recruiters gathered outside a gas station
in the town of Huejutla de Reyes, about 130 miles north of Mexico City.
Among those offering jobs at distant farms was Luis Garcia, 37. Garcia,
a stocky Nahuatl Indian with silver-rimmed teeth, had risen from child
picker to field boss to labor contractor for Agricola San Emilio. He lived
just outside town, in a hilltop house behind tall gates, and was known
to locals as "Don Luis." "We all owe our livelihoods to the farmworkers,"
he said. "We have to treat them well, or the gringos don't get their tomatoes." Labor contractors are key players in the agricultural economy, the
link between export farms in the north and peasants in Huasteca and
other impoverished regions. An estimated 150,000 make the pilgrimage
every harvest season. The contractors, working for agribusinesses, transport laborers to and from the farms. Often, they also oversee the camps
and distribute workers' pay.

Many contractors abuse their power, according to indigenous leaders and federal inspectors. They lie about wages and living conditions at
the camps. Under pressure from growers, they sometimes refuse to bring
laborers home, even at the end of their contracts, if there are still vegetables to be picked. Earlier this year, 25 farmworkers walked 20 miles across
a Baja California desert after a contractor left them on the roadside, short
of their destination. At the gas station in Huejutla de Reyes, villagers
listened warily to the recruiters' pitches. One was said to be representing a contractor wanted on human trafficking charges. Another worked
for a contractor notorious for wage theft and other abuses. Garcia had
his own brush with controversy several years ago, when dozens of pickers accused him of holding them captive and abusing them at an onion
farm in Chihuahua. "They said I beat people. Lies, all lies," Garcia said,
bristling. "I wouldn't be here today talking to you if it was true, would I?"
He depicted himself as a reformer who wanted to establish a trade association to set standards and drive out unscrupulous contractors. But he saw
no need to do more for workers. "The more protected they are, the less
they work," he said. As he spoke, recruiters tried to outbid one another
for laborers, boosting their offers of spending money for the two-day bus
trip to Sinaloa.

Garcia won the day's competition. With his smooth baritone, he persuaded about 40 people to get on his bus. Garcia read their contract aloud
to the workers, including the provision that they wouldn't be paid until

the end of their three-month term. He later acknowledged that federal law requires weekly payments but said that there were other issues to consider. "Paying them every week is a problem because it causes lots of issues with drinking and drugging and violence," Garcia said. "Huasteca people are fighters when they're drunk." Proud of his success in a cut-throat business, Garcia portrayed himself as the product of a farm labor system in which the real bosses were U.S. companies. "The gringos are the ones that put up the money and make the rules," he said.

The U.S. companies linked to Agricola San Emilio through distributors have plenty of rules, but they serve mainly to protect American consumers, not Mexican field hands. Strict U.S. laws govern the safety and cleanliness of imported fruits and vegetables. To meet those standards, retailers and distributors send inspectors to Mexico to examine fields, greenhouses and packing plants. The companies say they are also committed to workers' well-being and cite their ethical sourcing guidelines. Retailers increasingly promote the idea that the food they sell not only is tasty and healthful but was produced without exploiting workers. But at many big corporations, enforcement of those standards is weak to nonexistent, and often relies on Mexican growers to monitor themselves, The Times found.

In some low-wage countries, U.S. retailers rely on independent auditors to verify that suppliers in apparel, footwear and other industries comply with social responsibility guidelines. For the most part, that has not happened with Mexican farm labor. American companies have not made oversight a priority because they haven't been pressured to do so. There is little public awareness of harsh conditions at labor camps. Many farms are in areas torn by drug violence, which has discouraged media coverage and visits by human rights groups and academic researchers. Asked to comment on conditions at Agricola San Emilio, Subway said in a statement: "We will use this opportunity to reinforce our Code of Conduct with our suppliers." The code says suppliers must ensure that workers "are fairly compensated and are not exploited in any way."

> "The U.S. companies linked to Agricola San Emilio through distributors have plenty of rules, but they serve mainly to protect American consumers, not Mexican field hands."

Safeway said: "We take any and all 20 claims regarding worker conditions seriously and are looking into each of the points you raise." In its vendor code of conduct, Safeway says that suppliers must offer a "safe and healthy work environment" and that it "will not tolerate any departure from its standards." Vendors are expected to "self-monitor their compliance," the code says.

Wal-Mart sought to distance itself from Agricola San Emilio, saying in a statement: "Our records show that we do not currently take from this facility." Asked if it had received produce from the farm in the past, Wal-Mart repeated its statement.

Executives at Agricola San Emilio and two firms that have distributed its produce — Triple H of Culiacan and Andrew & Williamson of San Diego — said Wal-Mart received shipments from the Mexican farm this year. John Farrington, chief operating officer at Andrew & Williamson, said that his company shipped San Emilio tomatoes to the retailer and that inspectors from Wal-Mart had been to the farm. Mari Cabanillas, an assistant camp supervisor at Agricola San Emilio, said Wal-Mart inspectors visited regularly, recommending cleanups and fresh coats of paint. "They try and improve conditions here," she said. "They're very strict."

As for Agricola San Emilio's pay practices, Daniel Beltran, the firm's director and legal counsel, said workers from the Huasteca region whose wages were withheld until the end of their three-month contracts had agreed to that arrangement. He said they could opt to be paid weekly, as others were. A dozen workers, however, said in interviews that they had no choice in how they were paid. Withholding workers' pay is illegal even if they agree to it, according to Mexico's federal labor law, a senior federal labor official and two labor lawyers. In regard to living conditions, Beltran said the company stopped providing beds because workers dismantled them for firewood. The laborers are from regions where it's common for people to sleep on the floor, he said.

He took issue with workers' claims that they were underfed. "Some people, even if you give them chicken or beef every day, they'll still want a different menu," he said, adding that workers could supplement company rations by purchasing food from vendors. SunFed, an Arizona firm that has distributed produce from Agricola San Emilio, said its representatives had inspected the fields and packinghouse at the farm but not the labor camp. "The Mexican government would be the first line of protection for Mexican workers," said Dan Mandel, president of SunFed, a distributor for supermarkets across the U.S. Enforcement of Mexican labor laws in Sinaloa is feeble. One state official insisted, incorrectly, that withholding wages until the end of a contract was legal.

Federal labor inspectors are clear on the law but said they were largely powerless to crack down on deep-pocketed growers, who can stymie enforcement with endless appeals. "They just laugh at us," said Armando Guzman, a senior official with Mexico's federal Secretariat of Labor and Social Welfare. "They mock authority and mock the letter of the law." Agricola San Emilio is no outlier. Harsh conditions persist in many camps. At Agricola Rita Rosario, a cucumber exporter near Culiacan in Sinaloa, workers said they hadn't been paid in weeks. Some were pawning° their belongings to pay for diapers and food when Times journalists visited a year ago. Laborers said company managers had threatened to dump their possessions in the street if they persisted in demanding their wages. "We have nowhere to go. We're trapped," said a 43-year-old man, looking around nervously. Rita Rosario, under new management, started paying workers their back wages this year before suspending operations, according to a U.S. distributor who did business with the farm.

Workers at Agricola Santa Teresa, an export farm nearby, were doing odd jobs outside the camp on Sundays to earn spending money because their wages had been withheld. The tomato grower supplies U.S. distributors whose customers include the Albertsons supermarket chain and the Los Angeles Unified School District. Told that workers hadn't been paid, Enrique Lopez, director of Santa Teresa, said it wasn't the company's fault. Santa Teresa pays them by electronic bank deposit every week, he said. Lopez said he suspected that the laborers handed over their ATM cards to the contractor who recruited them, a practice he said was customary for workers from indigenous regions. "That is the agreement they have," Lopez said. "We can't control that situation." An LAUSD spokeswoman, Ellen Morgan, said the district requires suppliers to inspect farms from which they buy produce, primarily to ensure food safety. She said the district was formulating a new procurement policy that would probably address labor conditions too. Albertsons declined to comment.

At Agricola El Porvenir, also near Culiacan, workers were required to disinfect their hands before picking cucumbers. Yet they were given just two pieces of toilet paper to use at the outhouses. At Campo San Jose, where many of them lived, workers said rats and feral cats had the run of the cramped living quarters and feasted on their leftovers. Laborers and their families bathed in an irrigation canal because the water had run out in the showers. In March, a snake was sighted in the canal, sparking a panic. Carmen Garcia stepped out of the fetid waterway after washing her 1-year-old grandson. His skin was covered with boils that she blamed on insect bites. "He itches constantly," Garcia said. "I want to get a blood test, but I can't get to a doctor." Agricola El Porvenir's legal counsel, Eric Gerardo, said the company rents Campo San Jose from another agribusiness to handle the overflow when its own camps fill up. Efforts to reach the owner of the other business were unsuccessful. "We don't invest in it because it's not ours," Gerardo said.

---

pawning: giving belongings as a deposit or security for money borrowed, usually with high interest rates or fees attached.

Twenty miles away, at Campo Isabelitas, operated by the agribusiness Nueva Yamal, families used buckets in their room to relieve themselves because, they said, the toilets were filthy and lacked water. Men defecated in a cornfield. Workers could be seen bathing in an irrigation canal; they said the camp's showers were out of water. Charles Ciruli, a co-owner of Arizona-based Ciruli Bros., which distributes Nueva Yamal tomatoes, visited the camp after being told about conditions there by The Times. Through an attorney, he said that the men's bathrooms "did not meet Ciruli's standards" and that repairs had been made to "reinstate running water." The attorney, Stanley G. Feldman, said in a letter that the women's showers and toilets were "fully functioning," with a paid attendant. Asked why workers were washing in the irrigation canal, Feldman wrote: "Ciruli cannot explain this with certainty, but it was told that it may be a cultural practice among some workers." He added: "Ciruli will consult with the on-farm social worker and doctor to determine if a worker education campaign may be appropriate in this case."

In June 2013, Bioparques found itself under rare government scrutiny. Three workers at one of the tomato grower's labor camps escaped and complained to authorities about the wretched conditions. Police, soldiers and labor inspectors raided the camp and found 275 people trapped inside. Dozens were malnourished, including 24 children, authorities said. People were desperate, but at least the camp had showers and stoves, said laborer Gerardo Gonzalez Hernandez. "To tell you the truth, Bioparques was a little better than other labor camps I've been to," Gonzalez, 18, said in an interview at his home in the mountains north of Mexico City. "That's why I didn't complain. I've seen a lot worse."

Understanding the Text

1. What does Marosi notice about the difference between how produce and people are treated on Mexico's farms?

2. What does the law dictate about how workers on Mexico's farms should be paid? What does Marosi say actually happens in practice?

3. How do the Mexican farms that Marosi describes recruit workers? What role does child labor play in the production of fruits and vegetables in Mexico?

4. What role do labor contractors play in the U.S./Mexico agricultural economy?

Reflection and Response

5. What role does Walmart play in this story? Why do you think Marosi specifically calls out Walmart?

6. Five major conclusions are offered in the second paragraph. Select one, and explore and analyze how Marosi supports the conclusion. Does the conclusion make you think differently about the food you buy? If so, why and how? If not, why not?

7. Marosi is clearly trying to gain sympathy for the farm workers he describes. What rhetorical choices does he use to achieve this effect? Does it work for you? Does his writing make you sympathetic to the workers' plight? If so, how? If not, why not?

Making Connections

8. Many U.S. companies (such as Triple H) claim that they are committed to fair working conditions and the well-being of farm workers, but Marosi shows that workers are routinely exploited. Go online and research a few companies that have ethical sourcing guidelines. How and why do these food suppliers publicize their participation in fair labor practices? Why do you think so many companies insist that they have policies that ensure fair labor practices even though Marosi found startling evidence to the contrary? Is this something American consumers should care about? Do you? If so, how will you act on your concerns?

9. Yuval Noah Harari ("Industrial Farming Is One of the Worst Crimes in History," p. 177) argues that the treatment of domesticated animals on industrial farms is among the worst crimes in history. Imagine that Marosi (or you) wants to argue that the treatment of Mexican farm workers is worse than the treatment of domesticated animals on industrial farms. What is the best way to make such an argument? What ethical principles would you rely upon? What evidence would you use to support your conclusions?

10. Marosi explores racial and class inequities in the global food system. How is the exploitation of Mexican farm workers that Marosi describes related to what Stephen Satterfield ("I'm a Black Food Writer. Here's Why We Need More Like Me," p. 131) describes in his essay? You may want to look up the work of Marosi and Satterfield to better understand their projects, affiliations, and understandings of the world they write about.

Biotechnology Isn't the Key to Feeding the World

Frances Moore Lappé

Frances Moore Lappé is an environmental activist and author who has written 19 books, including *Diet for a Small Planet* (1971) and *EcoMind: Changing the Way We Think, to Create the World We Want* (2011). The winner of many awards and the recipient of many honorary degrees, Lappé is known for her tireless dedication to democratic social movements and the fight against world hunger. Her extensive writings aim to change the way we think about agriculture, nutrition, and food production and consumption. In this essay, she argues that democracy — not biotechnology — is the key to finding a solution to the problem of world hunger. It is not that we do not have enough food, she explains; it is that we do not have a successful democratic process.

Biotechnology companies and even some scientists argue that we need genetically modified seeds to feed the world and to protect the Earth from chemicals. Their arguments feel eerily familiar.

Thirty years ago, I wrote *Diet for a Small Planet* for one reason. As a researcher buried in the agricultural library at the University of California, Berkeley, I was stunned to learn that the experts — equivalent to the biotech proponents of today — were wrong. They were telling us that we had reached the Earth's limits to feed ourselves, but in fact there was more than enough food for us all.

Hunger, I learned, is the result of economic "givens" that we have created, assumptions and structures that actively generate scarcity from plenty. Today this is more, not less, true.

Throughout history, ruminants had served humans by turning grasses and other "inedibles" into high-grade protein. They were our four-legged protein factories. But once we began feeding livestock from cropland that could grow edible food, we began to convert ruminants into our protein disposals.

Only a small fraction of the nutrients fed to animals return to us in 5 meat; the rest animals use largely for energy or they excrete. Roughly one-third of the world's grain goes to livestock; today it is closer to one-half. And now we are mastering the same disappearing trick with the world's fish supply. By feeding fish to fish, again, we are reducing the potential supply.

We are shrinking the world's food supply for one reason: The hundreds of millions of people who go hungry cannot create a sufficient "market demand" for the fruits of the Earth. So more and more of it flows into the mouths of livestock, which convert it into what the better-off can afford. Corn becomes filet mignon. Sardines become salmon.

Enter biotechnology. While its supporters claim that seed biotechnology methods are "safe" and "precise," other scientists strongly refute that, as they do claims that biotech crops have actually reduced pesticide use.

But this very debate is in some ways part of the problem. It is a tragic distraction our planet cannot afford.

We are still asking the wrong question. Not only is there already enough food in the world, but as long as we are only talking about food—how best to produce it—we will never end hunger or create the communities and food safety we want.

We must ask instead: How do we 10 build communities in tune with nature's wisdom in which no one, anywhere, has to worry about putting food—safe, healthy food—on the table? Asking this question takes us far beyond food. It takes us to the heart of democracy itself, to whose voices are heard in matters of land, seeds, credit, employment, trade, and food safety.

"Hunger is not caused by a scarcity of food but by a scarcity of democracy."

The problem is, this question cannot be addressed by scientists or by any private entity, including even the most high-minded corporation. Only citizens can answer it, through public debate and the resulting accountable institutions that come from our engagement.

Where are the channels for public discussion and where are the accountable polities?

Increasingly, public discussion about food and hunger is framed by advertising by multinational corporations that control not only food processing and distribution but farm inputs and seed patents.

Two years ago, the seven leading biotech companies, including Monsanto, teamed up under the neutral-sounding Council for Biotechnology Information and are spending millions to, for example, blanket us with full-page newspaper ads about biotech's virtues.

Government institutions are becoming ever more beholden to these 15 corporations than to their citizens. Nowhere is this more obvious than in decisions regarding biotechnology—whether it is the approval or patenting of biotech seeds and foods without public input or the rejection of mandatory labeling of biotech foods despite broad public demand for it.

The absence of genuine democratic dialogue and accountable government is a prime reason most people remain blind to the many breakthroughs in the last 30 years that demonstrate we can grow abundant, healthy food and also protect the Earth.

Hunger is not caused by a scarcity of food but by a scarcity of democracy. Thus it can never be solved by new technologies, even if they were to be proved "safe." It can be solved only as citizens build democracies in which government is accountable to them, not to private corporate entities.

Understanding the Text

1. To what is Lappé referring when she writes about "our four-legged protein factories"?

2. What does she mean by "protein disposals"?

3. On what does Lappé blame world hunger? What does she think is the best way to decrease or eliminate it?

Reflection and Response

4. Lappé argues that proponents and opponents of biotechnology are distracted and thus not focused on the right issue. What is the right issue for Lappé, and how does she make and support her position on the issue? Do you agree with her? Why or why not?

5. What connections does Lappé argue exist among food availability, hunger, farming practices, biotechnology, and democracy? How does she describe their current relationships? How would she change them if she could?

Making Connections

6. Identify the other selections in this book that discuss biotechnology. Try to place them on a continuum. Who agrees with Lappé? Who does not? And to what extent?

7. In what ways does Lappé's argument about the future of food complicate Robert Paarlberg's position ("Attention Whole Foods Shoppers," p. 292)? Who makes the best case? Whose evidence seems the strongest? Explain your response using textual references.

8. Lappé argues that global hunger problems are "not caused by a scarcity of food but by a scarcity of democracy" (par. 17). What role does Abaki Beck ("How One Tribe Is Fighting for Their Food Culture in the Face of Climate Change," p. 279) see for democracy in the fight for food justice? What values or beliefs do Lappé and Beck share? What relationship do you think should exist between the future of food and the political process?

Recycling Energy

Bob Quinn and Liz Carlisle

Bob Quinn grew up on his family farm in Montana. After he earned a PhD at UC Davis in plant biochemistry, he returned to the farm to start experimenting with organic wheat. Not only did he use regenerative organic farming to grow food in rural Montana, he also started producing renewable energy. Although initially his goal was to make a living farming, eventually his interests expanded to include health, the environment, and the state of the economy in rural America. And, along the way, his business grew into a multimillion-dollar heirloom grain company. At one point during his journey, he developed a book idea. He sought out Liz Carlisle to be his coauthor. Carlisle studied folklore and mythology at Harvard University before receiving her PhD in geography from UC Berkeley. Now she teaches at UC Santa Barbara in the Environmental Studies Program. She has won awards for conducting academic research that makes a social impact, and she also writes for a public audience in many magazines and newspapers. Carlisle wrote *Lentil Underground: Renegade Farmers and the Future of Food in America* (2015) about sustainable farming before coauthoring *Grain by Grain: A Quest to Revive Ancient Wheat, Rural Jobs, and Healthy Food* (2019) with Quinn. In this essay, excerpted from their book, we learn about the journey Quinn took as he tried move to renewable energy in order to make his farm sustainable.

When I started looking at farming from a net value perspective, I suddenly had to get really honest with myself. I couldn't measure my success solely by my production—that was the commodity mindset. Instead, I had to pay equal attention to my consumption. I had gone some distance down this road by switching to whole, organic heritage grain and growing my own locally adapted fruit and dryland vegetables. I no longer used chemical fertilizer or herbicide, and on my dryland farm we had never used irrigation. But I was still a major consumer of a commodity far more destructive than my conventional wheat had ever been: fossil fuel.

Dependence on fossil energy is so rampant in the American food system that it raises the question, Is agriculture in this country truly a productive activity, or a consumptive one? Researchers estimate that it takes 7 to 10 units of fossil energy to produce 1 unit of food energy in the US food system.[1] Much of that energy being gobbled up by our food system is spent beyond the farm gate, in processing, transportation, storage, and preparation.[2] But American farms use a lot of fossil fuel too: on average, US farmers use 2 kilocalories of fossil energy for every 1 kilocalorie of crop energy they harvest.[3] What kind of business model is that?

The reason American agriculture has gotten away with essentially spending more than it earns is that, particularly since World War II, fossil fuel has been artificially cheap. It's been subsidized by our government. And it's been subsidized again by the public, since we get stuck with the consequences of the industry's unpaid environmental costs. Hence, thanks to the burdens we all bear with our taxes and our bodies, fossil energy has been made to appear inexpensive and abundant, leading to its ubiquitous use in our cars, in our industries, in our consumer products—and on our farms.[4] The result is that, for all the claims that American agriculture has been improved and modernized over the course of the past century, our farming systems have actually become less efficient. In 1910, American growers of one of nature's most energy-efficient crops—corn—produced 5.8 units of energy for every 1 unit they used. By 1983, that ratio had dwindled to just 2.5.[5]

How are American farmers spending all this energy? About one-third of the fossil fuel footprint of contemporary US commodity farms can be chalked up to synthetic nitrogen fertilizer. Another third is due to other inputs: mainly pesticides, but also irrigation—it takes a lot of energy to pump water across thousands of acres of farmland.[6] That means two-thirds of the energy problem with American agriculture can be solved by converting to organics and minimizing supplementary water. So far, so good, I told myself—these were changes I'd made to my operation. But what about that last third?

The last third of fossil energy consumption on American farms is, by and large, just as prevalent on organic farms as on conventional ones—if not more so. This is the diesel fuel we put in our tractors.[7]

Running my farm on diesel didn't sit well with me. As a wheat grower, I'd worked hard to get off the commodity treadmill and control more of my own destiny. That's why I'd started the grain business and gone organic—so I could control my input costs and take my crop to market myself, for a price I thought was fair. But so long as I relied on fossil fuel supplied by cartels, my profit margins were still at the mercy of global commodity prices. My farm's dependence on fossil fuel also cut into the other values I was trying to add: environmental regeneration and social benefit. I didn't see much of that in the way multinational petroleum corporations did business. There had to be a better way.

Given that I was a farmer, the most obvious way for me to source alternative fuel was to grow my own. We can raise lots of different oilseed crops on the northern Great Plains. My neighbors have tried sunflower and canola and safflower. So I thought, Why don't we find one of those crops that works well as a biofuel?° We can all add it into our rotations; then some local group can get together and build a facility to crush it into a fuel for our tractors. If a bunch of farmers went in on it, it wouldn't be that expensive. And all the money would stay in the community instead of going to some cartel.

I didn't think canola was the way to go. It did great in Canada, just north of us, or to our west, where the influence of the nearby Rocky Mountains made for cooler weather. But here, it would often bloom in the hottest part of the summer and the flowers would be destroyed because they were too fragile to withstand the heat. My neighbors who had grown safflower complained that it matured so late that you had to go get your combine back out of the shed as winter was approaching. It's not uncommon for farmers in my area to pull eighteen-hour days during harvest season in July and August and then hit winter wheat seeding hard in September. By Halloween, we're all ready for a break.

But then came along a brand-new option, a crop being promoted by a researcher at a nearby experiment station. This oilseed crop could be planted in March in very cold soils, which meant it would bloom in June, before the heat came on. It was called camelina.

To see if camelina would like it at my place, I grew a test plot of half 10 an acre. That turned out pretty well, so I scaled up to twenty acres in my second year, and I did another thirty-five acres or so the following year. I had a brief misadventure with my first attempt to press the camelina into oil. It was a good reminder about the real value of cheap goods: I bought a cheap press, and I couldn't get the thing to work at all. As a last-ditch effort, I invited all my best mechanic friends to come over one Saturday morning and help me. By Saturday afternoon, all we had to show for our efforts was a gallon jug of brownish oil that smelled like coffee. Burnt coffee.

So I got a higher-quality oil press, which worked like a dream. My son, thirteen at the time, was able to run it by himself. I had already purchased the other piece of equipment I needed—a digester to convert the pressed camelina oil into biodiesel so we could run it in our tractor. Our homegrown energy experiment was ready to launch! But the more I learned about biodiesel, the more I started having second thoughts.

To convert vegetable oil into biodiesel, you need to use lye.° When you wash out the lye, you end up with wastewater—and a by-product, glycerin.° I didn't know where I could find a market for high volumes of glycerin. This whole idea wasn't looking quite so closed-loop after all.

Then a friend from the educational farm at the University of Montana came to my rescue. He said I didn't need to make biodiesel. I could use

---

biofuel: fuel deriving from living matter, usually seen as a source of renewable energy.
lye: a strong alkaline solution used for cleaning.
glycerin: a sweet, odorless, clear liquid often used to make soap.

straight vegetable oil. All I had to do was modify my tractor so that it would preheat the vegetable oil to 160 degrees. This would reduce the viscosity° of the oil, so it would go into the engine hot and act just like diesel.

The catch was, there were only certain kinds of vegetable oil that could go straight into a tractor. Camelina oil was *poly*unsaturated, meaning the long fatty acid chains in each molecule had multiple double carbon bonds. From a chemical standpoint, those multiple double bonds made the camelina oil susceptible to oxidation, which meant it could gunk up my engine and rapidly go rancid in storage. What I needed was an oil that was *mono*unsaturated—just one double carbon bond. That's when I learned about high-oleic safflower.

I'd never thought much about the balance of fats in a safflower seed. 15 As far as I knew, the main market for safflower was birdseed, and I didn't think the birds were all that picky about types of fat. But what might not matter to the birds was critically important for my tractor, my friend from UM told me.

Most of the safflower grown for birdseed, my friend explained, is high in *linoleic* acid—a polyunsaturated fatty acid, similar to those found in camelina. But there were other varieties of safflower bred to be high in *oleic* acid, which had the monounsaturated fat I was looking for.

Figuring I'd found the solution to my fuel problem, I sold my digester and planted forty acres of high-oleic safflower. (The unused camelina seed went to a chicken feed outfit in Washington, and a natural food retailer in Boston bought the camelina oil I had already pressed.) That first crop made me really nervous, because it took so long to mature. I was used to wheat and barley, fast-growing grains that cover the field within just a few weeks of planting. Not safflower. It took its time. But once it started to bloom, oh my goodness. The field was a glistening sea of golden yellow blossoms, which turned to orange as the crop ripened. I walked into the rows of flowering energy factories to check on their progress toward harvest and was immediately checked by the sensation of little pins pricking me. The safflower had grown stickers everywhere, all over the leaves and even the flowers. It was like a thistle. I had another surprise as we harvested the crop, when the air conditioner in my combine suddenly quit working. Inside the seed heads of the safflower, I discovered, were large quantities of very fine fibers—which were plugging up the air conditioner's filters. They shut it right down. But once I learned to clean the air filters every day and wear heavy gloves and leather chaps in the field, I found safflower quite an agreeable crop.

---

viscosity: a measure of a fluid's resistance to flow; if a fluid has a large viscosity, it resists flow because its molecular makeup results in a lot of friction.

Yes, it meant a little bit longer season, but the plants produced well, and the seeds were readily converted to oil in the press we'd purchased for camelina. Now all I had to do was convert my tractor, and I was ready to run my farm on homegrown fuel.

Then my hired man threw me a curveball. He took some of my high-oleic safflower oil to one of the restaurants in Big Sandy. They tried using it as cooking oil and loved it. The restaurant owner asked if we would consider selling to him and said he'd be willing to pay us nearly $2 per pound. I did the math and determined that was almost $16 per gallon. And I was getting ready to pour this oil into my tractor to replace diesel fuel, which cost about one-fourth as much. Now I had a genuine sustainability dilemma on my hands. I knew the best decision for our business was to sell the oil to restaurants. But I didn't want to give up on my original goal of replacing fossil fuel with something homegrown and renewable. This was the frustration I found myself confessing to Ian Finch, director of sustainability for University of Montana Dining Services.

Safflower field in late bloom with the Missouri River Breaks National Monument in the background.

Photo by Hilary Page

Ian had been up to my farm before, as part of a UM field course that 20
often visited us in the summer, so he knew all about the ancient wheat
and the dryland vegetables. But he was surprised to hear I was now growing safflower — and he wanted to know more. In 2012, we arranged a
meeting at his office in the University Center at UM. Sitting around the
table were me, Ian, and my son-in-law Andrew Long, who had recently
moved back to the farm with my youngest daughter, Bridgette, to run
the oil business. I had offered Andrew the job right out of his MBA,
thinking we could use some help with our launch and he could use the
experience on his résumé. I'd asked Andrew for only a one-year commitment, figuring he might want to move on to one of the big-city jobs he'd
trained for. But after a year, he told me he was having more fun than any
of his classmates — so he and Bridgette settled in right next door to me,
in the house my folks vacated when they went into assisted living in
Great Falls. Andrew was a sharp guy, and he was just as interested as I was
in building a creative partnership with the University of Montana.

UM Dining relied on large quantities of vegetable oil to serve the
campus thousands of meals per day, Ian told Andrew and me. They had
been using a blended product from a plant in northeastern Montana,
but that plant had recently closed. It wasn't hard to see the flaw in the
business model. This plant had been extracting oil from oilseeds using
hexane — to get the very last drop of oil out of the seed. They maximized
the production, all right, but the result was that their mash became a
toxic waste product. You couldn't even feed it to animals. They ruined
their by-product trying to squeeze the last little bit of marginal value out
of the first product. They were in a race to the bottom, always competing
with cheaper and cheaper oils, from larger and larger plants. Textbook
value subtraction commodity mindset.

When this conventional vegetable oil plant shut down, UM Dining
went looking for another Montana supplier, which is why they called
me. The campus already had a Farm-to-College program, which was Ian's
domain, and they were committed to sourcing in-state and sustainably
whenever possible. But our cost of production was higher than that of
the conventional plant, which meant our prices were higher too. The
conventional plant, like most cooking oil manufacturers, had mixed
together whatever vegetable oils it could source most cheaply and
covered up any shortfalls in quality with a host of additives. In contrast,
we were using organically grown high-oleic safflower, which was more
expensive. And, of course, we hadn't yet decided to go into the culinary
oil market, anyway.

"How about we just give it a try?" Ian proposed, figuring there was no
harm in an experiment. We agreed to drop off thirty-five gallons of our

oil so the chefs in UM's various kitchens and cafés could trial it in their recipes. As the trial progressed, the chefs made some remarkable discoveries. The first thing they noticed was that there was less transfer of flavors from one dish to another than they'd had with their conventional oil. If they used high-oleic safflower oil to cook fish and then chicken and then potatoes, they didn't end up with fishy-tasting potatoes. The stability of the oil meant they could use it longer—getting more bang for their buck. Intrigued by this finding, UM ran tests to find out just how long they could use safflower oil before it degraded. They found that the safflower oil held up significantly longer than blended cooking oil products or canola oil—meaning it had not only a longer cooking life but a longer shelf life too. That made sense to me—the whole reason we'd gone with high-oleic safflower was that it was more stable. I was thinking about tractors, not woks, but biochemically, it was the same principle.

The UM chefs loved the flavor of the safflower oil, and they tried all sorts of things with it that I never would have imagined. They fried in it, as they had done with their previous blended oil product. But they also used it for baking, grilling—even as an ingredient in salad dressings. UM had previously stocked different oils to do each of these things, and the overhead associated with all that inventory was adding up. The versatility of safflower oil meant they could cut that inventory by more than half.

But the person who really convinced UM Dining that safflower oil 25 was the way to go was their registered dietitian. While trying to move students away from fried foods, UM Dining had learned that discontinuing these items entirely meant students would just go off campus to get them elsewhere. So UM decided on a pragmatic strategy: if fried foods were a nonnegotiable part of their students' diet, Dining Services wanted to do what it could to make those chicken nuggets and tater tots as healthy as possible. Safflower oil, the dietitian found, was one of the healthiest oils to deep-fat fry in—and our cold-pressed product was free of the TBHQ (tertiary butylhydroquinone) and other chemical ingredients that commodity oil suppliers regularly added to their products as anti-foaming agents and preservatives, despite mounting evidence that these are dangerous to consume in any quantity.[8]

Had UM run a traditional cost-benefit analysis on their safflower oil experiment, they would have concluded that our oil was too expensive. It cost twice as much as canola oil or a blended product, and even the longer cooking life and reduced inventory costs weren't enough to completely make up the difference. But UM didn't run a traditional cost-benefit analysis. They looked at the full spectrum of safflower oil's value: from the crop's role in organic rotations and the rural Montana economy to the long-term health of their students. From that standpoint, safflower oil came out a clear winner. UM asked if we would consider becoming their regular vegetable oil supplier. It was a great opportunity for us, I told Ian, but I was still frustrated about ending up on the wrong side of my fuel versus food dilemma.

Competition between fuel production and food production is a major sustainability concern with biofuels. Normally the worry is that fuel use will trump food use, as has happened with corn ethanol, which has led to croplands being converted to fuel cars instead of feeding people. When we start asking farms to fuel our cities, I think we are inevitably going to run into this problem. In my case, I had a less ambitious goal: using a small part of my farm to fuel just the farm itself. And I was concerned that the UM Dining deal would put me back in the commodity conundrum: exporting something off the farm (a potential energy source) that I would then have to import from someone else (a cartel). On the cusp of achieving a closed-loop fuel solution, I didn't want to sell my energy independence down the river.

Then I had an idea: why not go ahead and sell the oil to UM but recover the waste oil and burn it in my diesel engine? I asked Ian if he might consider such an arrangement.

What if we thought of it as a sort of rental agreement, I proposed. After all, the UM chefs weren't exactly *using* most of the oil. When they cooked in it, they didn't use the oil up; they just employed it to perform a service: transforming raw food into a meal. When it was done performing that service and had degraded beyond its usefulness in the kitchen, it became a liability. A waste product. They had to pay to dispose of it.

So instead of letting all that oil go to waste, I suggested, why not send 30 it back to me and Andrew? UM could return it to my farm in the same containers we delivered it in—transforming their liability (waste oil) into our asset (fuel). We didn't need to choose between fuel value and food value—we could utilize both!

The oil we get back from UM is enough to provide about one-eighth of the fuel needs for our farm, and we're now actively looking for other customers to "rent" the remaining seven-eighths of our homegrown energy en route to the fuel tank. Vegetable oil is not so great as a fuel in the winter because it becomes too viscous in extreme cold. But we don't farm in the winter.

"Eliminating our dependence on fossil fuel would shield farmers from the worrying ups and downs of diesel prices — and make us much more valuable net contributors to the real wealth of our communities and our planet."

In addition to fuel value and food value, we've added a third source of value to our safflower crop: feed. Because we extract our oil using a cold press at low temperatures instead of hexane, we end up with a mash by-product that is nontoxic and still 3 or 4 percent oil. At 21 percent protein, it makes a good supplementary feed for cattle, and we're now selling it to Organic Valley for their dairy cows.

What this all means is that with high-oleic safflower, we can use our farm production first for food, then for feed, then for fuel. We call this business The Oil Barn, and with my son-in-law now at the helm, we've started making some small retail bottles of the oil too, so people can try it in their homes. Our latest idea is to pair the oil with my daughter Allison's homegrown red wine vinegar as a Montana-made salad dressing.

The Oil Barn is still a pretty modest demonstration, but I think oilseed crops used first for food and then for fuel could be a viable substitute for at least some of the diesel we use on farms. Infrastructure like the oil press and cleaning equipment we've installed could be purchased by a farmer cooperative, which could serve as both its own supplier and its own customer. Eliminating our dependence on fossil fuel would shield farmers from the worrying ups and downs of diesel prices—and make us much more valuable net contributors to the real wealth of our communities and our planet.

Of course, farmers aren't the only ones worried about dependence on fossil fuels. I've had a number of urban people ask me if I think the Oil Barn model could provide sustainable fuel for their vehicles. But at that scale, I think the closed loop breaks down. As we've seen with most large-scale experiments with biofuels, importing huge quantities of energy from the countryside to our urban centers overtaxes land and rural communities. It's not as environmentally destructive as fossil fuel development, but it's still extractive—and it can displace food crops. So I don't think we should try to have farmers grow all the energy for cities. For cities, we need to tap into other renewable resources, like solar and wind. But farmers can help with that too—because if you've ever been to north central Montana farm country, you know that we are very rich in wind.

Notes

1. M. C. Heller and G. A. Keoleian, "Life Cycle-Based Sustainability Indicators for Assessment of the U.S. Food System," Center for Sustainable Systems Report No. CSS00-04 (Ann Arbor: University of Michigan School of Natural Resources and Environment 6 December 2000), p. 42, http://css.umich.edu/sites/default/files/css_doc/CSS00-04.pdf.

2. Heller and Keoleian, "Sustainability Indicators."

3. D. Pimentel, "Impacts of Organic Farming on the Efficiency of Energy Use in Agriculture: An Organic Center State of Science Review" (Foster, RI: The Organic Center, August 2006), p. 5, www.organic-center.org/reportfiles /ENERGY_SSR.pdf.

4. International Panel of Experts on Sustainable Food Systems (IPES-Food), "From Uniformity to Diversity: A Paradigm Shift from Industrial Agriculture to Diversified Agroecological Systems," June 2016, www.ipes-food.org/images /Reports/UniformityToDiversity_FullReport.pdf.

5. D. Pimentel and W. Dazhong, "Technological Changes in Energy Use in U.S. Agricultural Production," in *Agroecology*, ed. C. R. Carroll, J. H. Vandermeer, and P. Rosset (New York: McGraw-Hill, 1990).

6. Pimentel, "Impacts of Organic Farming," p. 1.

7. Ibid.

8. M. Pollan, *The Omnivore's Dilemma: A Natural History of Four Meals* (New York: Penguin Books, 2006), pp. 113–14.

Understanding the Text

1. What role does fossil fuel play in farming?

2. Why and how has farming become less efficient during the past century?

3. What is the different between energy development that is extractive and energy development that is renewable?

Reflection and Response

4. Why do you think Quinn explains the chemistry of the various kinds of oil in such detail? Why do they matter to his story? Why should they matter to farmers and citizens more widely?

5. Think about the initial ethical dilemma Quinn faced regarding high-oleic safflower oil — whether to use it as fuel or sell it. What would you do in this situation? Why? What values are implicit in your stated choice? What do you think of the eventual outcome?

Making Connections

6. This essay is written from the perspective of Bob Quinn, but it comes from a book he coauthored with Liz Carlisle. Do some research on their project and their backgrounds. What role did Carlisle play in this project? Why do you think Quinn wanted a coauthor? Why did he choose her specifically? Would you consider this a successful partnership? Why or why not?

7. Compare Quinn's farming methods to Matt Barnard's (discussed by Wang in "The Future of Farming Is Looking Up," p. 331). What motivations, values, and methods do they share? Which solution is interesting to you? Why?

8. What do Quinn and Carlisle suggest as priorities for the future of food production? What significant values and beliefs do they share with Jonathan Foley ("Can We Feed the World and Sustain the Planet?," p. 212), Barbara Kingsolver ("You Can't Run Away on Harvest Day," p. 150), and Bren Smith ("The Least Deadly Catch," p. 270)? How might these beliefs be used to develop new practices and/or concrete policy changes?

9. How do Quinn and Carlisle describe the relationship between scientific knowledge and the experiences of real farmers? How does their representation of this relationship differ from the one offered by Blake Hurst ("The Omnivore's Delusion," p. 184)? Explain, using specific textual evidence from both essays.

The Future of Farming Is Looking Up

Selina Wang

Selina Wang studied economics and government at Harvard University, where she was named a John Harvard Scholar for being in the top 5 percent of her class. She went on to become an award-winning journalist who covers global technology, venture capital, and cross-border investments. She writes for *Bloomberg News* and is a regular contributor on Bloomberg Television. With *Bloomberg News*, she has worked in New York City, Hong Kong, and San Francisco. In this essay, Wang describes an indoor, vertical farming method and suggests that it may just be the future of farming.

Before stepping into Plenty Inc.'s indoor farm on the banks of San Francisco Bay, make sure you're wearing pants and closed-toe shoes. Heels aren't allowed. If you have long hair, you should probably tie it back.

Your first stop is the cleaning room. Open the door and air will whoosh behind you, removing stray dust and contaminants as the door slams shut. Slide into a white bodysuit, pull on disposable shoe covers, and don a pair of glasses with colored lenses. Wash your hands in the sink before slipping on food-safety gloves. Step into a shallow pool of clear, sterilized liquid, then open the door to what the company calls its indoor growing room, where another air bath eliminates any stray particles that collected in the cleaning room.

The growing room looks like a strange forest, with pink and purple LEDs illuminating 20-foot-tall towers of leafy vegetables that stretch as far as you can see. It smells like a forest, too, but there's no damp earth or moss. The plants are growing sideways out of the columns, which bloom with Celtic crunch lettuce, red oak kale, sweet summer basil, and 15 other heirloom munchables. The 50,000-square-foot room, a little more than an acre, can produce some 2 million pounds of lettuce a year.

Step closer to the veggie columns, and you'll spot one of the roughly 7,500 infrared cameras or 35,000 sensors hidden among the leaves. The sensors monitor the room's temperature, humidity, and level of carbon dioxide, while the cameras record the plants' growing phases. The data stream to Plenty's botanists and artificial intelligence experts, who regularly tweak the environment to increase the farm's productivity and enhance the food's taste. Step even closer to the produce, and you may see a ladybug or two. They're there to eat any pests that somehow make it past the cleaning room. "They work for free so we don't have to eat pesticides," says Matt Barnard, Plenty's chief executive officer.

Barnard, 44, grew up on a 160-acre apple and cherry orchard in 5 bucolic Door County, Wis., a place that attracts a steady stream of fruit-picking tourists. Now he and his four-year-old startup aim to radically change how we grow and eat produce. The world's supply of fruits and vegetables falls 22 percent short of global nutritional needs, according to public-health researchers at Emory University, and that short-fall is expected to worsen. While the field is littered with the remains of companies that tried to narrow the gap over the past few years, Plenty seems the most promising of any so far, for two reasons. First is its technology, which vastly increases its farming efficiency—and, early tasters say, the quality of its food—relative to traditional farms and its venture-backed rivals. Second, but not least, is the $200 million it collected in July from Japanese telecom giant SoftBank Group, the largest agriculture technology investment in history.

With the backing of SoftBank CEO Masayoshi Son, Plenty has the capital and connections to accelerate its endgame: building massive indoor farms on the outskirts of every major city on Earth, some 500 in all. In that world, food could go from farm to table in hours rather than days or weeks. Barnard says he's been meeting with officials from some 15 governments on four continents, as well as executives from Wal-Mart Stores Inc. and Amazon.com Inc., while he plans his expansion. (Bezos Expeditions, the Amazon CEO's personal venture fund, has also invested.) He intends to open farms abroad next year; this first one, in the Bay Area, is on track to begin making deliveries to San Francisco grocers by the end of 2017. "We're giving people food that tastes better and is better for them," Barnard says. He says that a lot.

Plenty acknowledges that its model is only part of the solution to the global nutrition gap, that other novel methods and conventional farming will still be needed. Barnard is careful not to frame his crusade in opposition to anyone, including the industrial farms and complex supply chain he's trying to circumvent. He's focused on proving that growing rooms such as the one in South San Francisco can reliably deliver Whole Foods quality at Walmart prices. Even with $200 million in hand, it won't be easy. "You're talking about seriously scaling," says Sonny Ramaswamy, director of the National Institute of Food and Agriculture, the investment arm of the U.S. Department of Agriculture. "The question then becomes, are things going to fall apart? Are you going to be able to maintain quality control?"

The idea of growing food indoors in unlikely places such as warehouses and rooftops has been hyped for decades. It presents a compelling solution to a series of intractable problems, including water shortages, the scarcity of arable land, and a farming population that's graying as young people eschew the agriculture industry in greater numbers. It also promises to reduce the absurd waste built into international grocery routes. The U.S. imports some 35 percent of fruits and vegetables, according to Bain & Co., and even leafy greens, most of which are produced in California or Arizona, travel an average of 2,000 miles before reaching a retailer. In other words, vegetables that are going to be appealing and edible for two weeks or less spend an awful lot of that time in transit.

So far, though, vertical farms haven't been able to break through. Over the past few years, early leaders in the field, including PodPonics in Atlanta, FarmedHere in Chicago, and Local Garden in Vancouver, have shut down. Some had design issues, while others started too early, when hardware costs were much higher. Gotham Greens in Brooklyn, N.Y., and AeroFarms in Newark, N.J., look promising, but they haven't raised comparable cash hoards or outlined similarly ambitious plans.

While more than one of these companies was felled by a lack of 10 expertise in either farming or finance, Barnard's unusual path to his Bay Area warehouse makes him especially suited for the project. He chose a different life than the orchard, frustrated with the degree to which his life could be upended by an unexpected freeze or a broken-down tractor-trailer. Eventually he became a telecommunications executive, then a partner at a private equity firm. In 2007, two decades into his white-collar life, he started his own company, one that concentrated on investing in technologies to treat and conserve water. After an investor suggested he consider putting money into vertical farming, Barnard began to research the subject and quickly found himself obsessed with shortages of food and arable land. "The length of the supply chain, the time and distance it takes," he says, meant "we were throwing away half of the calories we grow." He spent months chatting with farmers, distributors, grocers, and, eventually, Nate Storey.

The grandson of Montana ranchers, 36-year-old Storey spent much of his childhood planting and tending gardens with his six siblings. Their Air Force dad, who eventually retired as a lieutenant colonel, moved them to another base every few years, and the family gardened to save money on groceries. "I was always interested in ranching and family legacy but frustrated on how to do it," Storey says. "If you're an 18-year-old kid and you want to farm or ranch, most can't raise $3 million to buy a farm or a ranch."

A decade ago, as a student at the University of Wyoming, he learned about the same industry-level inefficiencies Barnard observed. He began experimenting with vertical farming for his doctoral dissertation in agronomy and crop science, and in 2009 patented a growing tower that would pack the plants more densely than other designs. He spent $13,000, then a sizable chunk of his life savings, to buy materials for the towers and started building them in a nearby garage. By the time he met Barnard in 2013, he'd sold a few thousand to hobbyist farmers and the odd commercial grower.

Storey became Barnard's co-founder and Plenty's chief science officer, splitting his time between Wyoming and San Francisco. Together they made Storey's designs bigger, more efficient, and more readily automated. By 2014 they were ready to start building the farm.

Most vertical farms grow plants on horizontal shelves stacked like a tall dresser. Plenty uses tall poles from which the plants jut out horizontally. The poles are lined up about 4 inches from one another, allowing crops to grow so densely they look like a solid wall. Plenty's setups don't use any soil. Instead, nutrients and water are fed into the top of the poles, and gravity does much of the rest of the work. Without horizontal shelves, excess heat from the grow lights rises naturally to vents in the ceiling. "Because we work with physics, not against it, we save a lot of money," Barnard says.

Water, too. Excess drips to the bottom of the plant towers and collects in a recyclable indoor stream, and a dehumidifier system captures the condensation produced from the cooling hardware, along with moisture released into the air by plants as they grow. All that accumulated H_2O is filtered and fed back into the farm. All told, Plenty says, its technology can yield as much as 350 times more produce in a given area as conventional farms, with 1 percent of the water. (The next-highest claim, from AeroFarms, is as much as 130 times the land efficiency of traditional models.) 15

Based on readings from the tens of thousands of wireless cameras and sensors, and depending on which crop it's dealing with, Plenty's system adjusts the LED lights, air composition, humidity, and nutrition. Along with that hardware, the company is using software to predict when plants should get certain resources. If a plant is wilting or dehydrated, for example, the software should be able to alter its lighting or water regimen to help.

Barnard, tall and lanky with a smile that crinkles his entire face, becomes giddy when he recounts the first time Plenty built an entire growing room. "It had gone from pretty sparse to a forest in about a week," he says. "I had never seen anything like that before."

When he and Storey started collaborating, their plan was to sell their equipment to small growers across the country. But to make a dent in the produce gap, they realized they'd need to reproduce their model farm with consistency and speed. "If it takes you two or three years to build a facility, forget about it," Storey says. "That's just not a pace that's going to have any impact." That meant they'd have to engineer the farms themselves. And that meant two things: They'd need more than their 40 staffers, and they'd need way more money.

It wasn't easy for Barnard to get his first meeting with Son, in March. One of Plenty's early investors had to beg the SoftBank CEO, who allotted Barnard 15 minutes. He and the investor, David Chao of DCM Ventures, jammed one of the 20-foot grow towers into Chao's Mercedes sedan and took off for Son's mansion in Woodside, Calif., some 30 miles from San Francisco. Son looked

> "Although Plenty bears little resemblance to a quaint family farm, the tastes bring me back to the tiny vegetable patch my grandparents planted in my childhood backyard."

bewildered as they unloaded the tower, but the meeting stretched to 45 minutes, and two weeks later they flew to Tokyo for a more official discussion in SoftBank's boardroom. The $200 million investment, announced in late July, will help Plenty put a farm in every major metro area with more than 1 million residents, according to Barnard. He says each will have a grow room of about 100,000 square feet, twice the size of the Bay Area model, and can be constructed in under 30 days.

Chao says SoftBank wants "to help Plenty expand very quickly, 20 particularly in China, Japan, and the Middle East," which all struggle with a lack of arable land. Other places on the near-term list include Canada, Denmark, and Ireland. Plenty is also in talks with insurers and institutional investors such as pension funds to bankroll its farm-building with debt. Barnard says the farms would be able to pay off investors in three to five years, vs. 20 to 40 years for traditional farms. Think of it more like a utility, he says.

Plenty, of course, isn't as sure a bet as Consolidated Edison Inc. or Italy's Enel SpA. The higher costs of urban real estate, and the electricity needed to run all of the company's equipment, cut into its efficiency gains. While it's adapting its technology for foods including strawberries and cucumbers, the complications of tree-borne fruits and root crops likewise neutralize the value of its technology. And Plenty has to contend with commercial farms that have spent decades building their relationships with grocers and suppliers and a system that already offers many people extremely low prices for a much wider variety of goods. "What I haven't seen so far in vertical farm technologies is these entities getting very far beyond greens," says Michael Hamm, a professor of sustainable agriculture at Michigan State University. "People only eat so many greens."

Barnard says he's saving way more on truck fuel and other logistical costs, which account for more than one-third of the retail price of produce, than he's spending on warehousing or power. He's also promising that the company's farms will require long-term labor from skilled, full-time workers with benefits. About 30 people can run the South San Francisco warehouse; future models, which will be about two to five times its size, may require several hundred apiece, he says. While robots can handle some of the harvesting, planting, and logistics, experts will oversee the crop development and grocer relationships on-site.

Retailers shouldn't need much convincing, says Mikey Vu, a partner at Bain who studies the grocery business. "Grocers would love to get another four to five days of shelf life for leafy greens," he says. "I think it's an attractive proposition."

Gourmets like Plenty's results, too. Anthony Secviar, a former sous-chef at The French Laundry, a Michelin-starred restaurant in the Napa town of Yountville, says he wasn't expecting much when he received a box of Plenty's produce at his home in Mountain View, Calif. The deep green of the basil and chives hit him first. Each was equally lush, crisp, flavorful, and blemish-free. "I've never had anything of this quality," says Secviar, who while at The French Laundry cooked with vegetables grown across the street from the restaurant. He's now on Plenty's culinary council and is basing his next restaurant's menu around the startup's heirloom vegetables. "It checks every box from a chef's perspective: quality, appearance, texture, flavor, sustainability, price," he says.

At the South San Francisco farm, the greens are fragrant and sweet, 25 the kale is free of store-bought bitterness, and the purple rose lettuce carries a strong kick. There's enough spice and crunch that the veggies won't need a ton of dressing. Although Plenty bears little resemblance to a quaint family farm, the tastes bring me back to the tiny vegetable patch my grandparents planted in my childhood backyard. It's tough to believe these spicy mustard greens and fragrant chives have been re-created in a sterile room, without soil or sun.

Understanding the Text

1. How is Plenty Inc. different from the farm Matt Barnard grew up on? What is similar?

2. What kind of farm is Plenty Inc.? Why are there so many infrared cameras and sensors in Plenty Inc.'s growing room?

3. How is Plenty Inc. being funded? Why is this significant? And what is its expansion plan?

Reflection and Response

4. What is so compelling about indoor or vertical farming? What problems does it help solve? Does it create any? Would you invest in it if you had the means? Why or why not?

5. Why do you think Wang includes so much of Barnard's life story in this essay about indoor farming?

6. What expertise did Storey and Barnard each bring to their partnership? Why do you think this is important to the success of Plenty Inc.?

Making Connections

7. What would Joon Yun, David Kessler, and Dan Glickman ("We Need Better Answers on Nutrition," p. 301) think of Plenty Inc.? Use evidence from the texts to support your response.

8. If, in fact, Plenty Inc. can produce "as much as 350 times more produce in a given area as conventional farms, with 1 percent of the water" (par. 15), this could be a major benefit in areas where the climate crisis and water scarcity are reducing food production. Research the areas that could benefit most from this kind of farming technology. Make an argument aimed at investors that explains why they should or should not invest in this kind of food production for the areas you identify. Use at least three sources to support your position.

9. According to Wang, "Gourmets like Plenty's results, too. . . . The deep green of the basil and chives hit him first. Each was equally lush, crisp, flavorful, and blemish-free" (par. 24). Think about the philosophies of eating that Michael Pollan ("Eat Food: Food Defined," p. 10), Wendell Berry ("The Pleasures of Eating," p. 46), and Thich Nhat Hanh and Lilian Cheung ("Are You Really Appreciating the Apple?," p. 59) offer. How would they react to scientific advancements that lead to the production of vegetables indoors — ones that are described in such delicious detail as Wang describes those at Plenty Inc.? Are these greens natural? Do they have the potential to change how we think about the natural world and our relationship to it? Describe at least three potential ways of thinking through these problems before drawing conclusions of your own.

Being a college student means being a college writer. No matter what field you are studying, your instructors will ask you to make sense of what you are learning through writing. When you work on writing assignments in college, you are, in most cases, being asked to write for an academic audience.

Writing academically means thinking academically — asking a lot of questions, digging into the ideas of others, and entering into scholarly debates and academic conversations. As a college writer, you will be asked to read different kinds of texts; understand and evaluate authors' ideas, arguments, and methods; and contribute your own ideas. In this way, you present yourself as a participant in an academic conversation.

What does it mean to be part of an *academic conversation*? Well, think of it this way: You and your friends may have an ongoing debate about the best film trilogy of all time. During your conversations with one another, you analyze the details of the films, introduce points you want your friends to consider, listen to their ideas, and perhaps cite what the critics have said about a particular trilogy. This kind of conversation is not unlike what happens among scholars in academic writing — except they could be debating the best public policy for a social problem or the most promising new theory in treating disease.

If you are uncertain about what academic writing *sounds like* or if you're not sure you're any good at it, this section offers guidance for you at the sentence level. It helps answer questions such as these:

How can I present the ideas of others in a way that demonstrates my understanding of the debate?

How can I agree with someone, but add a new idea?

How can I disagree with a scholar without seeming, well, rude?

How can I make clear in my writing which ideas are mine and which ideas are someone else's?

The following sections offer sentence guides for you to use and adapt to your own writing situations. As in all writing that you do, you will have to think about your purpose (reason for writing) and your audience (readers) before knowing which guides will be most appropriate for a particular piece of writing or for a certain part of your essay.

The guides are organized to help you present background information, the views and claims of others, and your own views and claims — all in the context of your purpose and audience.

Academic Writers Present Information and Others' Views

When you write in academic situations, you may be asked to spend some time giving background information for or setting a context for your main idea or argument. This often requires you to present or summarize what is known or what has already been said in relation to the question you are asking in your writing.

SG1   Presenting What Is Known or Assumed

When you write, you will find that you occasionally need to present something that is known, such as a specific fact or a statistic. The following structures are useful when you are providing background information.

As we know from history, _____.

X has shown that _____.

Research by X and Y suggests that _____.

According to X, percent of are/favor _____.

In other situations, you may have the need to present information that is assumed or that is conventional wisdom.

People often believe that _____.

Conventional wisdom leads us to believe _____.

Many Americans share the idea that _____.

_____ is a widely held belief.

In order to challenge an assumption or a widely held belief, you have to acknowledge it first. Doing so lets your readers believe that you are placing your ideas in an appropriate context.

Although many people are led to believe X, there is significant benefit to considering the merits of Y.

College students tend to believe that _____ when, in fact, the opposite is much more likely the case.

SG2   Presenting Others' Views

As a writer, you build your own *ethos*, or credibility, by being able to fairly and accurately represent the views of others. As an academic writer, you will be expected to demonstrate your understanding of a text by summarizing the views or arguments of its author(s). To do so, you will use language such as the following.

X argues that _____.

X emphasizes the need for _____.

In this important article, X and Y claim _____.

X endorses _____ because _____.

X and Y have recently criticized the idea that _____.

_____, according to X, is the most critical cause of _____.

Although you will create your own variations of these sentences as you draft and revise, the guides can be useful tools for thinking through how best to present another writer's claim or finding clearly and concisely.

SG3   Presenting Direct Quotations

When the exact words of a source are important for accuracy, authority, emphasis, or flavor, you will want to use a direct quotation. Ordinarily, you will present direct quotations with language of your own that suggests how you are using the source.

X characterizes the problem this way: ". . ."

According to X, _____ is defined as ". . ."

". . . ," explains X.

X argues strongly in favor of the policy, pointing out that ". . ."

Note: You will generally cite direct quotations according to the documentation style your readers expect. MLA style, often used in English and in other humanities courses, recommends using the author name paired with a page number, if there is one. APA style, used in most social sciences, requires the year of publication generally after the mention of the source, with page numbers after the quoted material. In *Chicago* style, used in history and in some humanities courses, writers use superscript numbers (like this[6]) to refer readers to footnotes or endnotes. In-text citations, like the ones shown below, refer readers to entries in the works cited or reference list.

MLA	Lazarín argues that our overreliance on testing in K-12 schools "does not put students first" (20).
APA	Lazarín (2014) argues that our overreliance on testing in K-12 schools "does not put students first." (p. 20)
Chicago	Lazarín argues that our overreliance on testing in K-12 schools "does not put students first."[6]

Many writers use direct quotations to advance an argument of their own:

> Standardized testing makes it easier for administrators to measure   *Student writer's idea*
> student performance, but it may not be the best way to measure it. Too much
> testing wears students out and communicates the idea that recall is the
> most important skill we want them to develop. Even education policy advisor   *Source's idea*
> Melissa Lazarín argues that our overreliance on testing in K-12 schools "does
> not put students first" (20).

SG4   Presenting Alternative Views

Most debates, whether they are scholarly or popular, are complex—often with more than two sides to an issue. Sometimes you will have to synthesize the views of multiple participants in the debate before you introduce your own ideas.

> On the one hand, X reports that _____, but on the other hand, Y insists that _____.
>
> Even though X endorses the policy, Y refers to it as ". . ."
>
> X, however, isn't convinced and instead argues _____.
>
> X and Y have supported the theory in the past, but new research by Z suggests that _____.

Academic Writers Present Their Own Views

When you write for an academic audience, you will indeed have to demonstrate that you are familiar with the views of others who are asking the same kinds of questions as you are. Much writing that is done for academic purposes asks you to put your arguments in the context of existing arguments—in a way asking you to connect the known to the new.

When you are asked to write a summary or an informative text, your own views and arguments are generally not called for. However, much of the writing you will be assigned to do in college asks you to take a persuasive stance and present a reasoned argument—at times in response to a single text, and at other times in response to multiple texts.

SG5   Presenting Your Own Views: Agreement and Extension

Sometimes you agree with the author of a source.

X's argument is convincing because _____.

Because X's approach is so _____, it is the best way to _____.

X makes an important point when she says _____.

Other times you find you agree with the author of a source, but you want to extend the point or go a bit deeper in your own investigation. In a way, you acknowledge the source for getting you so far in the conversation, but then you move the conversation along with a related comment or finding.

X's proposal for _____ is indeed worth considering. Going one step further, _____.

X makes the claim that _____. By extension, isn't it also true, then, that _____?

_____ has been adequately explained by X. Now, let's move beyond that idea and ask whether _____.

SG6   Presenting Your Own Views: Queries and Skepticism

You may be intimidated when you're asked to talk back to a source, especially if the source is a well-known scholar or expert or even just a frequent voice in a particular debate. College-level writing asks you to be skeptical, however, and approach academic questions with the mind of an investigator. It is OK to doubt, to question, to challenge—because the end result is often new knowledge or new understanding about a subject.

Couldn't it also be argued that _____?

But is everyone willing to agree that this is the case?

While X insists that _____ is so, he is perhaps asking the wrong question to begin with.

The claims that X and Y have made, while intelligent and well-meaning, leave many unconvinced because they have failed to consider _____.

A Note about Using First Person "I"

Some disciplines look favorably upon the use of the first person "I" in academic writing. Others do not and instead stick to using third person. If you are given a writing assignment for a class, you are better off asking your instructor what he or she prefers or reading through any samples given than *guessing* what might be expected.

First person (*I, me, my, we, us, our*)

I question Heddinger's methods and small sample size.

Harnessing children's technology obsession in the classroom is, I believe, the key to improving learning.

Lanza's interpretation focuses on circle imagery as symbolic of the family; my analysis leads me in a different direction entirely.

We would, in fact, benefit from looser laws about farming on our personal property.

Third person (names and other nouns)

Heddinger's methods and small sample size are questionable.

Harnessing children's technology obsession in the classroom is the key to improving learning.

Lanza's interpretation focuses on circle imagery as symbolic of the family; other readers' analyses may point in a different direction entirely.

Many Americans would, in fact, benefit from looser laws about farming on personal property.

You may feel as if not being able to use "I" in an essay in which you present your ideas about a topic is unfair or will lead to weaker statements. Know that you can make a strong argument even if you write in the third person. Third-person writing allows you to sound more assertive, credible, and academic.

 SG7   Presenting Your Own Views: Disagreement or Correction

You may find that at times the only response you have to a text or to an author is complete disagreement.

X's claims about _____ are completely misguided.

X presents a long metaphor comparing _____ to _____; in the end, the comparison is unconvincing because _____.

It can be tempting to disregard a source completely if you detect a piece of information that strikes you as false or that you know to be untrue.

Although X reports that _____, recent studies indicate that is not the case.

While X and Y insist that is _____ so, an examination of their figures shows that they have made an important miscalculation.

SG8 Presenting and Countering Objections to Your Argument

Effective college writers know that their arguments are stronger when they can anticipate objections that others might make.

Some will object to this proposal on the grounds that _____.

Not everyone will embrace _____; they may argue instead that _____.

Countering, or responding to, opposing voices fairly and respectfully strengthens your writing and your *ethos*, or credibility.

X and Y might contend that this interpretation is faulty; however, _____.

Most _____ believe that there is too much risk in this approach. But what they have failed to take into consideration is _____.

Academic Writers Persuade by Putting It All Together

Readers of academic writing often want to know what's at stake in a particular debate or text. Aside from crafting individual sentences, you must, of course, keep the bigger picture in mind as you attempt to persuade, inform, evaluate, or review.

SG9   Presenting Stakeholders

When you write, you may be doing so as a member of a group affected by the research conversation you have entered. For example, you may be among the thousands of students in your state whose level of debt may change as a result of new laws about financing a college education. In this case, you are a *stakeholder* in the matter. In other words, you have an interest in the matter as a person who could be impacted by the outcome of a decision. On the other hand, you may be writing as an investigator of a topic that interests you but that you aren't directly connected with. You may be persuading your audience on behalf of a group of interested stakeholders—a group of which you yourself are not a member.

You can give your writing some teeth if you make it clear who is being affected by the discussion of the issue and the decisions that have been or will be made about the issue. The groups of stakeholders are highlighted in the following sentences.

> Viewers of Kurosawa's films may not agree with X that _____.

> The research will come as a surprise to parents of children with Type 1 diabetes.

> X's claims have the power to offend potentially every low-wage earner in the state.

> Marathoners might want to reconsider their training regimen if stories such as those told by X and Y are validated by the medical community.

SG10   Presenting the "So What"

For readers to be motivated to read your writing, they have to feel as if you're either addressing something that matters to them, or addressing something that matters very much to you or that should matter to us all. Good academic writing often hooks readers with a sense of urgency—a serious response to a reader's "So what?"

> Having a frank discussion about _____ now will put us in a far better position to deal with _____ in the future. If we are unwilling or unable to do so, we risk _____.

> Such a breakthrough will affect _____ in three significant ways.

It is easy to believe that the stakes aren't high enough to be alarming; in fact, _____ will be affected by _____.

Widespread disapproval of and censorship of such fiction/films/art will mean _____ for us in the future. Culture should represent _____.

_____ could bring about unprecedented opportunities for _____ to participate in _____, something never seen before.

New experimentation in _____ could allow scientists to investigate _____ in ways they couldn't have imagined _____ years ago.

SG11 Presenting the Players and Positions in a Debate

Some disciplines ask writers to compose a review of the literature as a part of a larger project—or sometimes as a freestanding assignment. In a review of the literature, the writer sets forth a research question, summarizes the key sources that have addressed the question, puts the current research in the context of other voices in the research conversation, and identifies any gaps in the research.

Writing that presents a debate, its players, and their positions can often be lengthy. What follows, however, can give you the sense of the flow of ideas and turns in such a piece of writing.

_____ affects more than 30% of children in America, and signs point to a worsening situation in years to come because of A, B, and C. Solutions to the problem have eluded even the sharpest policy minds and brightest researchers. In an important 2003 study, W found that _____, which pointed to more problems than solutions. [. . .] Research by X and Y made strides in our understanding of _____ but still didn't offer specific strategies for children and families struggling to _____. [. . .] When Z rejected both the methods and the findings of X and Y, arguing that _____, policy makers and health-care experts were optimistic. [. . .] Too much discussion of _____, however, and too little discussion of _____, may lead us to solutions that are ultimately too expensive to sustain.

Student writer states the problem.

Student writer summarizes the views of others on the topic.

Student writer presents her view in the context of current research.

Appendix: Verbs Matter

Using a variety of verbs in your sentences can add strength and clarity as you present others' views and your own views.

When you want to present a view fairly neutrally

acknowledges	observes
adds	points out
admits	reports
comments	suggest
contends	writes
notes	

X points out that the plan had unintended outcomes.

When you want to present a stronger view

argues	emphasizes
asserts	insists
declares	

Y argues in favor of a ban on _____; but Z insists the plan is misguided.

When you want to show agreement

agrees
confirms
endorses

An endorsement of X's position is smart for a number of reasons.

When you want to show contrast or disagreement

compares	refutes
denies	rejects
disputes	

The town must come together and reject X's claims that _____ is in the best interest of the citizens.

When you want to anticipate an objection

admits
acknowledges
concedes

Y admits that closer study of _____, with a much larger sample, is necessary for _____.

Acknowledgments *(continued from page iv)*

Donald Barlett and James Steele, "Monsanto's Harvest of Fear," originally published in *Vanity Fair.* Copyright © 2008 by Donald Barlett and James Steele, used by permission of The Wylie Agency LLC.

Abaki Beck, "How One Tribe Is Fighting for Their Food Culture in the Face of Climate Change," *Talk Poverty,* February 27, 2019. Copyright © 2019 by Center for American Progress. Used with permission.

Wendell Berry, "The Pleasures of Eating." Copyright © 2010 by Wendell Berry, from *What Are People For?* Reprinted by permission of Counterpoint.

David Biello, "Will Organic Food Fail to Feed the World?" *Scientific American,* April 25, 2012. Reproduced with permission. Copyright © 2012 Scientific American, a division of Nature America, Inc. All rights reserved.

Alejandra Borunda, "Grocery Stores Are Packed with Plastic. Some Are Changing," *National Geographic,* April 22, 2019. Copyright © 2019 by National Geographic. Used with permission.

Taffy Brodesser-Akner, "Why I've Never Learned How to Cook," *Bon Appetit,* October 3, 2017. Copyright © 2017 by Conde Nast. Used with permission.

Jonathan Foley, "Can We Feed the World and Sustain the Planet?" *Scientific American,* November 2011. pp 84–89. Reproduced with permission. Copyright © 2011 Scientific American, a division of Nature America, Inc. All rights reserved.

David H. Freedman, Excerpted from "How Junk Food Can End Obesity," *The Atlantic,* July/August 2013. © 2013 The Atlantic Media Co., as first published in *The Atlantic Magazine.* All rights reserved. Distributed by Tribune Content Agency, LLC.

"Heartland" from *The Omega Principle: Seafood and the Quest for a Long Life and a Healthier Planet* by Paul Greenberg, text copyright © 2018 by Paul Greenberg. Used by permission of Penguin Press, an imprint of Penguin Publishing Group, a division of Penguin Random House LLC. All rights reserved.

Georgina Gustin, "Can a Climate Conscious Diet Include Meat or Dairy?" *Inside Climate News,* September 18, 2019. Copyright © 2019 by Inside Climate News. Used with permission.

Ch. 2: "Are You Really Appreciating the Apple?" (pp. 39–43) from *Savor* by Thich Nhat Hanh, Lilian Cheung. Copyright © 2010 by Thich Nhat Hanh and Lilian Cheung. Used by permission of HarperCollins Publishers.

Yuval Noah Harari, From *Sapiens,* "Industrial Farming Is One of the Worst Crimes in History" September 25, 2015, ynharari.com. Reprinted by permission of the author.

Blake Hurst, "The Omnivore's Delusion: Against the Agri-intellectuals," *The American,* July 30, 2009. Copyright © 2009 American Enterprise Institute. Reprinted by permission.

Rowan Jacobsen, "The Biography of a Plant-Based Burger," *Pacific Standard,* July 28, 2017. Copyright © 2017 by Pacific Standard. Used with permission.

Dhruv Khullar, "Why Shame Won't Stop Obesity," *Bioethics Forum,* March 28, 2012. Copyright © 2012 The Hastings Center. Reprinted by permission.

Excerpt from "You Can't Run Away on Harvest Day" (pp. 219–25, 228–29, 232–35) from *Animal, Vegetable, Miracle* by Barbara Kingsolver, Camille Kingsolver, Steven L. Hopp. Copyright © 2007 by Barbara Kingsolver, Steven L. Hopp, and Camille Kingsolver. Used by permission of HarperCollins Publishers.

Frances Moore Lappé, "Biotechnology Isn't the Key to Feeding the World," *International Herald Tribune,* July 5, 2001. Reprinted by permission of Small Planet Institute.

"Stop the Rot" from *The Fate of Food: What We'll Eat in a Bigger, Hotter, Smarter World* by Amanda Little, copyright © 2019 by Amanda Little. Used by permission of Harmony

Books, an imprint of Random House, a division of Penguin Random House LLC. All rights reserved.

Richard Marosi, "Product of Mexico: Hardship on Mexico's farms, a bounty for U.S. tables," *Los Angeles Times*, December 7, 2014. Copyright © 2014 Los Angeles Times. Reprinted with permission.

Jill McCorkle, "Her Chee-to Heart" from *We Are What We Ate: 24 Memories of Food*, edited by Mark Winegardner. Copyright © 1998 Share Our Strength, Inc. Reprinted by permission of Dunow, Carlson & Lerner Literary Agency on behalf of the author.

Bill McKibben, "The Only Way to Have a Cow," *Orion Magazine*, April 1, 2010. Reprinted by permission of the author.

Margaret Mead, "The Changing Significance of Food," *American Scientist*, 58(2) March/April 1970. pp 176–181. Reprinted by permission of Sigma Xi, the Scientific Research Society.

Marion Nestle, "Eating Made Simple," *Scientific American*, September 2007. pp. 60–69. Reproduced with permission. Copyright © 2007 Scientific American, a division of Nature America, Inc. All rights reserved.

Robert Paarlberg, "Attention Whole Foods Shoppers," *Foreign Policy*, April 26, 2010. Copyright © 2010 by Foreign Policy. Used with permission.

Joe Pinsker, "Why So Many Rich Kids Come to Enjoy the Taste of Healthier Foods," *The Atlantic*, January 28, 2016. © 2016 The Atlantic Media Co., as first published in *The Atlantic Magazine*. All rights reserved. Distributed by Tribune Content Agency, LLC.

"Eat Food: Food Defined" from *In Defense of Food: An Eater's Manifesto* by Michael Pollan, copyright © 2008 by Michael Pollan. Used by permission of Penguin Press, an imprint of Penguin Publishing Group, a division of Penguin Random House LLC. All rights reserved.

Bob Quinn, and Liz Carlisle, "Recycling Energy" from *Grain by Grain: A Quest to Revive Ancient Wheat, Rural Jobs, and Healthy Food* by Bob Quinn and Liz Carlisle. Copyright © 2019. Reproduced by permission of Island Press, Washington, D.C.

From *Gulp: Adventures on the Alimentary Canal* by Mary Roach. Copyright © 2013 by Mary Roach. Used by permission of W. W. Norton & Company, Inc.

Stephen Satterfield, "I'm a Black Food Writer. Here's Why We Need More Like Me," originally appeared in *Chefsfeed*, February 17, 2017. Copyright © 2017 by Stephen Satterfield. Used with permission.

"Why the French Fries Taste So Good" from *Fast Food Nation: The Dark Side of the All-American Meal* by Eric Schlosser. Copyright © 2001 by Eric Schlosser. Reprinted by permission of Houghton Mifflin Harcourt Publishing Company. All rights reserved.

Smith, Bren "The Least Deadly Catch: Ocean Farming in the Climate Change Era," transcript of speech at Bioneers 2016. Used with permission.

Nicole Walker, "Experiment with eggs by making a hollandaise in the time of global warming" and "How to cook a planet," pp. 32–49; 145–46 from *Egg*. Copyright © 2017 by Nicole Walker. Used with permission from Bloomsbury Academic, an imprint of Bloomsbury Publishing, Inc.

Selina Wang, "The Future of Farming Is Looking Up," *Bloomberg*, September 6, 2017. Copyright © 2017 by Bloomberg Publishing. Used with permission.

Lily Wong, "Eating the Hyphen," *Gastronomica: The Journal of Critical Food Studies*, Vol. 12, no. 3, Fall 2012, pp. 18–20. Copyright © 2012 by the Regents of the University of California. Published by the University of California Press. Reprinted by permission.

Barry Yeoman, "The Hidden Resilience of 'Food Desert' Neighborhoods," *Sapiens*, August 30, 2018. Copyright © 2018 by Sapiens. Used with permission.

Joon Yun, David A. Kessler, and Dan Glickman, "We Need Better Answers on Nutrition," *The New York Times*, February 28, 2019. Copyright © 2019 by The New York Times. Used with permission. All rights reserved. Used under license.

Index of Authors and Titles